Hiroshi NAITO
1992-2004
From Protoform to Protoscape
1

Hiroshi NAITO 1992-2004
From Protoform to Protoscape 1

First published in Japan on March 19, 2013
Third published on March 30, 2022

TOTO Publishing (TOTO LTD.)
TOTO Nogizaka Bldg., 2F
1-24-3 Minami-Aoyama, Minato-ku
Tokyo 107-0062, Japan
[Sales] Telephone: +81-3-3402-7138 Facsimile: +81-3-3402-7187
[Editorial] Telephone: +81-3-3497-1010
URL: https://jp.toto.com/publishing

Author: Hiroshi Naito
Publisher: Takeshi Ito
Editor: TOTO Publishing, Naito Architect & Associates
Art Direction & Design: Tsuyokatu Kudo, Shu Watanabe
Printing Director: Noboru Takayanagi
Printer: Tokyo Inshokan Printing Co., Ltd.

Except as permitted under copyright law, this book may not be reproduced, in whole or in part, in any form or by any means, including photocopying, scanning, digitizing, orotherwise, without prior permission. Scanning or digitizing of this book through a third party, even for personal or home use, is also strictly prohibited. The list price is indicated on cover.

ISBN978-4-88706-332-7

oshi NAITO

内藤廣の建築
1992-2004
素形から素景へ
1

	目　次		Contents

006	海の博物館		210	住居No.22	
	Sea-Folk Museum			House No.22	
			218	倫理研究所富士高原研修所	
				Fuji RINRI Seminar House	
046	素形から素景へ 1				
	From Protoform to Protoscape 1		238	最上川ふるさと総合公園センターハウス	
				Mogamigawa Park Center House	
058	住居No.14　筑波・黒の家		248	ちひろ美術館・東京	
	House No.14, Tsukuba			Chihiro Art Museum Tokyo	
070	住居No.15　杉並・黒の部屋		264	住居No.27	
	House No.15, Suginami			House No.27	
078	住居No.18　伊東・織りの家		273	英文作品解説	
	House No.18, Ito			English Project Descriptions	
092	住居No.19　金沢の家		282	作品データ	
	House No.19, Kanazawa			Data on Works	
108	安曇野ちひろ美術館		284	作品年表	
	Chihiro Art Museum Azumino			Project Chronology	
132	茨城県天心記念五浦美術館		286	略歴	
	Tenshin Memorial Museum of Art, Ibaraki			Profile	
150	住居No.21　千歳烏山の家		289	初出一覧	
	House No.21, Setagaya			Original Publication Data	
160	十日町情報館		290	クレジット	
	Tokamachi Public Library			Credits	
176	牧野富太郎記念館				
	Makino Museum of Plants and People				

海の博物館
Sea-Folk Museum

1992
三重県鳥羽市 Mie

完成する以前は、遠くから世間を眺めていたようなものだ。
大切な物を失わないで、いかに建築に接し続けることができるか、
という試練の場を与えられたような気持ちだった。

Before it was completed, I felt like I had been looking at the world from afar.
It was as if I had been put to a trial in which I had to continue to cling on to
architecture without losing hold of something important.

素形への遡行

博物館の館長の石原義剛さんとの出会いがすべての始まりだったと言ってもいい。石原館長の父の石原円吉さんは、三重県の漁業組合長を務めた後、衆議院議員にもなった人で、伊勢志摩で漁民から慕われたことで知られる。その遺志を継いで、1971年に鳥羽市内で漁民の文化を扱う博物館を立ち上げた。最初の博物館は海際で老朽化が激しく、漁労用具など収蔵物の急増で手狭になっていたことから移転を考えていた。

石原館長は、痩せぎす、ともかく頭の回転が速い人だが、生来の負けず嫌い、人の言うことを聞かない。知識の幅が広く行動的でどこへでも出かけていく徹底した経験主義の人だ。だから、常識的な社会通念や役所的な仕組みには徹底的に反発する気骨の人でもある。三重県の原発誘致反対運動の旗振り役でもあった。漁民のためにならない、というのが信念だった。また、伊勢人独特の徹底した倹約精神の持ち主でもある。一方で、次々とアイデアが思い浮かぶ人で、打ち合わせのたびに考え方が変わる。自分でも、「振りの石原」と言って笑う。だから建築に関しては、なかなか肝心な与件が定まらない。魅力的だがこの上なくやっかいな相手だ。

一言でいえば海の博物館は、この石原館長の性格と思いを写し取って出来上がっている。徹底したローコスト、「金はない」と口癖のように言う。一方で、海の近くで塩害に晒される劣悪な環境下で百年を越える耐久性を求める。この相矛盾する2点が提示された課題だった。

設計が始まったのは1985年、バブル経済が産声を上げた時期だ。時代とはまったく逆の課題がのしかかってきた。収蔵庫の坪42万というコストは、当初はとても不可能なことに思われた。おまけに、次々とアイデアが加えられる。内部を自由に使いたいので柱なしの体育館みたいな建物がいい。絶対に守らなければならない収蔵庫は、過去の津波の資料から海抜12.5mに置き、火災から守るためRC造にすること。経験から勾配屋根とし、塩害があるので金属材料で葺かないこと。

配置も含めて設計はまとまらない。二転三転した。このまとまらなさに縛りを掛けたのがコストだった。最も大切な要求を中心に、枝葉末節を切り捨ててコストを突き詰めていけば答えは収斂していく。このローコストで多くの答えは出るはずもないからだ。

担当をしたのは渡辺仁だった。渡辺は今でいうオタク。人間関係に関しては不器用で、状況判断についてはまったく音痴に近い。しかし、目的を達成するために必要な設計に対するこだわりと集中力は人並み外れていた。そして、施工で大活躍した大工の大西勝洋さんが、この変わり者を息子同然にかわいがってくれたことが大きかった。この建物は彼らの共作と言ってもいい。

竣工後、収蔵物は増え続けた。当初2万点あまりだったものが、20年を経て今や6万点を超えているという。収蔵庫は満杯で、漁具の部屋の棚は中2階のようにして増床した。使われなくなった漁労用具が、この博物館を目指して押し寄せてきている。それだけ時代の推移が激しい。どれも貴重な民族資料ばかりだが、引き受けなければ粗大ゴミとなって消滅してしまう。受け入れざるを得ない。漁船、漁網、漁具など、今や貴重な漁労用具を収蔵する全国有数の博物館になった。

収蔵物に反比例するように、博物館の財政は年々厳しくなっている。本来なら公共がやるべきところを、最大限努力したところで自前の財団では運営が厳しいのは当然だ。大いなる矛盾である。これからどうするのか。海の博物館は正念場を迎えている。(Eng. p.274)

建築は人間がなにがしかの目的を達成するための
手段にすぎない。単なる手段にすぎない建物に特別の意味を
見出した時、人はそれを建築と呼ぶ。

Architecture is just a means for people to achieve certain objectives.
When people find special meaning within a building that is nothing
more than a means, they call it architecture.

切妻の屋根に特に関心はない。それ以外の屋根の
形式にも同じように特別な思いもない。切妻が
単純な形式だからそれを選択することが多いだけだ。
I have no particular interest in gabled roofs. I have no particular
feelings about roofs of any other form either. I often choose the gabled
roof merely because it is a simple form.

自分の思考と社会の常識との間に、
いつも微妙な速度的なズレがある。

There is always a subtle discrepancy of pace between my thoughts and the widely accepted ideas of society.

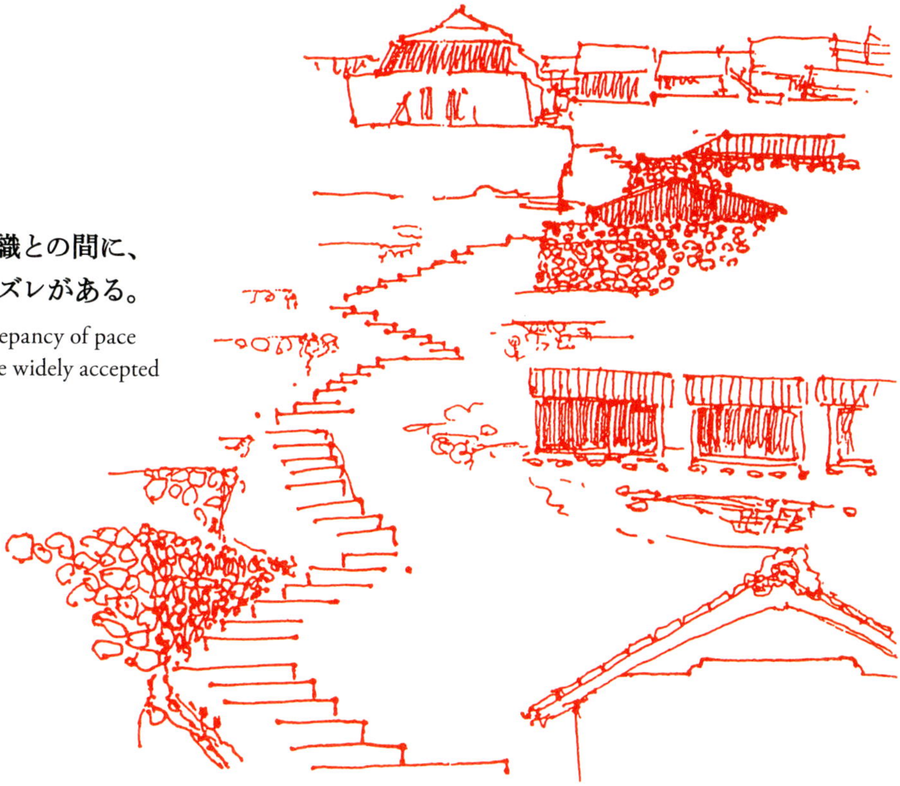

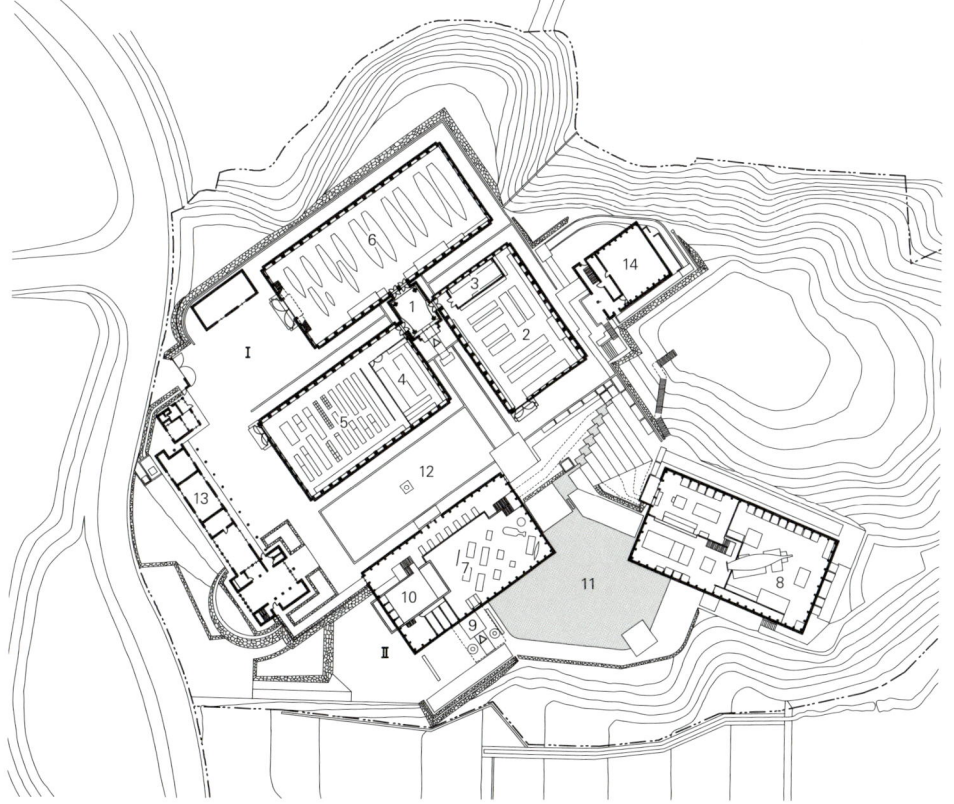

I **Repository**
1 windbreak room
2 storage room A (fishing nets)
3 storage room B (clothes, paper)
4 storage room C (tubs, casks, baskets)
5 storage room D (fishing tools)
6 storage room E (boats)

II **Exhibition Hall**
7 exhibition wing A
8 exhibition wing B
9 main entrance
10 lecture room

11 water court
12 courtyard
13 research laboratory
14 workshop room

Plan 1/1500

013   Sea-Folk Museum

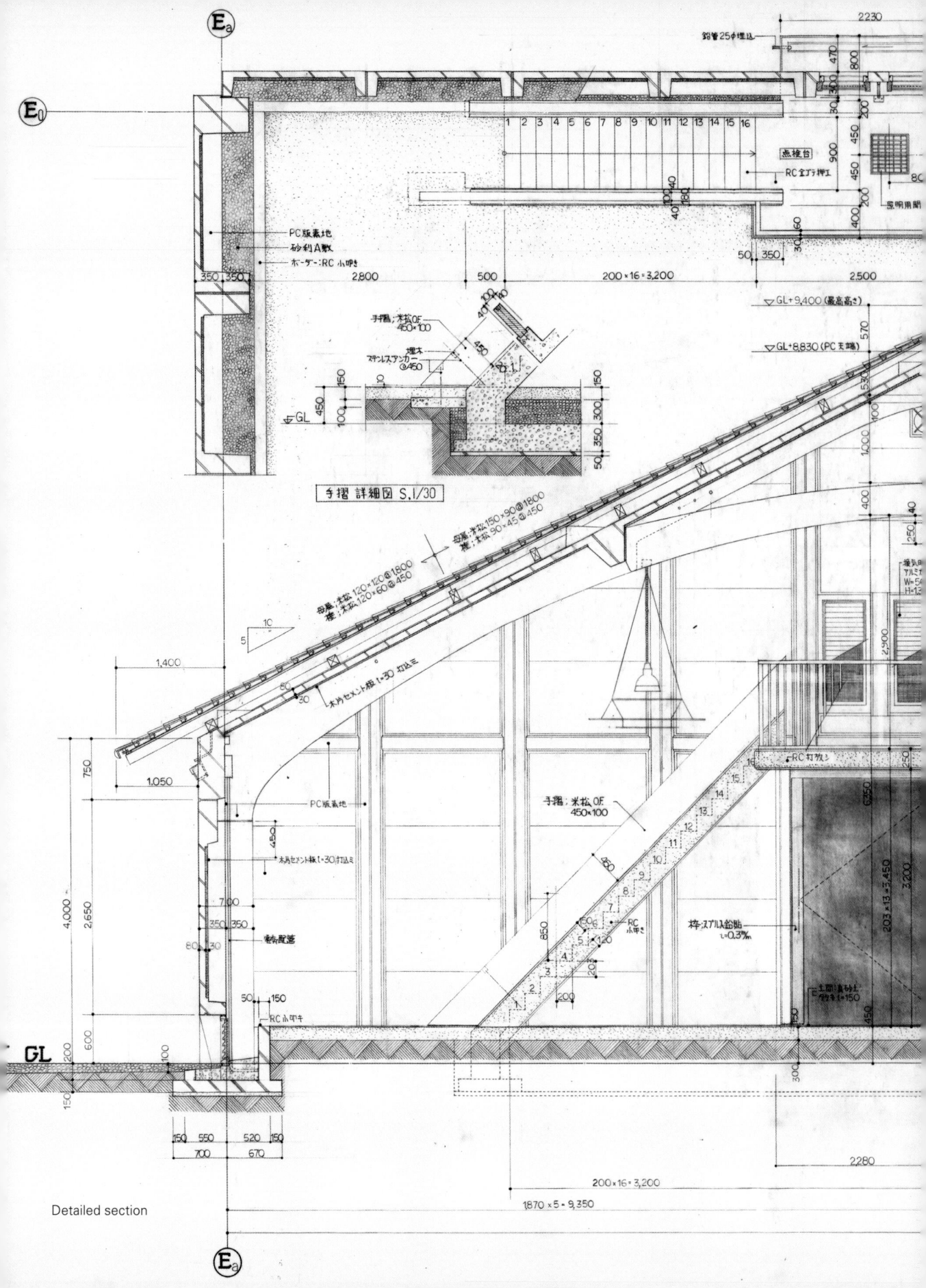

Detailed section

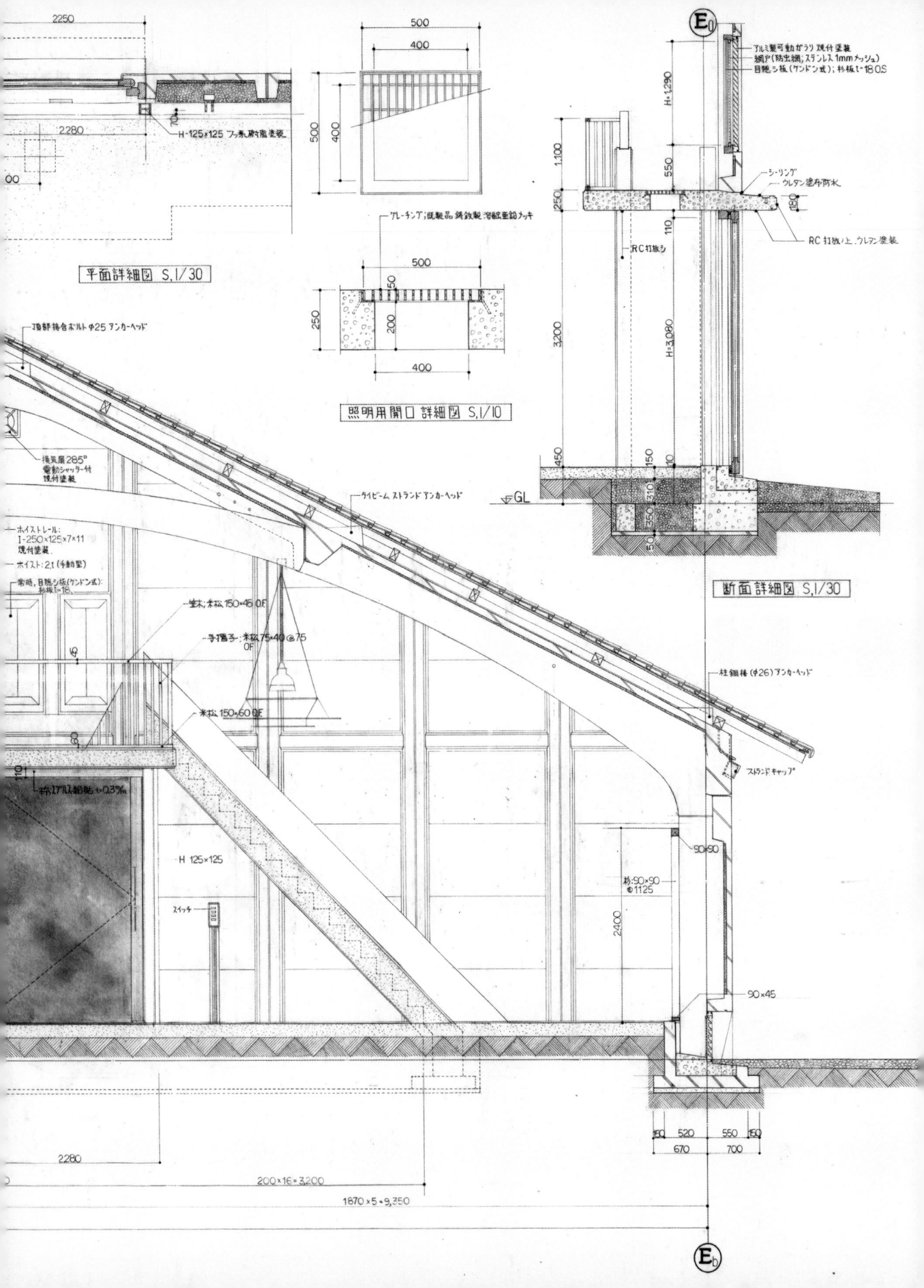

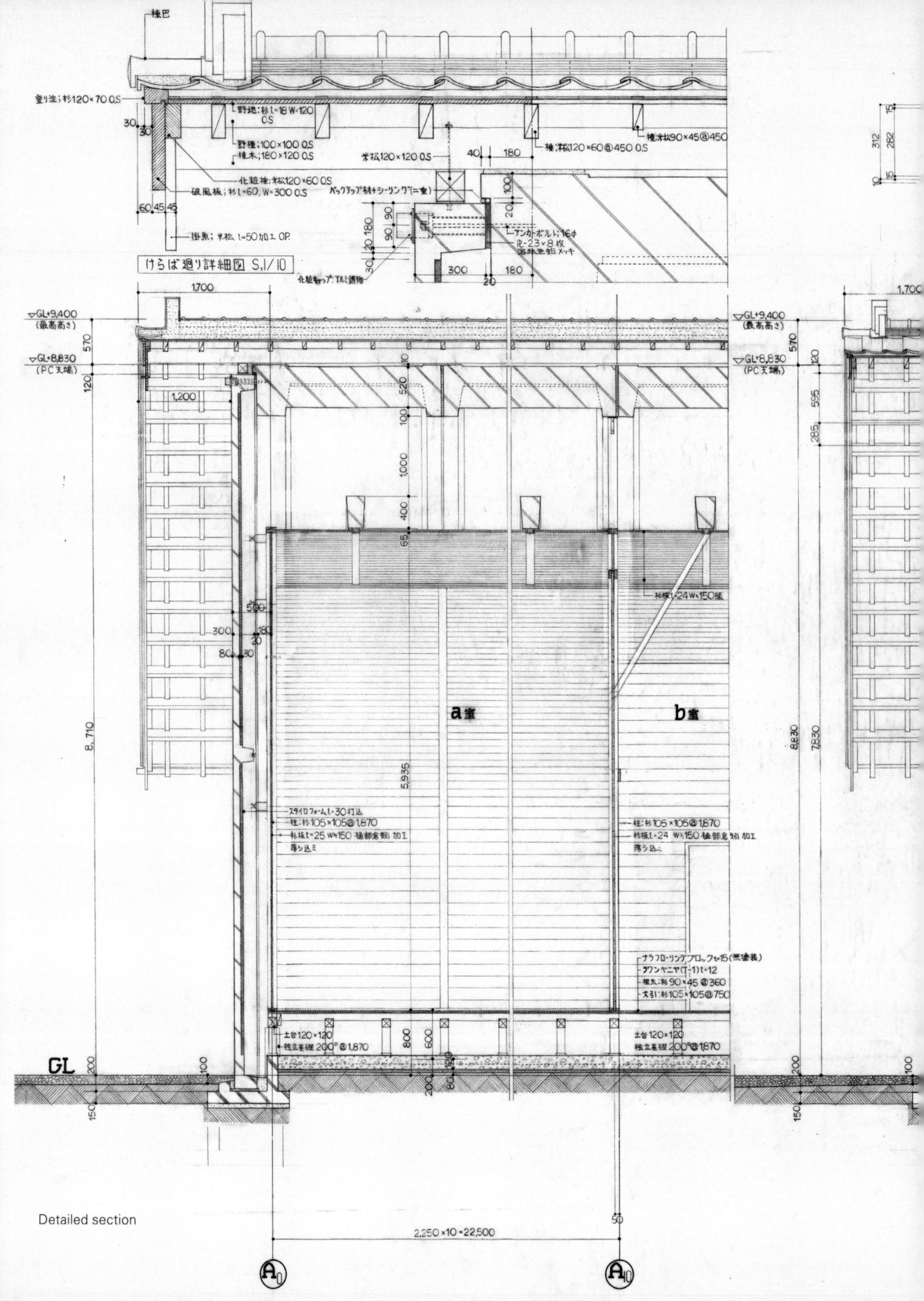

Detailed section

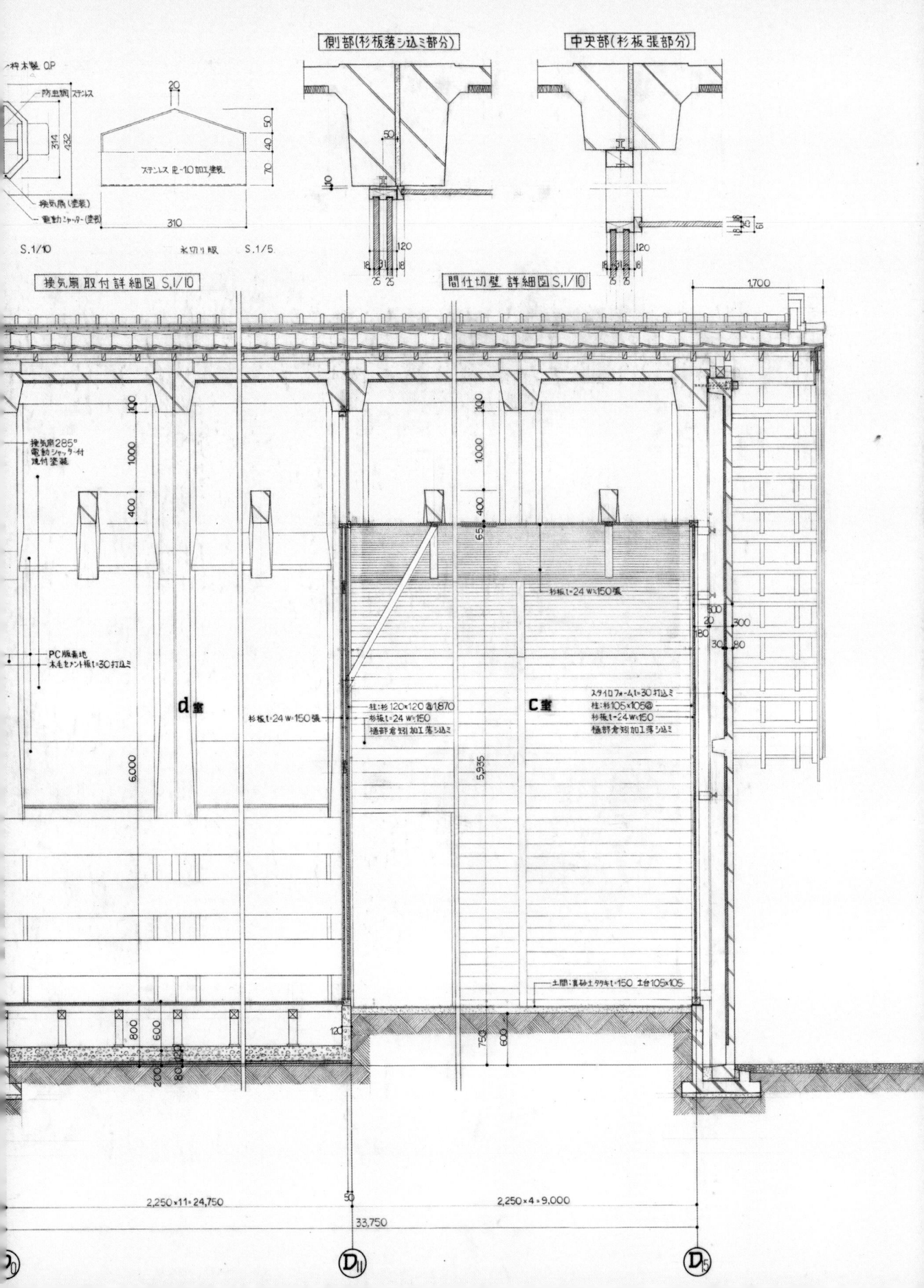

収蔵庫の建方風景
A scene of the repository under construction.

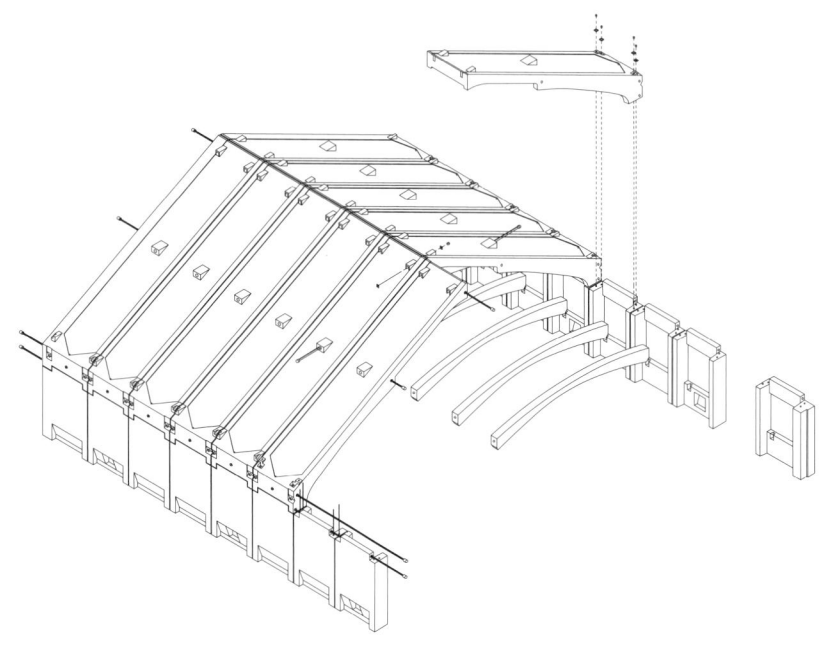

架構組立図
屋根勾配は瓦から決まる。それに合わせてPCa架構を決めた。スパンは短手18.5m、長手方向は最大40m。基礎のコストダウンを図るため、架構の3つのヒンジを剛接合的に扱った。工場で部材を作るので、トレーラーで搬送可能な幅2.25mのモジュールで分割し架構を組み立てた。ひとつのモジュールは5つのパーツで構成されている。組み立てた上でこれにポストテンションを加えて一体化するとともに、架構に対する応力も補正する。

Structural System
The precast concrete structure was designed to the roof's pitch that was determined by the tiles. It spans 18.5 meters in the short direction and a maximum of 40 meters in the long direction. The three hinges of the frame were treated as rigid joints in order to lower the cost of the foundations. The structure was segmented into modules 2.25 meters wide to be transportable by trailer from the factory in which they were prefabricated. Each module consists of five parts. Post-tensioning was applied to integrate the assembled modules and to balance the loads of the structure.

建築家が自分の仕事を作品と呼ぶのが嫌いだ。
I hate how architects describe their work as "pieces".

特別なものに驚きを覚えるのは当然のことだが、
当たり前のものの中に美しさを見出せないようであれば、
われわれに希望はない。

It is natural that we are astonished by the extraordinary, but there is no hope for us if we cannot find beauty within the ordinary.

言葉は、本来、建築の存在とは無縁のものだ。
言葉を連ねながら書くというのも矛盾しているが、言葉を介せずに、
建築が力をもつことができたら、どんなにか素晴らしいことだろう。

Words, fundamentally, are unrelated to the existence of architecture. As contradictory
as it is for me to be expressing this through the very use of words, how wonderful
would it be if architecture could wield strength without a need for them?

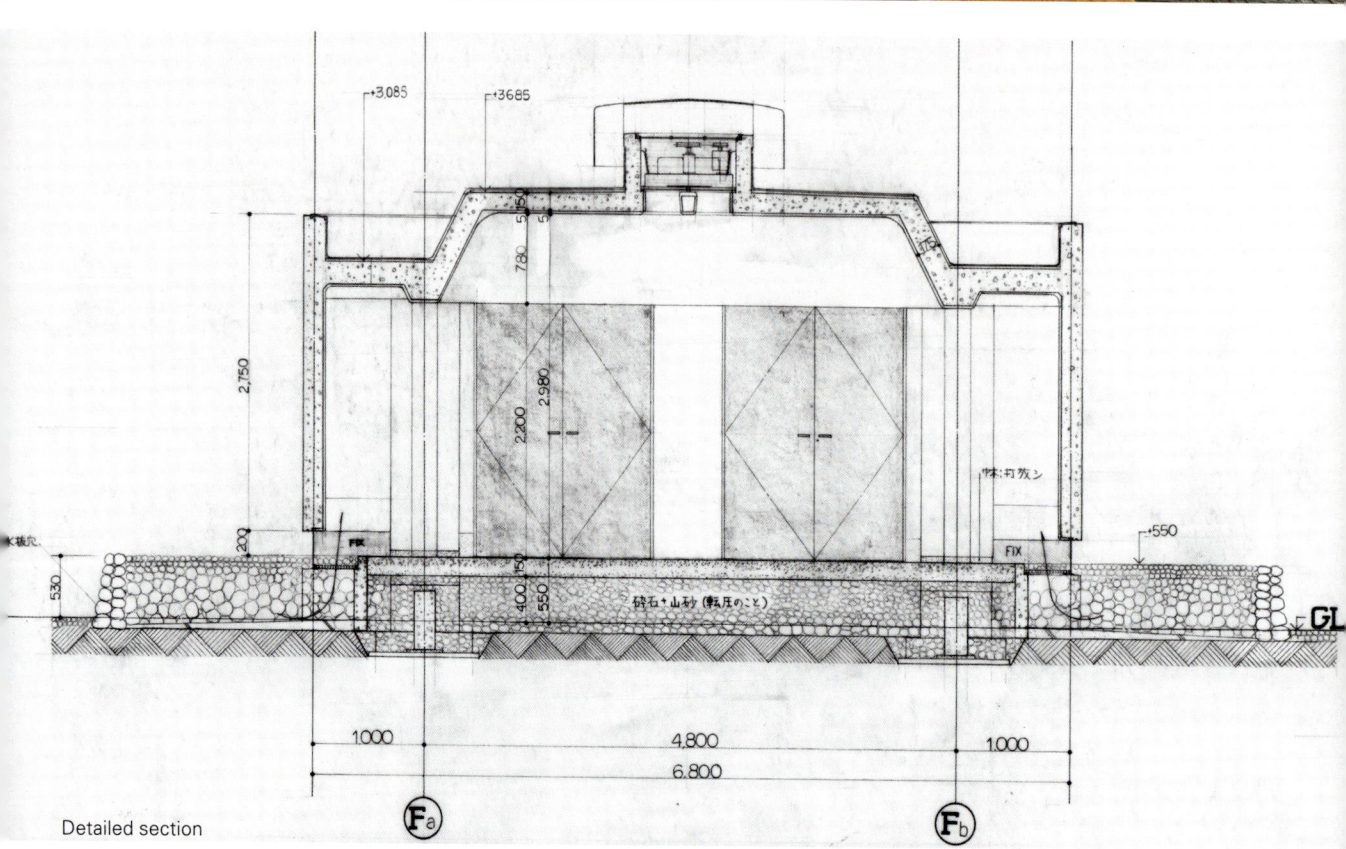

ガラスの下端から砂利を通して外気が入る、
たたき土間の風除室
Outdoor air enters inside by passing through
the gravel beneath the glass perimeter of
the earthen-floored windbreak room.

Detailed section

028 Hiroshi NAITO 1992-2004

時間にこだわれば思考の速度は停滞し、建物は
面白みを欠いていく。消費されやすい空間価値からも遠ざかる。

When being respectful of time, the pace of one's considerations slow and
buildings shed their spectacle appeal. It also distances them from the kind of
spatial values that are easily consumed.

海の博物館 Sea-Folk Museum
展示棟 Exhibition Hall

わたしにはわたしの建築に対するアプローチが
あるわけで、自分らしくない、自分の考えとは違うやり方で
無理にやってもうまくいかない。
Since I have my own personal approach towards architecture,
I cannot achieve a successful outcome by forcing myself to attempt
an approach that is not like mine or which differs from my ideas.

スタイルや様式として屋根を考えている
つもりは全然ない。

I do not at all think of the roof as a stylistic element.

Hiroshi NAITO 1992-2004

「海の博物館」以来の自分の仕事を俯瞰してみると、
結果として幾つかの共通した特徴がある。形態としての傾向があり、
一定の類似性の中にいることが分かる。
When I look back on my work since the Sea-Folk Museum, I notice
that several common characteristics have emerged among them. It is evident that
there is a trend to their forms and they fit within a certain set of similarities.

構造をそのまま見せるのは、そのための必然性と
意思がなければやってはいけないことではないか。
Exposing structure is something that should not be done
unless there is a necessity and purpose for doing so.

地球上のどこであれ、その場所にいる人が誇りをもてるような
建築をエンジニアリングの延長で作り出したい。
Wherever on this earth it may be, I want to create as an extension of
engineering an architecture that the people of that place can feel proud about.

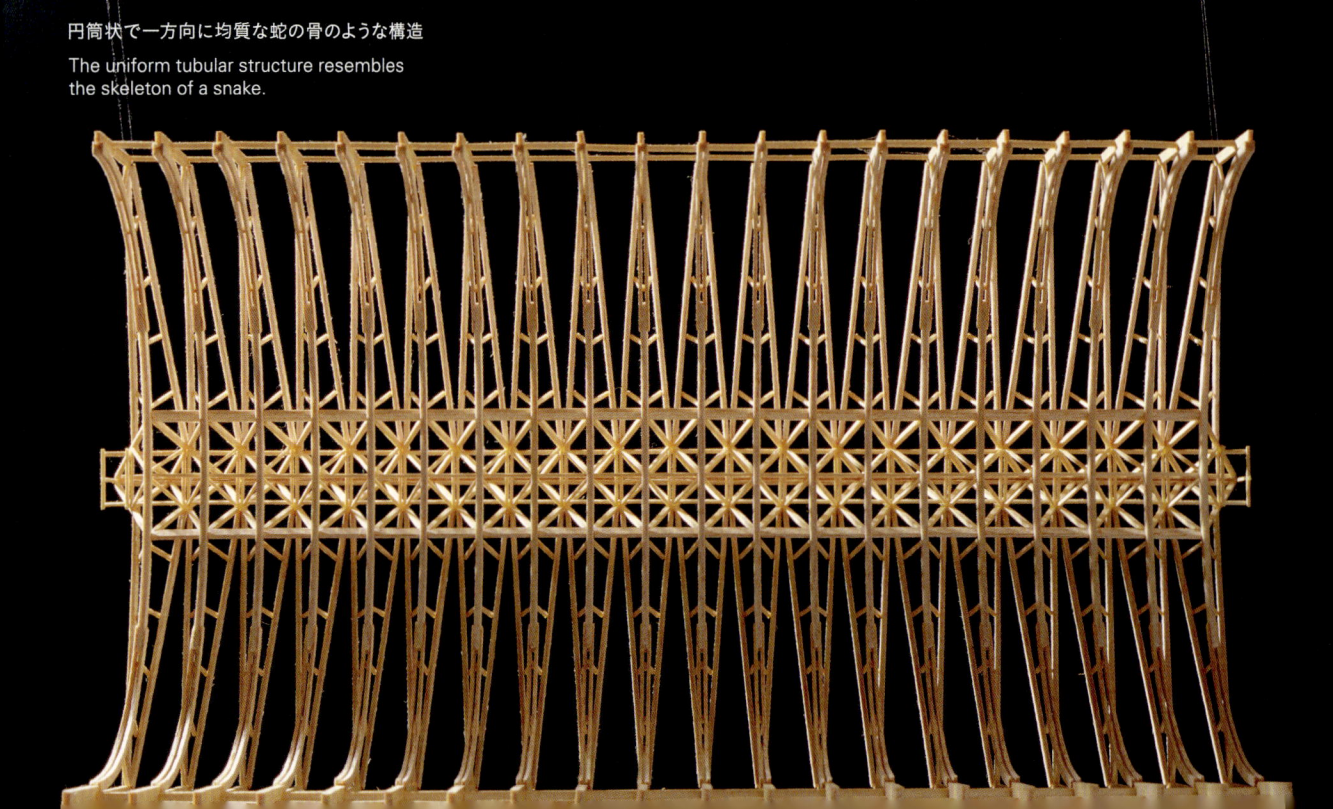

円筒状で一方向に均質な蛇の骨のような構造
The uniform tubular structure resembles the skeleton of a snake.

建築が手段であるのと同様、
構造も手段の範囲に留まるべきだと思う。
Similarly to architecture, I think structure should
also stay within the realm of being a means.

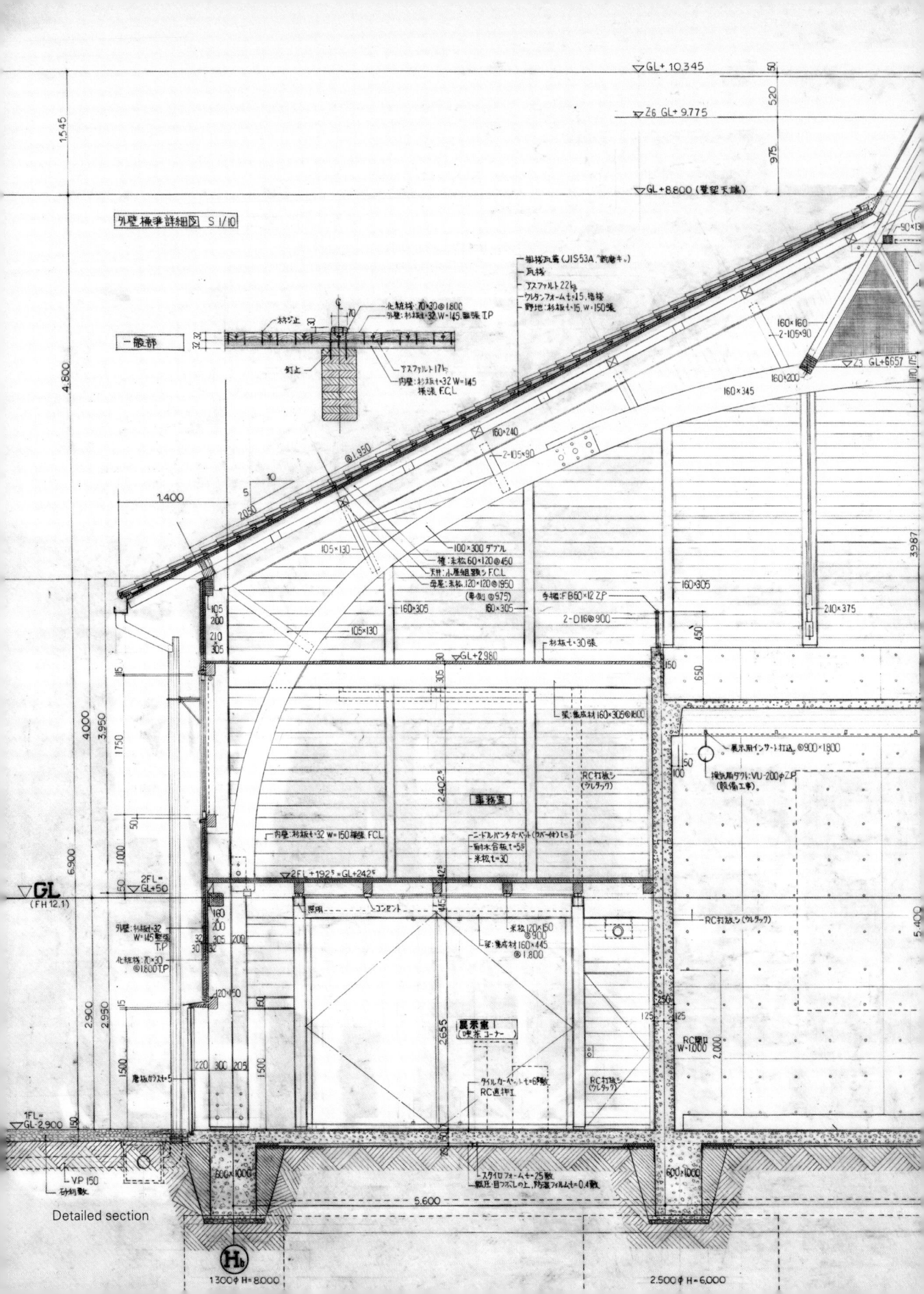

Detailed section

屋根・軒棟矩計詳細図 S/10

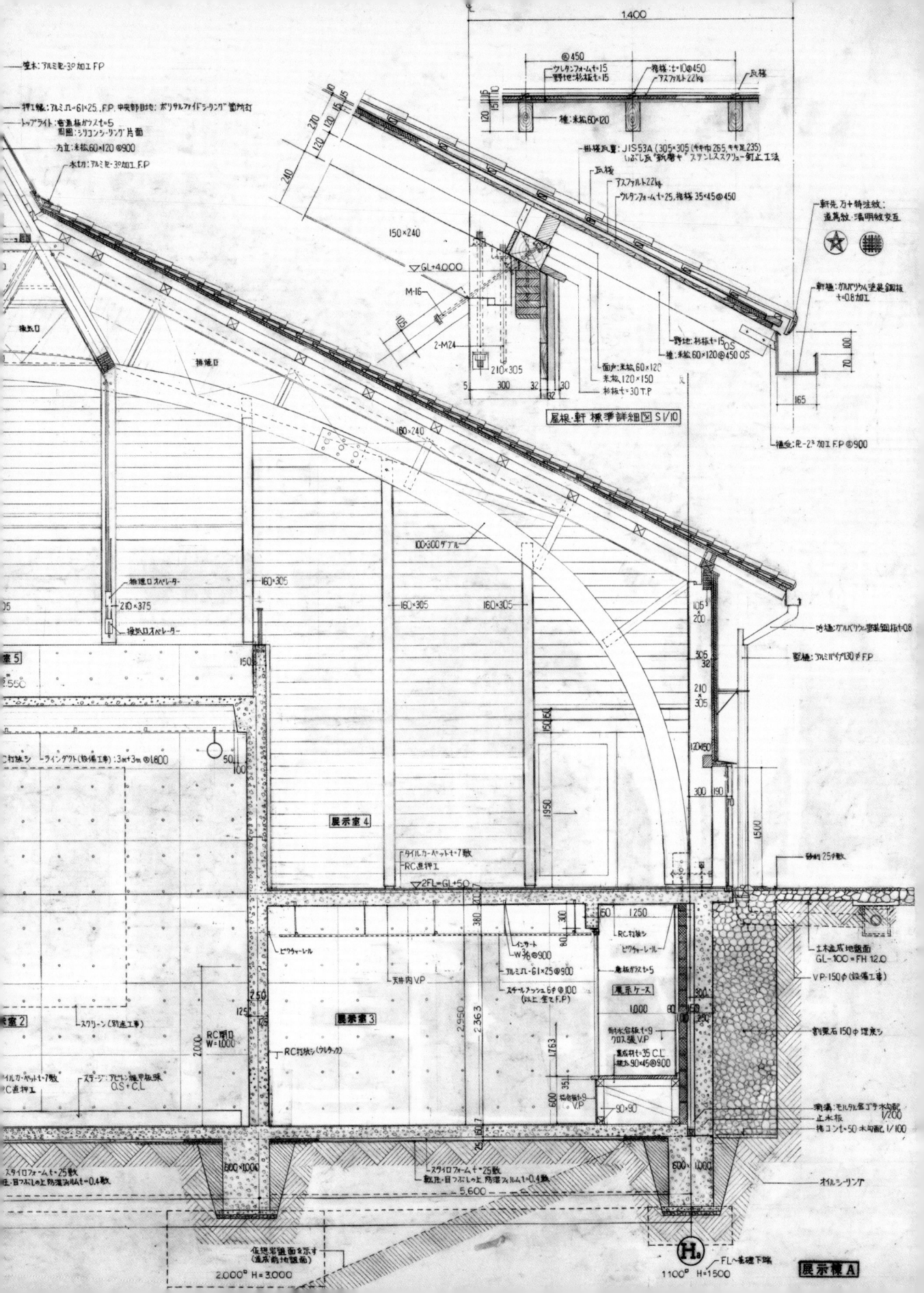

展示棟A

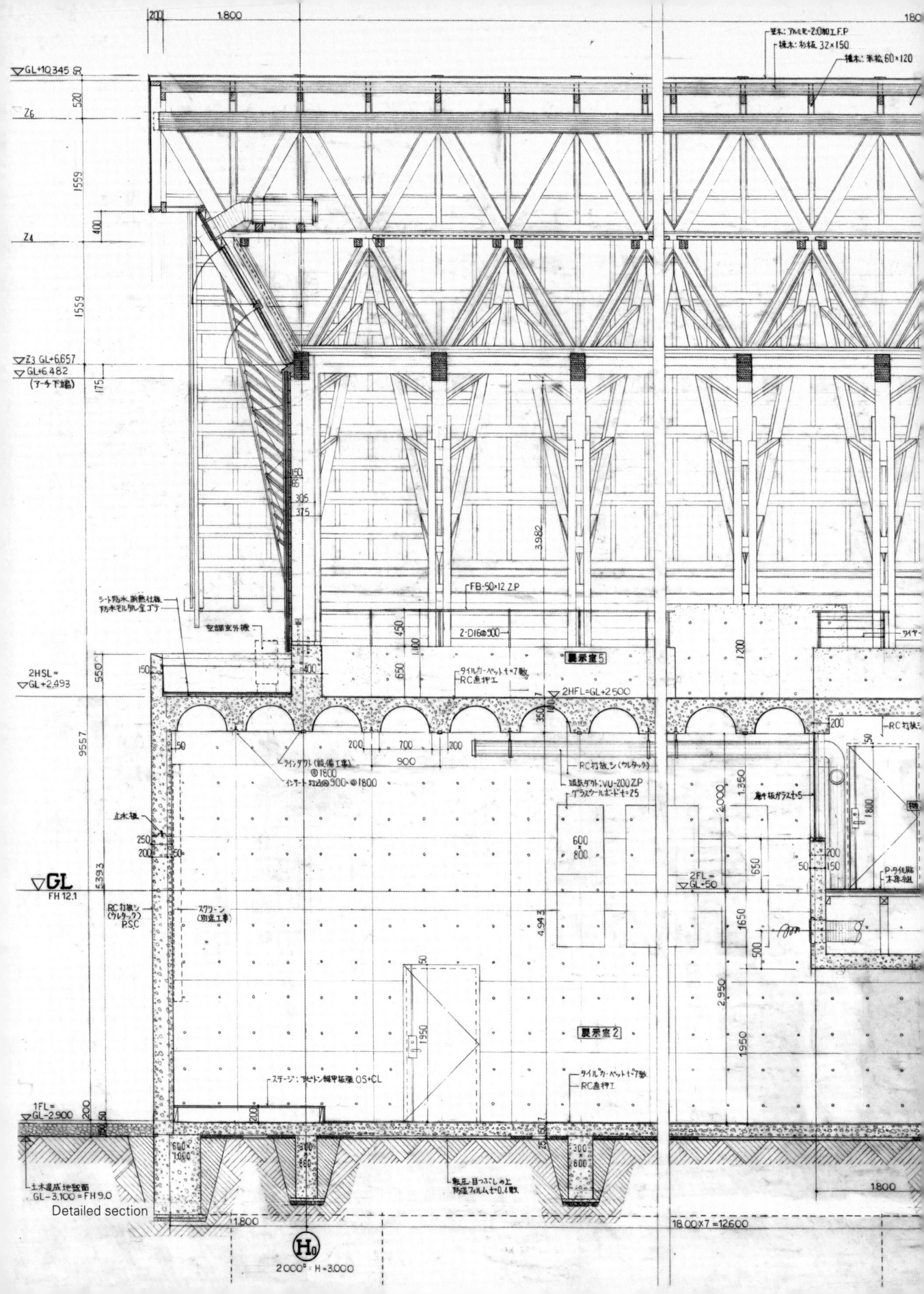

Detailed section

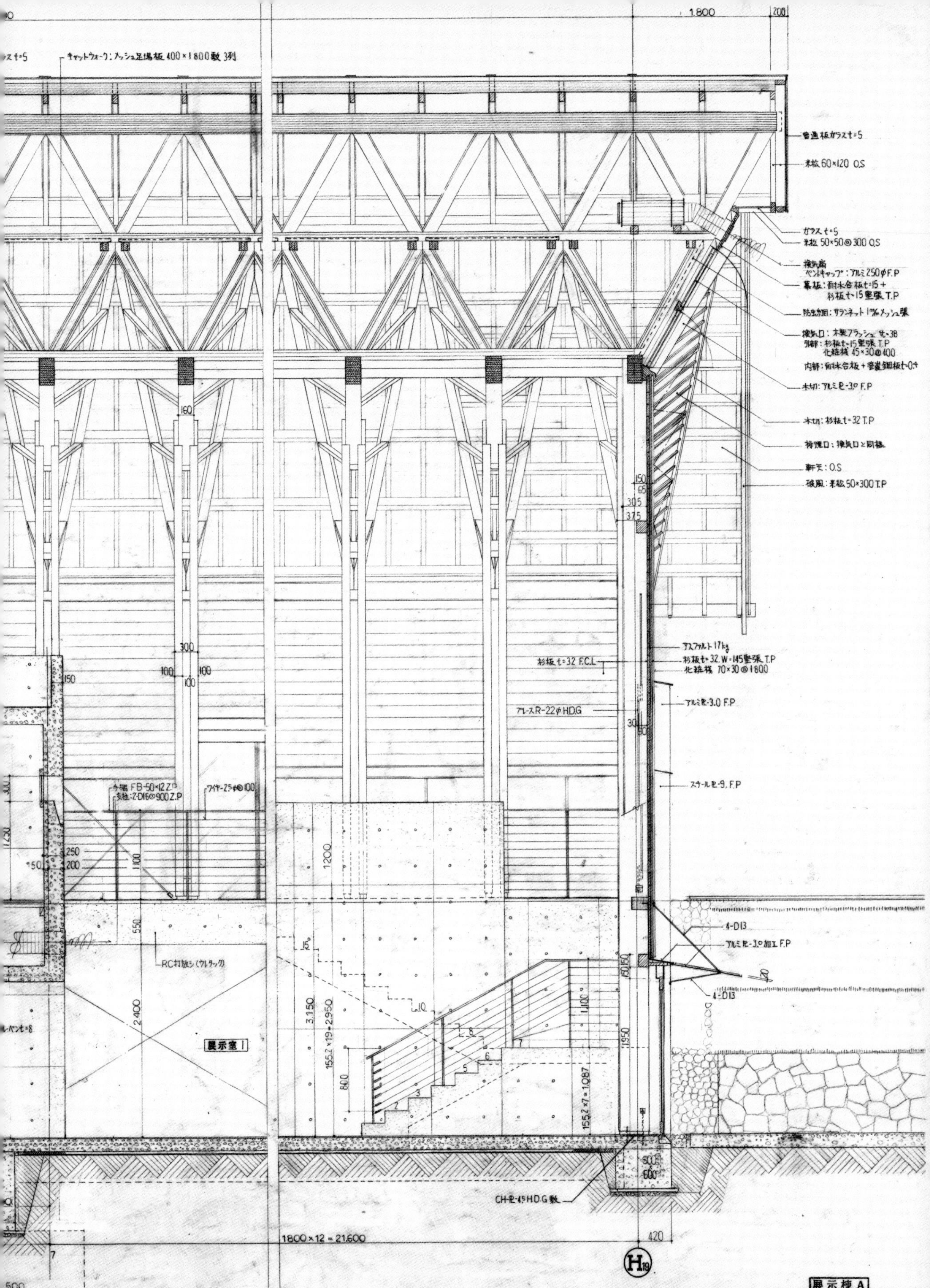
1,800
200
キャットウォーク：メッシュ足場板 400×1800 敷 3列
普通板ガラス t=5
米松 60×120 O.S
ガラス t=5
米松 50×50 @300 O.S
排気筒 ベンドキャップ：アルミ 250φ F.P
幕板：耐水合板 t=15 + 杉板 t=15 竪張 T.P
防虫網：サランネット 1% メッシュ張
換気口：木製フラッシュ t=38
外部：杉板 t=15 竪張 T.P 化粧桟 45×30 @400
内部：耐水合板 + 亜鉛鉄板 t=0.4
水切：アルミ PL-3.0 F.P
水切：杉板 t=32 T.P
排煙口：換気口と同様
軒天：O.S
破風：米松 50×300 T.P
アスファルト 17kg
杉板 t=32 F.C.L
杉板 t=32 W=145 竪張 T.P
化粧桟 70×30 @1800
アルミ PL-3.0 F.P
ブレースR-22φ HDG
スチール PL-9, F.P
手摺 FB-50×12 Z.P
支柱：Z-D16 @900 Z.P
ワイヤー 2.5φ @100
RC打放し（ウレタンク）
展示室1
155.2×19 = 2,950
3,150
155.2×7 = 1,087
4-D13
アルミ PL-3.0 加工 F.P
CH-PL-4.5 HDG 敷
1800×12 = 21,600
420
H19

展示棟A

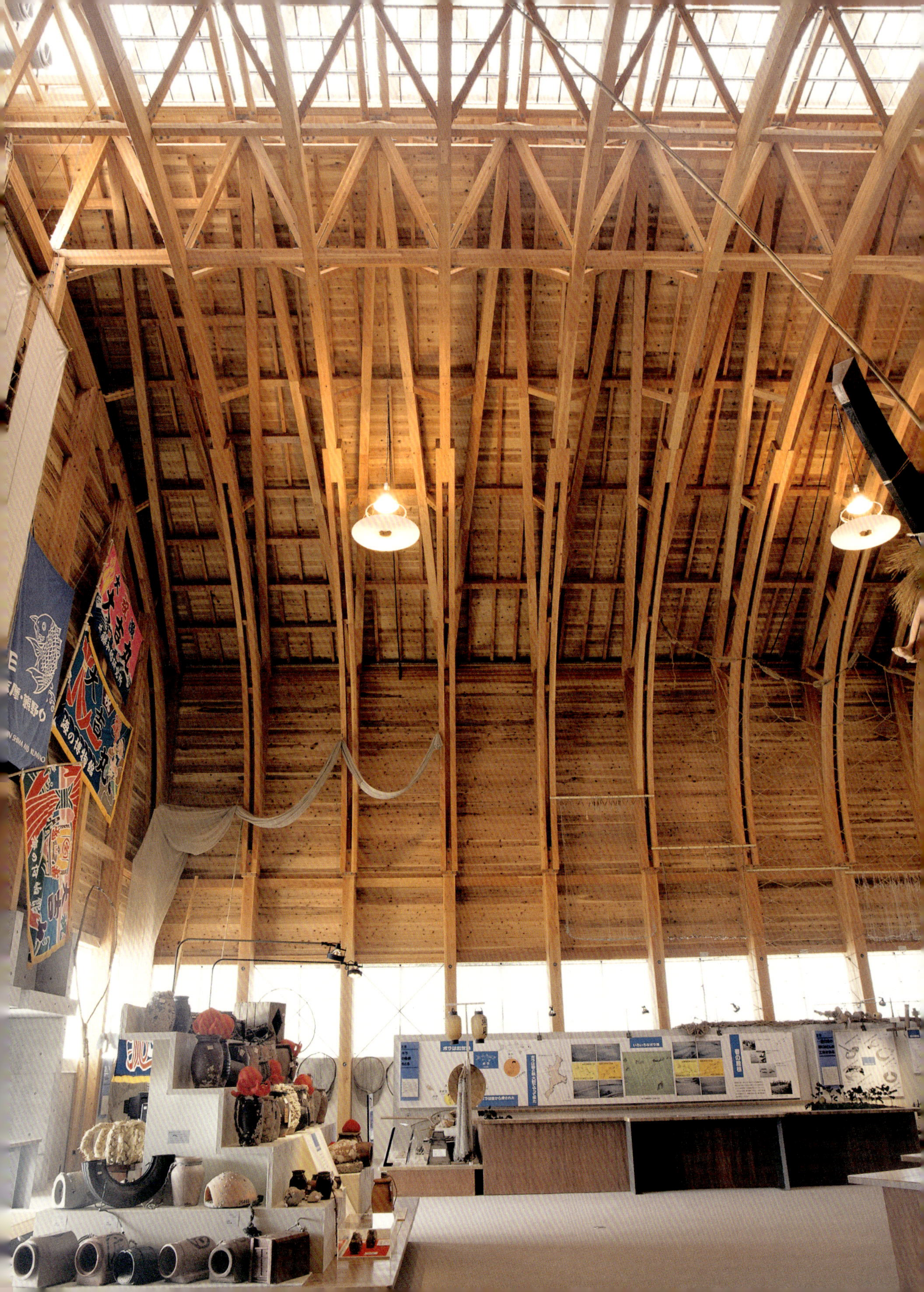

自分のやっている行為が、激動する状況と
連動していないのではないか、という不安にときたま襲われる。

At times I am overcome by an anxiety that my actions might not be in sync with the drastically changing situations.

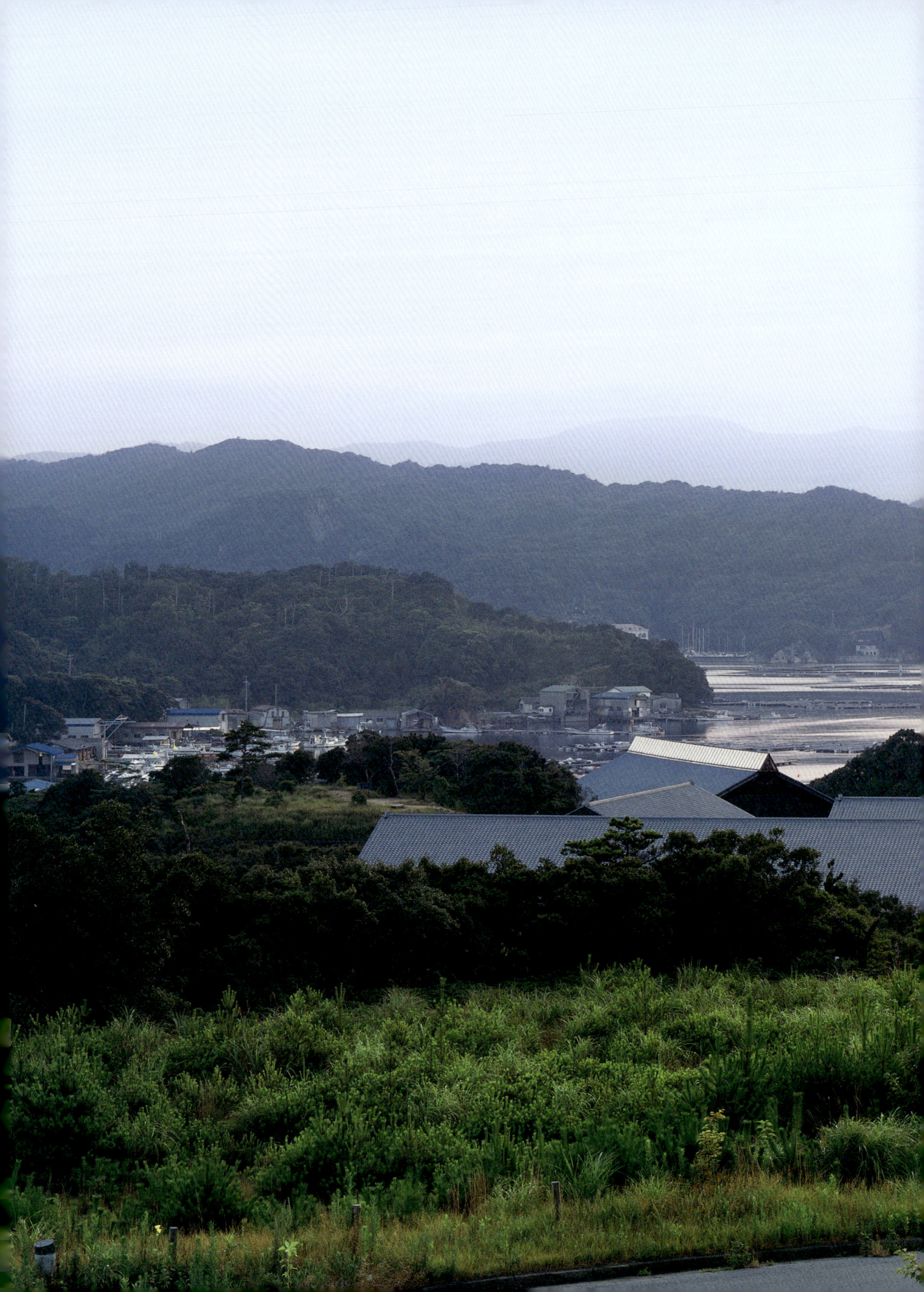

海は直観に満ちている。そこに在るのは、さまざまな
生の矛盾を包含する、すべての始まりであり
すべての終わりでもある純粋無垢で非情な不条理だ。

The sea is full of inspiration. What exists there is a pure and
heartless irrationality that encompasses the various contradictions
of life and is both the beginning and end of everything.

再考または反建築論

　もし建築という価値が、多くの若者や巷の人たちの希望をつなぐものではなく、当たり前の暮らしを幻滅させ、ありもしない束の間の夢想に駆り立てるようなものなら、それは否定されるべきものだと考える。

　建築は不自由さを生み出す装置ではない。それによってより豊かになるための装置である。建築それ自体に価値はない。建築に過剰な価値を求めようとするから、家を建てることや建物を建設することが息苦しくなるのだ。もしそうなら、いっそ、そんなものはすべてきれいさっぱり廃棄してみたらどんな世の中が描けるだろう、などと想像してみる。

　建築を目指す者なら誰でもそうであるように、わたしは建築という価値に何らかの希望を見出そうとして四苦八苦してきた。そして残念なことに、いまだに確たる自信はもてていない。だから、多くの悩める学生や若者、何事かを成し遂げようとしている志のある建築家たちと、まったく同じところにいまだに立ち続けていると言ってもいい。

　1980年代の中頃、つまりわたしの30代の中頃のこと、「海の博物館」の設計に取り掛かる前、本気で建築を辞めようと思ったことがある。自分に与えられた生の時間は一度しかないのだから、なにがしかの希望が見出せないのなら、手遅れにならないうちに別の道を探すべきだと思っていた。狂ったような高

素形から素景へ 1

内藤　廣

　度経済成長の世相とそれに歩調を合わせる建築界の空気に、わたし自身の気分が次第についていけなくなっていた。その時のわたしには、当時良いとされていた建築の価値、とりわけ作品という価値に、つまり建築を通して表現されねばならないとされていた価値に、まったく希望がもてないでいた。

　そんなわたしを、かろうじて建築につなぎとめたのは、「海の博物館」という状況だった。建物ではなく状況と書いたのにはそれなりの意味がある。あの建物が作り出した過酷な状況は異様だった。それは、わたし自身の生きる道を否応なく建築へと固定した。それがわたしにとって良いことだったのかどうか。そんなことは分からない。人生とはそういうものだろう。常に明確な結論など出ずに、次の状況に送り込まれる。そして今、再び多くの人と共にとんでもない状況にのみ込まれつつある。

渚にて

　被災からひと月後の4月中旬、陸前高田の渚に立った。その時、海は鏡のように凪いでいた。空は雲ひとつなく晴れ渡り、紺碧の空を映した穏やかな水面が遙か彼方まで広がっていた。まだ仮設の防潮堤もなく、まるで大きな湖の湖畔にたたずんでいるかのようだった。背後には、学校のグラウンドのような何もない大地が山裾まで広がっていた。1m近く下がってしまった大地と水面とがほぼ同じ高さでつながっている。海、大地、空、あまりに単純な、そしてまったく人のいない寂寥とした風景だった。

　この風景を前に、言葉にならない啓示のようなものがあった。いまだにそれが何であるかを説明することはできない。この風景は、中途半端な感傷や思い入れを、そして一切の言葉を拒絶する。この国の在り方も暮らしに対する考え方も、そしてそれを支える建築に対する考え方も、これを境に大きく変わ

A Reconsideration or else Renunciation of Architecture

What is the value of architecture? That it gives hope to people in their lives, as they are, or that it perpetuates false, fleeting dreams so that people grow disenchanted with their lives? If the latter, then architecture should be renounced.

Architecture is not a device for encumbering our freedom but a means of making our lives richer. Architecture has no value in itself. It is because we continually attach excess value to architecture that building a house or constructing a building becomes oppressive and suffocating. If architecture is only an encumbrance, then how much better the world might be if we simply rid ourselves of it, once and for all.

Like anyone taking architecture as an aim, I have gone to great trouble to find a source of hope in architecture. Unfortunately, I cannot confidently claim to have found it, even now. In this respect, I have come no farther than any student or young person mired in uncertainty, or any aspiring architect who seeks to accomplish something of worth.

In the mid-1980s, prior to undertaking the design for Sea-Folk Museum—when I was still in my thirties—I seriously considered giving up architecture. These valuable years of my life would never come again, I reasoned, so if I cannot discover in architecture something having value to people then I had better choose another career before it was too late.

Amid the madness of a high economic growth era, and that of an architectural world rushing to keep

From Protoform to Protoscape 1

Hiroshi NAITO

pace with it, I gradually began to lose my motivation. I found no hope at all in what others considered the positive value of architecture at the time, which was above all its value as a created work—the value, this is to say, of having to express something through architecture.

It was the situation I tackled with the Sea-Folk Museum that, in the nick of time, kept me in architecture. I say "situation" instead of "building" for a special reason. The harsh conditions surrounding that building compelled me to commit my life to architecture. Whether this was good for me or not, I have no idea. But life is that way. One is always being swept along to the next situation without any kind of clear conclusion. And now, with countless others, I am once again being swallowed up by deplorable circumstances.

On a Beach

In mid-April, one month after the earthquake and tsunami, I stood on a beach in Rikuzentakata, Iwate. The ocean was calm and mirror-like. The sky too was cloudless, and the ocean reflecting the blue of the sky stretched to the horizon. There were no temporary seawalls, either, so it was much like standing at the edge of an immense lake. Behind me, an empty flat area like an elementary school athletic ground extended to the foot of the mountains. The flat area of land, which had sank nearly a meter, was nearly at the same elevation as the water. Ocean, land, sky—elements of a simple and utterly uninhabited, desolate landscape.

With this landscape before me, I felt something like a divine revelation, inexpressible in words. Even now I cannot explain it. The landscape forbade any half-considered thoughts or sentiments, and forbade any words at all. After this, everything would change—the way we see our country, the way we see our lives, and the way we see the architecture that has structured our world. After this, it could only change. My

るだろう。いや、変えていかねばならない。漠然とはしていたが、確かにそう感じた。

あれから1年半、復興は遅々として進まない。なぜこうまでうまくいかないのか。その根は、おおよそ1960年あたりにあると考えている。この頃、誰もが経済的に豊かになることを求め、それこそが実現されるべき目標であり夢だと考えていた。社会は向かっていく大きな方向を定め、さまざまな法制度を整えた。建物を作っていくための建築基準法、戦災で灰塵と化した都市を再整備するための都市計画法、工業製品を作っていくためのJIS規格、それらが道具として出そろうのもこの時期である。今、これらの道具立てが復興を阻んでいる。そして、言うまでもなく原発の設置に手を付けたのもこの頃である。

すべては経済復興と高度経済成長に照準が合っていた。半世紀にわたって作り上げてきた社会制度は、たとえそれが愚かなものであれ、そうやすやすとは変わらない。その様は絶望的ですらある。復興に関して、あらゆる人が必死になって取り組んでいるにもかかわらずうまく事が運ばないのなら、制度そのものが間違っていると言わざるを得ない。

本書で取り上げようとしている建物にわたしが取り組んでいた1980年頃から20年余りの間は、いわば1960年頃に始まった社会形成の延長上にある。そしてその絶頂期でもあった。この時期の過ごし方そのものにも問題があったことは、今になってみればよく分かる。そしてあらゆる建築家は、時代の寵児たろうとして、この時期を蕩尽したのである。

堀田善衞(よしえ)は、「ギリシャ人は背中から未来に入っていく時間感覚をもっていた」と述べたが、今まさにわれわれもこのことに学ばなければならない。3.11を経た今以上に、それにふさわしい時期はないように思える。

変化について

1980年から2000年までの20年を振り返るとき、この間、ベルリンの壁が壊れて東西冷戦が終わり、アフガン戦争や第一次湾岸戦争などが起こり、世界情勢が一挙に流動化し始めた。国内では、バブル経済とその崩壊、そして阪神淡路大震災、同じ年に地下鉄サリン事件。時代を画するような大きな事柄が数年を置かずして起きた。いつの時代もそうだったのかもしれないが、慌ただしい激動の世紀末だった。身の回りの暮らしも大きく変わった。

しかし、これだけのことが起きて、建築という価値がどれほど変わったろうか。建築という価値は、何事もなかったかのように再生産され続けているかのように見える。また、わたし自身はどれほど変われたのだろうか。それとも変われなかったのか。

建築家の主張は、ころころと変わるべきではないと思っている。生み出された建物は、そのまま長い時間を生きていくのだから、生み出した当人の考えがすぐに変わるようでは、建て主も建物も時代の変化と共に置き去りにされてしまう。建築家は自分の考えを主張し、それを建物に反映させようとするのだから、生み出した建物のためにもせめて建築家は軽々にその主義主張を変えるべきではないと思っている。

しかし一方で、9.11や3.11のように、時代は時として建築家に過酷な試練を与える。それによってさまざまなことに気付かされ、建築家の思考が変わっていくことも確かだ。それは変化というよりは成長といった方が良いかもしれない。設計を通して、建物と会話するプロセスを通して、世の中の大きな事件を通して、現場で出会う職方を通して、日々建築家の思考は鍛えられ成長している。変わりたくはないが成長せざるを得ない。現実を見つめ生きようとすればそうならざるを得ない。

本書で取り上げるのは、バブル経済の崩壊から9.11までに出来上がった建物群だ。それに先立つ1981年からの10年間の経験で、わたしの設計の方向は次第に明確になっていったので、幾つかの大きな出来事はあったが、建築に対する基本的な態度は変わることがなかった。

thoughts were vague, but they were something on this order.

A year and a half later, the pace of reconstruction is slow. Why is it going so badly? The problem is rooted in the 1960s. In those days, people thought only of obtaining economic wealth. That became a goal in itself and everyone's dream. Society established a grand direction for itself and prepared varying laws accordingly—the Building Standard Law for architecture, the City Planning Law for rebuilding the cities reduced to ashes in the war, and the Japanese Industrial Standards for producing industrial goods. These laws were readied, at that time, as tools for a national goal. Those provisions are currently obstructing reconstruction in Tohoku. It was also in that period that Japan began to tamper with nuclear power.

In every aspect of society, economic resurgence and high level growth became a transcending aim. A social system constructed and maintained for over a half-century will not change easily, even if that system is fool-headed. It now appears hopeless. If post-disaster reconstruction is not moving forward effectively despite all the efforts people are putting into it, then clearly, the system is itself the problem.

That social system, launched in the 1960s, reached its zenith in the two decades commencing from the 1980s when I undertook the buildings in this book. Looking back at it now, much of the problem lies in how we spent those two decades. The architects who were the golden boys of the times absolutely squandered those twenty years.

Yoshie Hotta has said of the ancient Greeks that they approached time with their "back to the future." This is the lesson we must learn. There is no more suitable a time than now, after the 3.11 Earthquake.

Concerning Change

In the two decades from 1980 to 2000, the Berlin Wall collapsed and Cold War ended; war commenced in Afghanistan and the First Gulf War broke out, and change swept through the world. In Japan, an asset-inflated bubble economy formed and collapsed, the Great Hanshin Earthquake struck and, in the same year, the Sarin gas attack on the Tokyo subway occurred. In these two decades, events of great magnitude took place in rapid succession. Perhaps any period of history has been as rocked by change, but these years marked a tumultuous end to the century. Technology also changed our lives, dramatically.

Yet, how much did architecture truly change, even with all that happened? It appears to have simply gone on being produced and reproduced, oblivious to the profound events in the world. For all that, how much did I myself change? Or did I change?

An architect should not continually change his position, because the buildings he creates must serve people long into the future. If the designer frequently shifts in his thinking, the client and building too will be forgotten and left behind, as times change. An architect articulates his ideas and strives to reflect them in his buildings. For the sake of the buildings, therefore, he should remain consistent in his thinking.

On the other hand, the times often bring the architect harsh trials, such as 9.11 and 3.11. The architect takes heed of new factors, and his thinking changes as a result. But this is perhaps maturation, not a change in thinking. Many things temper the architect's thinking and cause him to grow and mature—the labor of design, the process of dialogue with the building, great events occurring in the world, and encounters with craftsmen at the construction site. One does not want to change, but growth is inevitable. This must be, if one will live in recognition of reality.

The buildings collected in this book were completed in the years from the bubble economy's collapse to the events of 9.11. Prior to those years, I had already obtained a clear direction as a designer from my experiences in the decade beginning from 1981. Therefore, my basic approach to architecture, although affected by events in the world, did not change.

The Approach Run

In the early 1980s, soon after launching my own office, I designed two buildings in the same span of a few years. One was a residence for multiple generations that would later receive the curious name "Symbiotic House" (House No.1). The other, Gallery TOM, was a building for a small gallery where people with visual impairments could touch and appreciate sculpture.

助走

　独立したばかりの80年代の初頭、後で「共生住居」という妙な名前を付けた多世代で住まう自宅の設計と、「ギャラリーTOM」という目の不自由な人が彫刻に触れることができる小さなギャラリーの建物を同時期に設計していた。

　「共生住居」は坪35万で作り上げねばならなかった超ローコスト住宅である。それを無謀にもRCで作ろうとした。版状の壁柱とフラットスラブで全体を構成し、床を仕上げて、後は建具をはめるだけ、という簡素極まる作り方だった。形のことなど構っていられなかった。ともかく、あらゆることがモノとコストのせめぎ合いだった。地味なたたずまいは、当然のことながらさして注目されることもなかった。

　それとは対照的に、「ギャラリーTOM」の建物は、形を優先させた造形的な作り方だった。ファーストイメージは粘土模型で作り、それを形にしていった。RCの箱の上に鉄骨のボックス梁を斜めに架け渡した特異な形をしている。技術的な知識を積み重ねた今なら難なくこなせると思うが、当時、この形をやるには知識と経験が足りなかった。ボックス梁はドブ漬けの熱で微妙に歪み、トップライトの雨仕舞いに無理が生じ、雨が漏った。イメージとモノに乖離が生じたのである。以後、10年以上、メンテナンスに追われることになる。

　これに懲りて、イメージよりモノに、形よりも技術に重きを置く作り方をするようになった。つまり、ど

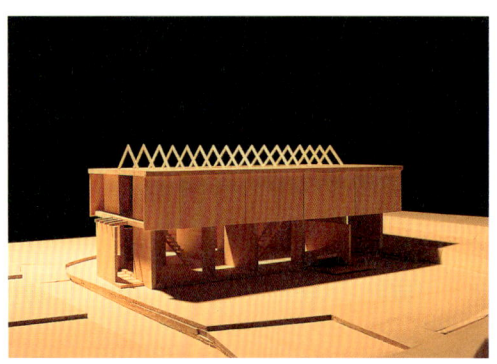

House No.1

ちらかといえば「共生住居」で見出した方法に近い作り方をするように変わった。ここに留まったことが、この後、時代とのズレを生むことになっていく。

バブルの前と後

　「共生住居」と「ギャラリーTOM」を終えてまもなく、「海の博物館」に取り掛かった頃の1985年、われわれ建築に関わる者にとっては直接的に影響を受ける大きな出来事があった。ニューヨークのプラザホテルで行われた先進5カ国蔵相・中央銀行総裁会議でプラザ合意が取り交わされ、通貨が変動相場制になった。それまで1ドル242円だった円ドルレートが、1988年までの2年あまりで120円になった。

　プラザ合意をきっかけとして、わが国ではバブル経済が始まり、世の中は空前の建設ブームになっていった。土地の値段は信じられないくらいの高騰を続け、建物の値段は土地価格の1年分の利息にすぎないと言われた。建物の価値は、高価な土地の上に置かれたオマケみたいなものになった。早く作って早く売る、これがこの時代の空気だった。

　建物の価値を認めないのだから、転売できればどのようなものでも構わない、ということになり、奇妙な形をした建物が氾濫した。それらの建物には、ポストモダニズムという名前が付けられた。ポストモダニズムは、もともと供給側の論理が勝った啓蒙的なモダニズムに対して、人間の側からの異論を唱えたものだった。そのスタイルは、バブル経済が生み出した巨大な消費社会の流れに瞬く間にのみ込まれてし

House No.1 was a super low-cost house that had to be constructed at 106,000 yen per square meter. Despite that, I rashly chose to construct it using reinforced concrete. My method was extremely simple. Composing a structure of wall-type columns and flat slabs, I finished the floor only and inserted factory-made interior walls afterward. I had no leeway to think about the building's shape and appearance. The design labor was a continual struggle between costs and materials. A building of plain appearance, it naturally did not attract much attention.

In contrast, I gave priority to plastic form in Gallery TOM. Modeling my image in clay, I translated it into a building. The result—a building of unique shape, with steel box beams placed at a diagonal over a reinforced concrete box. Today, when I have acquired some technical knowledge, I could manage such a building fairly easily, but at the time, I had neither the knowledge nor experience necessary. The steel box beams developed a slight warp during hot-dip galvanizing, so that the sealing system for the skylights was overtaxed, and leaked rainwater. Thus, a schism formed between my image and the actual, physical building. For over ten years, thereafter, I was burdened with the building's maintenance.

Learning from this, I came to value materials over image, and technique over form. In other words, I formulated a method closer in character to my approach in House No.1. My commitment to this method would later place me at odds with the times.

Gallery TOM

Before and After the Bubble Economy

In 1985, around the time when I set to work on the Sea-Folk Museum, soon after completing House No.1 and Gallery TOM, an event of major consequence for people in architecture took place. The Plaza Accord was concluded by the finance ministers and central bank governors of five developed nations at New York's Plaza Hotel, and Japan's currency shifted to a floating exchange rate system. As a result, the yen, which had stood at 242 yen to the dollar, rose to 120 yen by 1988, in just two years.

Prompted by the Plaza Accord, an asset-inflated bubble economy formed in Japan and ignited an unprecedented construction boom. Land prices skyrocketed, and a building, it was said, cost no more than a year's interest on the price of the land. In value, a building was like a premium thrown in for good measure on the high price of the land. Build quickly, sell quickly—was the mood of the times.

Because the building itself was considered of no value, any kind of building was acceptable as long as it could be resold, and buildings of bizarre appearance proliferated. The name "post-modernism" became attached to such buildings. Originally, post-modernism had expressed the user's counter argument to modernism, which gave preference to the supplier's logic. As an architectural style, it was snatched up by the massive consumerist surge set off by the bubble economy and interpreted in any way convenient, so that it lost its creative edge, became stripped of meaning and, in a twinkling, was consumed. At the time, most people in Japan's architectural industry believed in post-modernism and supported this trend. Its power was irresistible.

まった。本来の正当な主張が都合良く解釈され、前衛性を失い、形骸化し、瞬く間に消費されていった。当時、建築界のほとんどがポストモダニズムを信奉し、その積極的な支持者だった。その勢いは抗しがたいほどだった。

　かく言うわたしも、その流れに合わせようと努力はしてみたが、どうも肌に合わなかった。いわば、ポストモダニズムの失格者として、不適格者として、この時期を過ごすことになった。その後、バブル経済の崩壊と共にその流れは断ち切られ、何事もなかったかのように忘れ去られた。情けないことに建築界は変わり身が早い。

諦めの前と後
　この間わたしは、不幸にも、見方を変えれば幸運にも、三重県の鳥羽市のさらに郊外で、「海の博物館」という金のない民族系博物館の地味な仕事に埋没していた。1985年から1992年までの7年間である。ちょうどバブル経済が始まる頃に設計が始まり、完成後まもなく突然のようにバブルが弾けたから、世の中から隔離された隠れ里で、隠棲するようにこの時期を過ごしていたことになる。

　設計に取り掛かったあたりで、わたしの中に大きな変化があった。それはある種の「諦め」のようなものだったかもしれない。もともと器用に立ち回れるほうではない。この難しいプロジェクトを貫徹するには、世の中の流れに合わせるなどということは諦め、それとは逆の方角へと向かう決意が必要だった。未練を捨てる。この「諦め」は、自らを取り巻く状況の受容であり自らの内面への挑戦でもあった。

　設計には、当初から極限のローコストが求められた。このための方法は、すでに「共生住居」へのトライアルである程度身に付けていた。来る日も来る日も見積もりの書類ばかりを見ていた。世の中では坪単価200万とか300万の奇妙な形をした建物が自慢げに語られる中で、わたしが全精力を注ぎ込んで取り組んでいたのは、博物館の収蔵庫、坪単価42万の建物だった。どうすればコストを限界まで下げられるか。最低限の機能とは何か。それを実現するにはどうしたらいいのか。設計から現場まで、釘やボルトの1本まで徹底的にモノに即して内容を詰めていかざるを得なかった。伊勢志摩の空気を吸い、職人に学び、金の計算をし、担当だった渡辺仁と共に設計に没頭した。その果てしない作業の中で、わたし自身も変わっていった。

　1992年の「海の博物館」の完成まで、仕事の機会にはまったく恵まれなかった。経済的にも精神的にもとても苦しい時期だった。しかし、それ以降の10年間は、幸運にも幾つかの恵まれた機会を得ることができた。いわば、バブル経済が隆盛の時期は、それとはまったく無縁の場所で仕事をしていたが、バブル経済崩壊以降は仕事に恵まれたと言ってもいい。どういう訳か、わたしは景気の良い時は世の中と波長が合わない。それは今も同じだ。

　ベルリンの壁が壊れ、東西冷戦による核戦争の危機感が遠のき、核による世界の突然の終末というイメージが忘れられていった。イデオロギーという言葉に代わって、エコロジーという耳ざわりの良い言葉が主役になった。終末に対するイメージは、「核戦争による突然死」から「環境破壊による緩慢な死」へとシフトしていった。シナリオが変わったのである。そして、バブルが弾けて、ポストモダニズムの建物が衣のようにまとった余計なデザインは、一瞬のうちに時代遅れのものになった。

方法としての「素形」
　1995年、「海の博物館」（以下、海博）と当時取り組み始めていたプロジェクトをTOTOギャラリー・間で発表することになった。これらの建物をどのように説明してよいのか分からなかった。そこで「素形」という造語を作った。誰もが心の奥底にもっている建築の原形質のようなものがあるとしたら、それに「素形」という名前を与えてみたい。そして、それを探し求めているのだ、と語った。作っている時は夢中で、そんなことは考えもしなかったが、振り返って、その間の自分の無意識の中に常にあったものを語った。

I, who write this, made an initial effort to conform to that trend, but it sat uncomfortably with me and I ended up spending this period as an architectural misfit. Thereafter, with the bubble's collapse, this lavish trend came to an abrupt end and was forgotten for good. Deplorably, the architectural world changes quickly.

Before and After Giving Up

During this period, unfortunately—or fortunately, depending on the perspective, I became caught up in a modest job of building a folk museum having little financial resources, in an outlying area of Toba, a tiny rural city in Mie Prefecture. The project, "Sea-Folk Museum," required seven years, from 1985 to 1992. In the year of the bubble economy's inception, I embarked on the design, and soon after the building's completion, the bubble burst. I spent the entire era in a remote forgotten village divorced from the world at large, as if living in seclusion from society.

When embarking on the design, I experienced a profound inner change. It was a kind of "giving up." I had never been a maneuverer, and so, to pull off this difficult project, it became necessary for me to abandon the times and resolve to move in an entirely different direction. I had to give up my regrets. This "giving up" was also an active acceptance of my situation and the taking up of an inner challenge.

From the outset, a drastically low-cost design solution was demanded. I had already obtained a method for this during my "trial" in designing House No.1. Day after day, I found myself staring at nothing but estimate sheets. In the world at large, pompous buildings of bizarre design were being erected for 600,000 to 900,000 yen per square meter, and meanwhile, my energies were consumed in constructing a museum repository at 127,000 yen per square meter.

How could I cut costs to the bone? What were the minimum necessary functions? How could I carry this project to realization? From the design stage to the construction site, I weighed every detail of planning and sought to justify every bolt and nail. Breathing the salt air of the Shima Peninsula, learning from the craftsmen, and calculating costs, I absorbed myself in the design along with the project coordinator, Hitoshi Watanabe. And amid this relentless, hard labor, I myself changed.

Until the Sea-Folk Museum's completion in 1992, I received no other important work opportunities. It was a difficult period for me, both economically and mentally. Yet, in the decade that followed, I was fortunate to receive a number of commissions. Under the bubble economy, with Japan at the height of its prosperity, I had labored in a region nearly untouched by that prosperity. Then, after the bubble's collapse, I began to get work. For some reason, the world and I are not on the same wavelength in times of prosperity. This is still true, today.

With the fall of the Berlin Wall and the Cold War's end, fears of a nuclear war faded, and the image of an abrupt nuclear Armageddon was forgotten. Instead of "ideology," a pleasant word, "ecology," came to be heard. Our image of the world's ending went from "sudden death from nuclear war" to "slow death from environmental destruction." The scenario changed, and after the bubble's collapse, those ostentatiously appareled post-modernist buildings instantly fell from fashion.

The "Protoform" Method

In 1995, I had opportunity to exhibit the Sea-Folk Museum and other buildings underway at the time, at TOTO GALLERY MA. Not knowing how I should explain these buildings, I created the term *sokei* ("protoform"). If there existed an "architectural protoplasm" everyone carried in the depths of their being, I proposed, then I wanted to call it "protoform," and this is what I was searching for. When working, I had little time to think about such things, but now, I was able to reflect and speak of what had continually been at the back of my mind. I also felt I should declare my opposition to the social conditions produced by the bubble economy. I basically still take this same approach, today.

The knowledge I acquired from the Sea-Folk Museum, then, I applied and further developed in every one of the buildings I undertook in the 1990s. In Tokamachi Public Library, I utilized the precast concrete (PCa) technique I obtained from the Sea-Folk repository to endure heavy snows. In Tenshin Memorial

バブル経済が産み出した当時の世相に反旗を翻すような気持ちもあった。この取り組み方は、基本的には今も変わっていない。

　90年代に手掛けた建物は、どれも「海博」で得た知識を展開し応用したものだ。「十日町情報館」は、豪雪に耐えるために「海博」の収蔵庫で得たプレキャストコンクリート（PCa）の知識を使った。「茨城県天心記念五浦美術館」は海の近くの劣悪な環境と超短期間だった工期に対応するためにPCaを使った。「安曇野ちひろ美術館」では、「海博」の展示棟で得た木構造の知識を駆使した。「牧野富太郎記念館」では、「海博」の堅さを破ってより有機的な自由曲面を木造で作ることに挑んだ。「倫理研究所富士高原研修所」では、「海博」の展示棟の時期にはやりたくてもできなかった木造のジョイントの開発に取り組んだ。

　「海博」の地味な作業の中で身に付け鍛え上げたのは、建築的な価値を成立させるための方法や筋道であって、そこに現れた表面上のスタイルではない。方法と筋道が同じであっても、建物をめぐる条件はひとつとして同じものはなく、それ故それぞれの建物はあくまでも個別解であり、一つひとつ答えは違う。土地の性格を読み、風土を知り、用途によって構造形式を厳密に決め、設備環境の風土との相性を計り、コストをコントロールする。方法やアプローチは変わらないが、それぞれ条件は異なるのだから、現れてくるものが同じ形にならないのは当たり前のことだ。これらの建物は、外見はそれぞれ違うが、どれも「海博」で取り組んだ方法をそのままに、それぞれその状況下での最適解を提示したつもりだ。

「つまらなくて価値のあるもの」

　「素形」から10年、それまでを振り返るようなかたちで、2002年に「つまらなくて価値のあるもの」という文章を書いた。「素形」を思い描いて生み出してきたものが、このようであってほしい、というような願望を述べたものだ。本書に収録した建物がもっている大きな傾向を述べたものとも言える。

　バブル経済が産み落とした「おもしろくて価値のないもの」にとどめを刺しておきたかった。たとえ形としては「つまらなく」ても「価値のあるもの」が作り出せたら、と考えてきた。「つまらなさ」を目指すわけではない。「価値のあるもの」を作り出すことこそが重要で、そのために「おもしろさ」が犠牲になるとしてもそれを恐れてはいけない、ということを言いたかった。

　一体それはどのようなものなのか。最近ではあまり聞かなくなったが、わが国は、「つまらないものですが」と言って贈り物をする不思議な文化をもっていた。アメリカナイズされた近代的な社会では、こうした卑屈な謙譲表現は似合わないとされ、遠ざけられるようになった。しかし、わたしは違う見方をしている。

　たしかに微妙な心理を伴った謙譲表現ではあるが、手渡すモノよりもその背後にある気持ちの方が遥かに重く、その気持ちに比べれば「つまらない」モノなのだ、という言い方なのではないかと思う。モノでは語り尽くせない背後にある気持ちを言うために、あえて自分の気持ちに比してモノを「つまらない」と言うのではないか。そうだとすれば、これほど素晴らしい表現はない。わたしもこれに習おうとした。

　建築に引き付けて言うとこういうことになる。建物よりもその背後にある建物を成り立たせている思考や生業が豊かなものであるなら、当然、建物は「つまらないもの」として堂々と語られるべきなのだ。わたしがここで言いたい「つまらなさ」は、そういう価値の在り方だ。建築に「つまらなさ」を許すためには、その見えない背後を豊かにしなければならない。建てようとした人の思い、建てることに汗をかいた人の思い、建物が建てられる土地の思い、そうしたものが織り交ぜられ昇華されて真に価値あるものが生まれてくる。織物が複雑で大きくなればなるほど、建物は重層的で重くなり、カッコよさや新奇さからは遠くなる。つまり「つまらなく」なっていくのである。

　近代文明も近代建築も、分かりやすく、軽く、透明で、矛盾がなく、清潔で、衛生的であることを求める。その上で、新しく、面白くなければならないことになっている。わたしからすれば、そう思い込まされているにすぎない。「つまらなさ」は、向上心や進歩を求める気持ちに対する怠慢であるとされ、ジャーナ

Museum of Art, Ibaraki, I used PCa in response to a harsh ocean environment and super-short construction period. In Chihiro Art Museum Azumino, I gave play to the knowledge of wood construction I obtained from the Sea-Folk exhibit building. In Makino Museum of Plants and People, I broke with the rigidity of Sea-Folk and undertook to create a more organic free-form shell using wood construction. In Fuji RINRI Seminar House, I developed a wood joint that was far beyond my capability at the time of the Sea-Folk exhibit building.

In giving myself to the arduous work of Sea-Folk, I forged a method and logic for producing architectural valuc, not a visual style. Even if the method and logic are the same, the conditions posed by a building always differ, and hence, every building is a unique solution embodying a different answer. Reading the geographical features, grasping the cultural climate, finding the right structural form for the desired utility, ensuring that the equipment environment is compatible with the natural environment, and controlling costs—the method and approach do not change, but the conditions differ fundamentally, so naturally, the resulting building looks different in each case. The afore-mentioned buildings all differ in appearance, but in each I have set forth the optimal solution under the conditions, I feel, using the method I forged at Sea-Folk.

Uninteresting—with Real Value

In 2002, I wrote an essay reviewing the decade that had followed my "Protoform" exhibition. Its title, "Uninteresting with Real Value," expressed how I hoped buildings born from a vision of "protoform" would be. In the essay, I discussed in a general way the defining features of the buildings collected in this book. I felt I wanted to deliver a coup de grace to the kind of buildings engendered by the bubble economy, buildings that were "interesting with no real value." I had come to feel I wanted to create buildings that had value, even if it meant a building uninteresting in appearance. This is not to say an "uninteresting" appearance was my aim. Rather, to create something of value was important, and if, to that end, one must sacrifice an interesting appearance, then one should not be afraid to do so.

But what kind of a building does this mean? Although not often heard of late, we have a curious custom in Japan of offering someone a gift with the words, "It's only something uninteresting, but…" Today, in our modern Americanized society, the expression is shunned as one of excessive humility, but I take a different view of it.

While for certain an expression of humility reflecting a subtle psychology, it essentially means that the feeling behind the gift is far more important, and that compared to that feeling, the gift is "uninteresting." A material gift cannot adequately express the feeling behind the gift, so the giver, to communicate that feeling, can only contrast it with the gift, which is inadequate and "uninteresting." If my interpretation is correct, then there could be no finer expression. I set out to learn from it.

This meant applying it to architecture. More than the building itself, the thought and labor going into the building are what have special richness. If so, then naturally, the building should be declared to be something inadequate, "something uninteresting," without hesitation. This is the value I mean by the word "uninteresting." For an uninteresting building to be acceptable, richness must lie behind it—in the ideas of the people who set out to build it, in the thinking of the people who labored to construct it, and in the thoughts and memories of the land on which the building has been brought to stand. All become interwoven and exalted in the building, and true value is born. The broader the fabric and more complex its weave, the more layered and weighty the building becomes, and the less striking or novel in appearance. The more "uninteresting" it becomes, in other words.

Modern civilization and modern architecture value clarity, lightness, transparency, freedom from contradiction, cleanliness, and hygiene. In addition, the qualities of being new and interesting are considered important, but in my view, this is baseless. An uninteresting appearance is considered evidence of lacking an aspiring, progressive spirit and is scorned, not only in journalism but even in education.

But, this is absurd. Experience tell us that, when we go all out in pursuit of what has importance—in pursuit of something of value, in other words—increasingly, new elements come into play, and the building

リズムはもちろん教育現場でも劣位に置かれてきた。

　しかし、それはおかしい。経験からすると、大切なことを必死に追い求めると、つまり「価値のあるもの」を求めると、それを実現するための要素が幾重にも重なってきて、自分がやりたい形からは遠くなっていく。要素が増えるたびに連立方程式の変数が増えていく。ちょうどメモリーがいっぱいになるほどパソコンの反応が遅くなるように、思考の速度は遅くなり、形は明快さを失っていく。そして、それが理解できない人からは「つまらない」としか見えなくなっていく。

　この「つまらなさ」に耐えること、それが「海博」を設計した日々で身に付けたことであり、その後の10年間、プロジェクトを通して守り続けた態度である。本書に収録された建物は、なにがしかの「価値あれ」と願う気持ちから生まれ出た「つまらない」かもしれない建物たちだ。

　本書で取り上げる建物は、どれも完成してから10年以上の歳月を経ており、いわば独立した人格として自立しつつある。すでに建物が過ごすべき大きな時間の流れの中にいる。生み出されたものは、生み出した当人の手を離れることによって、コミュニケーションの媒介物になる。建築家は、生み出した当事者のひとりとして、当時の施主と共にこれらを見守る立場にいるわけだが、建物はそれ自身、独自の言葉を語り始めている。

　「素形」は心の奥底に潜むものであり、そこに至るには形のバリエーションがもたらす「おもしろさ」を求めない勇気が必要だ。「素形」に価値を求めない人からは、それは「つまらない」ものと見えるに違いない。しかし、それらの人たちにこそ、苦闘の末に実現した建物を、あえて「つまらないものですが」という言葉を添えて捧げたいと思っている。

「素形」としての家・「素形」としての故郷

　3.11を経て、家を流され故郷を追われた人たちに接するたびに感じることは、彼らが思い描き求めているのは、「素形」としての家であり「素形」としての故郷なのだ、ということである。失われたもの、失われた暮らし、そして失われた時を思い浮かべるとき、手掛かりまで奪われてしまえば、そこに浮かんでくるのは、家であれ故郷であれ、それは共同体の夢のようなものであるはずだ。意識の底にあるものが「素形」であり、手掛かりすら奪われれば、それは夢のようなものになる。その夢が現実を生きることを支えるということもあるのだ。

　これらが誘発するものが何であるかは分かっている。ノスタルジーを梃にしたリージョナリズムやナショナリズムだ。ここに時代が傾斜していくことは容易に想像できる。それを承知の上であえて言いたい。われわれの世代は、それを戦前の悪しき記憶としてこれらを遠ざけてきた。そしてこれらは、戦勝国であるアメリカからもち込まれたピカピカの資本主義が、脱脂粉乳の匂いのするモダニズムという名前の付いた消しゴムで、古き時代の悪弊として消し去ろうとしたものでもある。どれも西欧近代が全力で否定し駆逐しようとしてきたものばかりだ。思えば、「戦後」ではなく、「黒船来航以来」と言ってもいいかもしれない。かつて若かった団塊の世代が、激しく攻撃したのもこれらのイメージであったはずだ。

　しかし、今、多くのものを失った三陸や福島の無数の人たちを前に、わたしたちはなすすべを知らず、言葉を失っている。わたしには、個人個人の暮らしの夢となる「素形」の建築、共同体の夢となる風景、それを新たに「素景」と呼んでみたいのだが、それこそが現代において実現されるべき価値であるように思えてならない。

　手掛かりを失った大地にモダニズムは似合わない。被災地の切実な願いに応えるには、新たな時代の新たな方法が必要である。たとえ、ノスタルジーであっても自閉的になることなく、リージョナリズムであっても偏狭になることなく、ナショナリズムであっても独善に陥ることなく、そんな針の穴を通すような建築的思考の隘路を見つけ出さねばならないのではないか。そのすべを、この文章を読み本書を手にして下さった多くの建築家と共に手に入れたいと思っている。

gets farther and farther from the form we set out to achieve. As more elements enter in, the number of variables grows and, just as a computer slows when its memory is full, the speed of one's thoughts slows and one's form loses its clarity. And, in the eyes of those who do not understand this, it will only look "uninteresting."

I achieved the stamina necessary to persevere and achieve that "uninteresting building" during my days designing the Sea-Folk Museum, and it became an attitude I maintained in my projects for the next ten years. In this book, then, are those, perhaps, "uninteresting" buildings that have resulted from my wish to create something having real value.

In every case, over a decade has passed since the building's completion, and it is becoming an independent personality. It is already amid the great flow of time that buildings must entrust themselves to. By leaving the hands of the one who has nursed it to form, a thing becomes a medium for communication. As one who helped birth these buildings, the architect is in a position to watch over them, along with their owners, but the buildings themselves are now speaking in their own words.

"Protoform" is something lying in the depths of one's being. To reach it, courage is needed to avoid succumbing to a desire for an "interesting" appearance born from formal variation. To those who do not look for value in "protoform," such a building will simply appear uninteresting. It is to such people, however, that I offer these buildings, achieved through effort and trouble, with the words, "It's only something uninteresting, but…"

The Protoform House, the Protoform Hometown

What I have felt since 3.11, every time I meet people whose houses were swept away by the tsunami and who lost their ancestral home, is that what they see as necessary is a protoform house and a protoform hometown.

What comes to mind for such people, when they remember the possessions they lost, the way of life they lost, and the time they lost—what comes to mind, when all connection with their former lives is gone—is a house and a hometown, and surely, these are like the dream of a community. Protoform is something lying in one's deepest consciousness, and when one no longer has anything to hold on to, it appears in mind, like a dream. As a dream, then, it gives one the strength necessary to face reality.

We know what the dream of a community can invite—regionalism and nationalism leveraged by nostalgia. It is easy to imagine that the times might slide in this direction. With awareness of that in mind, I will venture to say this—our generation has intentionally distanced itself from such thinking, from an association of it with bad memories of pre-war times. And it was bright and shiny capitalism from America, the victor nation, that sought to erase such thinking as a corrupt practice of older times, using an eraser called "modernism" having the smell of powdered milk. Regionalism and nationalism are the very things that modern Western society invested terrific energy into renouncing and vanquishing. This it had done, in truth, since the arrival of Perry's Black Ships in the 19th century. It was also this image that people of Japan's baby boom generation attacked so fiercely when they were young.

But now, when confronted with the countless people of Tohoku's Sanriku and Fukushima who lost so much, we are helpless and at a loss for words. At such a time, I feel strongly that the value we must produce lies in "protoform architecture" that can fulfill the individual person's dream of a way of life, and in a "landscape" that can fulfill the dream of a community—something I would like to call "protoscape."

Modernism does not befit the land when its people have lost everything they had to hang on to. To meet the fervent hopes of the disaster-stricken areas, the new methods of a new age are needed. If nostalgia, then an unselfish nostalgia; if regionalism, then a regionalism broad-minded and tolerant; and if nationalism, then a nationalism without righteousness. This is the hard and narrow path of architectural thinking we must find. I am hopeful many of the architects who pick up this volume will join me in looking for it.

住居No.14 筑波・黒の家
House No.14, Tsukuba

1993
茨城県新治郡 Ibaraki

常時2件ほどは住宅設計を続けるよう自分に課してきた。建築は住宅が最も難しく、これを手放した瞬間に建築家は駄目になると考えるからである。

I have always given myself the task to constantly keep working on the design of a house or two. This is because I believe that the house is the most difficult type of architecture and letting go of the house would mean the end for an architect.

House No.14, Tsukuba

建て主が名付けた黒の家

これもローコストの極みのような住宅だ。建て主の井上雅之さんと中井川由季さんは前衛陶芸家として活躍する夫婦で友人である。この夫婦の純粋無垢な世間離れした人柄が気に入っていた。井上さんの作品は、師匠の中村錦平さんの作風を受けて、派手な金や赤の色彩を施した「ナンジャコリャ」と誰もが叫んでしまうようなオブジェ焼きの作風だった。中井川さんの方は、木の実のようでもあり内臓のようでもある不思議な形と手触りが特徴だ。ふたりとも、作るものが大きい。2m近くの作品も少なくない。

その当時住んでいた家が計画道路に引っ掛かって立ち退かざるを得なくなり、筑波の山の中に敷地を見つけて移住するというので、わたしが設計をすることになった。ふたりとも作家として名が知られ始めていた頃だが、前衛陶芸などそうそう売れるわけもない。器を作ればそれなりの収入は得られるはずなのだが、絶対に器は作らない。「作るのは陶芸によるオブジェなのだ」と頑固なまでに決めている。陶芸家ではなく芸術家であることにこだわっている。その頑さが気に入ったのだから仕方がない。金はなかった。「海の博物館」を終えて一息ついていた頃、またしてもため息が出るようなローコストである。

初めに思い付いたのは、わたしが若い頃に住んでいた借家である。農家が大工に頼んで建てた粗末で簡素極まりない一軒家だったが、住むのに不自由はなかった。3間四方の平屋で、4畳半、6畳、キッチン、便所がその中に無駄なく鮮やかに詰め込まれている。大工さんが作りやすい1間半のモジュールの田の字型平面だった。大工さんが作りやすい間取りにすれば安くなるはずだ。そもそも、木造で上棟するまでのいわゆる骨組みの値段は安い。骨組みさえ出来上がれば、屋根を架け、あとは建具を入れれば住まいにはなる。そう考えれば、これは設計というよりは半設計で、半分以上は大工さん任せの建物にするのがいい、と考えた。

1間半・1間・1間半のグリッドで空間を構成した。釜など重いものが置かれるアトリエは1階にし、2階を生活のスペースとし、その2階には道路側からブリッジで入ることとした。2階はプライベートゾーンなので軒下を使ってテラスを張り出し、雨戸で適宜隠せるようにした。金が掛かるからと節約した雨戸のスリットにアクリルを入れたのは井上さんである。

大工の杉田定一さんは、われわれの意図をよく汲んでくれて、梁が集中する真ん中の4本の大黒柱を、設計ではやや太い四角い柱だったのをたくましい丸柱に替えてくれた。あまりに熱を入れたので竣工後に体調を崩して倒れ込んだほどだ。

わたしの事務所では、住宅に作品名を付けるのを嫌って、設計した順番で「住居No.14」とそっけなく呼ぶことにしていた。この住宅は「住居No.14」となるはずであった。井上さんは、せっかく建てたのにそれでは寂しいと思ったのだろう。「黒の家」と自ら名付け、これが通称となった。

その後、阪神淡路大震災で被災された父君を引き取るため、別棟で小さな木造平屋を建てた。さらに何年かして駐車場の小屋を建てた。アトリエと庭を得て制作フィールドが広がり、陶芸家の作品は巨大化の一途をたどった。ふたりの旺盛な創作は今も止むことがない。(Eng. p.274)

Site Plan 1/1500

できないことはない、できないなら、できない
世の中が悪い、といった暴言を吐いた記憶がある。
I recall a memory of having once made a rash remark that
"there is nothing that can't be done—and if something
can't be done, it's the world that's at fault".

2階リビング・ダイニング
The living/dining room on the second story.

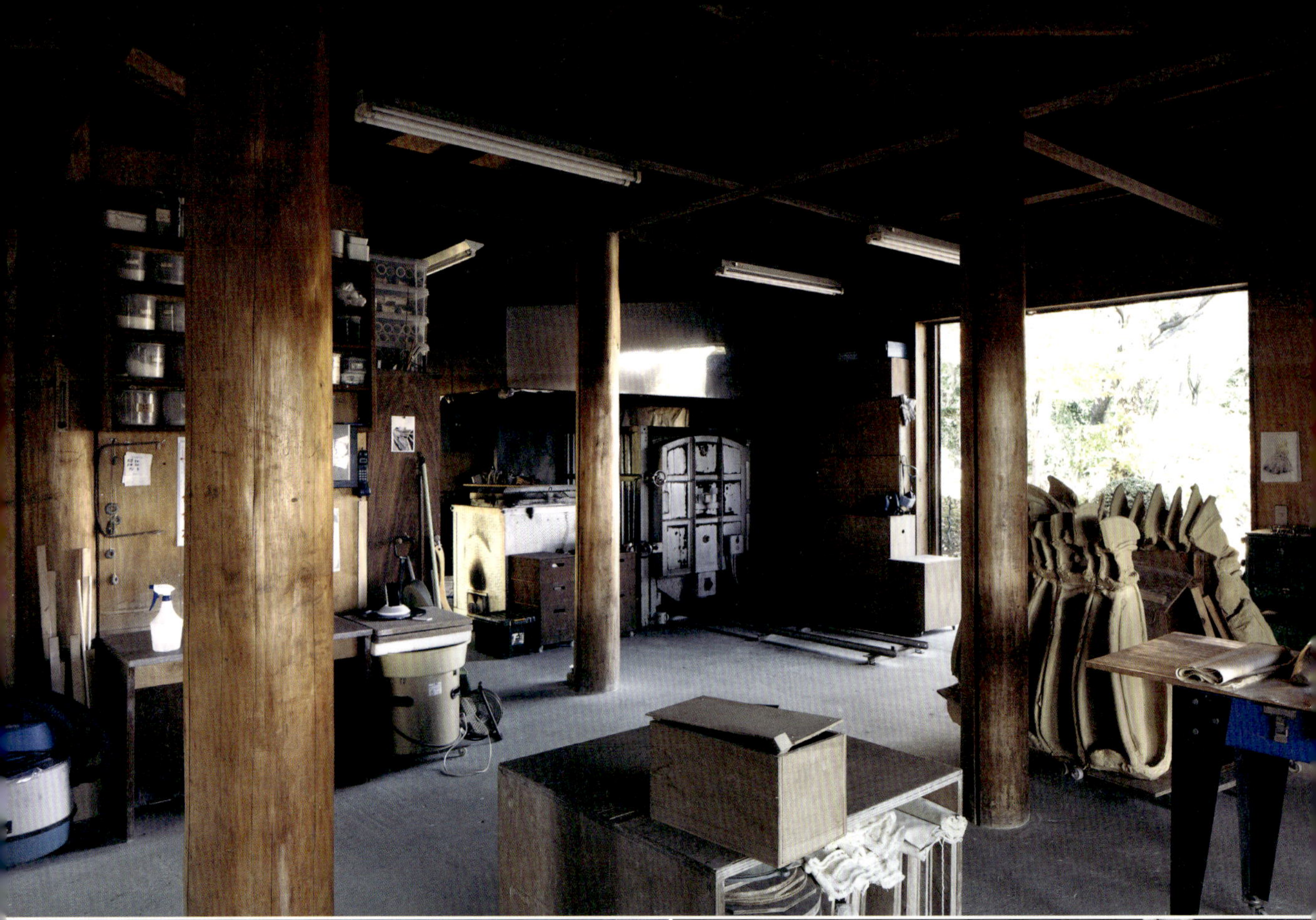

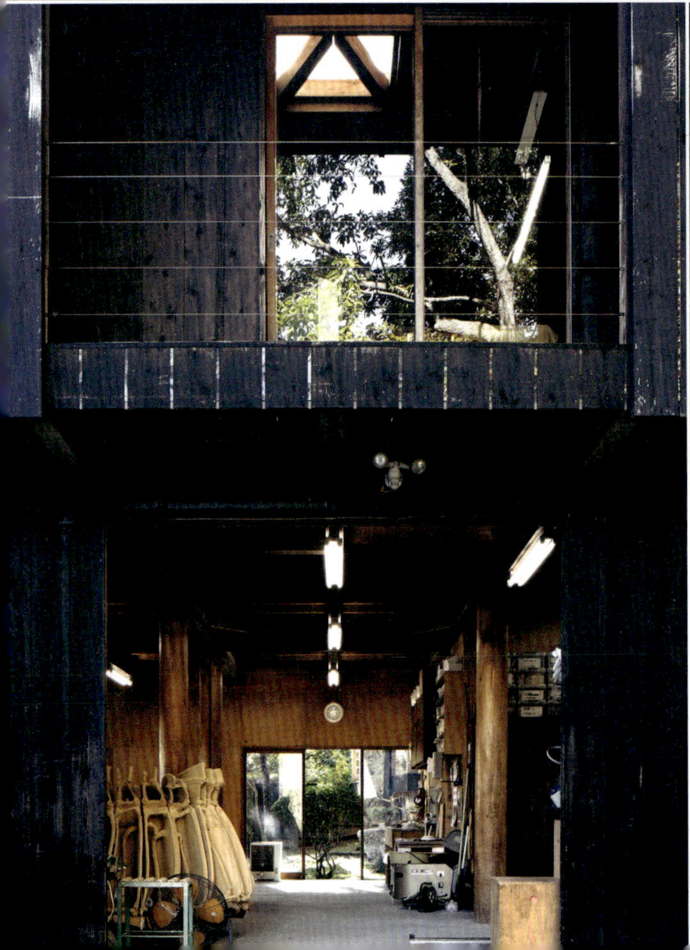

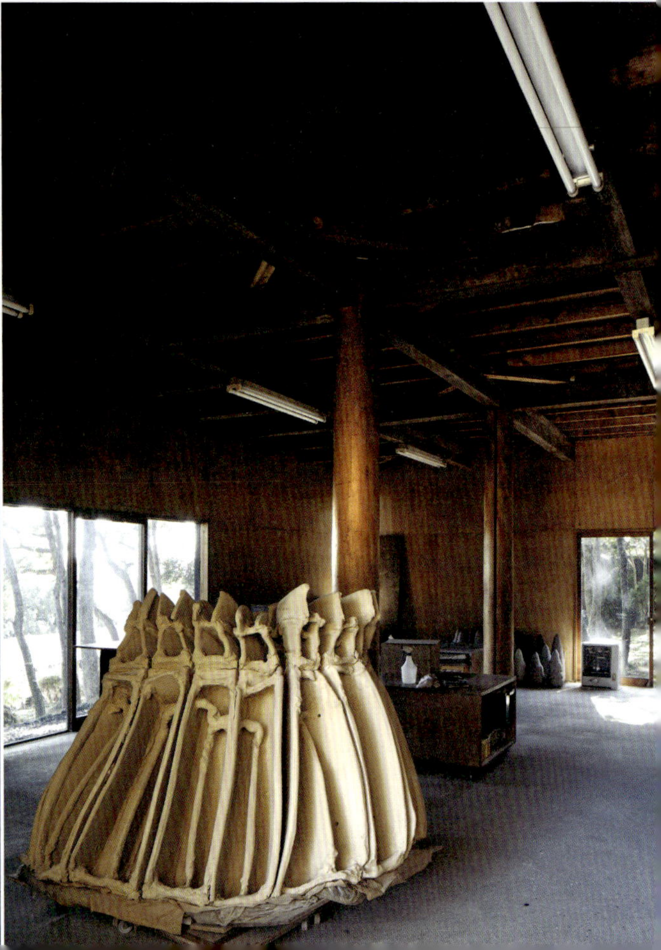

2F Plan

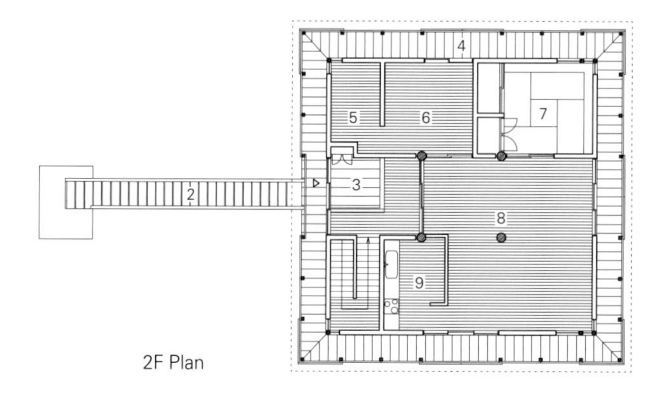

1 atelier
2 entrance bridge
3 entrance hall
4 corridor
5 storeroom
6 study
7 tatami room
8 living/dining room
9 kitchen

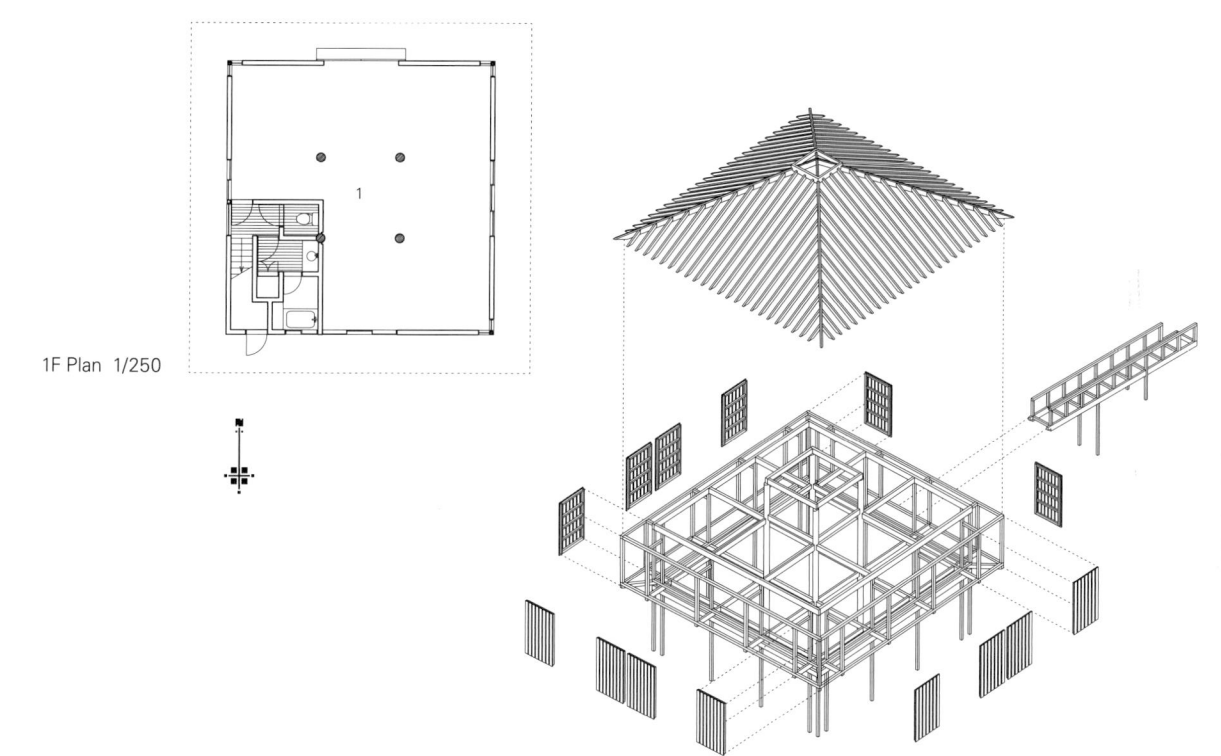

1F Plan 1/250

Section 1/250

全体構成図

中央に4本の梁間2.7mスパンで丸柱を配し、その外に3.15mスパンで架構を組んだ。コストダウンを図るため、大工さんが無理せず組めるスパンで全体を構成した。丸柱に絡む梁は四方差しにならぬよう段違いで差している。正方形平面で中央が暗くなるため、屋根頂部にトップライトを設けた。

Spatial Composition

Four rounded columns spaced at 2.7-meter intervals were positioned at the center and a frame with 3.15-meter spans was constructed around them. The entire structure was configured with spans that could easily be assembled by the carpenters in order to lower costs. The beams that meet the rounded columns were staggered to avoid four-way cross joints. A skylight was opened at the top of the roof above the darkest area at the center of the square plan.

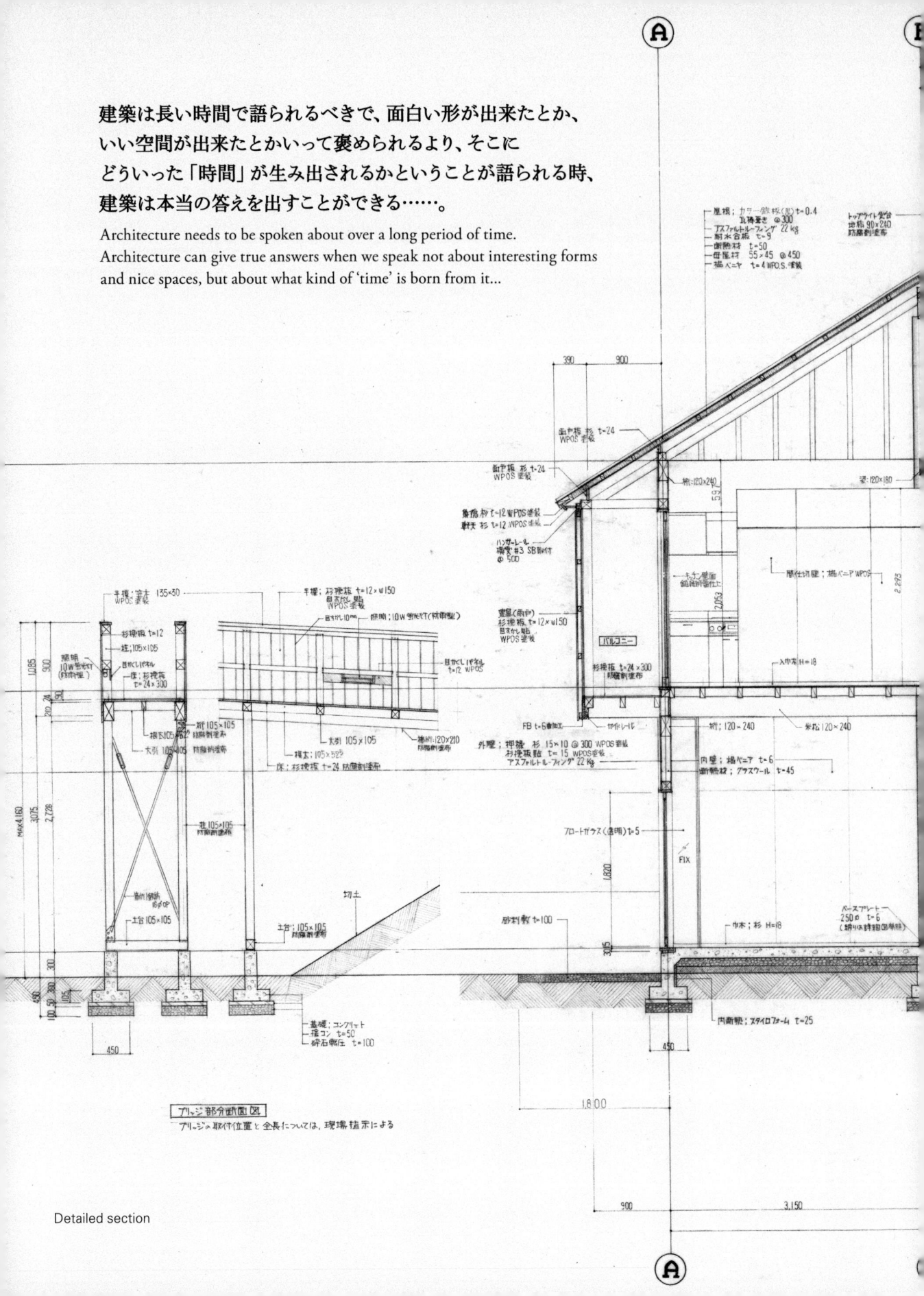

建築は長い時間で語られるべきで、面白い形が出来たとか、
いい空間が出来たとかいって褒められるより、そこに
どういった「時間」が生み出されるかということが語られる時、
建築は本当の答えを出すことができる……。

Architecture needs to be spoken about over a long period of time.
Architecture can give true answers when we speak not about interesting forms
and nice spaces, but about what kind of 'time' is born from it...

Detailed section

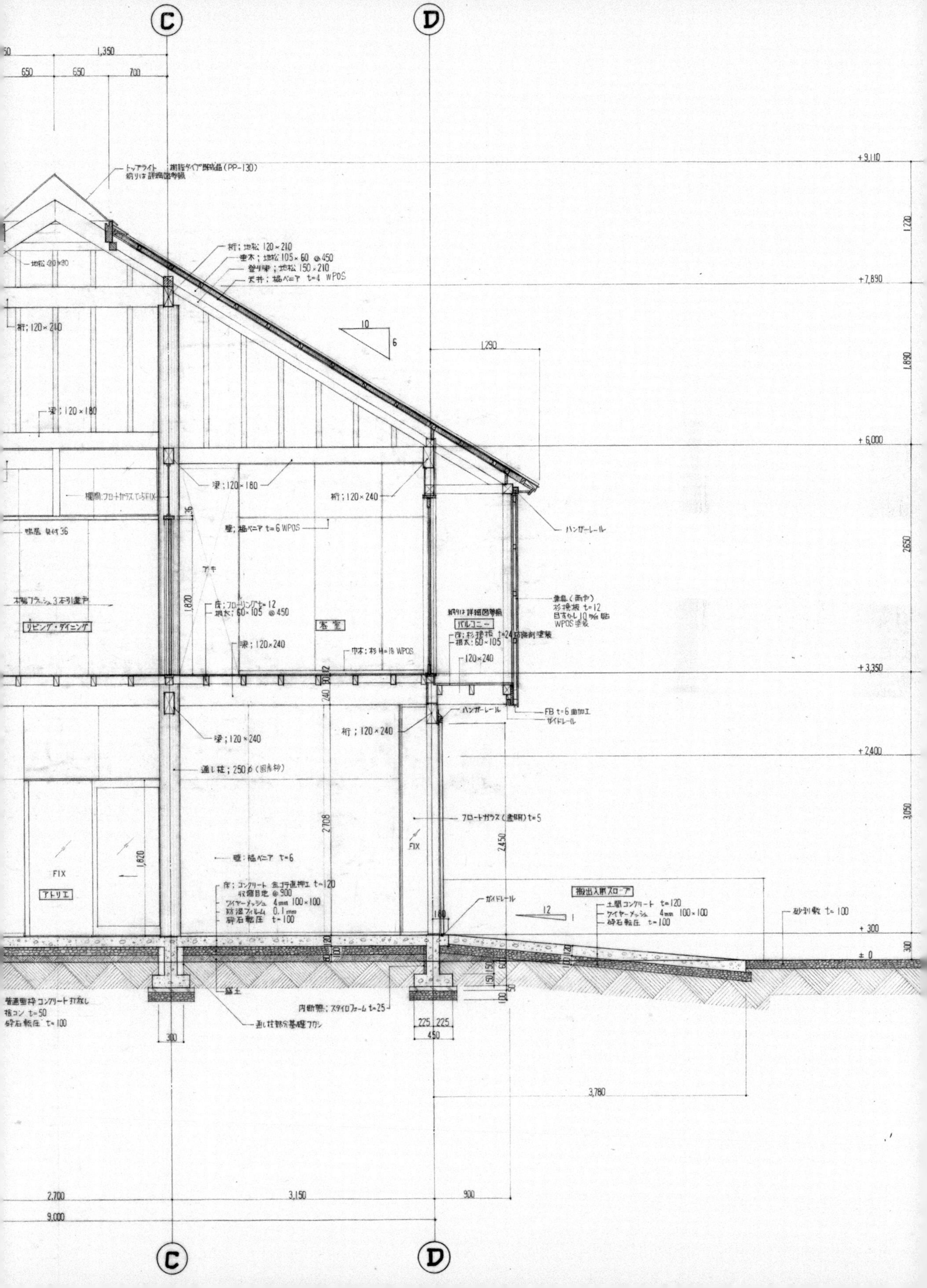

C
D
1,350
650
650
700
トップライト　樹脂タイプ既成品（PP-130）
納りは詳細図参照
+9,110
+7,890
+6,000
+3,350
+2,400
+300
±0
1,220
1,890
2,650
3,050
300
桁；地松 120×210
垂木；地松 105×60 @450
登り梁；地松 150×210
天井；桐ベニア t=4 WPOS
地松 90×90
桁；120×240
梁；120×180
10
6
1,290
梁；120×180
桁；120×240
欄間：フロートガラス t=5 FIX
ハンガーレール
敷居 見付36
壁；桐ベニア t=6 WPOS
アキ
木製フラッシュ3本引違戸
リビング・ダイニング
床；フローリング t=12
根太；60×105 @450
梁；120×240
客室
巾木；杉 H=18 WPOS
1,820
納りは詳細図参照
バルコニー
床；杉挽板 t=24 防腐剤塗装
根太；60×105
120×240
雨戸（雨戸）
杉挽板 t=12
目すかし10mm貼
WPOS塗装
FB t=6 曲加工
ガイドレール
ハンガーレール
梁；120×240
桁；120×240
通し柱；250φ（国産杉）
フロートガラス（透明）t=5
FIX
2,708
2,450
1,820
FIX
アトリエ
壁；桐ベニア t=6
床；コンクリート 金ゴテ直押エ t=120
収縮目地 @900
ワイヤーメッシュ 4mm 100×100
防湿フィルム 0.1mm
砕石転圧 t=100
ガイドレール
搬出入用スロープ
土間コンクリート t=120
ワイヤーメッシュ 4mm 100×100
砕石転圧 t=100
12
1
砂利敷 t=100
普通型枠コンクリート打放し
捨コン t=50
砕石転圧 t=100
盛土
内断熱；スタイロフォーム t=25
通し柱部分基礎フカシ
300
225
225
450
3,780
2,700
3,150
900
9,000
C
D

雨戸のスリットから差し込む回廊の光
Sunlight shines into the corridor through the slits of the shutters.

素直に思っていることが素直に伝わればいい。
All is well if my honest thoughts are honestly conveyed.

住居No.15　杉並・黒の部屋
House No.15, Suginami

1993

東京都杉並区　Tokyo

もし、身近に接する現前の壁が、表層の欲求を満たすために、
初めから世界との脈略を断っているのであれば……、
わたし個人としては、それを引き剥がしたいと思う。

If there was a wall before me that shuts off its connection to the world from the start, just in order to fulfill a superficial desire…personally, I would feel an urge to tear it right off.

黒くないのに黒の部屋

バリバリのキャリア官僚から辣腕編集者へ、華麗なる転身をした森山明子さんからマンションの部屋の改造を頼まれた。10年来の友人の依頼を断るわけにもいかない。築20年近くの建物で、森山さんはこの一角に部屋を持っているが、同じ建物に小さな別の部屋を手に入れたので客間として改装したい、との申し出であった。現地を見てみると、これ以上普通になりようもないほどどこにでもあるいわゆる2LDKの部屋である。入り口は既製品の鉄扉、シルバーのアルミサッシ、ビニールクロス、ユニットバス。これに手を加えて何とかものにするのはなかなか苦しい。

総工費500万、大振りの草間彌生のカボチャの絵を掛けたい、中川幸夫のガラス作品を置きたい、それに見合った空間にしてね、あとは全部任せたからね、内容はあえて見ない、といういかにも森山さんらしいサバサバした依頼であった。ものづくりにとってこれが一番厳しい注文の仕方だ。こんな依頼をされたのは前にも後にもこれきりだ。やや不安はあったが、言葉通り彼女には案を見せなかったし作っている最中も見に来なかった。

草間彌生と中川幸夫、なまじの壁を作っても様になるはずもない。幸い、試しにビニールクロスと下地のプラスターボードを剥がしてみると、コンクリートのなかなか存在感のある壁が出てきた。これを使わない手はない。サッシとの取り合いには気を使ったが、あとはひたすら虚飾と欺瞞に満ちたビニールクロスの壁を剥がして空間を作った。それだけの部屋だが、むき出しになるなんて夢にも思わないで作られたコンクリートの壁の存在感がなかなかいい。生々しく、荒々しく、奥行きがあって、温かい。片田舎の田圃で老いた農夫に会ったような気持ちにさせてくれる。壁をむき出しにした後は、収納を建て込み、畳を敷いただけである。

出来上がって、草間彌生のカボチャも居心地が良さそうだし中川幸夫のオブジェもこれはこれで据わりが良い。「黒の家」のすぐ後だったので、気楽なつもりで「黒の部屋」と呼ぶことにしたが、この名前がなぜかピッタリはまっている。部屋に漂う空気がそれを感じさせるのだろう。この部屋で思い浮かべるとしたら黒以外の色は考えられない。黒をどこにも使っていないのに、どうして「黒の部屋」なんですか、と聞かれたことは一度もない。(Eng. p.275)

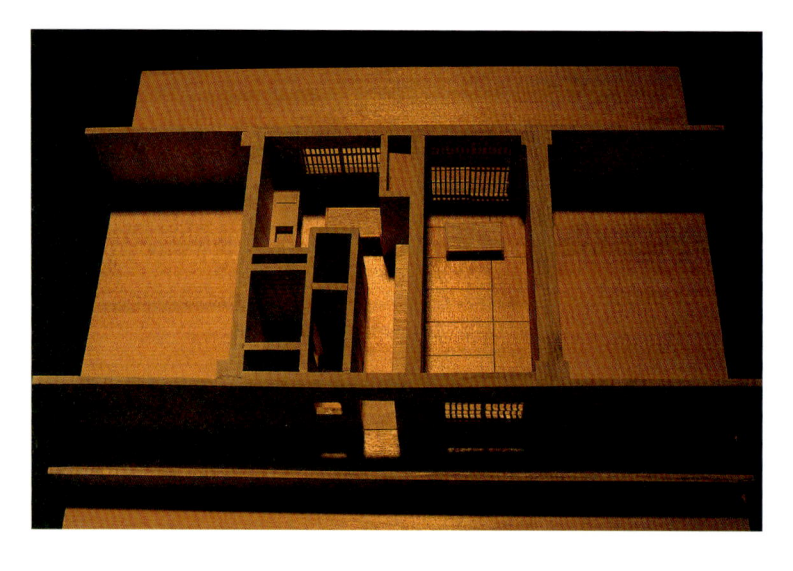

Site Plan 1/500

形態を操作することで、建築の表現が魔術のような効果を
生み出すことは知っている。この力を使って、
何かのメッセージを発することには抵抗がある。
I am well aware that the manipulation of form can generate magical
effects for the expression of architecture. I am reluctant to project any sort
of message through the use of such a power.

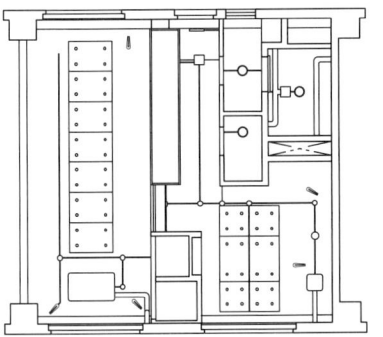

1 entrance
2 tatami room
3 dining room
4 washroom
5 bathroom
6 balcony

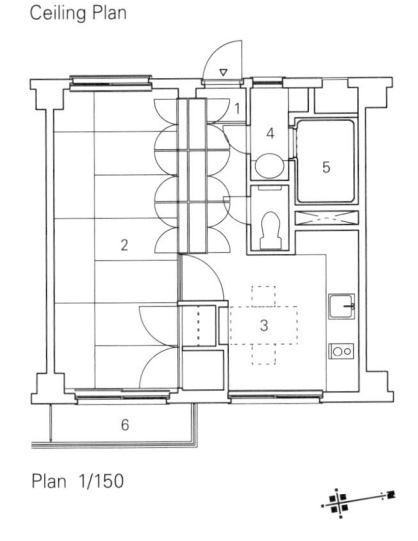

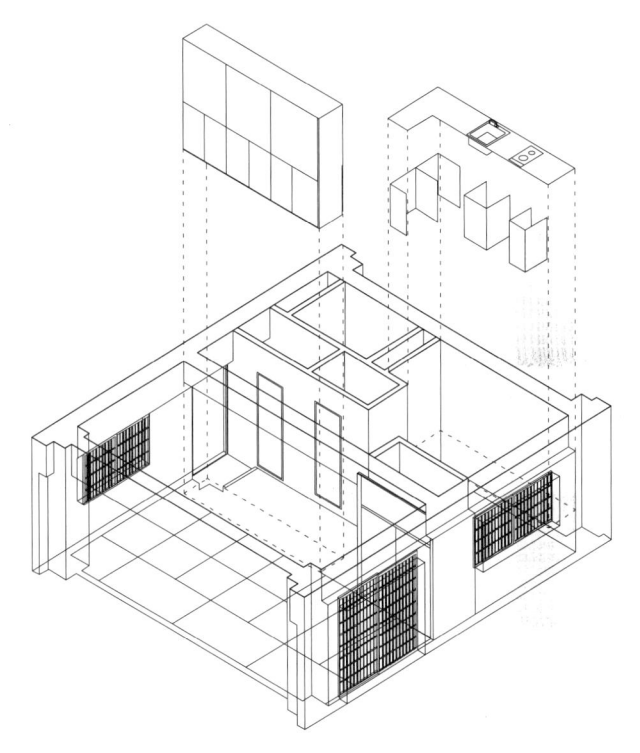

Ceiling Plan

Plan 1/150

Section 1/100

全体構成図
既存改修であるため、水回りの配置は変えなかった。残した既存の壁は目の粗い吹き付け塗装とした。和室に面した押し入れは記憶を留める意味で枠だけ残して色を塗った。全体を二分するように棚を接地し、これに展示棚と雑収納を配した。剥き出しにした天井には、居住性を考慮してグラスウールの吸音パネルを取り付けた。

Spatial Composition
The former positions of the rooms requiring plumbing were not altered because this was a renovation project. A coarse-grained coating was sprayed on the existing walls that were not removed. The frame of the closet of the traditional Japanese-style room was preserved and repainted to maintain a memory of the original space. The plan is divided into two by a shelf unit that serves as a display rack and storage cabinet. The exposed ceiling was installed with fiberglass sound-absorption panels in consideration of comfort.

ミニマムな設えのキッチンカウンター
The minimally-designed kitchen counter.

過去や記憶にこだわることは手間が掛かる。
労力も気力も使う。まったく新しい地平に自由に想像力を
働かせるような解放感もない。記憶を引きずれば、羽ばたくはずの
空想は失速し、思考は滞留する。しかし、その滞留のさなかに、
思考は時間の淀みやその肌触りを感じ取る。だとすれば、
その滞留こそが豊かさの資質と言えるのではあるまいか。

It is time-consuming to be concerned with the past and memories. It takes labor and energy. It also does not provide the sense of liberation like that of working freely on a fresh canvas. By dragging along memories, animated visions lose speed mid-flight and the flow of thoughts in the mind slows down. However, when the mind is in this state of stagnation, it is able to feel the settling of time and to take in its textures. Can we not say that such a state of stagnation is in fact a source of richness?

住居No.18　伊東・織りの家
House No.18, Ito

1995
静岡県伊東市 Shizuoka

まず一番最初にその敷地に立つ。
そこで思い付いたことがほとんどすべてだ。

I first begin by standing on the site. Almost everything comes from whatever ideas I conceive there.

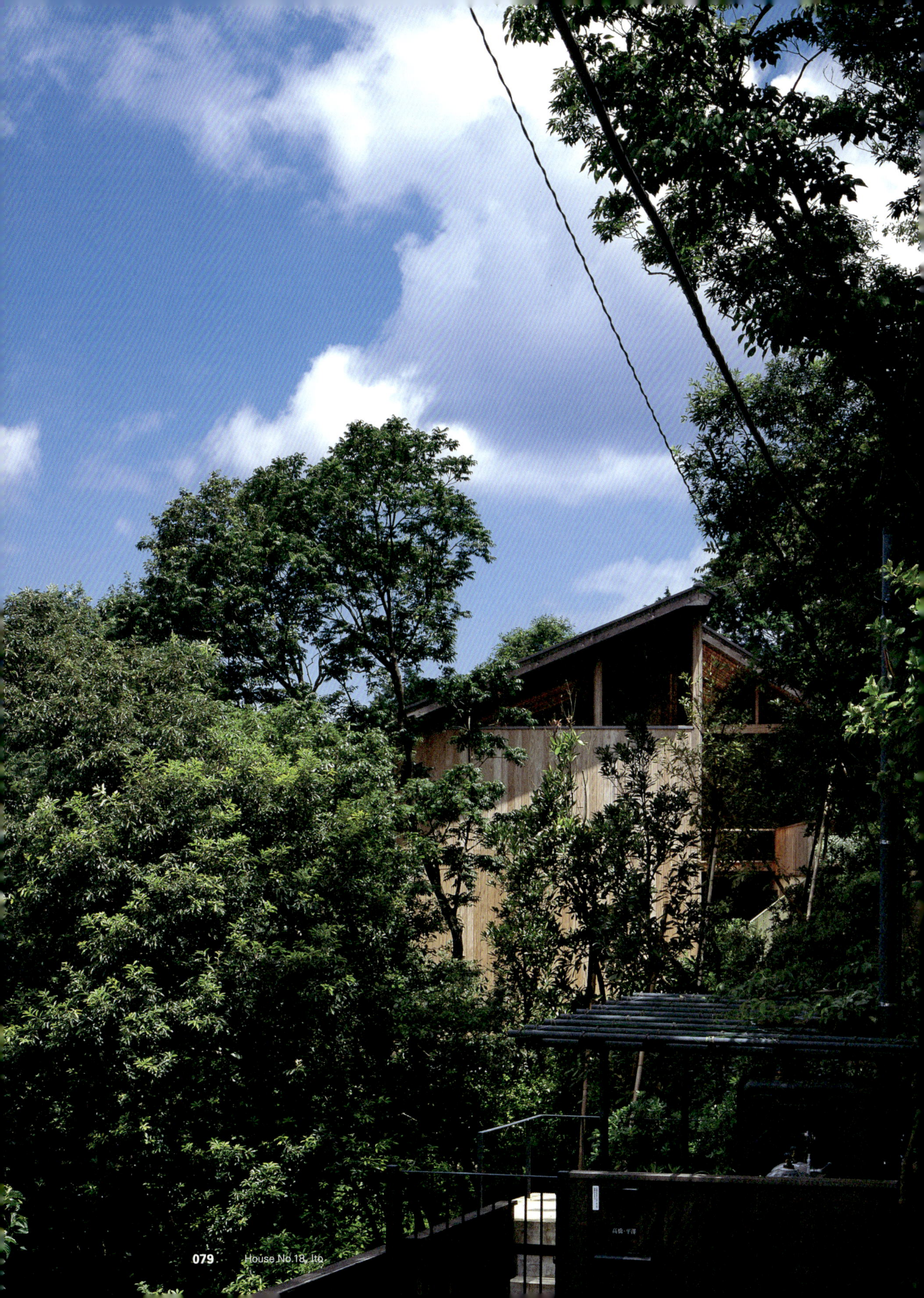

物語を織るような

知人の紹介で建て主のご夫婦に会った。ご主人の高橋正宏さんは横浜市役所に勤めるキャリアでたいへんな読書家。見るからに博識であることが分かる。奥さんの平澤エミ子さんは織物作家として知られる。小柄だが巨大な木製の機織りを操る。バイタリティーに溢れ、その元気さにいつも圧倒される。夫婦でエジプトに住んだ経験があり、その時の印象からザックリとした大きな空間で暮らしたいと考え、伊豆半島の宇佐見の斜面地を手に入れ、そこに移住することにしていた。

「そんなに急な斜面じゃないから全然大丈夫」という平澤さんの妙に明るい説明を受けて敷地を見に行って唖然とした。木にしがみつかないと立っているのも難しいほどのかなりの急斜面で、扇型の変形敷地で北側斜面である。おまけに入り口の接道部が狭いので、工事は困難を極めることが予想された。折しも伊豆で群発地震があり、それも気になって基礎部分にかなりのコストが食われることが予想された。

設計は難航した。そもそも高橋さんは建築学科の出で建物について詳しく、平澤さんはライフスタイルに対する作家特有のこだわりをもっていた。建築家は建て主の意図を汲みつつ現実化しなければならないのだが、そもそも敷地の難易度は建て主が考えているより遥かに高い。コストもある。なかなかイメージとコストの折り合いがつかない。

いつも思うのだが、住宅の設計はどのようなものであれ格闘技である。幾度か破談の局面を迎えた。事務所の担当者の太田理加が、切れそうになるわたしをなだめ、施主をなだめ、施工者を懐柔し、実に粘り強く対応してこの建物は出来上がった。ご苦労様でした。施工のために鉄骨の仮設鋼台を建て、杭を打ち、スラブと擁壁をRCで造り、シンプルな木造2階屋をその上に置いた。

やはり作品名が欲しいのだろうか。「織りの家」という名前は、担当者と平澤さんが話し合って決めた。建物の性格と施主の仕事を連想させる良い名前だと思う。築15年ほどになるが、工事でいったん荒れた敷地には木々が茂り、アプローチには草花が生い茂っている。「厚い板でしっかりした床が欲しい」という希望で設えた厚板の唐松の床は、アメ色に変わり実に良い味わいを出している。苦労して作り上げた空間が、建て主の暮らしの中で成熟していく様を、訪れるたびに体感することができるのはうれしい。(Eng. p.275)

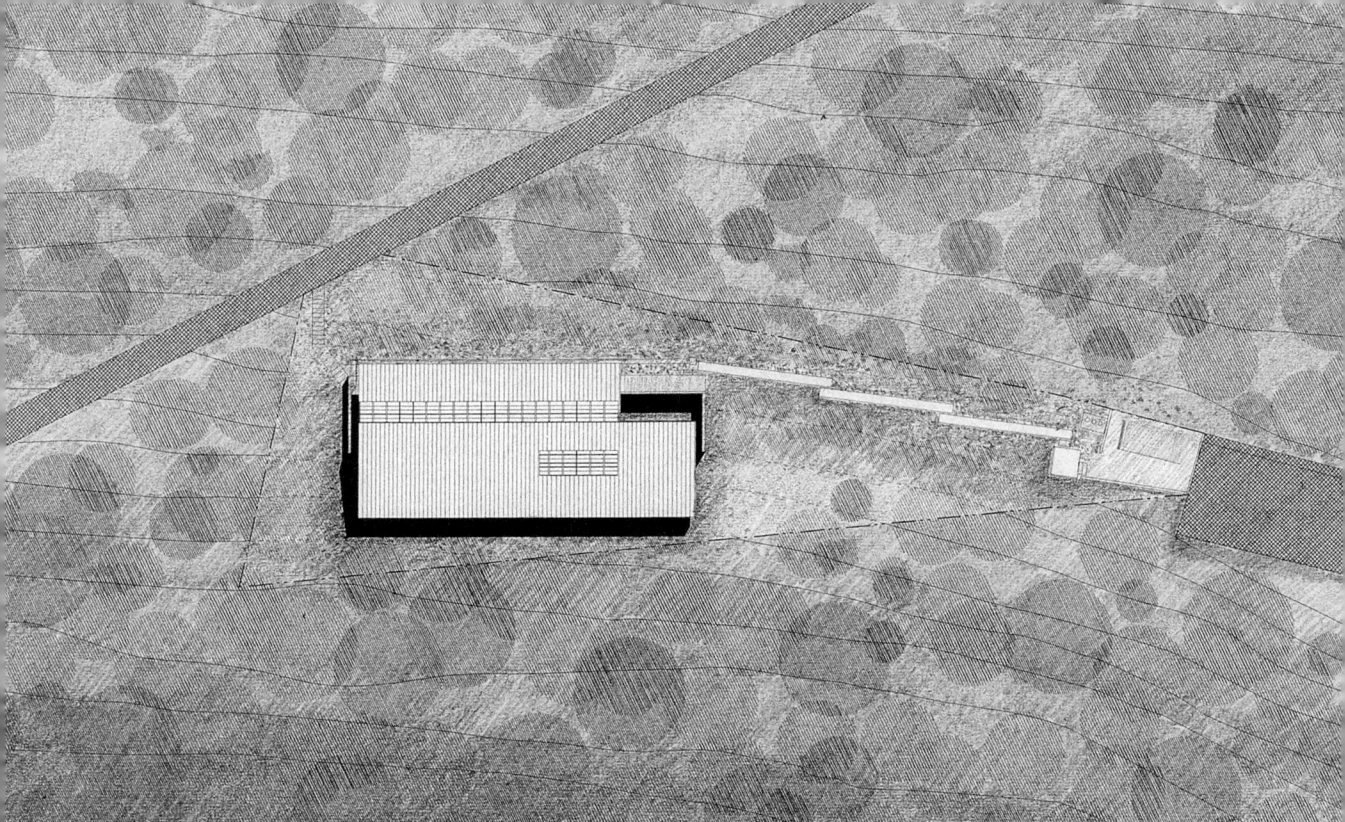

Site Plan 1/500

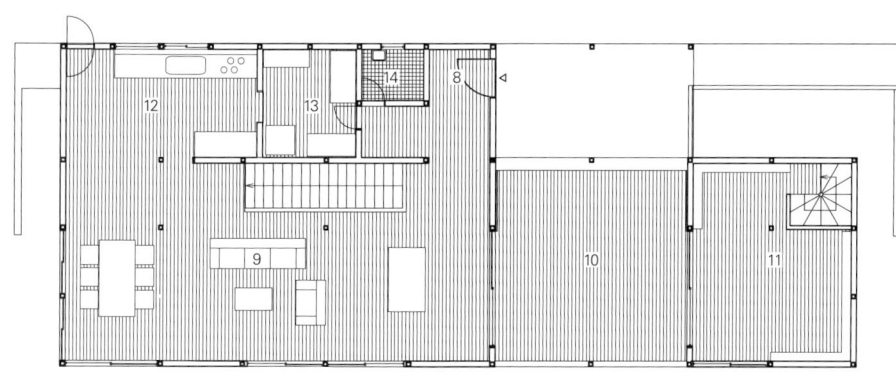

2F Plan

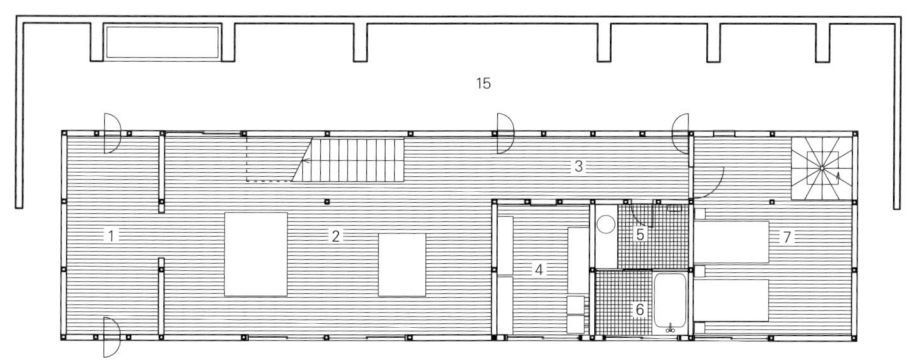

1F Plan 1/200

1 storeroom
2 atelier
3 corridor
4 workroom
5 washroom
6 bathroom
7 bedroom
8 entrance
9 living room
10 terrace
11 study
12 kitchen
13 pantry
14 toilet
15 dry area

081   House No.18, Ito

Exterior plan

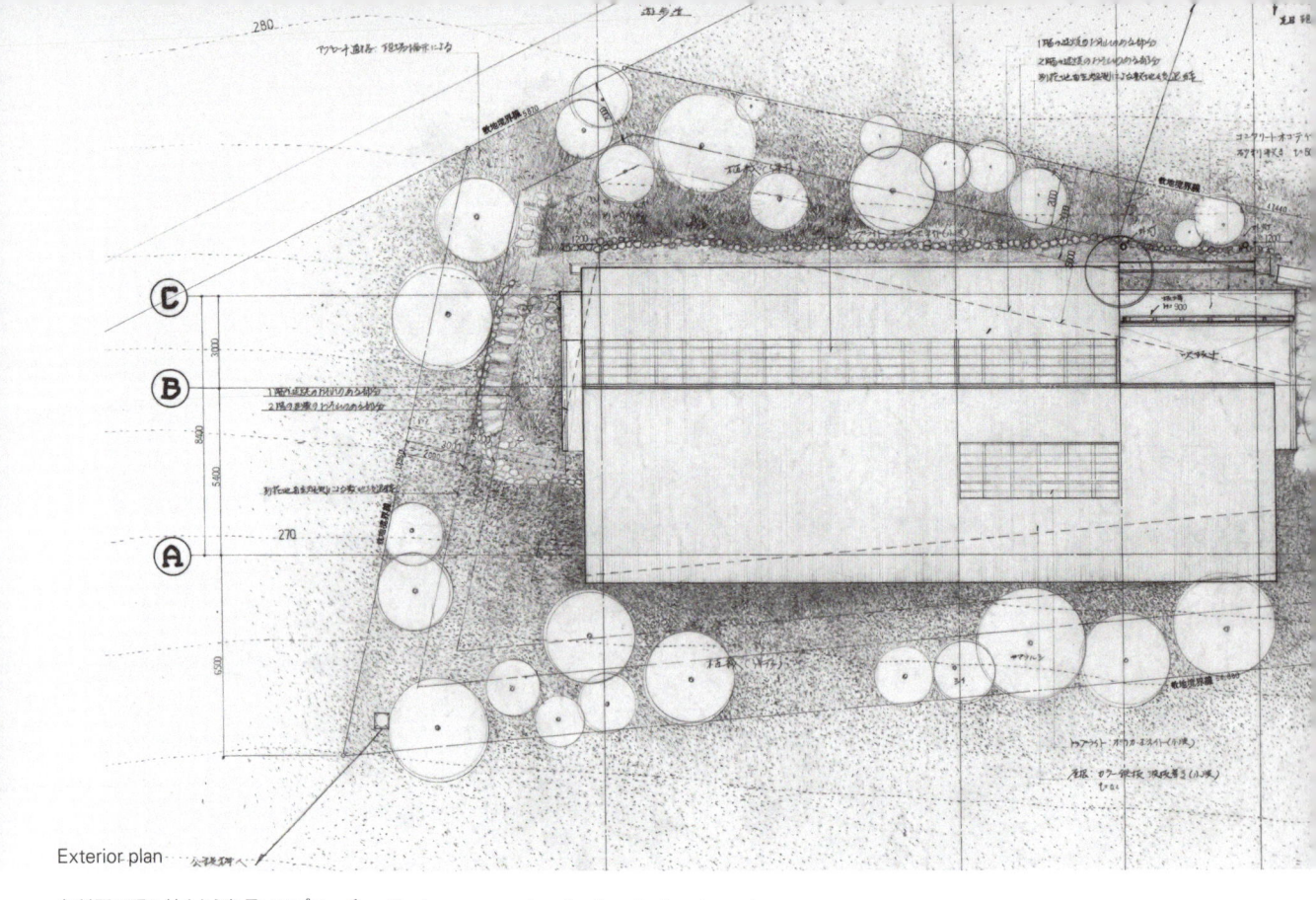

急斜面に張り付くような長いアプローチ　　The long approach path clings to the steep slope.

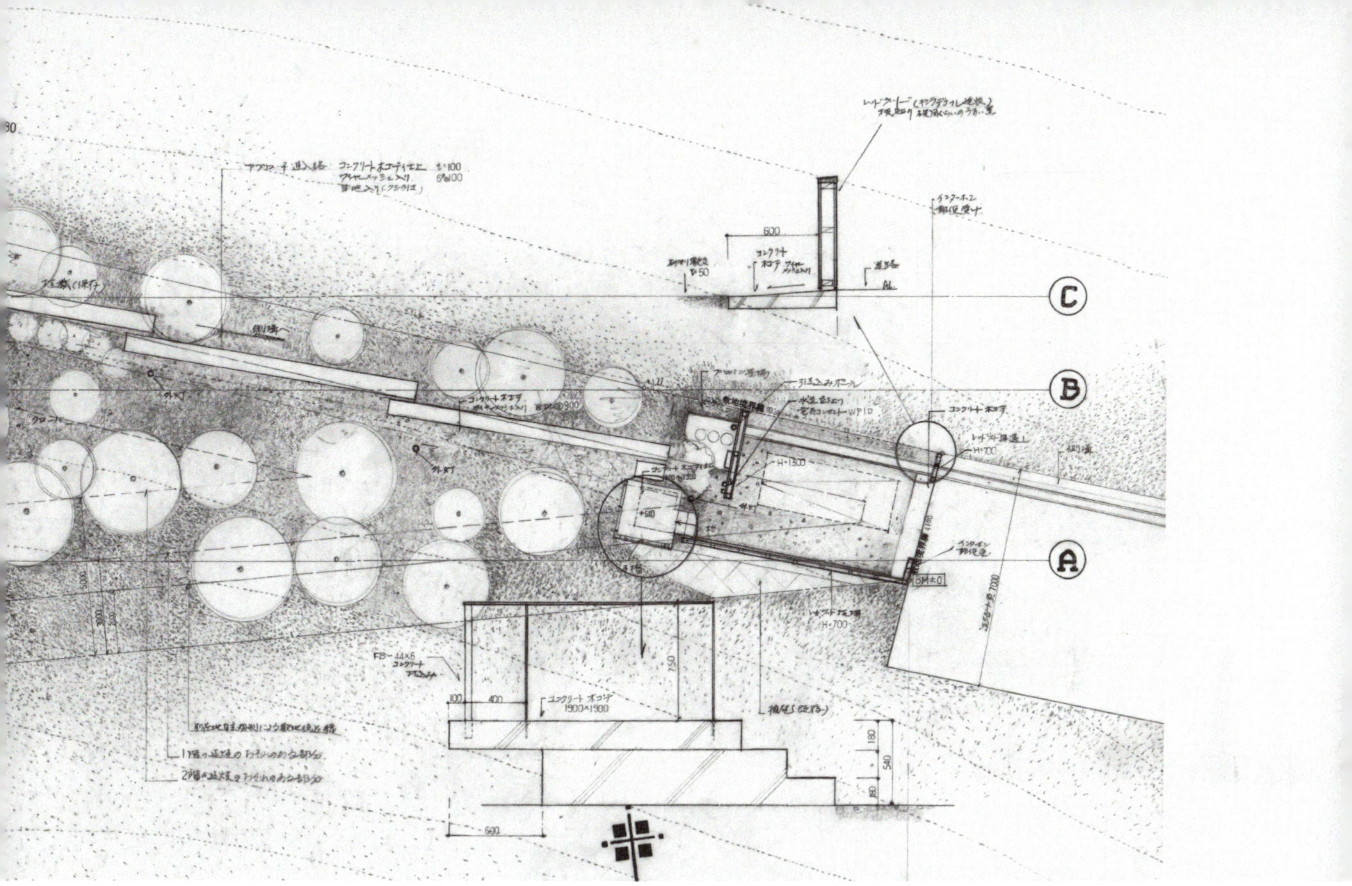
C
B
A

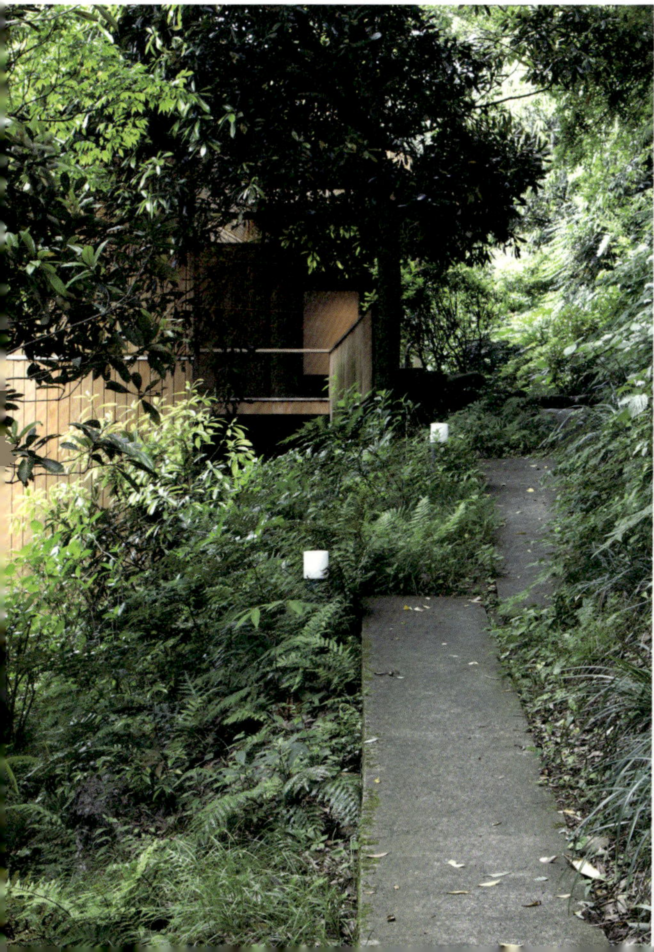

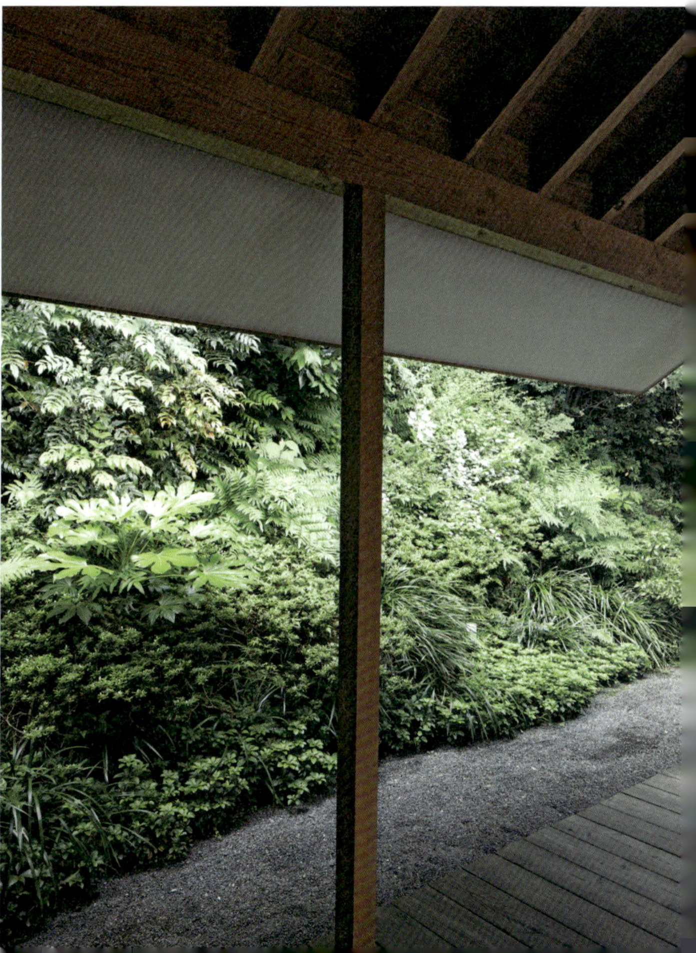

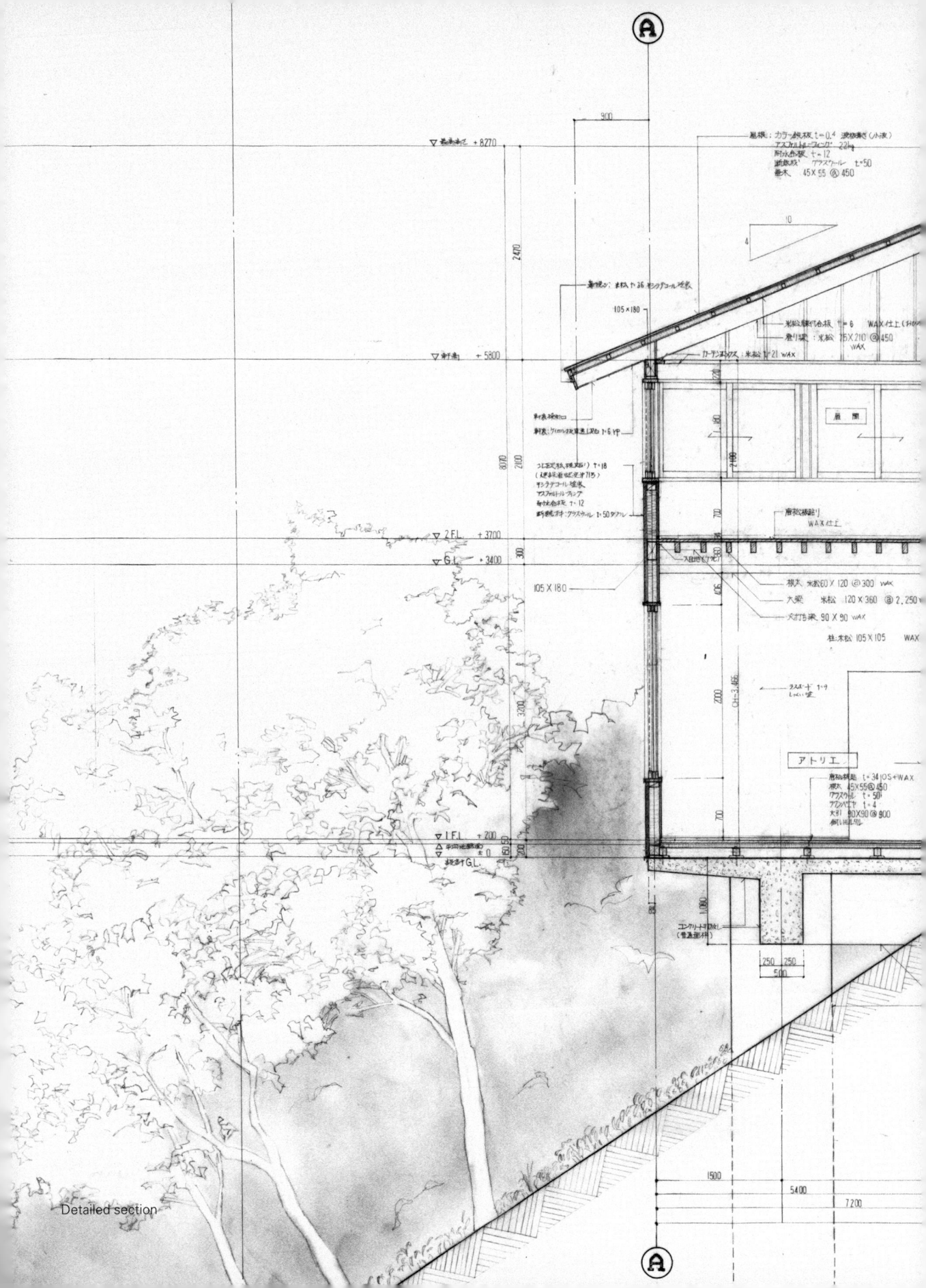

Detailed section

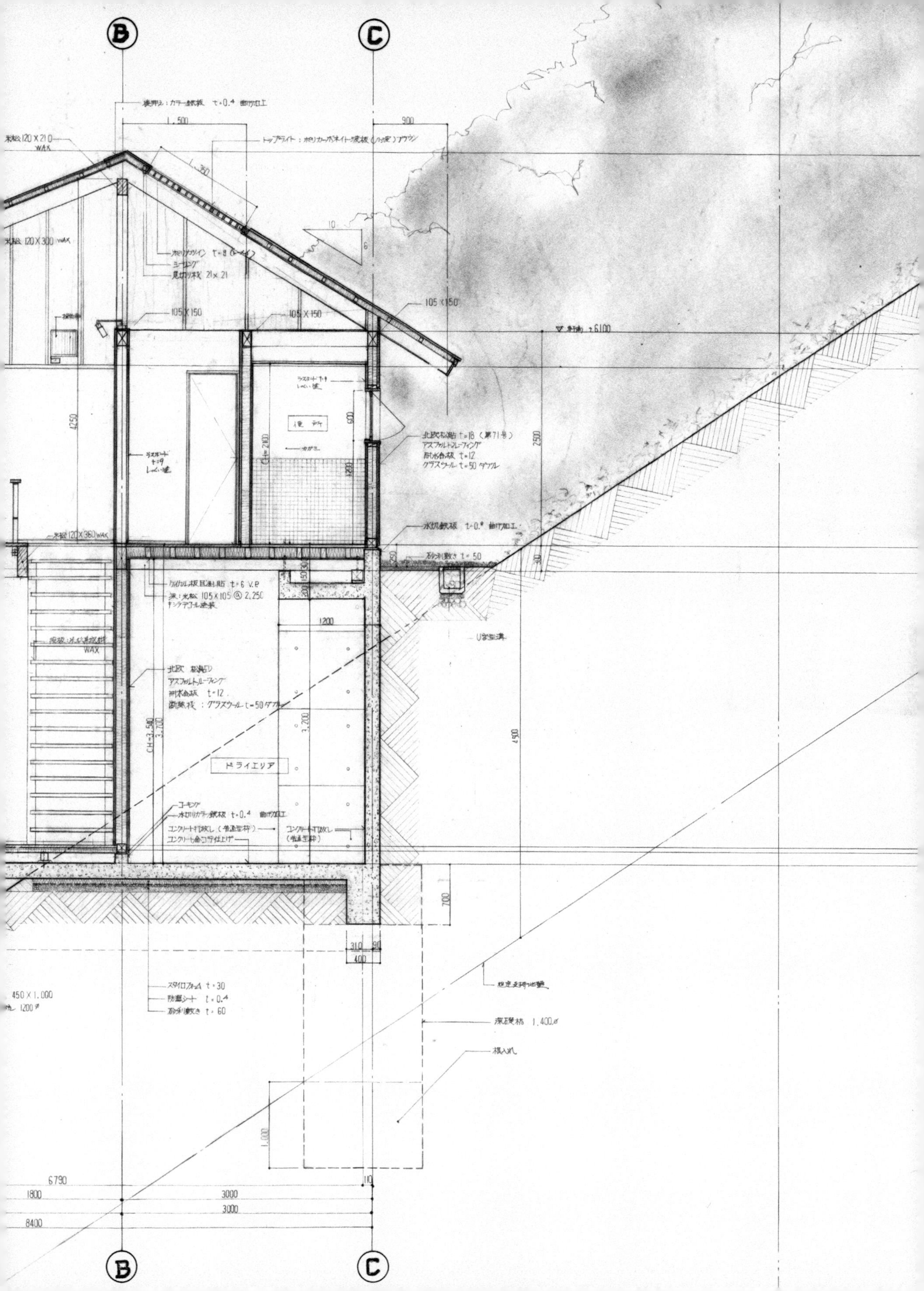
B
C
棟押え：カラー鉄板 t=0.4 曲げ加工
1,500
900
米松 120×210 WAX
トップライト：ポリカーボネイト波板（小波）ブラウン
米松 120×300 WAX
ポリカーボネイン t=8
見切り板 21×21
105×150
105×150
105×150
▽軒高 +6100
4250
便所
CH=2100
北欧松板貼 t=18
アスファルトルーフィング
耐水合板 t=12
グラスウール t=50 ダブル
2500
米松 120×360 WAX
水切鉄板 t=0.4 曲げ加工
砂利敷き t=50
カルカル板目透貼 t=6 V.P
1200
U字型溝
北欧 松板貼り
アスファルトルーフィング
耐水合板 t=12
断熱材：グラスウール t=50 ダブル
CH=3,540
3,700
3,200
ドライエリア
4500
コーキング
水切りカラー鉄板 t=0.4 曲げ加工
コンクリート打放し（普通型枠）
コンクリート金ゴテ仕上げ
700
310
90
400
スタイロフォーム t=30
防湿シート t=0.4
砂利敷き t=60
450×1,000
1200φ
深礎杭 1,400φ
杭入れ
1,000
6790
1800
3000
3000
8400
110

自然とリアルな関係がまずあって、結果的に美しい風景となる。
A beautiful landscape arises as the result of establishing a real relationship with nature.

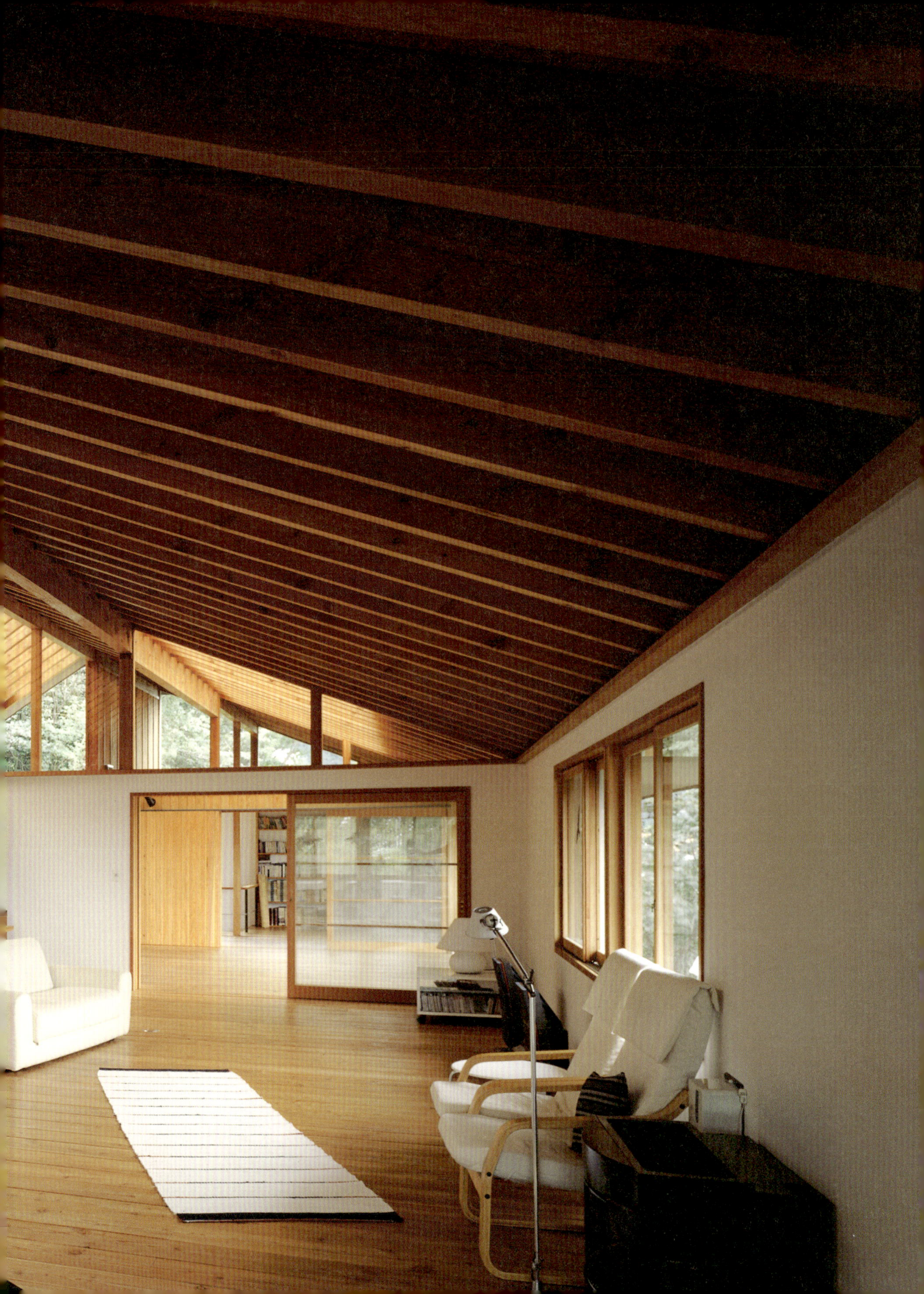

棟の南側に沿って設けたトップライト
A skylight runs along the south side of the roof ridge.

伊豆の海を見下ろす居心地のいいテラス
The comfortable terrace overlooks the waters of Izu.

施主の状態や思い、敷地の条件などを突き合わせて、それに
可能な限り従前の答えを用意する。しかし、それだけでは
何かが足りない。多くの場合、建物を建てる目的は単純化できない。

I compare the client's situation and their wishes with the conditions of the site to prepare a solution that provides for them as best as possible. This alone, however, is not enough. In many cases, the objective for making a building cannot be simplified.

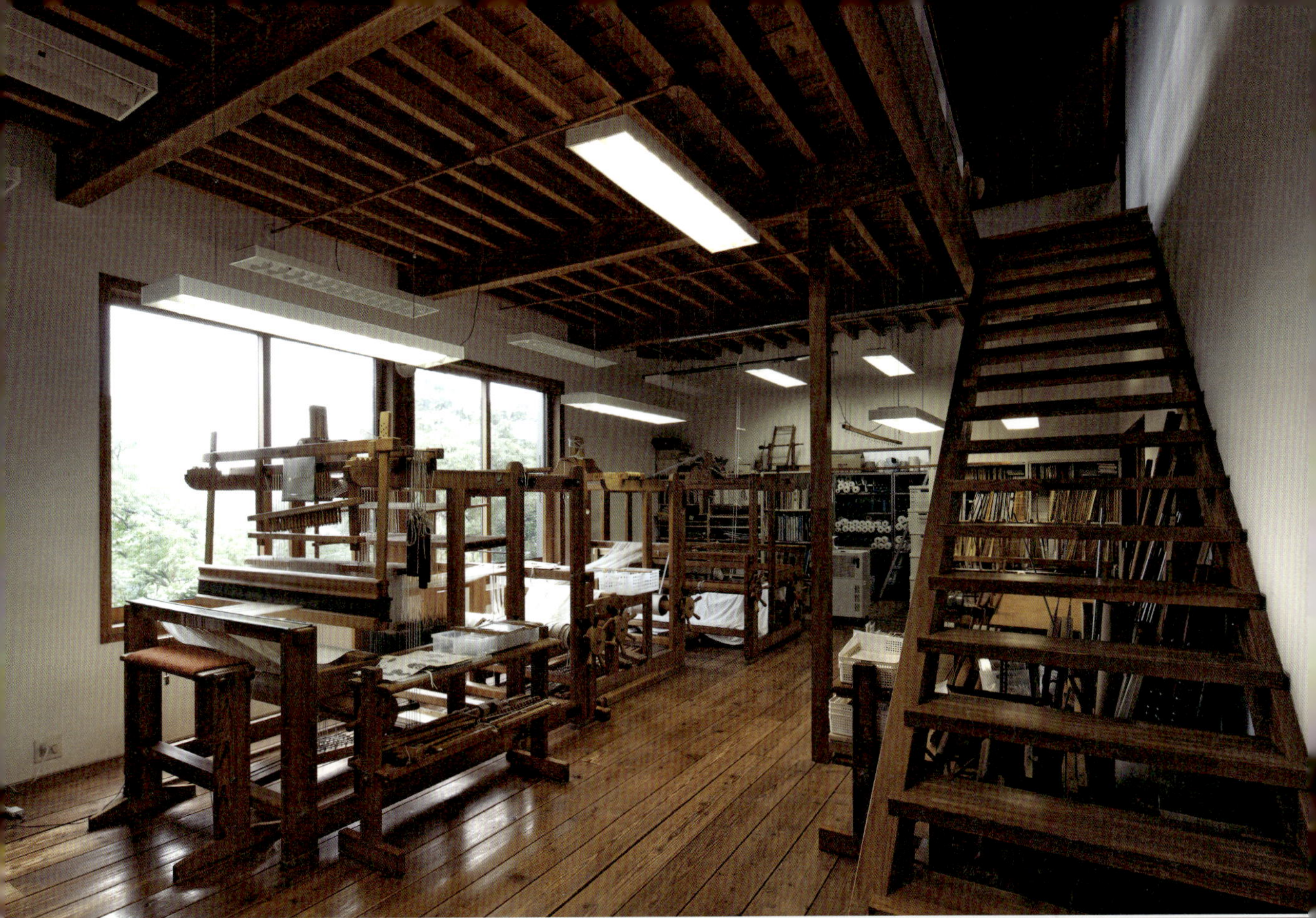

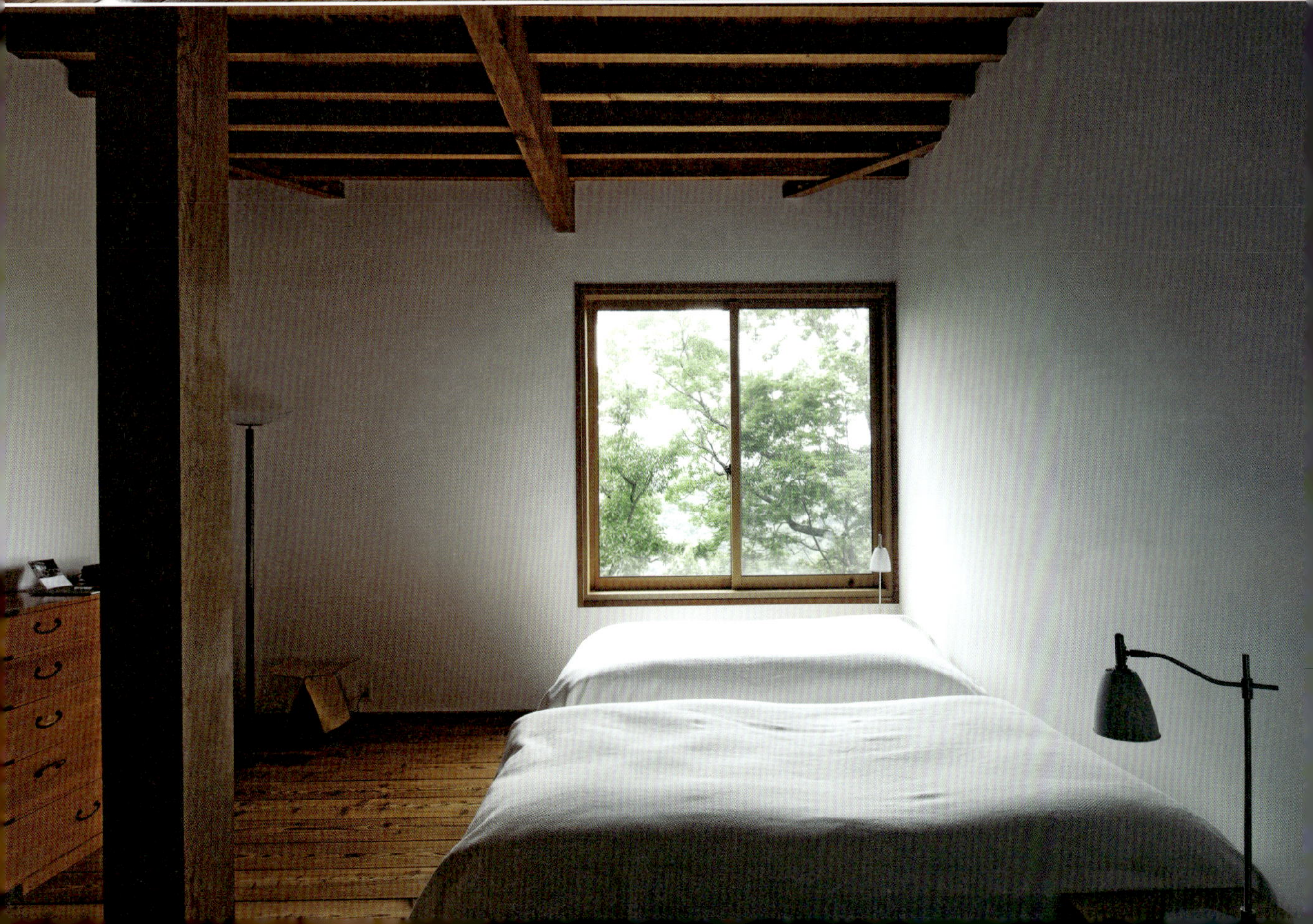

住居No.19　金沢の家
House No.19, Kanazawa

1996

石川県金沢市　Ishikawa

敷地と建物の関係という大きなストーリーがある。
There is a bigger story about the relationship between a site and a building.

ものづくりの迷宮

現代を代表する前衛陶芸作家として知られる中村錦平さん（以下、錦平さん。失礼）から、「金沢の実家を建て替えたいんだけど」という依頼があった。前述した「住居No.14 筑波・黒の家」の井上雅之さんの師匠だが、知己を得たのは錦平さんの方が早い。錦平さんの東京の自宅は、齋藤裕さんのデビュー作とも言える傑作。とても素晴らしい。これに迫るものを作るのはたいへんだな、と迷いつつ錦平さんの作品の磁力に引き込まれるように引き受けてしまった。

いつも予測が甘い。これが生来の欠点であり悪い癖だ。引き受けた後、さらにたいへんなことが分かった。施主が錦平さんも含めて4人居たのである。高齢の父君である2代目中村梅山（ばいざん）さんは、金沢でも名が知れた陶芸家だ。飄々として客には笑顔を絶やさない。ちょっと見では物腰が低い好々爺だが、ものを見る目はこの上なく厳しい人であることが端々に想像できた。奥の深い金沢の文化の粋を知る人と聞いていた。抹茶を出されたことがあるが、何気ない抹茶茶碗を手に取って、その手触りと重さ加減の絶妙さに驚き、口に付けてその微妙な口当たりにさらに驚いた。そういう人である。

長男の錦平さん、次男卓夫さん、三男康平さん、みな名が知られ活躍している陶芸家だが、作風はそれぞれまったく違う。この一族が住まう場所と工房を限られた敷地の中で作らねばならなかった。そして、梅山さんはもとより兄弟そろって建築に対して一家言もっている人ばかり。目眩のするような与件だった。とてもたち打ちできません。やめとけばよかった。

敷地の入り口付近にひとつ、少し入ったところにもうひとつ、かなりの樹齢を重ねた大きな松があり、これらは残すことにした。梅山さんが作った8畳に縁側のついた書院が旧宅の中心であった。贅沢なことも特別なことも何ひとつしていないが、素晴らしく密度のある濃厚な空間だった。どうしてそういうことが可能なのか、いまだにハッキリと説明できない。たぶん、高さや幅の微妙な寸法や部材の太さ加減なのだろう。これも、いったんは解体するが、そのまま復元することにし、新しくできる家の中心に据えることにした。つまり、変わらないのは2本の松と梅山さんの書院、あとは枝葉末節と考えた。

建物を配置できるエリアが限られているので、卓夫さんの住まいとアトリエを正面左手に3層、康平さんと梅山さんの住まいを右手に3層、正面中央を錦平さんが帰郷した時に使う書院とし、敷地の一番奥に康平さんのアトリエを設けた。居宅の1階部分はRC造とし、その他は鉄骨造にした。積雪があるので陸屋根で箱が並んだような建物になった。松の背景として目立たぬように、2階から上の外壁は亜鉛鋼板のハゼ葺きとした。

案の定、これも設計は困難を極めた。何しろ、どうしてそのような形になるのか、どうしてその素材を使うのか、それぞれ説明しなければならなかった。全員が興味津々なのだ。特に卓夫さんから質問攻めにあう。わたしの場合、形や素材を決めていくのは、どちらかと言うと論理性からではなく感覚的なところが大きいので、この説明には往生した。形や素材に対して多少なりとも説明がうまくなったとしたら、この建物が鍛えてくれたところが大きい。

住み手は文化の達人である。さすが住み方がうまい。素っ気ない建物が、作品を展示するギャラリーのようになった。建物の不足分を作品が埋めるように満たしている。やはり、建物も器なのだ。梅山さんの茶碗のように、何もない虚の部分の質感こそが大切なのだと改めて思った。(Eng. p.275)

Site Plan 1/500

Plan

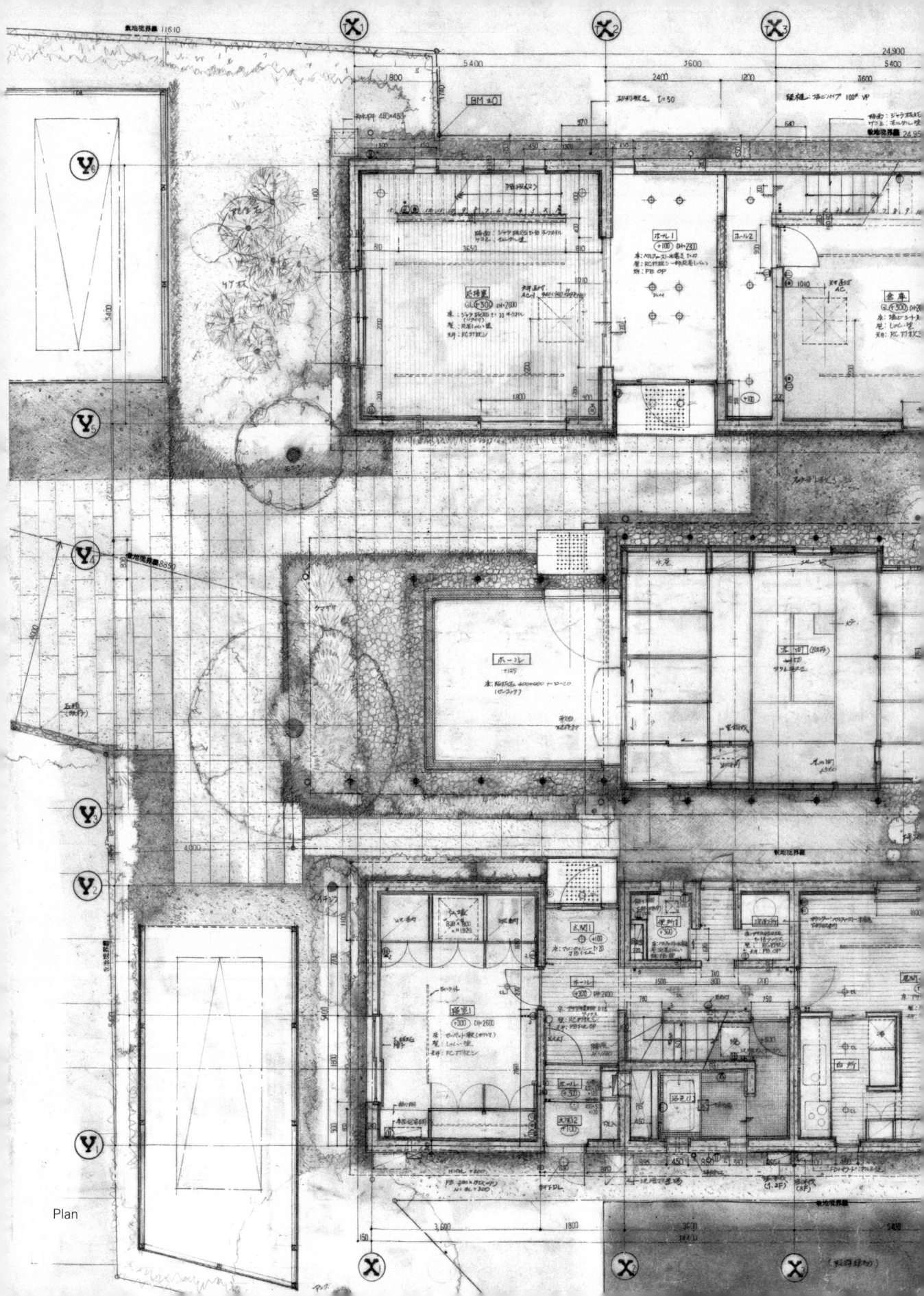

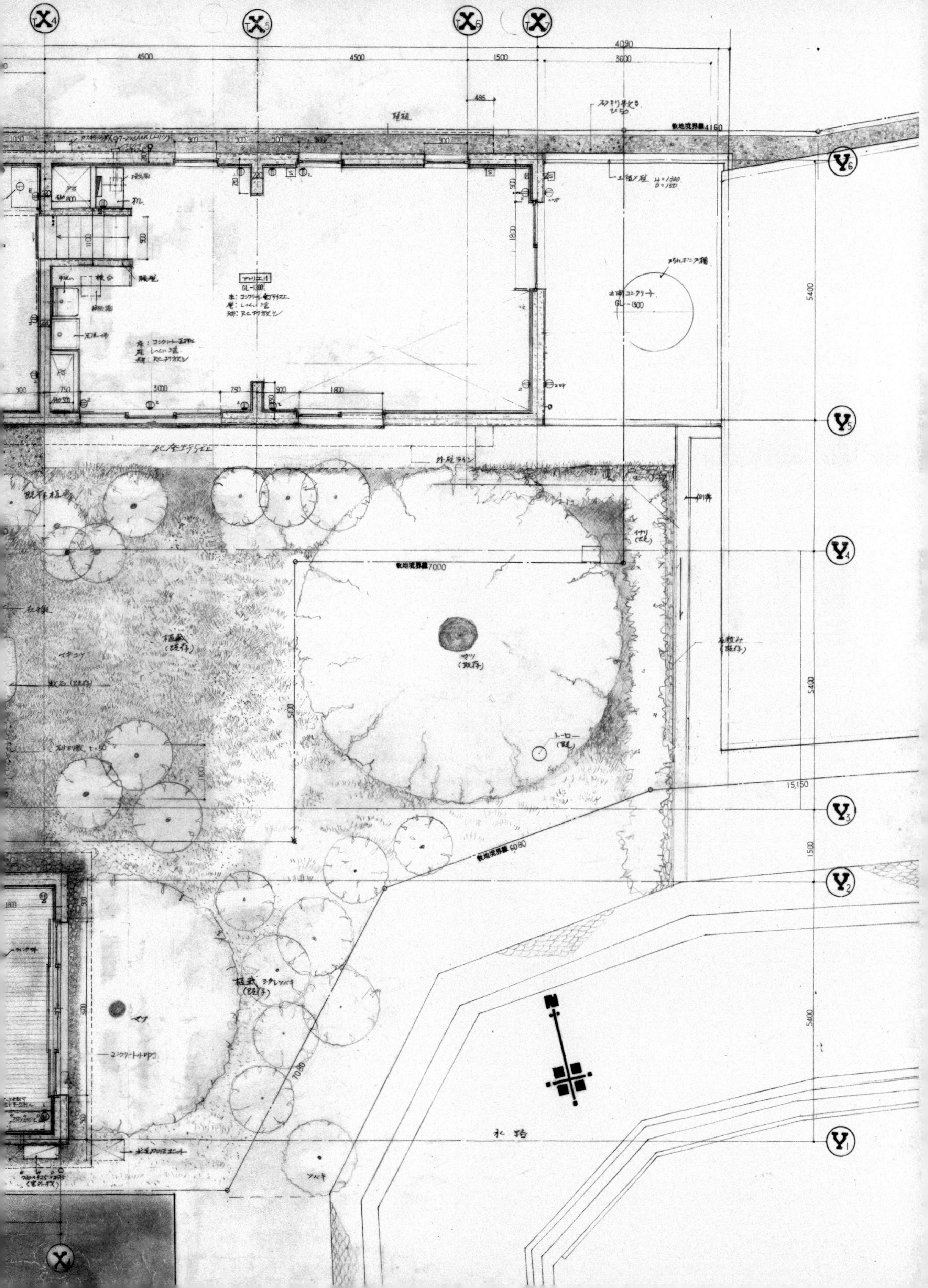
X4
X5
X6
X7
4500
4500
1500
4090
3600
485
敷地境界線
アトリエ
GL-1300
土間コンクリート
GL-1300
外壁ライン
Y6
Y5
Y4
Y3
Y2
Y1
5400
5400
1500
5400
15,150
敷地境界線 7000
マツ
(既存)
トーロー
(既存)
植栽
(既存)
敷地境界線 6090
7030
水路
ツバキ
N

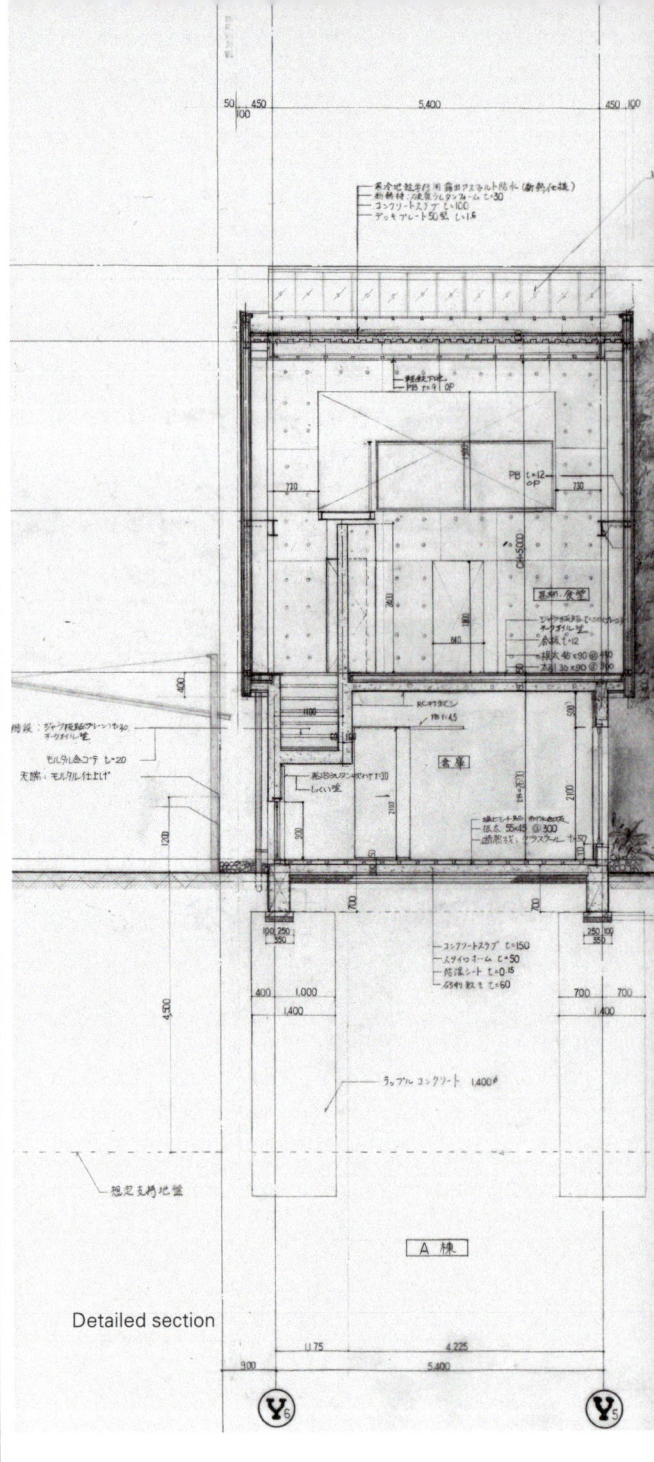

Detailed section

建物全体の構成から規定される細部と、
細部から規定される全体が重なり合い、
対立し合うところに、
建築が純粋になりきれないところがある。

There is a place that architecture cannot exist purely, where the details ruled by the composition of the building as a whole overlap and clash with the whole that is ruled by the details.

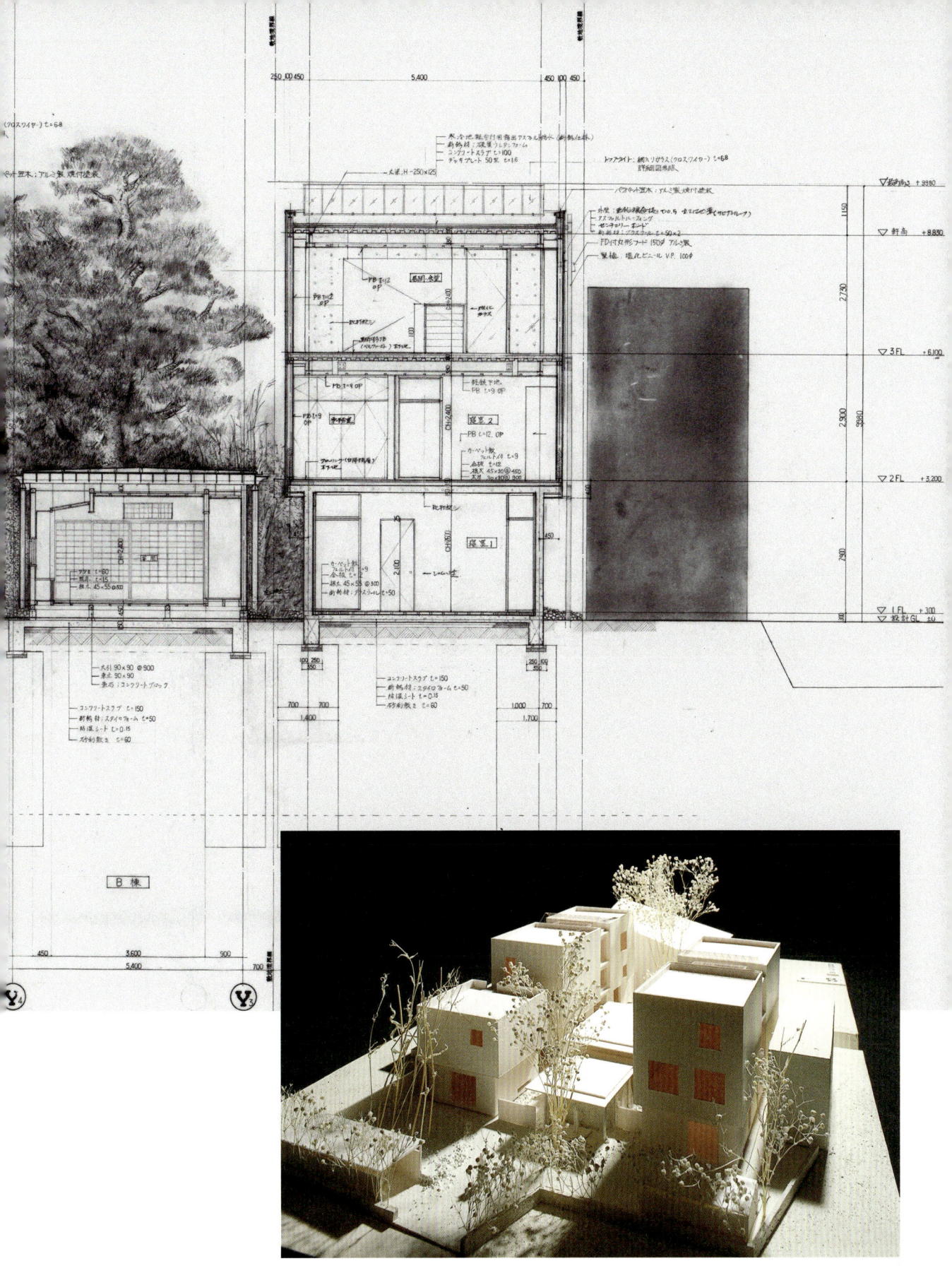

House No.19, Kanazawa

あの座敷を見ていると、建築家の限界のようなものを
考えてしまう。そういうものに対して、建築家がいくら
設計図を描いても、いくら模型を作っても、かなわない。

I am made to think about the limits of the architect when I look at a
traditional *zashiki* room floored with *tatami* mats. An architect cannot be
a match for it, no matter how many plans and models they may make.

梅山氏作の引手
Door pulls designed by Baizan.

紅殻漆喰壁に鉄骨シェルターを架けたB棟ホール
A steel canopy shelters the rouge plaster walls of the hall in Building B.

C棟キッチン
The kitchen in Building C.

3F Plan

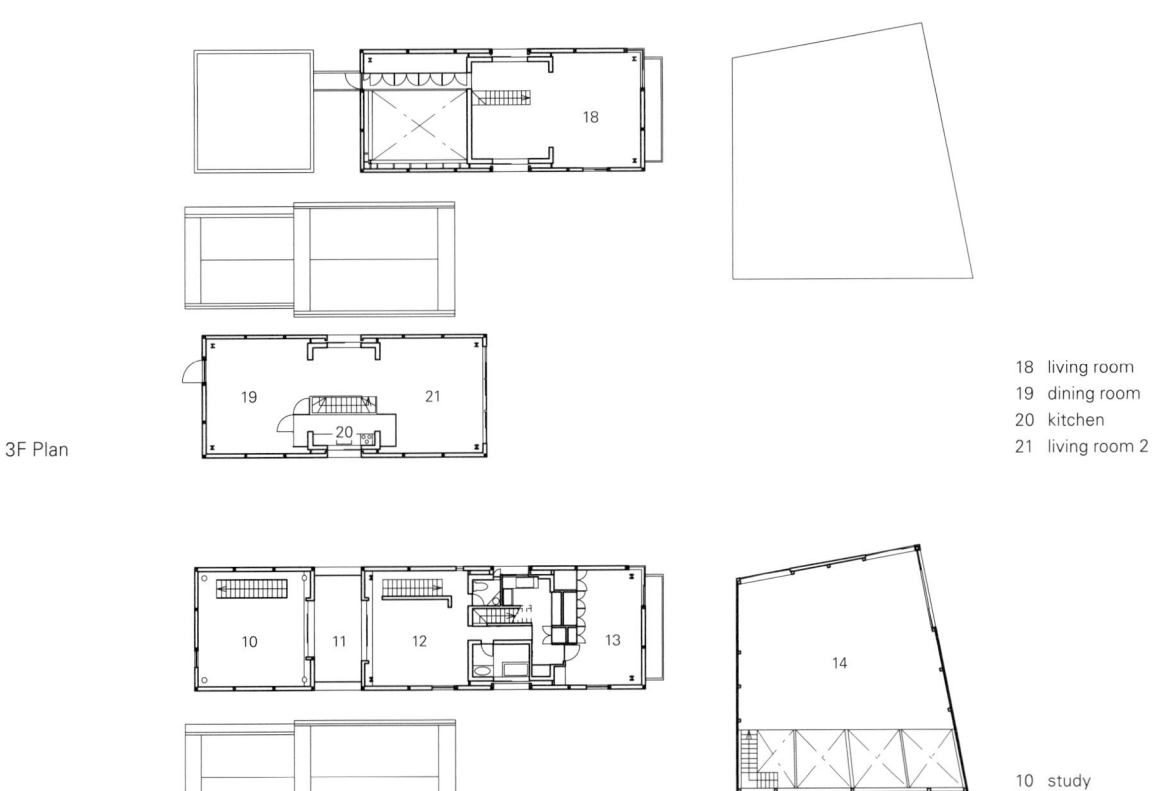

18 living room
19 dining room
20 kitchen
21 living room 2

2F Plan

10 study
11 terrace
12 dining room
13 bedroom
14 atelier
15 office
16 bedroom 2
17 children's room

1F Plan 1/400

1 drawing room
2 entrance hall
3 storeroom
4 atelier 1
5 atelier 2
6 hall
7 tatami room
8 bedroom 1
9 living room 1

103　House No.19, Kanazawa

A棟応接室
The drawing room in Building A.

A棟リビング
The living room in Building A.

A棟ダイニング
The dining room in Building A.

わたしがこうしたいということが、ある種、
住まう人の自発性に揺らぎを与えるのは嫌だ、という
信条があって、形態に関しても、物理的な説明を
繰り返していくので、すれ違いがあったかもしれない。

There must have been a disconnect between us because I held a principle which, in a sense, refused to let anything that I wanted to do affect the spontaneous activities of the residents, while I also kept giving them physical explanations of the forms.

A棟エントランスホール
The entrance hall in Building A.

安曇野ちひろ美術館
Chihiro Art Museum Azumino

1997

長野県北安曇郡松川村 Nagano

何げなく野原に建つ倉庫のようなものを作りたいと
どこかで思ったかもしれない。必要だから建てられたという、
事実だけを背負ったようなものに憧れる気持ちがある。

There may have been a thought somewhere in my mind to make something like a shed standing casually in a field. I am drawn to things that seem to be composed only of facts and which are built out of necessity.

黄金色の稲田から

照明デザイナーの面出薫さんに、美術館の建設を考えている松本猛さんと由理子さん夫妻を紹介された。ふたり共わたしとほぼ同年代だった。「海の博物館」を終えて1年ほど経った頃のことである。猛さんは絵本画家として知られるいわさきちひろの長男。いかにも育ちが良さそうな風貌。由理子さんは見るからに頭の回転が速い。美術館を運営統括する猛さんと、マネージングを仕切る由理子さんと二人三脚でこの美術館を育て上げてきた。

練馬のいわさきちひろの居宅跡に絵本美術館を立ち上げて15年が経ち、ちひろの生家があった安曇野にアネックスとして美術館建設を考えていた。聞けば指名コンペにするという。当時、わたしの事務所は仕事が立て込んできていたし、ふたりがあまりに建築とコンペに不案内な様子だったので、審査委員側に回ってサポートしたいと申し出た。ふたりで相談したのだろう。何日かして、応募側に回ってほしい、と連絡が来た。たしか15人ほどの建築家の名前が挙がっていたので、そのひとりとして気楽な気持ちで応募することにした。

絵本は幾つもの要素に分解できる。ちひろが描いたような絵本画、文学としての物語、それらを構成するエディトリアルデザイン。そう考えると、美術品を見せるためだけの従来の美術館では物足りないような気がした。プロポーザルコンペだったので考え方と概要だけだったが、「美術館と図書館の中間のような目立たない建物を作ったらどうか」と提案した。

審査委員は財団の理事の方々で、理事長であり劇作家であった飯沢匡さん、映画監督の山田洋次さん、俳優の黒柳徹子さん、国会議員だった松本善明さん、といったそうそうたるメンバーだった。提案した「どうにでもなるようないいかげんさ」が気に入られたのか、わたしが設計することになった。出会いとは奇妙なものである。

応募案を作成するに際して、敷地を初めて見に行ったときのことは忘れられない。快晴の秋空が広がり、遠くに初冠雪した白馬連山が見え、あたり一面は黄金色の稲穂に埋め尽くされていた。黄金の絨毯である。敷地は緩やかな棚田になっていて、用水路には澄んだ水が滔々と音をたてて流れていた。この風景の中に身を置き、陶然とした。

ここに、村営の公園を作りその中に美術館を建てる、そのことがとても不自然に思えた。このままの方がいいのではないか。そう素直に思った。普通ならこの時点で、コンペの応募者としては失格だ。この稲田を壊して公園と建物を建てるとしたら、その壊した以上のものを創らねばならない。これはかなりハードルが高い。設計に取り掛かってから煩悶する日々が続いた。建物を目立たせぬこと、ランドスケープの中で周囲と一体化させること、そのことばかりを考えてスタディを重ねた。

屋根の形は、全体のボリュームを小さく見せるには小さな切妻を連続させるのが、一番であることが分かった。これをモジュール化すれば、後で増築したとしても全体の印象は変わらない。地元の唐松材を使い、地元の砂を混ぜた左官壁を使い、鳥小屋のようでもあり農家の倉庫のようにも見える不思議な美術館が出来上がった。この場所での一番のごちそうは、山や川や田圃や澄んだ空気なのだから、建物は控えめな方が良いに決まっている。

開館後は予想を遥かに上回る多くの人が訪れる美術館になった。築16年になるがこの勢いはそのままだ。11年前に第一次の増築をし、コレクションである国際的な絵本画を展示する展示室と多目的室を設けた。さらに3年前に収蔵庫と研究スペースを増築した。当初1,580㎡だった建物が、増床を繰り返し、今は3,200㎡の立派な美術館になった。それでも、初めに考えた全体の印象は変わらない。訪れた人は気付かないかもしれない。

公園で子供たちが走り回り、遠距離運転で家族を連れてきた疲れたオトウサンが、美術館のテラスの寝椅子で気持ち良さそうに寝ている。たまに美術館を訪れると、そんな光景をよく見かける。建物の存在は背景のほんの一部でしかない。それでいいのだ。安曇野の素晴らしい景色と澄んだ空気と暖かな日差し。この場所でしか見られない幸せな光景である。ちひろさんも喜んでくれているのではないかと思う。(Eng. p.276)

Site Plan 1/1500

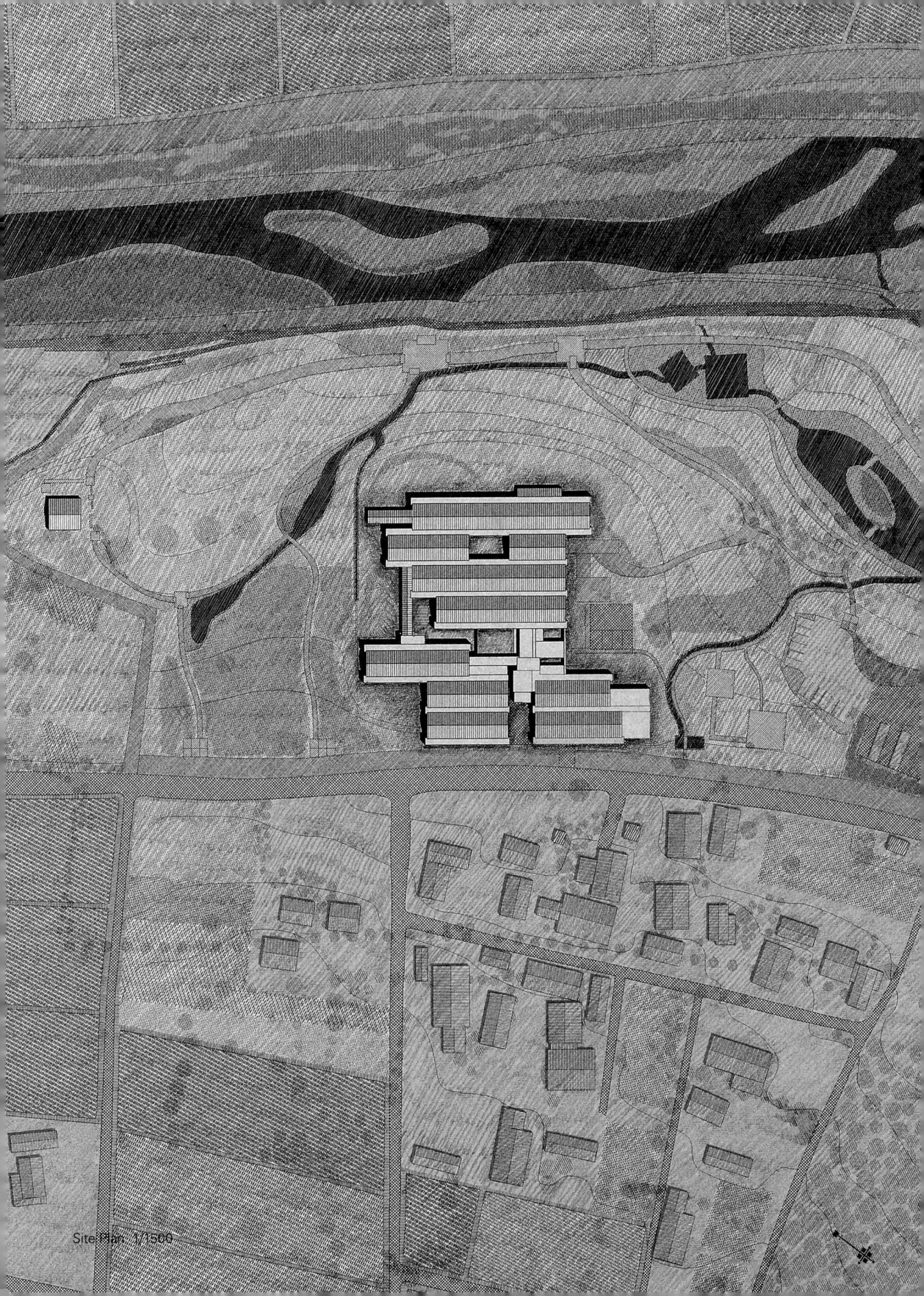

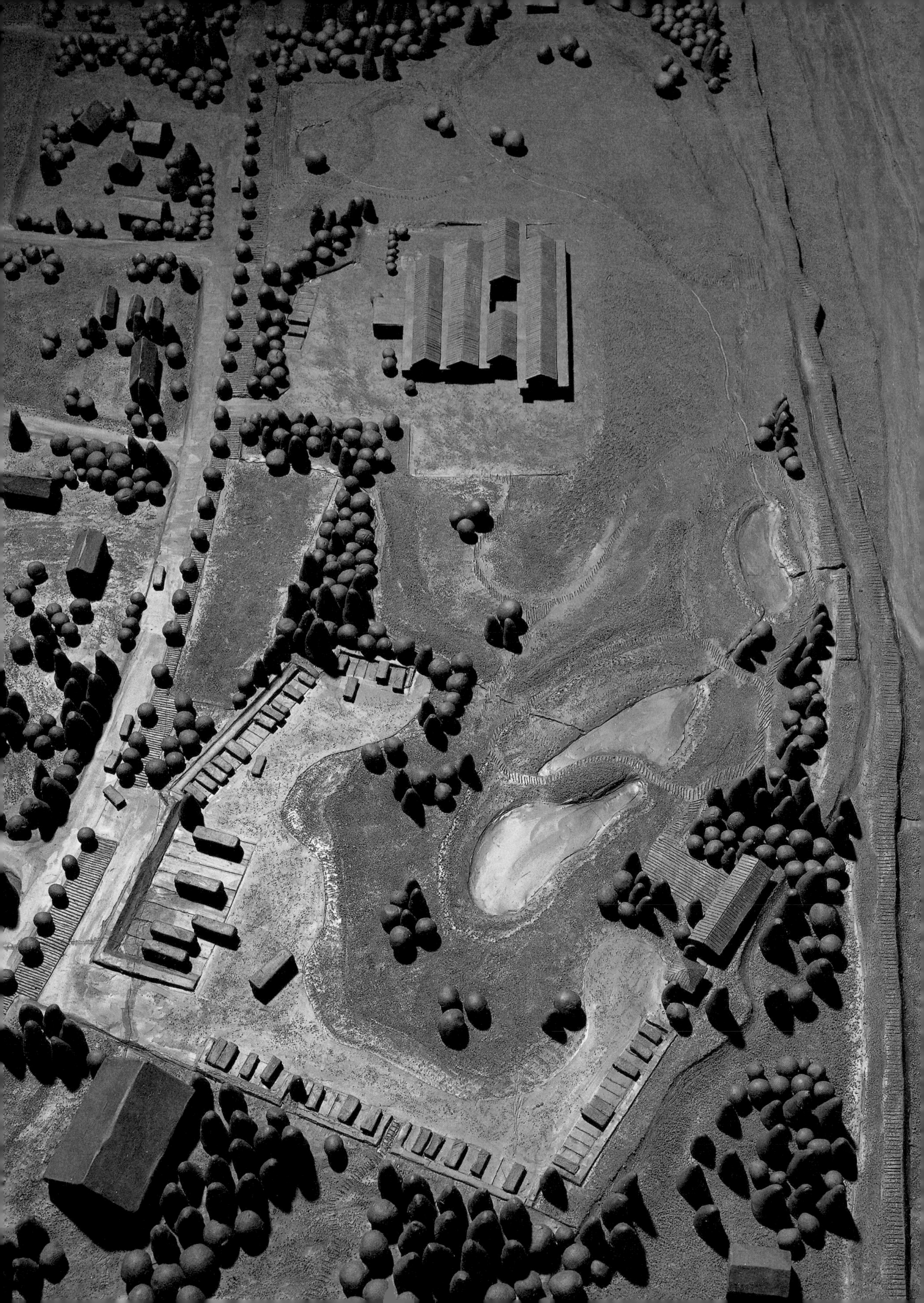

風景の中に溶け込んで、知られないように
ひっそりと当たり前に建っていればいい。

I want it to merge into the scenery and to stand there
quietly, anonymously, and unpretentiously.

Chihiro Art Museum Azumino

Plan 1/500

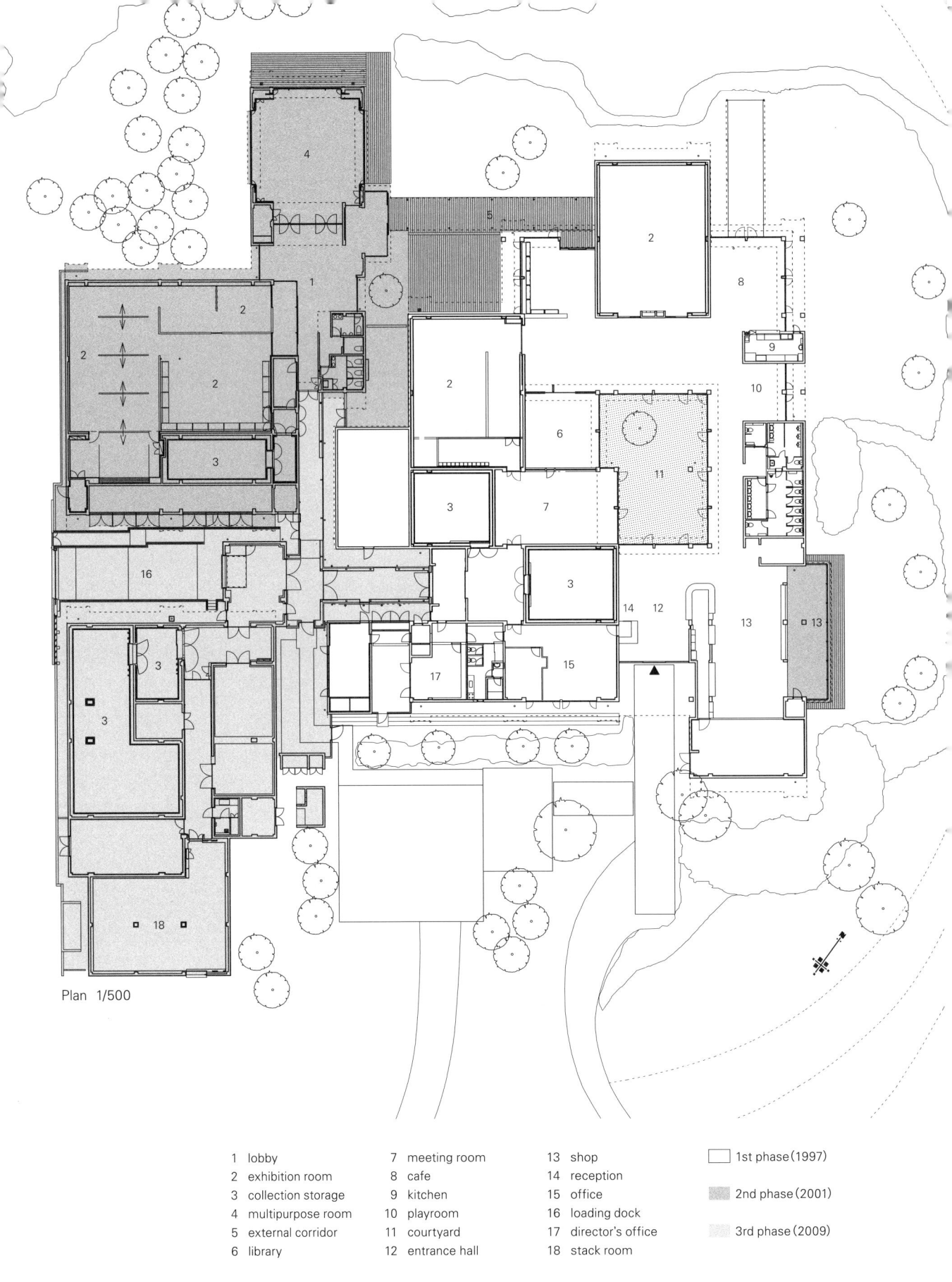

1 lobby	7 meeting room	13 shop	1st phase (1997)
2 exhibition room	8 cafe	14 reception	
3 collection storage	9 kitchen	15 office	2nd phase (2001)
4 multipurpose room	10 playroom	16 loading dock	
5 external corridor	11 courtyard	17 director's office	3rd phase (2009)
6 library	12 entrance hall	18 stack room	

この建物を倉庫のようだ、といった人は正しい。わたしの
建物の作り方はいかにも素っ気ない。使い手がその空間に対して、
何も行動を起こさなければ、たちまちただの倉庫になってしまう。

Those who said that this building is like a warehouse are correct.
The way I design buildings is certainly curt. They become warehouses in
a moment if their users do not interact with the spaces in some way.

どこでも裸同然でいることが素形なのではない。
倉庫や納屋がそうであるように、人の営みとその場所の条件に対して
過不足のない答えを出す中、意図せず現れるものが素形なのだ。

Protoforms are not simply described as the pure or innocent. A protoform is something which emerges naturally through the search for a solution that is neither too much nor too little and responds to the lives of the people and the conditions of its place, much like a warehouse or a shed.

117 Chihiro Art Museum Azumino

建築に何ができるか。そこに
希望のようなものはあるのかといつも考えている。
What can architecture do? I am always thinking about whether
there is any sort of hope in it.

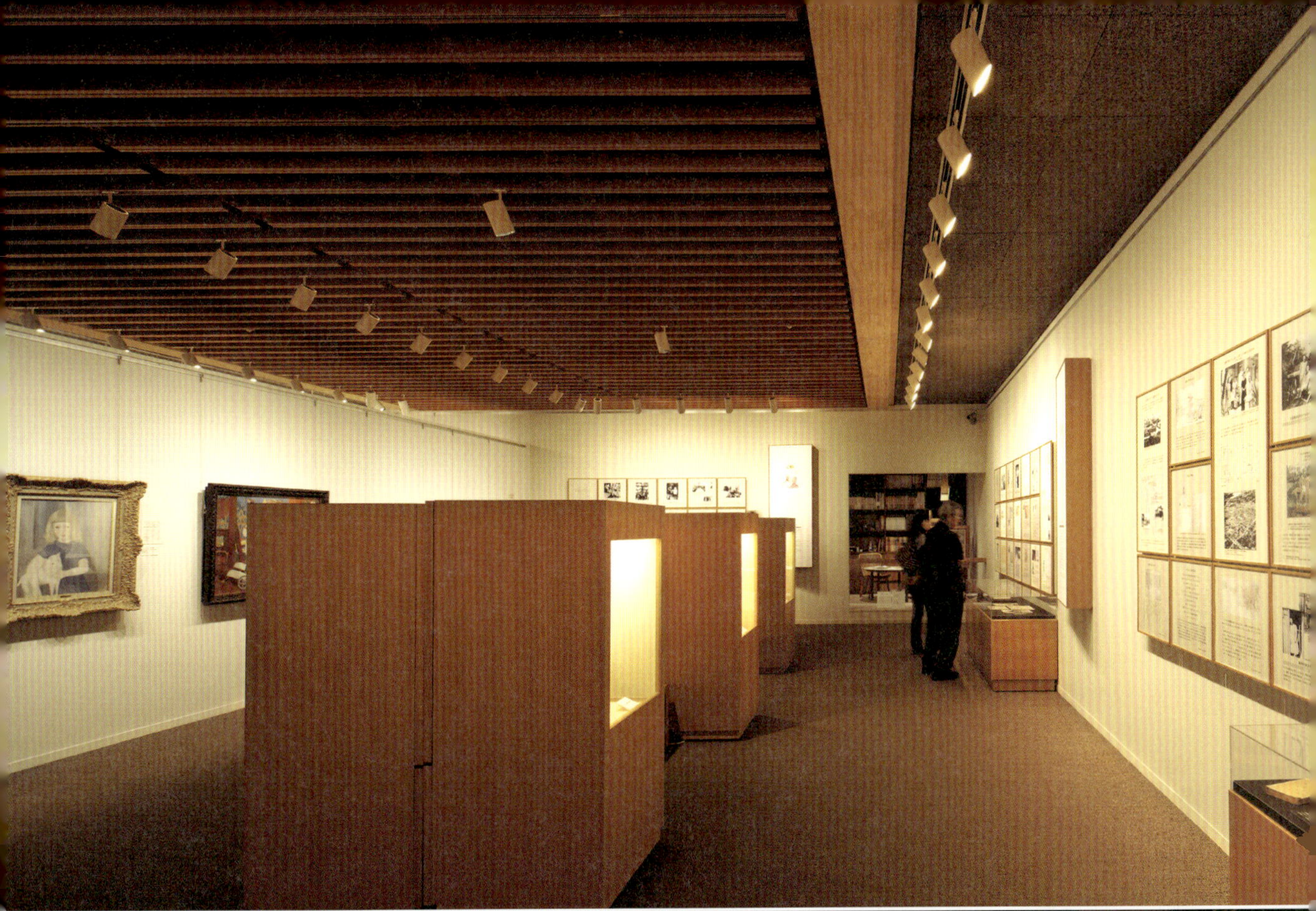

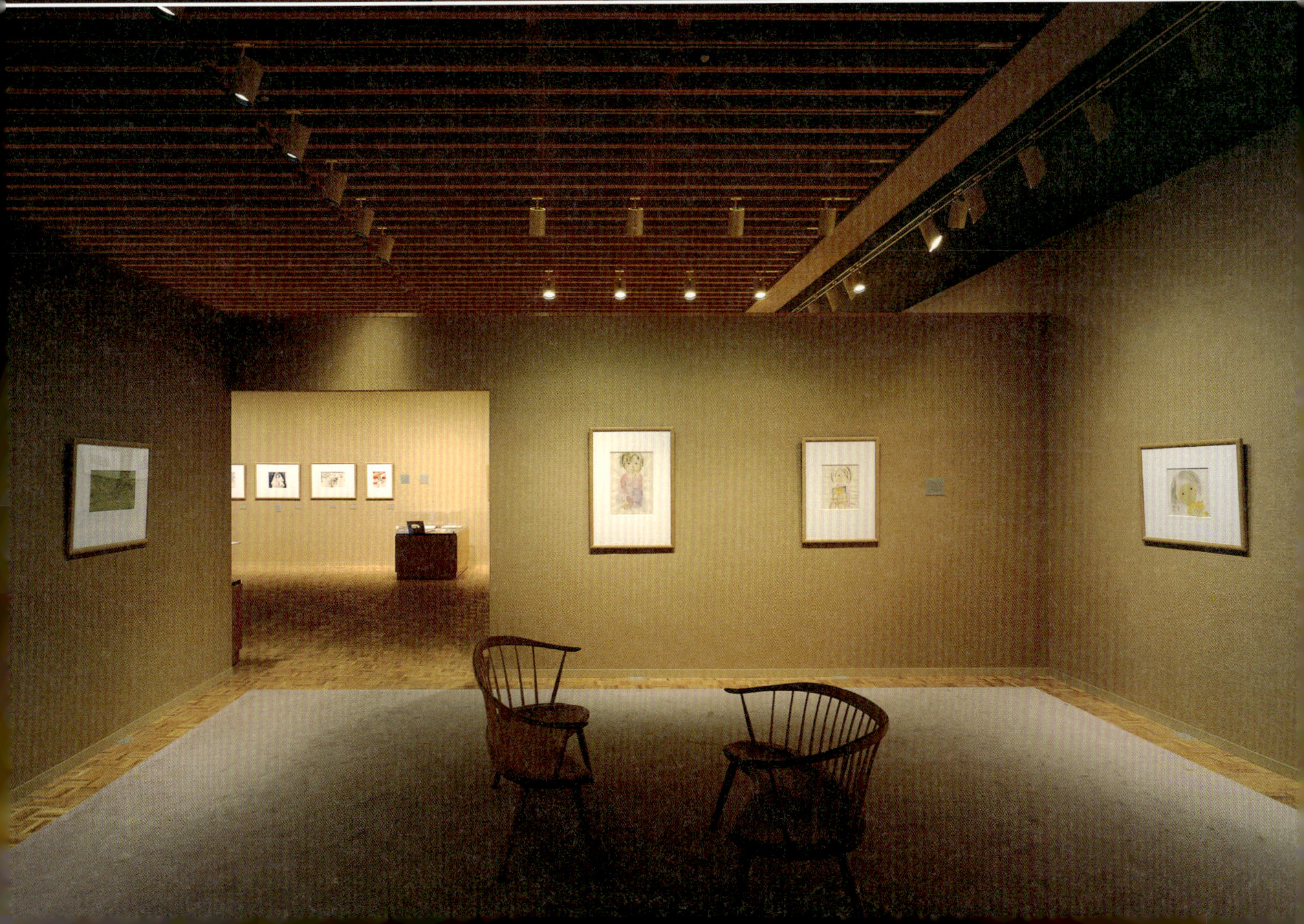

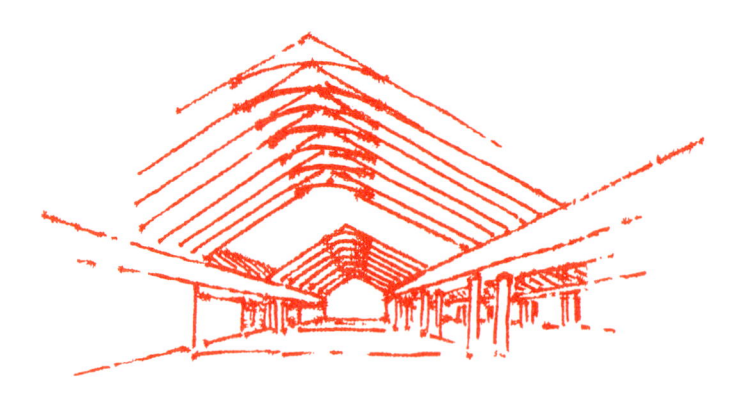

点在する展示空間と中庭をつなぐ中間領域
The intermediary area connects the interspersed exhibition spaces and the courtyard.

1 multipurpose room
2 lobby

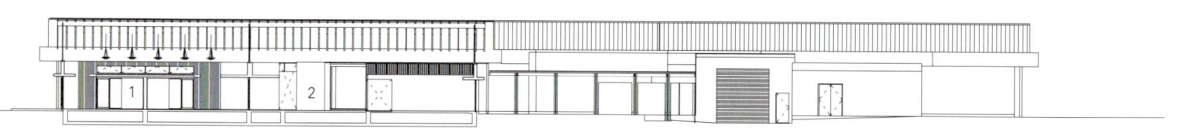

Section 1/500

何げない物、当たり前の物に、人の心が美しさを
見出せないのであれば、建築には何の希望も未来もない。
There is no hope or future for architecture if the hearts of people
cannot find beauty within the casual and ordinary.

辻褄合わせに手を出して形を操作してしまった部分もある。
この建物はそうした部分に曖昧さを残している。

There are parts where I admittedly manipulated the form for the sake of consistency. These areas have left the building with a sense of ambiguity.

Detailed section

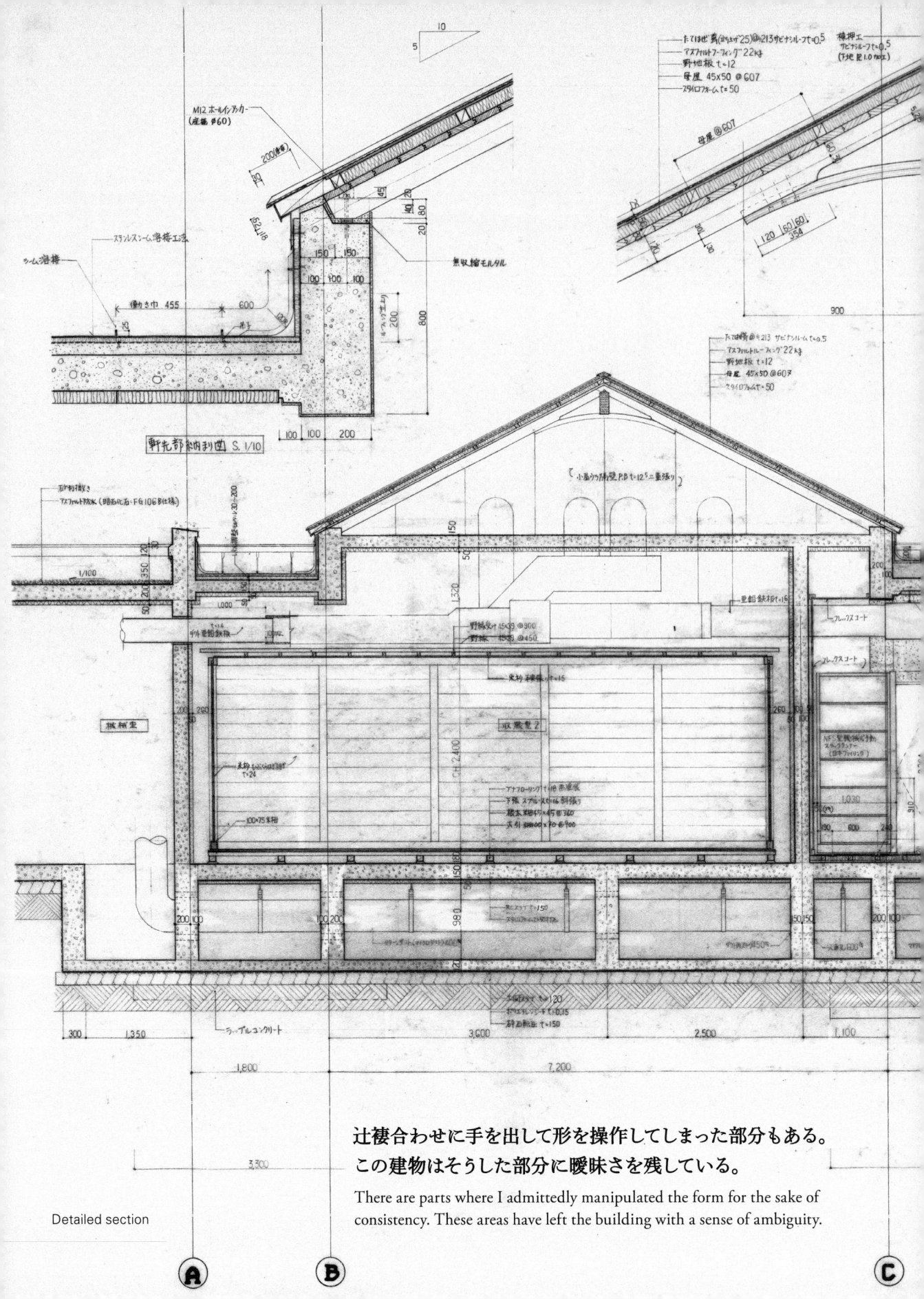

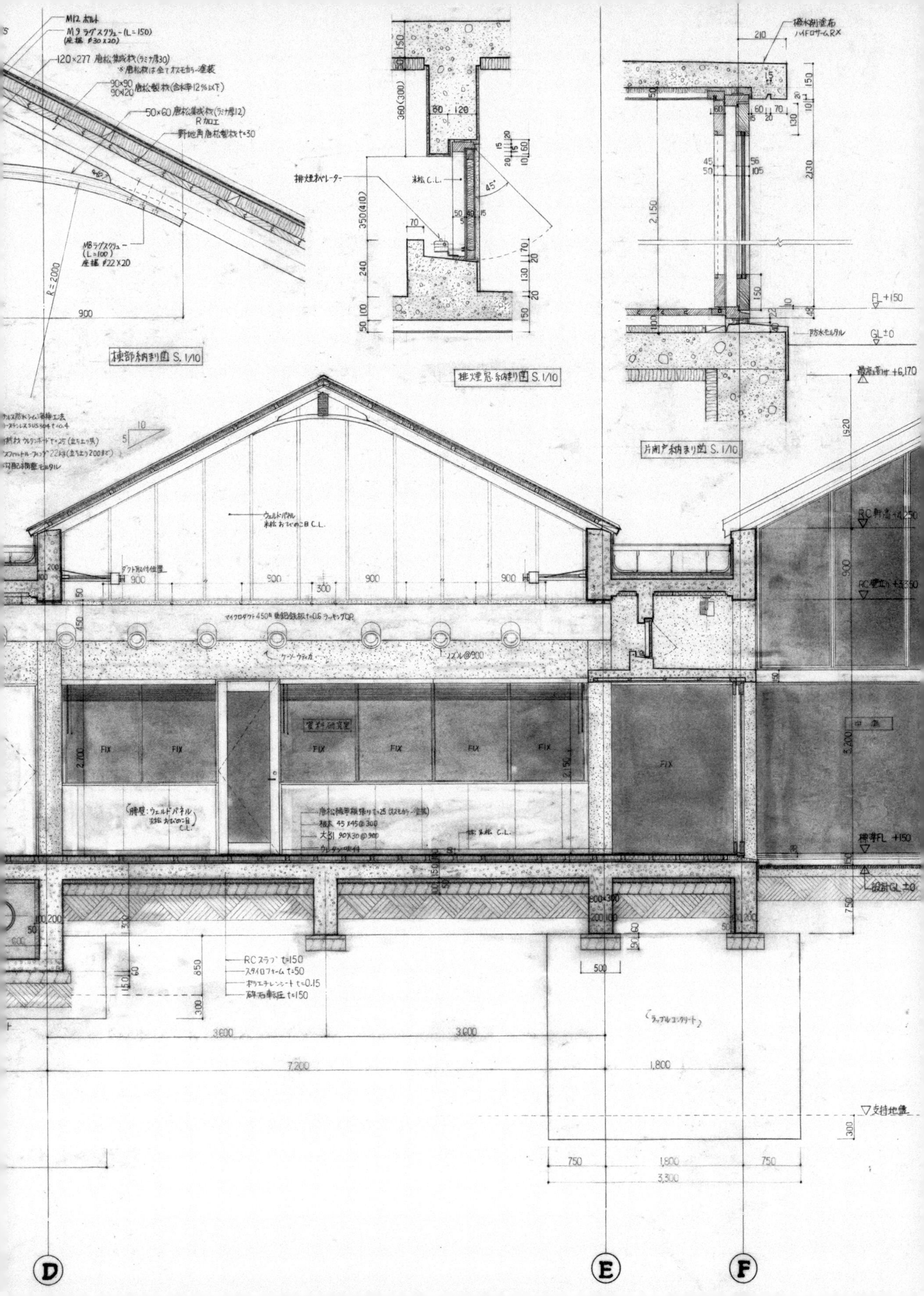

棟部納まり図 S. 1/10
排煙窓納まり図 S. 1/10
片開戸納まり図 S. 1/10
M12 ボルト
120×277 唐松集成材
野地角唐松製材 t=30
排煙オペレーター
米松 C.L.
撥水剤塗布
防水モルタル
ウェルドパネル 米松 おびのこ目 C.L.
ダクト取付位置
資料研究室
FIX
RCスラブ t=150
スタイロフォーム t=50
ポリエチレンシート t=0.15
砕石転圧 t=150
ラップルコンクリート
支持地盤
標準FL +150
設計GL ±0
RC軒高 +4,250
RC壁立上り +3,350
最高高さ +6,170
FL+150
GL±0
7,200
3,600
1,800
750
3,300
D
E
F

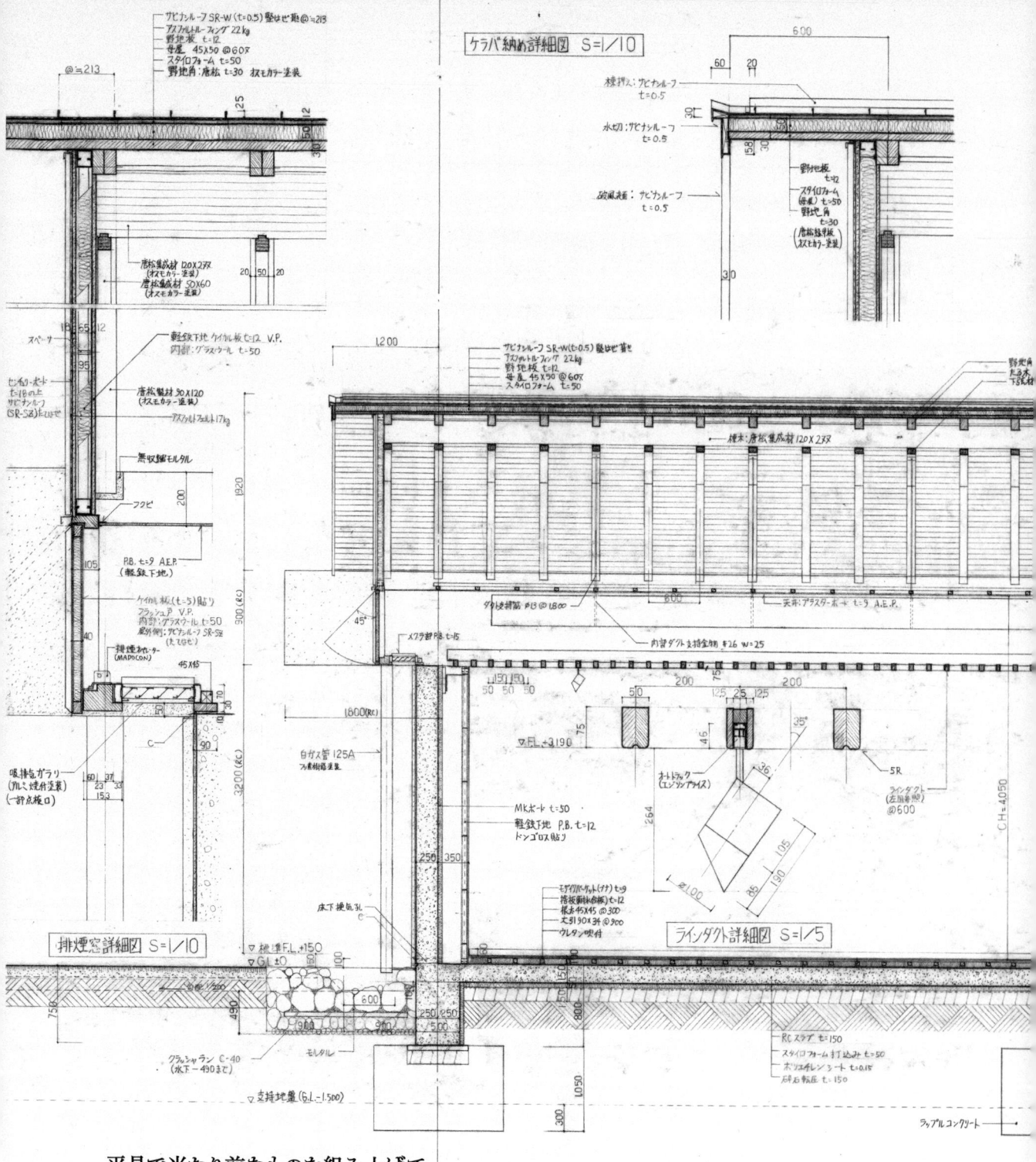

平易で当たり前なものを組み上げて
空間を作りたかった。建物は、身近な材料と分かりやすい
空間の大きさをつなぎ合わせて出来ている。

I wanted to make the spaces by compiling the plain and
ordinary. The building is composed of common materials and
spaces of an accessible size.

Detailed section

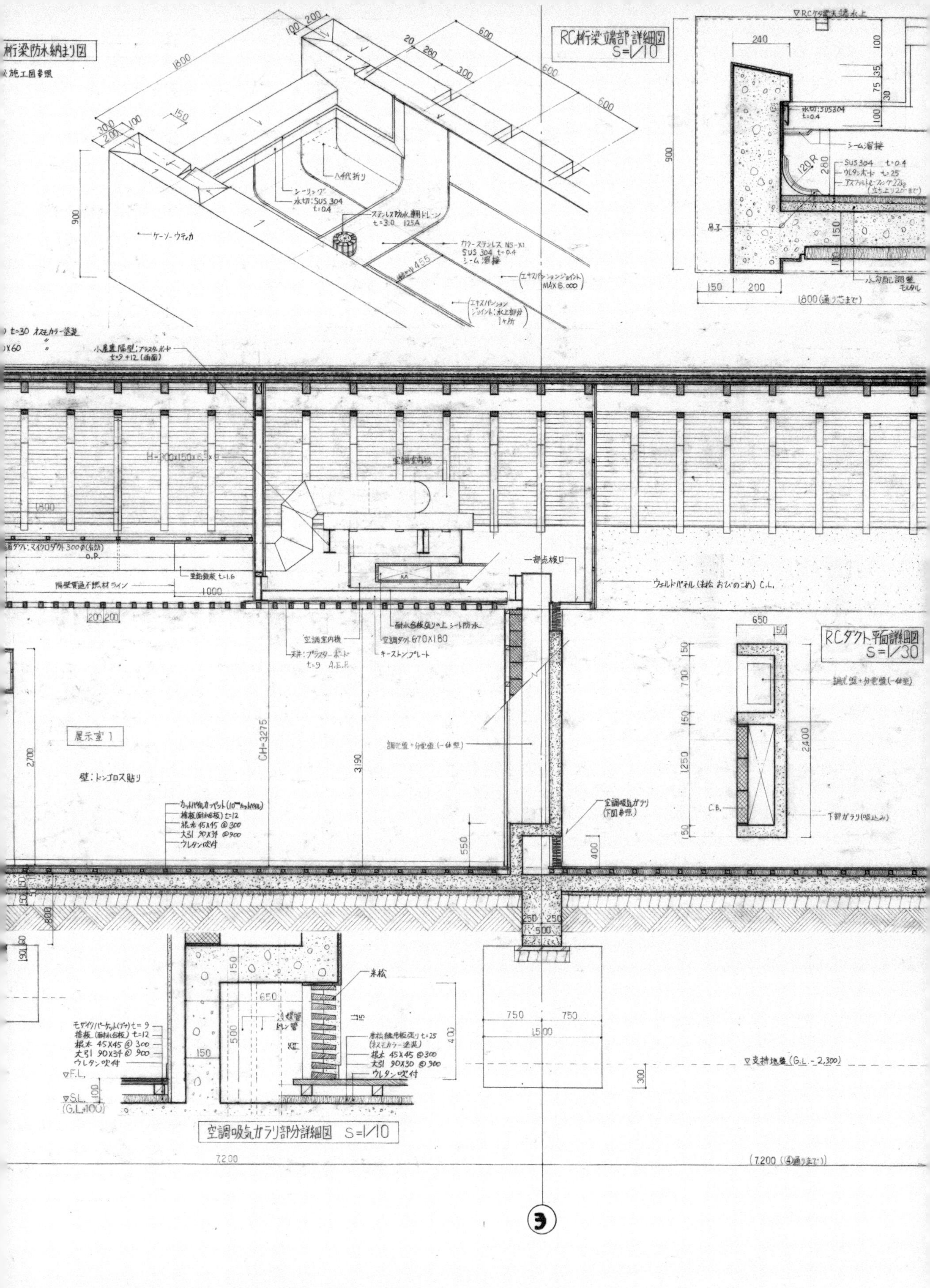
桁梁防水納まり図
施工図参照
1800
100 200
600
20 280
300
600
600
150
300 100
200
900
ケーソーウティカ
シーリング
水切:SUS 304 t=0.4
八代折り
ステンレス防水専用ドレーン t=3.0 125A
カラーステンレス NS-X1 SUS 304 t=0.4 シーム溶接
455
エキスパンションジョイント MAX 6.000
エキスパンションジョイント:水上部分 1ヶ所
RC桁梁端部詳細図 S=1/10
▽RCケタ梁天端水上
240
100
35
75
30
100
900
水切:SUS304 t=0.4
シーム溶接
120R
280
SUS304 t=0.4
ウレタンホード t=25
アスファルトルーフィング22kg (立ち上り20cmまで)
吊子
150
100
150
200
小勾配調整モルタル
1800(通り芯まで)
t=30 オスモカラー塗装
X60
小屋裏隔壁:プラスターボード t=9+12(両面)
H-300×150×6.5×9
空調室内機
1800
空調ダクト:マイクロダクト300φ(有効) O.P.
亜鉛鉄板 t=1.6
隔壁貫通不燃材ライン
1000
200 200
一部点検口
ウェルドパネル(米松 おびのこめ) C.L.
耐水合板張りの上 シート防水
空調室内機
空調ダクト 670×180
天井:プラスターボード t=9 A.E.P.
キーストンプレート
展示室1
2700
CH=3275
3190
壁:ドンゴロス貼り
調光盤+分電盤(一体型)
カッパ色カーペット(10°カット仕様)
捨板(耐水合板) t=12
根太 45×45 @300
大引 90×3寸 @900
ウレタン吹付
550
空調吸気ガラリ(下図参照)
400
RCダクト平面詳細図 S=1/30
650
150
150
700
150
1250
150
2400
調光盤+分電盤(一体型)
C.B.
下部ガラリ(吸込み)
150
300
800
90 60
250 250
500
米松
150
650
500
冷媒管 ドレン管
15
400
150
モザイクパーケット(ナラ) t=9
捨板(耐水合板) t=12
根太 45×45 @300
大引 90×3寸 @900
ウレタン吹付
唐松縁甲板張り t=25 (オスモカラー塗装)
根太 45×45 @300
大引 90×30 @900
ウレタン吹付
▽F.L.
100
▽S.L. (G.L+100)
750 750
1500
▽支持地盤(G.L.-2,300)
300
空調吸気ガラリ部分詳細図 S=1/10
7200
(7200 (④通りまで))
3

1　cafe
2　exhibition room (1st phase)
3　lobby
4　exhibition room (2nd phase)

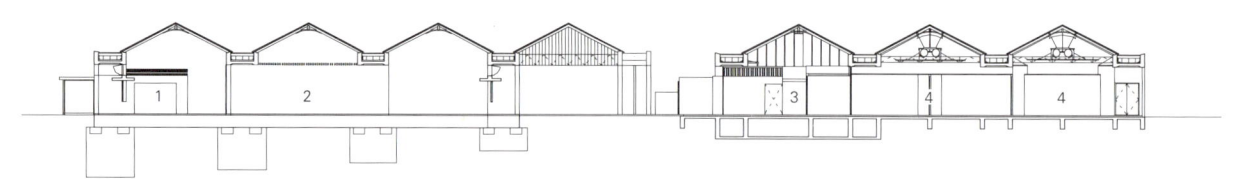

Section 1/500

1　exhibition room (2nd phase)
2　collection storage

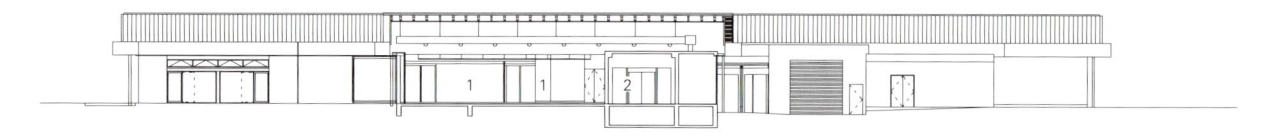

Section 1/500

126　Hiroshi NAITO 1992-2004

つまらなくて価値のあるもの。価値とは時間のことだ。
The mundane but valuable. Value is about time.

素朴で無駄のない小屋組架構
The simple and unadorned truss roof frame

展示室は、住宅の居室の延長のようなものになるだろう。
The exhibition rooms will probably become like the living rooms of a house.

内的な精神世界から広がりのある自然まで、部分と全体を
いかに無理なくつなぎ合わせるかが、大きなテーマになっている。
It has been a major theme of mine to try to connect together the part to whole
without strain, from the inner spiritual world to the expansive realm of nature.

過去から連なっている時間の流れの中に、
建物を素直に置けるかどうかだ。
The question is whether the building can be placed truthfully
within the continuum of time flowing from the past.

茨城県天心記念五浦美術館
Tenshin Memorial Museum of Art, Ibaraki

1997
茨城県北茨城市 Ibaraki

わたしの建築は敷地を抜いては成り立たない。
My architecture cannot come into being if removed of its context.

命を削った建物

岡倉天心が横山大観や菱田春草らと共に隠棲した五浦に、茨城県が天心を記念する美術館を作るというので指名設計競技が催され、幸いにも激戦を制して設計することになった。学生時代から、天心の『茶の本』はバイブルのように愛読していたから、この仕事はぜひともやりたかった。ボロボロになった文庫本を引っ張り出してきて読み直し、初心に帰って案を作った。

規定上、大づかみなゾーニング程度の提案しかできなかったが、展示室に至る空間の作り方を中心に提案した。また、従来の日本美術の展示の仕方がおかしいことを指摘した。本来、畳に反射した光が床の間を照らすように、横からの薄暗い間接光で見るべきものを、煌々と光を当てて見せるのは、作品本来の素晴らしさを削いでいるとしか思えなかったからだ。

当選して県庁に行くと、とんでもないことを聞かされた。「設計を半年で終わらせてほしい」。さらに、「着工から竣工までの工期は1年」と言われた。6,000㎡もの建物、それも海際の劣悪な条件の中でデリケートな日本美術を展示する空気環境を作らねばならない。ほとんど不可能なことに思えた。「もし、できない、と答えたらどういうことになりますか」と尋ねたら、「今の案をベースに他の設計事務所がやることになる」と言う。仕方がないので、「やります」と答えた。それまでのあらゆる知識と経験を総動員するしかなかった。ひたすら図面を作成する日々が続いた。設立準備室が設けられ、後に館長となる大久保武さん、学芸員となって主のような存在になる長山貞之さんらと打ち合わせを重ねた。

何せ工期がない。役に立ったのは「海の博物館」で得た知識だった。PCaを使えば、幾つかの工場で部材を分担して作り、近くの港から運び込んで組み立てればいい。また、品質が良いので高い対塩害性能も期待できる。PCa化するために複雑な平面をモジュール化し、構造家の渡辺邦夫さんと全体を組み上げた。建物は1,200ピースのPCa部材で構成される。ピース一つひとつに版図という詳細図が製作側で描かれる。膨大な作業だが、それをチェックするわれわれの側も膨大な作業となる。わたしも幾度となく夜を徹してチェックに当たった。

着工してみると、近くに大鷹の巣があるという。固い岩盤を掘削するのにダイナマイトを使えない。大鷹が逃げてしまうというのである。ひたすら削岩機で削らねばならないのだが、地下の機械室はかなり大きい。これで手間取った。そこをクリアしたら、今度はPCaに対する構造設計の不具合が発覚した。工場ではすでに製作に入っている。これを修正しなければならない。再び手間取ることになった。危機である。オープンの日はすでに決まっており、開館時には天心ゆかりの国宝級の日本画が特別展示されることになっていた。

竣工まであと3か月という正月の2日、どうしても気になってひとりで現場に行った時のことは忘れられない。ガランとした現場。ほとんど構造体しか出来上がっていない。これに3か月で、屋根を架け、外装をし、内装を仕上げなければならない。ここまで何とかやってきた事務所ももうこれで終わりか、と覚悟したのを覚えている。3月末、事務所のスタッフはもとより、建設会社と県の担当者の必死の努力で、何とか奇跡的に完成させることができた。すべてがギリギリで綱渡りだった。文字通り命を削った現場だった。

騒然とした中で作り上げた建物だが、開館後、県の北端という立地の悪さにもかかわらず、この建物は公立の美術館としては全国屈指の入館者の多さで知られるようになった。天心の知名度のみならず企画が素晴らしいからだと思う。すべての事情を知っていた大久保さんや長山さんの役割が大きかったはずだ。

3.11の時、幸いにも建物はほとんど無傷だった。次の日の早朝に電話を入れた時、守衛さんが、「大丈夫です。素晴らしい建物です」と言ってくれた時は本当にうれしかった。このことはとても誇りに思っている。しかし、離れたところにある駐車場の下に据えていた浄化槽がやられ、開館するのに数か月が掛かった。こんな時だからこそ公立の美術館を一刻も早く開館させたい、という美術館の姿勢に強く胸を打たれた。(Eng. p.277)

Site Plan 1/1500

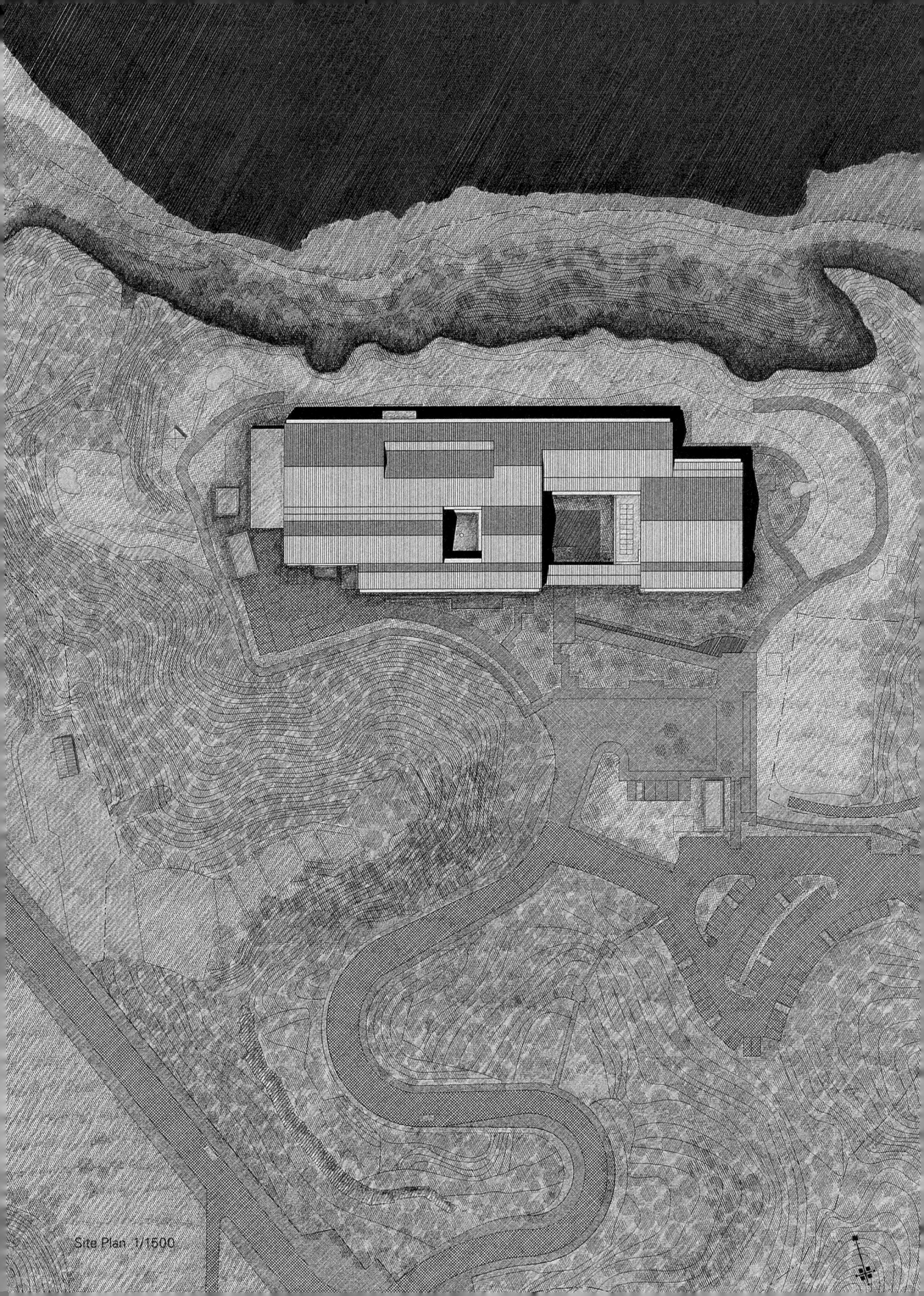

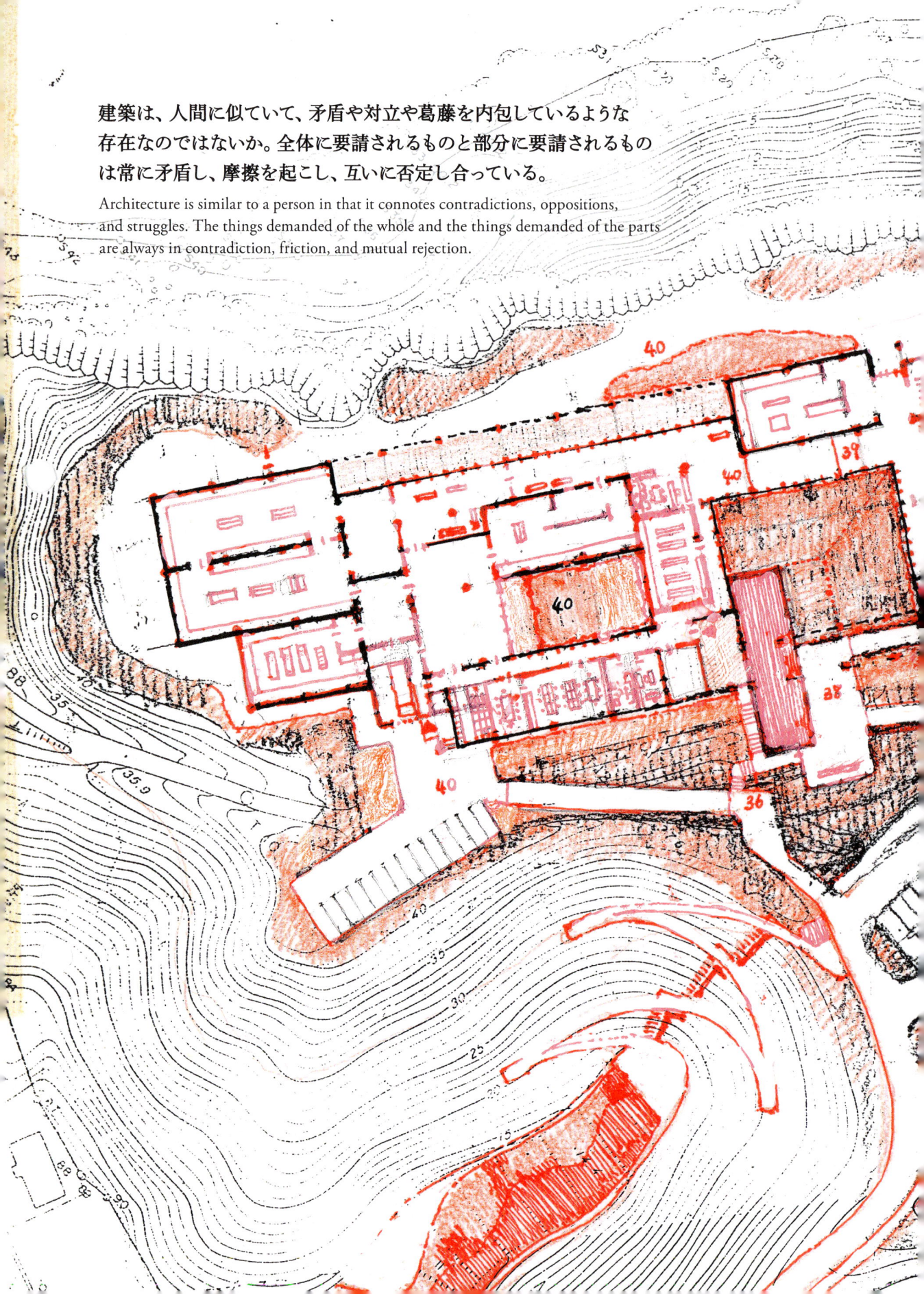

建築は、人間に似ていて、矛盾や対立や葛藤を内包しているような
存在なのではないか。全体に要請されるものと部分に要請されるもの
は常に矛盾し、摩擦を起こし、互いに否定し合っている。

Architecture is similar to a person in that it connotes contradictions, oppositions, and struggles. The things demanded of the whole and the things demanded of the parts are always in contradiction, friction, and mutual rejection.

38

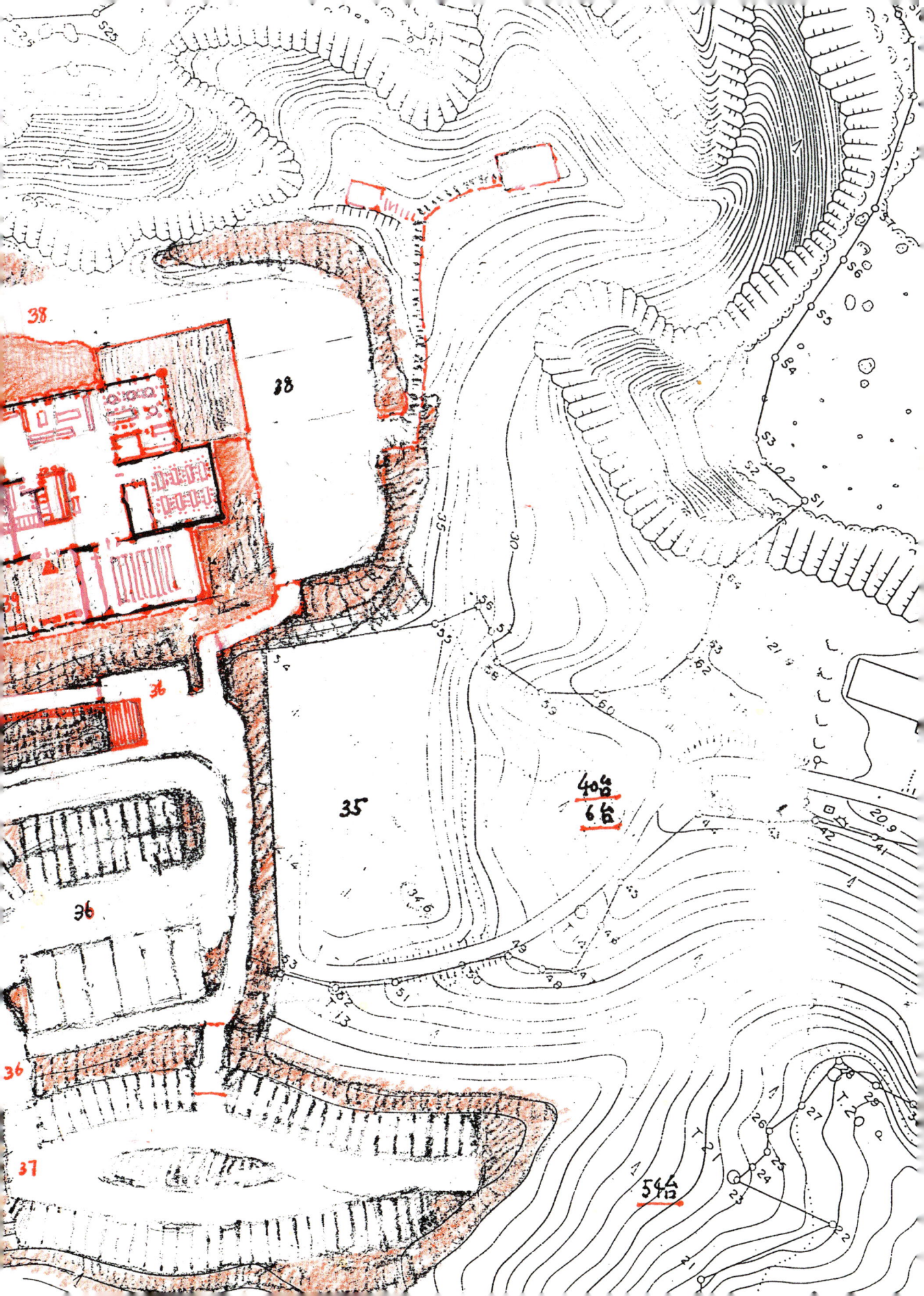

38

36

36

36

37

35

40台/6台

5台

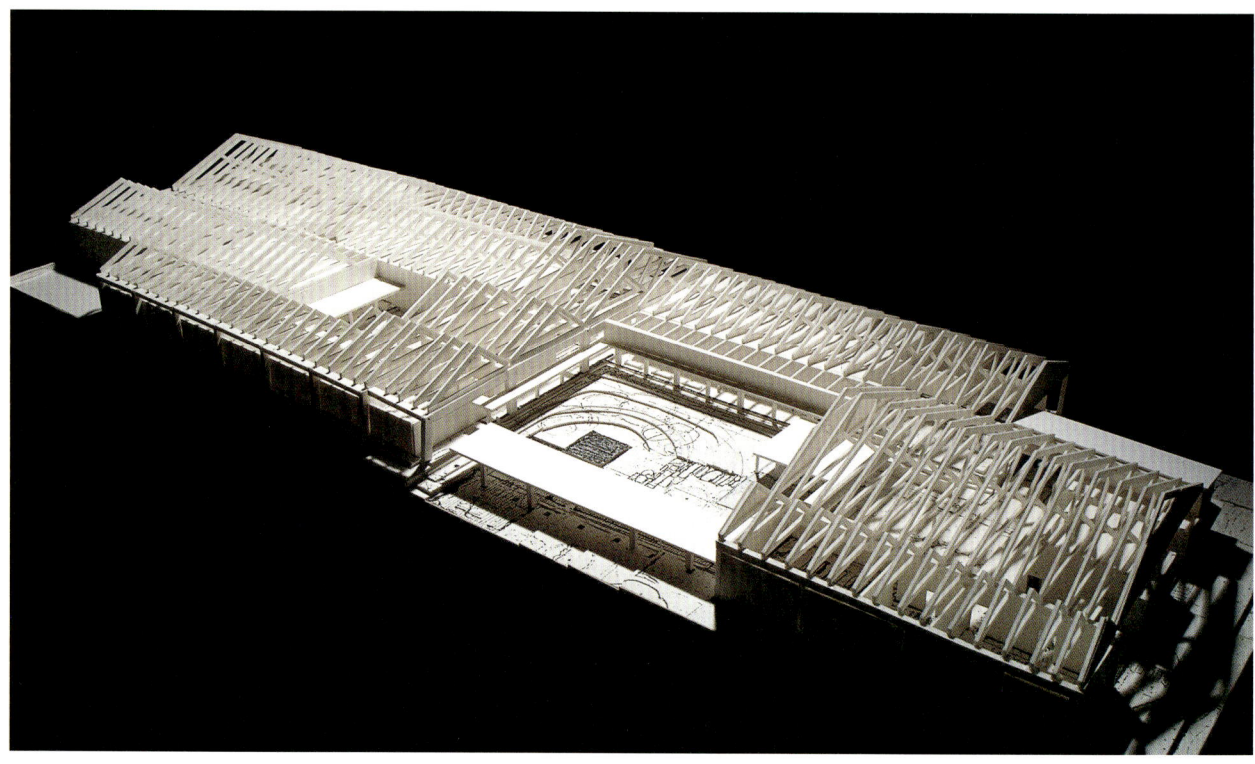

138   Hiroshi NAITO 1992-2004

建物は、崖の上に隠された
秘密の場所、のような存在になっていくはずだ。
The building should eventually become something of a secret place that is hidden above the cliff.

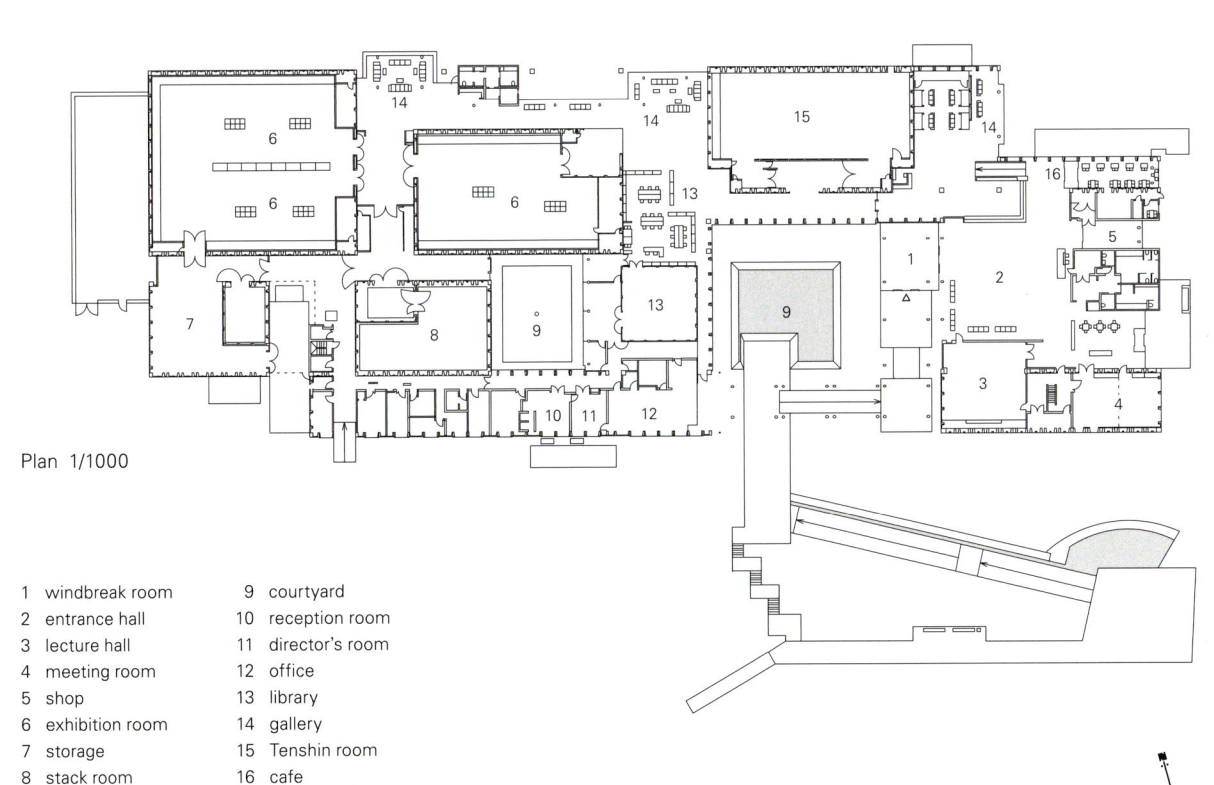

Plan 1/1000

1 windbreak room
2 entrance hall
3 lecture hall
4 meeting room
5 shop
6 exhibition room
7 storage
8 stack room
9 courtyard
10 reception room
11 director's room
12 office
13 library
14 gallery
15 Tenshin room
16 cafe

Tenshin Memorial Museum of Art, Ibaraki

切妻屋根は、その存在自体が不純だ。
初めから純粋さを拒否している。人間のわがままさと自然とを
調停し結びつける不純さを、それ自体が表明している。

The very existence of the gable roof is impure.
It rejects purity from the start. It in itself attests to the impurity of
a compromise made between human selfishness and nature.

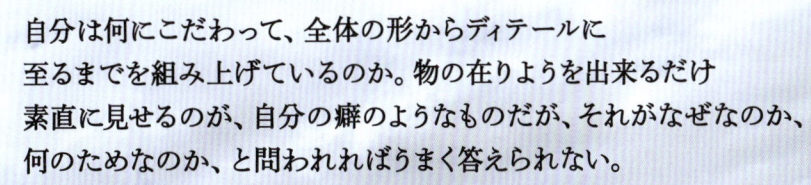

自分は何にこだわって、全体の形からディテールに
至るまでを組み上げているのか。物の在りようを出来るだけ
素直に見せるのが、自分の癖のようなものだが、それがなぜなのか、
何のためなのか、と問われればうまく答えられない。

What aspects am I particularly concerned about as I am working things out from the form of the whole down to the details? It seems that I have a habit to try to present things as they are as honestly as possible, but I cannot provide a good answer when asked why or for what purpose I do this.

整合性やら、ものをきれいに説明する理路やら、
そうしたこだわりの行き着く先は知れている。
そんなものの中に創造のリアルな生命は宿りはしない。

One can only go so far with being meticulous about
consistency or well-composed reasoning.
The true life of creativity does not dwell within such things.

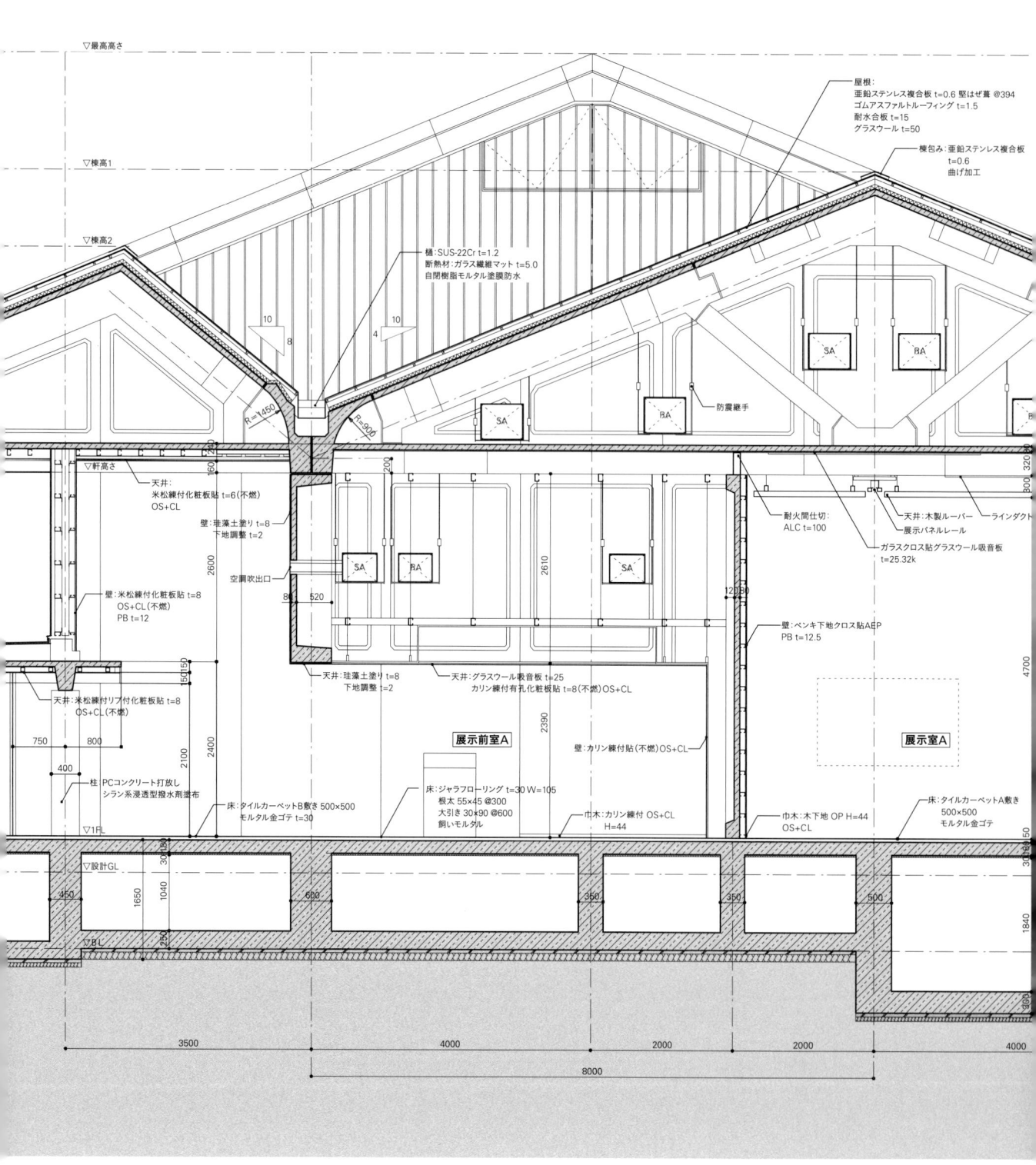

Detailed section 1/80

24mスパンのエントランスホールに架かるPCa

The precast concrete structure spans 24 meters across the entrance hall.

Hiroshi NAITO 1992-2004

矛盾や軋轢に満ちた不純さを許容する
建築というフィールドの中でも、物質世界に近い構造の分野は、
例外的に純度を保てる美しい場所のはずだ。

Within the domain of architecture that tolerates impurities full of
contradiction and friction, the field of structure that is closely tied to the
material world holds a particularly beautiful place in which purity can be
maintained at an exceptional level.

時間を生きることこそが建築の本来的な価値であり、
他の領域にない際立った特質ではないか。
The primary value of architecture is derived from how it lives through time. This is a distinct property that is not found in other realms.

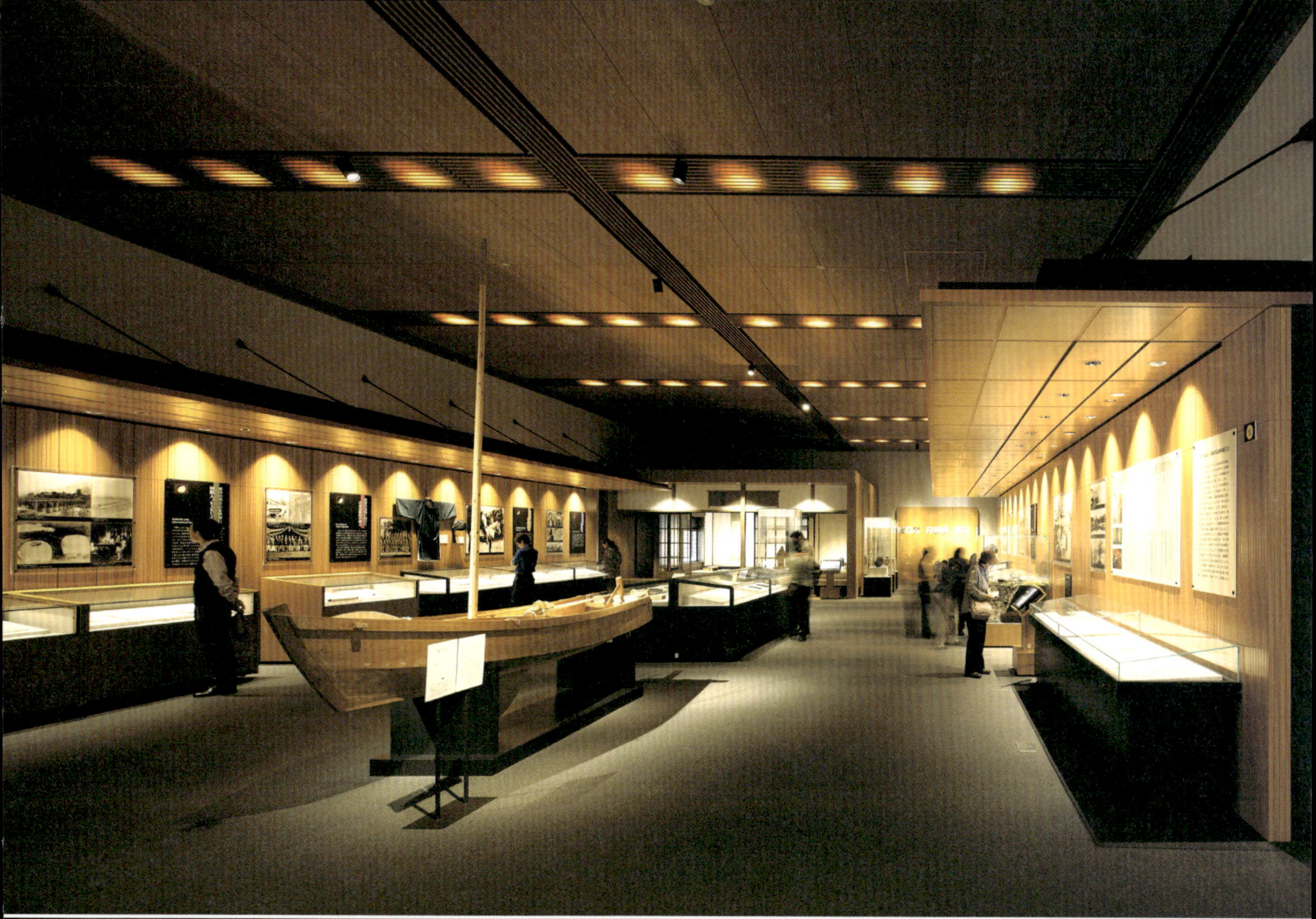

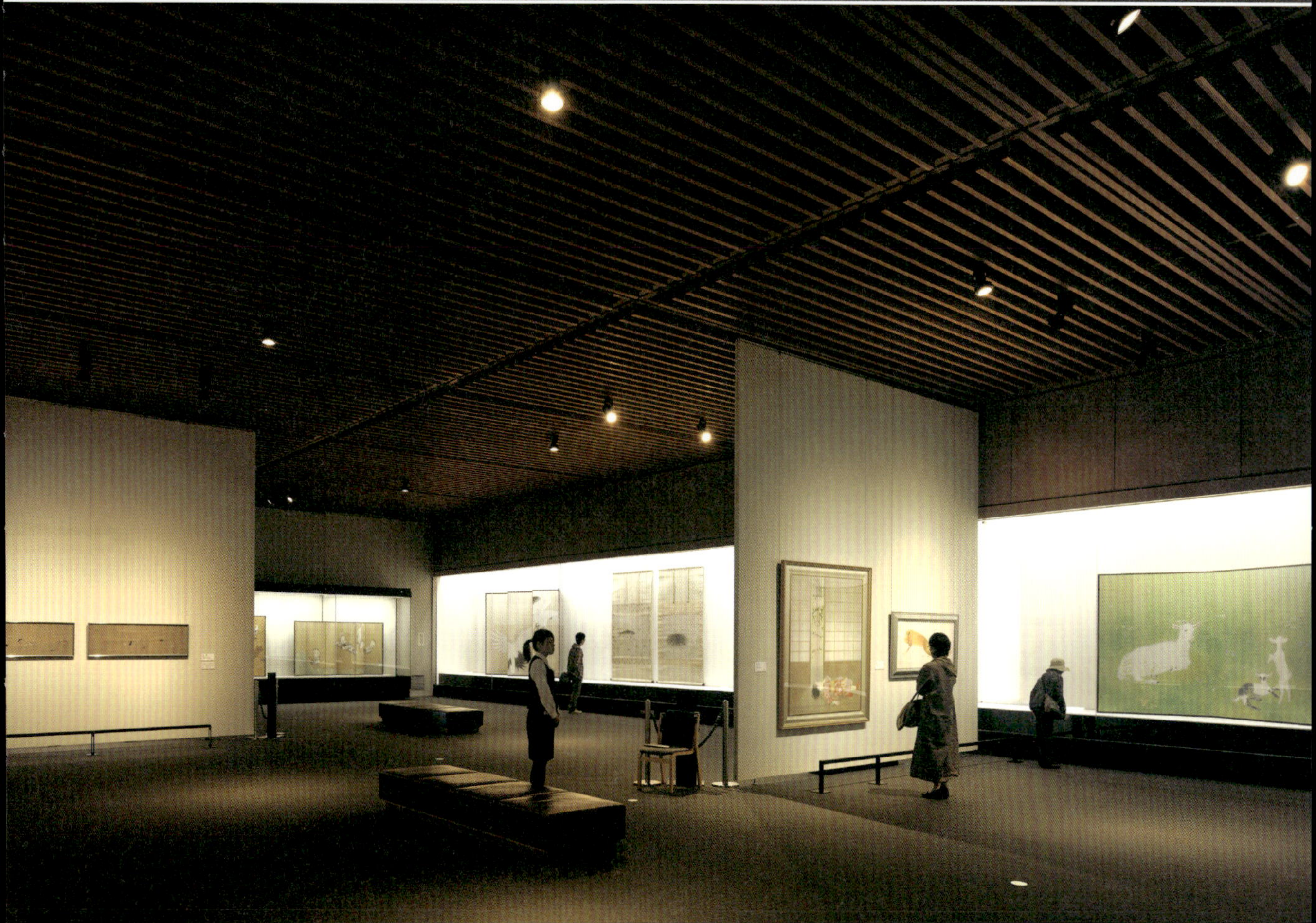

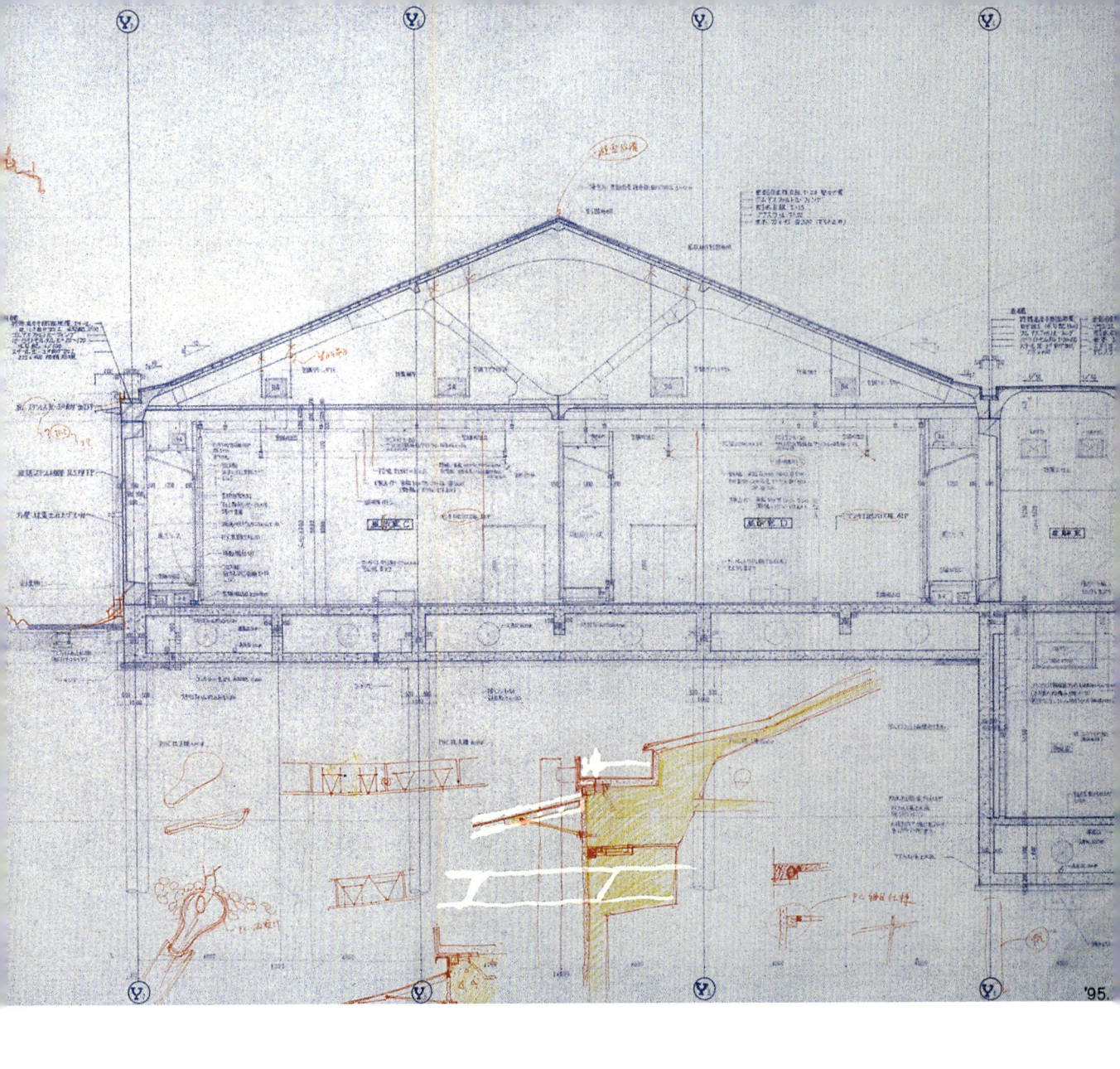

146 Hiroshi NAITO 1992-2004

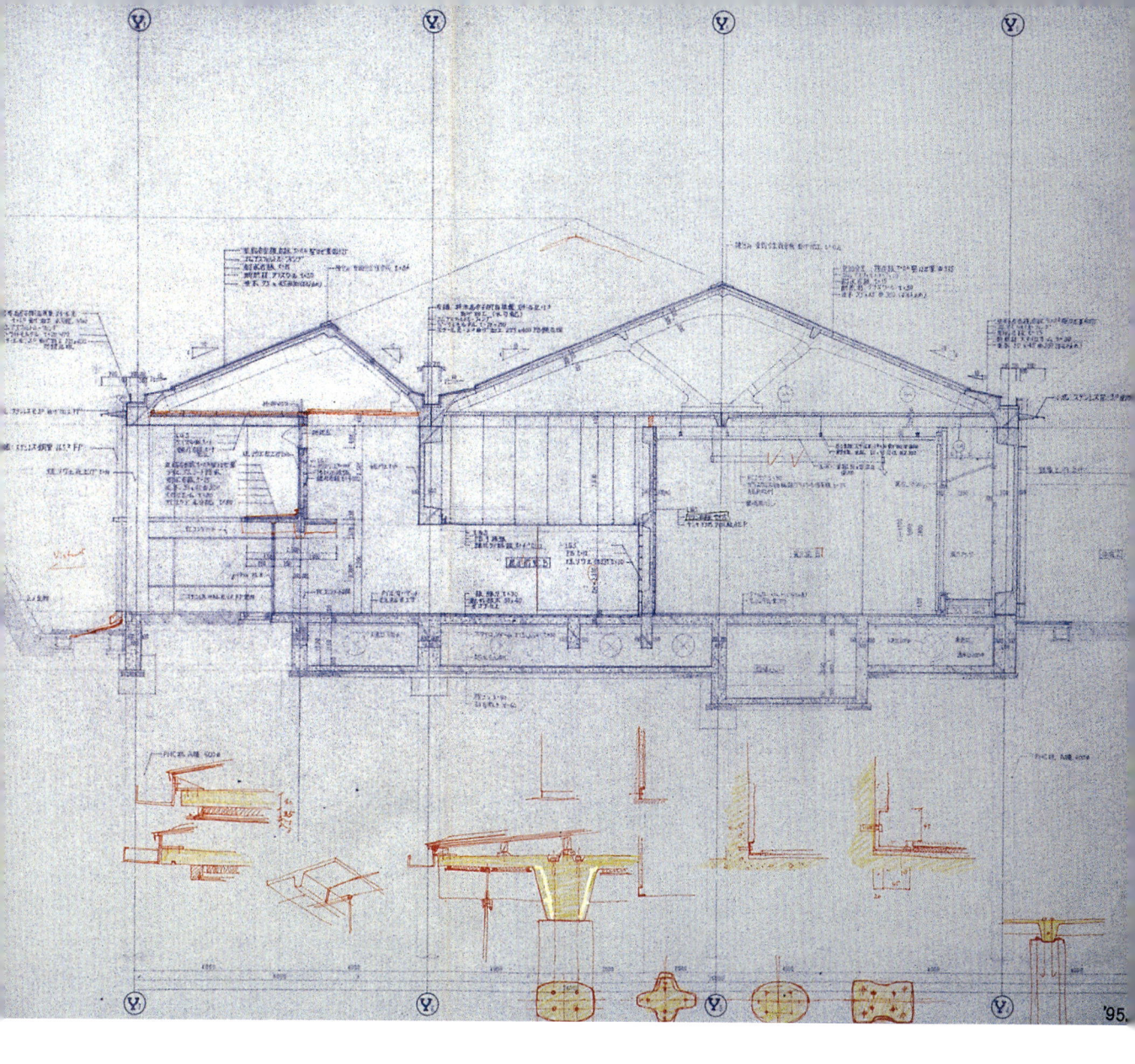

147 Tenshin Memorial Museum of Art, Ibaraki

建築を構成する諸要素の中で、その表面をいかに仕上げるのか、
ということほど、必然性から遠い部分はない。
Among the various elements that compose architecture, there is nothing that is
further from the essential than the matter of how its surface should be finished.

建築という「手段」が、それ自体が「目的」に
すり替わる瞬間がある。建築が「作品」と呼ばれる時だ。この時、
建築は在りのままの存在であることから離脱する。意味や価値が
転倒するのだ。建築は「手段」の範囲に留まるべきだ。

There is a moment when architecture switches from being a means to becoming the objective itself. This happens when architecture is called a "piece". At that moment, architecture breaks away from existing just as it is. Its meaning and value are toppled. Architecture must remain within the realm of being a means.

住居No.21 千歳烏山の家
House No.21, Setagaya

1997

東京都世田谷区　Tokyo

不純物として建築は、絶えず吹き付ける不条理の風にも、
自らの存在を貫く時の流れにも疲弊しない、確かな強さを携えること
ができるような気がする。その在り方が、矛盾に満ちた現在を
生きねばならない人間という存在に似ているからだ。

I have a feeling that architecture as an impurity carries a sure strength that enables it to withstand the unceasing winds of irrationality and time that pierces through it. I think so because its way of existence is similar to that of our own as humans living within the present that is full of contradiction.

旗竿敷地の路上生活

建て主の奥野憲一は、陶芸関係の雑誌の編集者で、後に西武百貨店の工芸画廊の責任者になった親しい友人のひとりだ。たいへんな酒飲みで、この上ない照れ屋で、その裏返しで強気なことを言う。その奥野が突然やって来て、「土地を買った」と重大事を告白するように満面の笑みをたたえて言った。友人の決断を聞いてよろこんだが、土地の図面を見て驚いた。ミニ開発の旗竿敷地の道路の部分だった。奥の宅地が接道することになって道路部分が売りに出され、それを買ったのだった。

「お前もついに路上生活者になるか」と冗談ともつかないようなことを言ってふたりで笑った。敷地の幅は4m、奥行き18m。おまけに北側斜線が効いている。いかに奥野でも、果たしてこれで人が住む場所が作れるのか不安になった。身なり風体には無頓着だが、仕事柄蔵書はかなりある。結婚したばかりで、夫人は漆芸のアーティストで作業場所も必要だ。子供は作る予定がなく、夫婦ふたりで住まうとのことだったが、設計中盤に事情が変わって定員が増えた。

トンネルが3段積み重なったようなラーメン状の木造の骨組みを作り、外壁を金属葺きで覆うことにした。奥行きはともかく部屋の幅は3mで極限まで狭く少しでも幅をかせぎたかったので、梁を表しにしてその間に板をかませて本棚とした。コストがなかったので、壁は普通の構造用合板を打ち付けただけだったので、本で仕上げてくれ、と頼んだ。また、斜線をかいくぐって3階部分を作るため、階高も2mとかなり低かった。担当したのはオランダ人のパディ・トメセン。190cmを超えるノッポで、梁に頭が付きそうだった。巨人が極小住宅を監理する現場の風景が忘れられない。大工さんが背の小さい人で、素人同然のパディを怒る光景が面白かった。

竣工後、病気の母を引き取ったのでふたりで住むはずの極小住宅の定員は4人になった。10年後、友人の奥野は病気で亡くなり、住宅は売りに出され、現在はこの一風変わった住宅を気に入ってくれた若いご夫婦が住んでいる。(Eng. p.277)

Site Plan 1/500

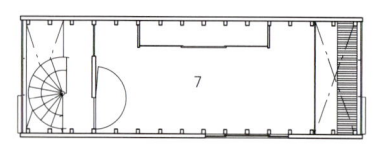

1 bedroom
2 washroom
3 bathroom
4 entrance
5 living/
  dining room
6 kitchen
7 atelier

3F Plan

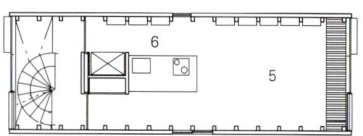

2F Plan

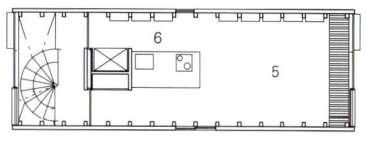

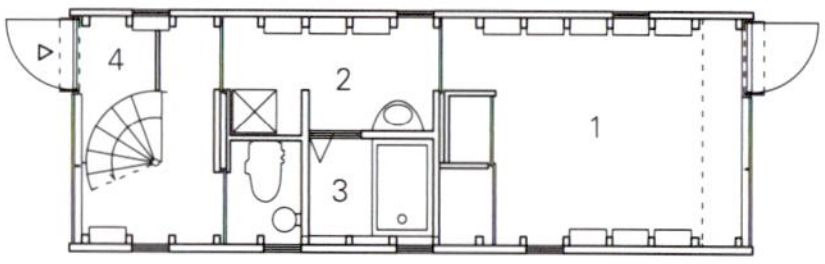

1F Plan 1/200

154　Hiroshi NAITO 1992-2004

常々思っているのは「建築というのはどこかで翻訳されなければならない」ということだ。
I always carry the thought that there is some point at which architecture must be translated.

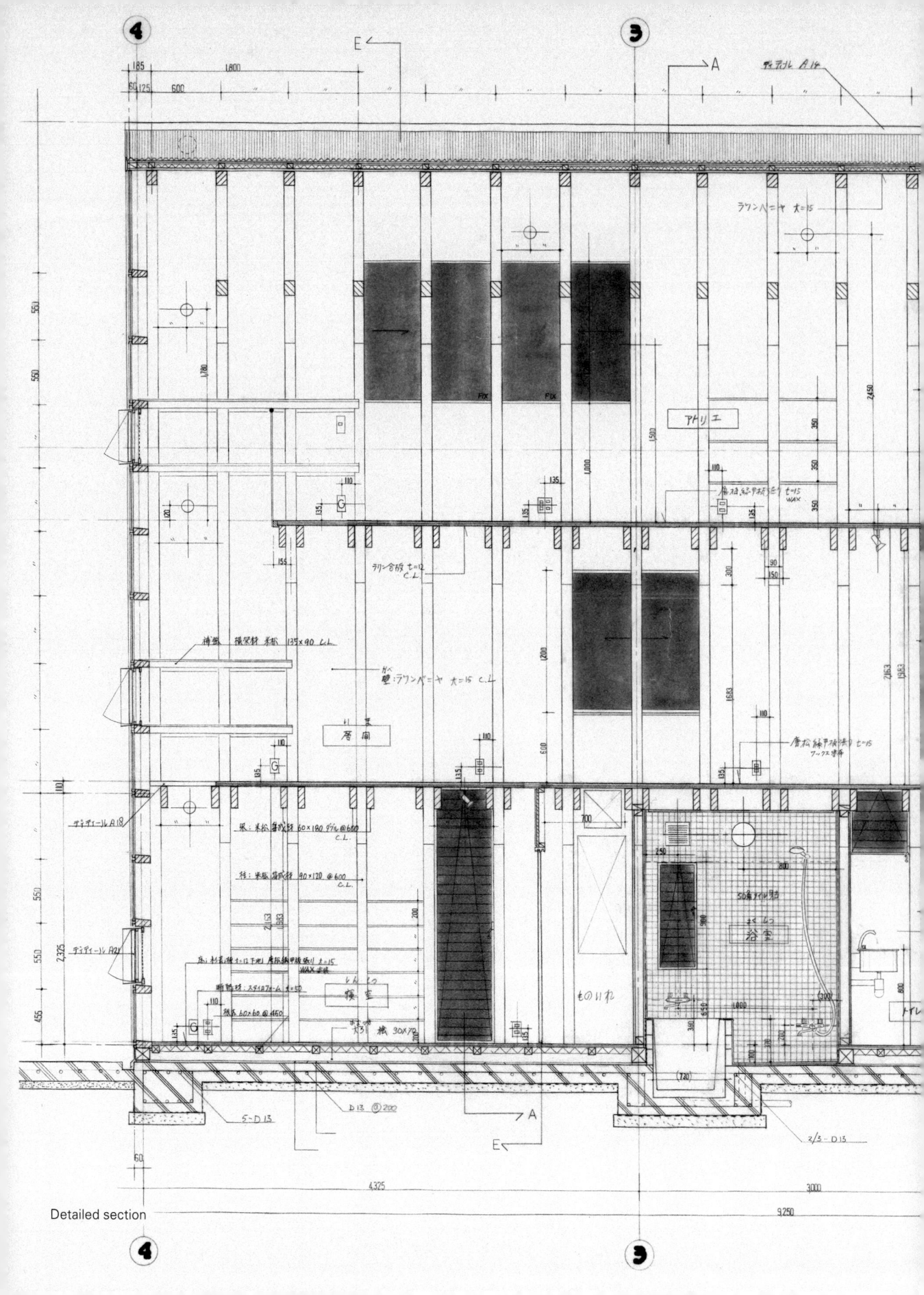

Detailed section

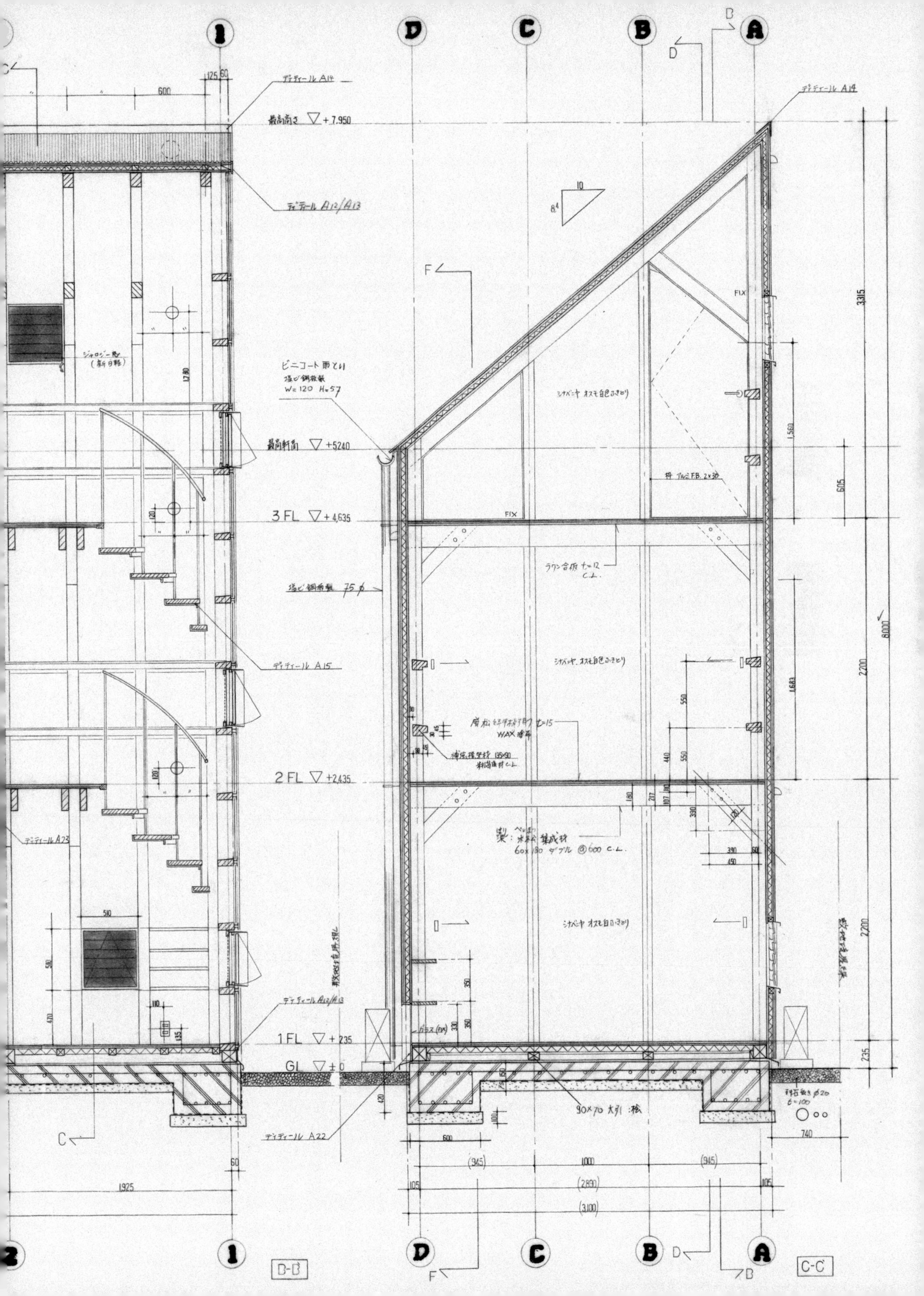

ディテール A14
最高高さ ▽+7,950
ディテール A12/A13
ジャロジー窓（新日軽）
ビニコート雨とい
塩ビ鋼板製
W=120 H=57
最高軒高 ▽+5240
3 FL ▽+4,635
塩ビ鋼板製 75φ
ディテール A15
シナベニヤ オスモ白色ふきとり
ラワン合板 t=12
C.L.
2 FL ▽+2,435
梁：ベイまつ 米松 集成材
60×180 ダブル @600 C.L.
ディテール A23
ディテール A12/A13
1 FL ▽+235
GL ▽±0
90×70 大引 桧
ディテール A22
B-B'
C-C'

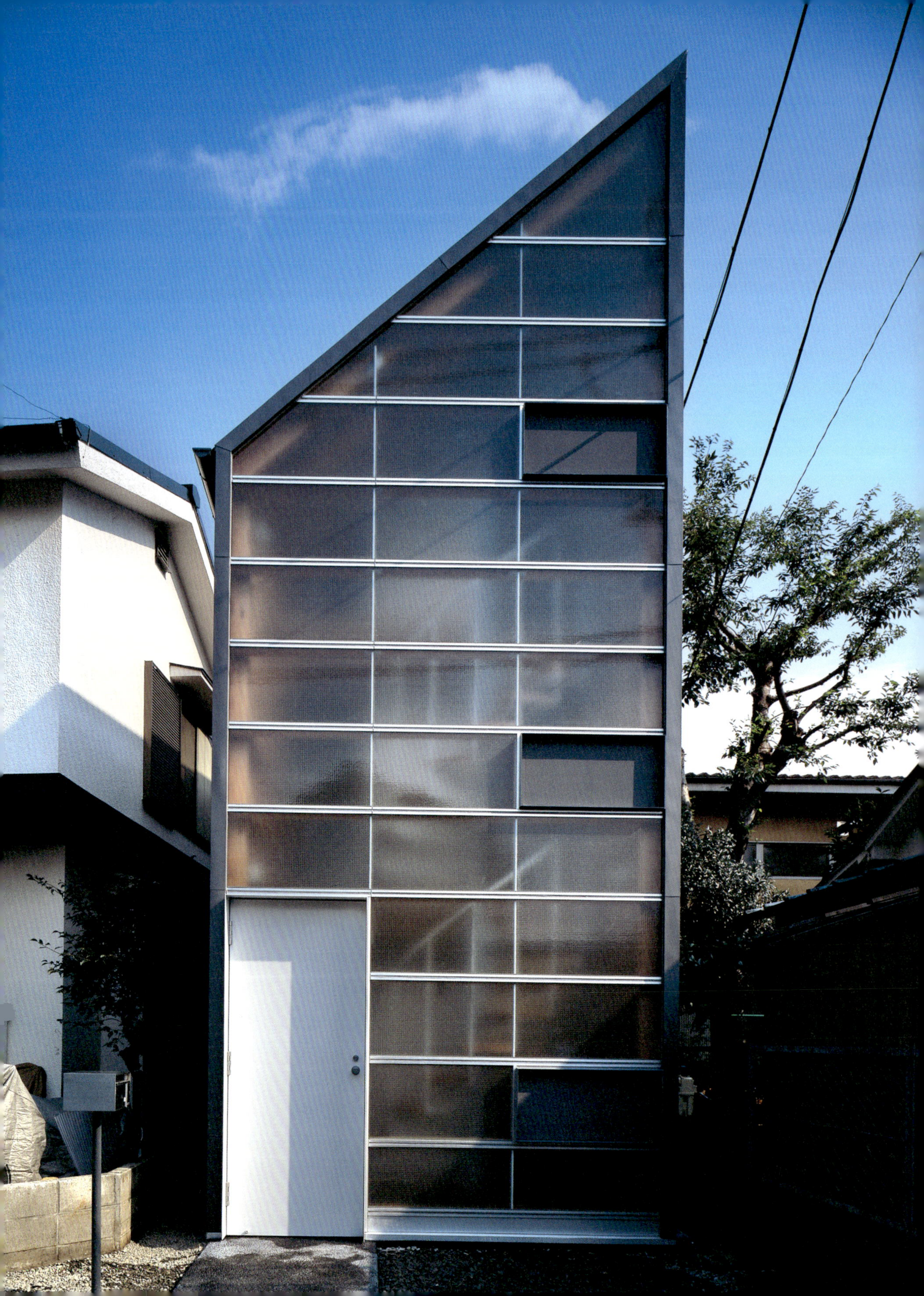

建築という価値は、いずれにせよ物質と意識の中間に、
純度を欠いたまま宙吊りにならざるを得ない。純度の高い抽象性や
物質性も、本来、建築という場にはそぐわない。

The value of architecture must inevitably be hung in midair in a state of impurity between the material and the consciousness. Highly pure states of conceptual abstraction and materiality are both fundamentally unsuited for the domain of architecture.

十日町情報館
Tokamachi Public Library

1999
新潟県十日町市 Niigata

現代は情報革命の時代だ。この建物でも、旧来の図書と
新しい情報の在り方がせめぎ合っている。しかし、
具体的な身体の置き場が確保されて初めて、情報世界に心が開く、
ということも確かなことだ。その逆はあり得ない。

This is the age of the information revolution. Information based on new technologies face off against the traditional media of the library in this building, too. However, one's mind can open to the information world only after a tangible place for their physical body to occupy has been secured. The opposite of this is impossible.

豪雪の街の大きな屋根

指名設計競技が行われ、この建物を設計することになった。4.5mを超える市街地積雪の記録をもつ豪雪地帯で有名な十日町市の図書館である。かつては織物業で栄えたところだが、今は見る影もない。市街地も人口も縮退している。街を歩くと何やら寂しい空気が漂い始めている。信濃川の河岸段丘の上に市街地があり、街外れの緩やかな傾斜地が敷地だった。

駅前にライオン堂という平屋建ての比較的大きなスーパーがあった。どういう案を提案しようかと考えあぐねている時に、ここをブラブラしてみた。その時、買い物客に交って、買い物をするでもなく、疲れたサラリーマンと思しき年配のオジサンたち、腰の曲がりかけた老人たち、そして時たま学生や若い人、そういう人たちが用もないのに時間つぶしをしていた。列車やバスの時間待ちなのだろうが、たぶんそれ以上に人の賑わいの中に身を置きたいのだろう。外は寒いし、それに街は寂しい。

そこで、「豪雪から守られた人が行き交う市場のような空間」を作ってはどうか、と考えた。図書館は本を読んだり借りたりするだけの場所ではもったいない。誰にとってもくつろげる居心地良い開かれた場所を作れば、自然と人は集まってくるはずだ。本を媒介に、さまざまな世代、さまざまな職業の人が集い群れるような建物であるべきだろう。

要は、雪に対するシェルターを作り、それを図書館として使う、という考え方だ。そうなるとしっかりとした屋根が必要になってくる。街を見て回ったのだが、体育館などの大きな屋根を持つ建物で、滑雪させる落雪型のものはどれも傷みが激しかった。雪がヤスリのように屋根の塗装面を傷つけてしまうからだ。落雪型の場合、落ちた大量の雪が解けるのに春先までかかるという不便さもある。そう考えると、雪を屋根の上に載せたままにしておく堆雪型の建物にするしかない。しかし、何せ豪雪地帯である。積雪を考えると、おおよそ1㎡あたり1トンの雪の荷重を見込まねばならない。おまけに、雪は屋根の上で均質に解けるとは限らない。偏荷重も考えねばならない。したがって、そうとう頑強な構造体を作る必要がある。このあたりは、有無をいわさず機能本意でいくしかない。大きなスパンで剛性の高い陸屋根を作るには、やはりPCaで、ということになる。それがベストだし、それしかない。

また、豪雪に対しては雪庇対策が重要だ。大きな雪庇だと、その固まりだけで1トン以上の重さになる。ただでさえ建物の弱点であるパラペットがやられてしまう。尖り屋根のような断面のパラペットを考案し、それに電熱線を通して雪庇を防いだので、外観はずいぶんモッタリしたものになった。立面はシャープさに欠ける。だが、この建物の肝は内部空間にあるのだから仕方がない。

出来上がったら、たぶん一番多い利用者は青少年だろう。設計が始まってから、幾つかの高校に出向いてヒアリングをした。10人ほど集まってもらっていろいろ聞いていく。学校が終わってからどうしてるんですか、と聞くと、「家に帰って勉強します」という答えが判で押したように返ってくる。ヒアリングには担任の先生が立ち会っていたのだが、これでは本音が聞けない。先生に退場してもらってからが面白かった。

途端に場の雰囲気が明るくなった。本当は、そこに居たほとんどの子が、「友達の家に行って雑談する、その時間が一番楽しい」らしい。どうして友達の家なの、と聞くと、「行く場所がないからだ」と言う。もし、みんなが気軽に集まれるような場所があったらそこに行きますか、と尋ねたら、全員が「もちろん」と声を合わせた。これでかねてより提案してきたことに自信がもてた。

それから、例えば東京から友達が来たらどこへ行くの、と聞いたら、「連れて行くところがない」と言う。つまり、自慢できるような、そして誇りのもてるような場所がないのだ。内容は図書館の設計だが、要は、人が集まれるような場所を作り、誇りのもてるような場所を作ることなのだということを再確認した。

大屋根に守られた大きな空間の中に、本の多さがどこからでも見えるように、本で囲まれた階段状の吹き抜けを作った。これなら東京の友達を連れてきても恥ずかしくないだろう。この建物の利用者は、年間30万人を超えるという。公共施設としてはたいへんな利用率だ。それは場を作るという意図がうまくいったからではないかと思っている。(Eng. p.278)

Site Plan 1/1500

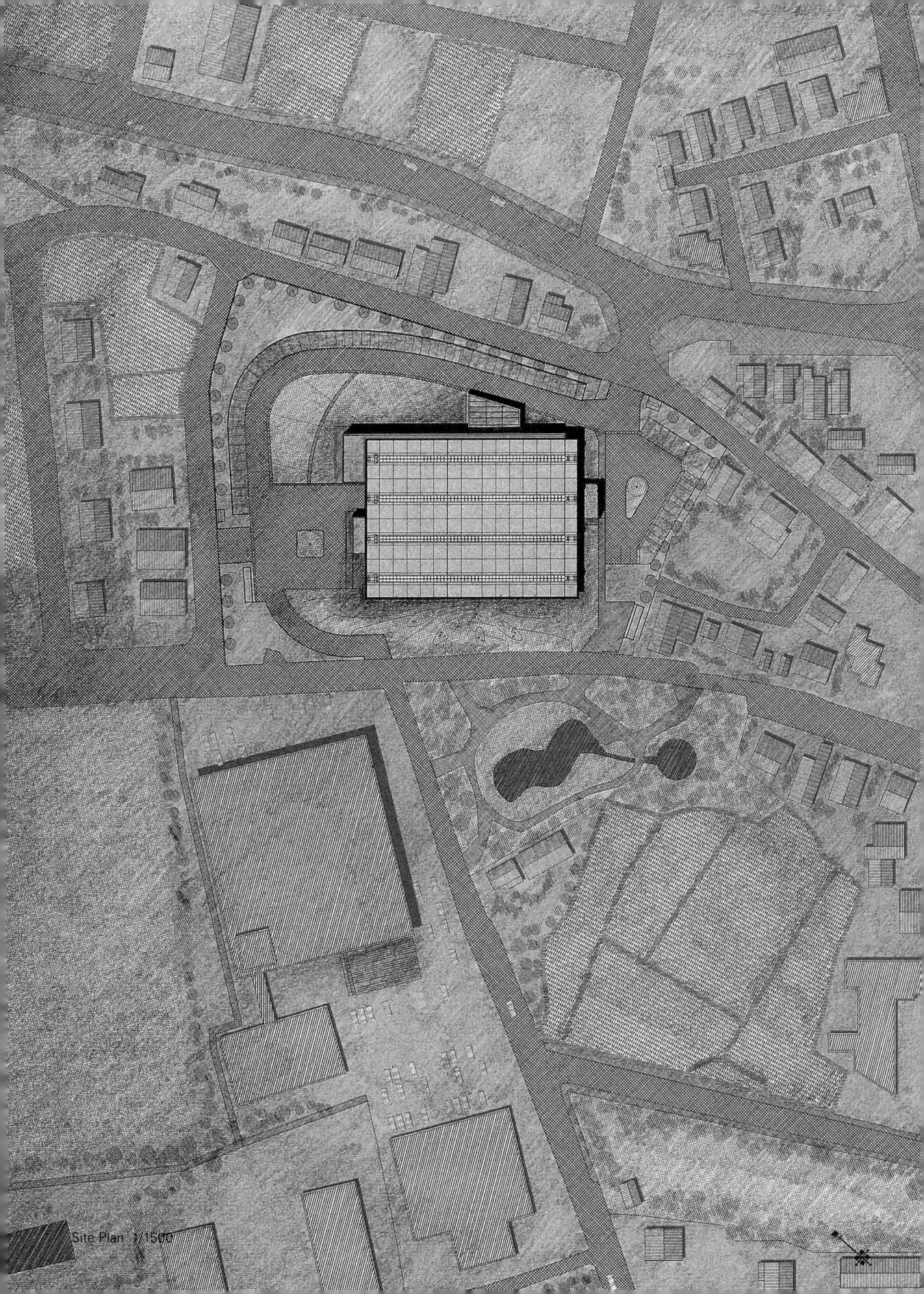

物珍しさはすぐに飽きられる。設計という
行為に課せられた大切な役割は、性能や機能を忠実に
満たしていく中で、変わりにくい価値、時間と共に
消費されない価値をいかに埋め込むことができるか、にある。

Newness quickly grows old. Aside from properly fulfilling performance and functional needs, an important part of the act of design rests upon how it embeds value that is not easily changed or consumed over time.

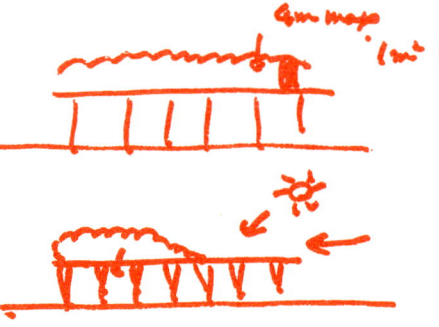

Tokamachi Public Library

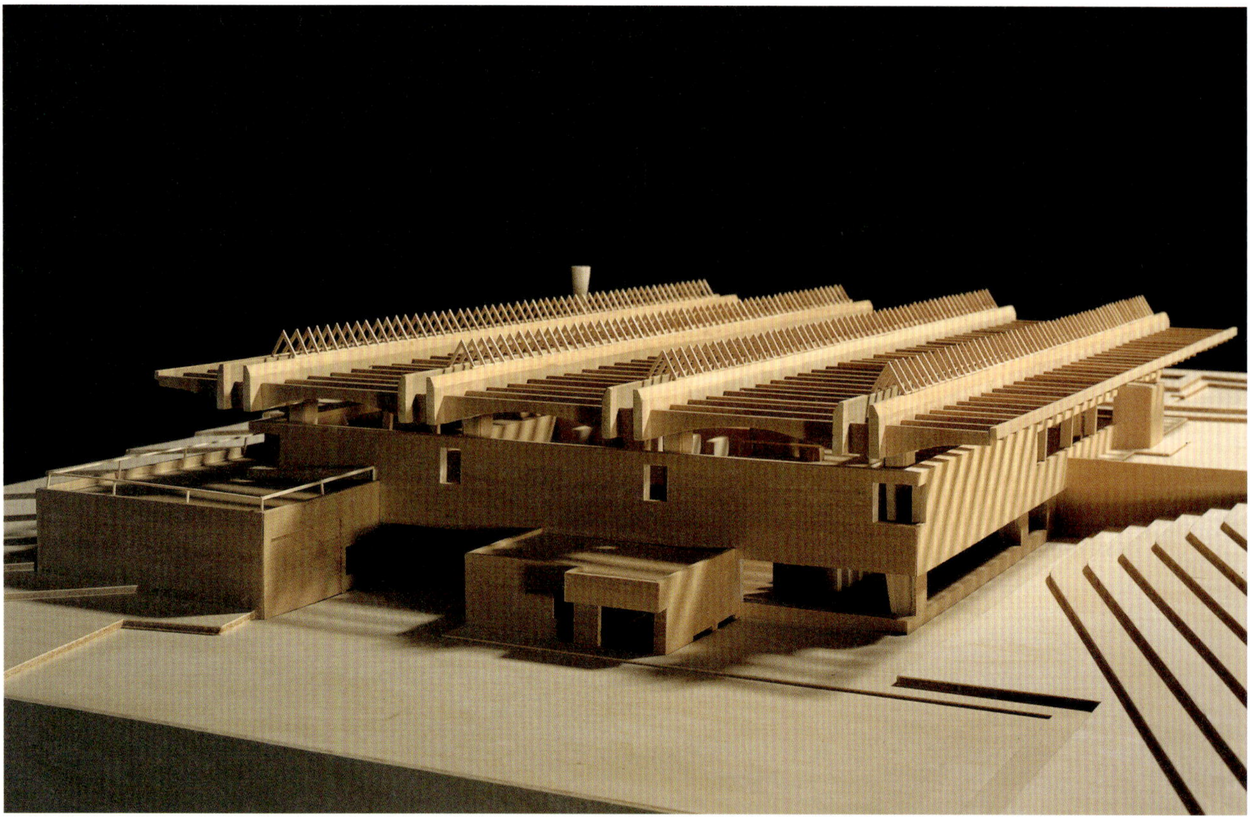
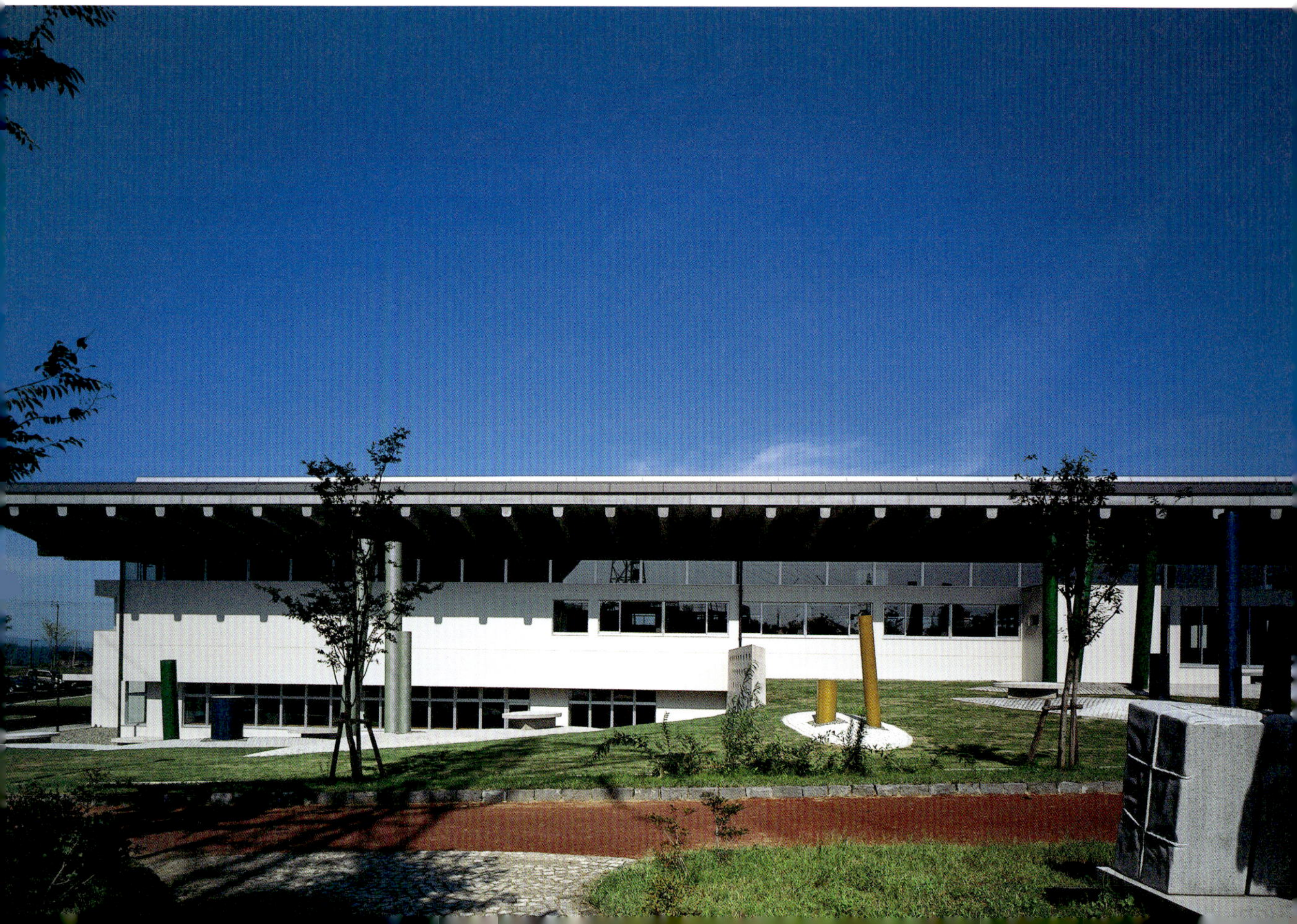

この建物で展開された考え方や方法は、
「海の博物館」に負うところが大きい。気候や環境に対して
技術的な最適解を求める、というアプローチの仕方は、
博物館を設計したときとまったく同じだ。

Many of the ideas and methods deployed in this building are indebted to
the Sea-Folk Museum. The approach taken here, in which the optimal
technical solutions were sought for in response to the climate and environment,
was exactly the same as that in the design of the earlier museum.

ミクロな部分を構成する要素が、全体計画から
部分へと降りてくるマクロな要素とうまく折り合わなければ
豊かな空間とは言えない。そうでなくては、人間のいる場所を
建築が保証したことにはならないからだ。

A space cannot be described as being rich unless the elements that form the parts on the micro-scale are brought to terms with the elements that span across the project from the macro-scale. Unless this is achieved, it cannot be said that the architecture has secured a place for people to inhabit.

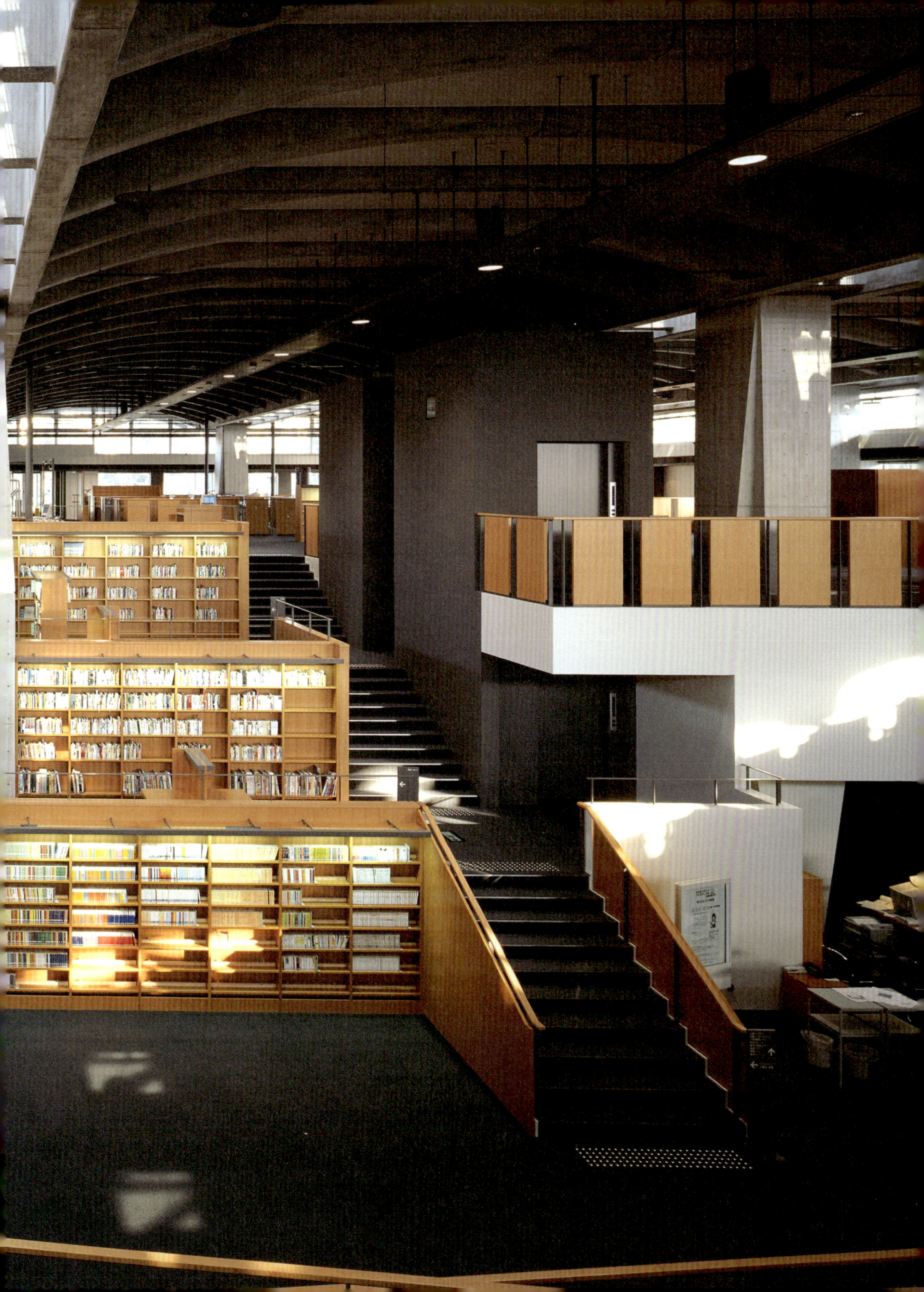

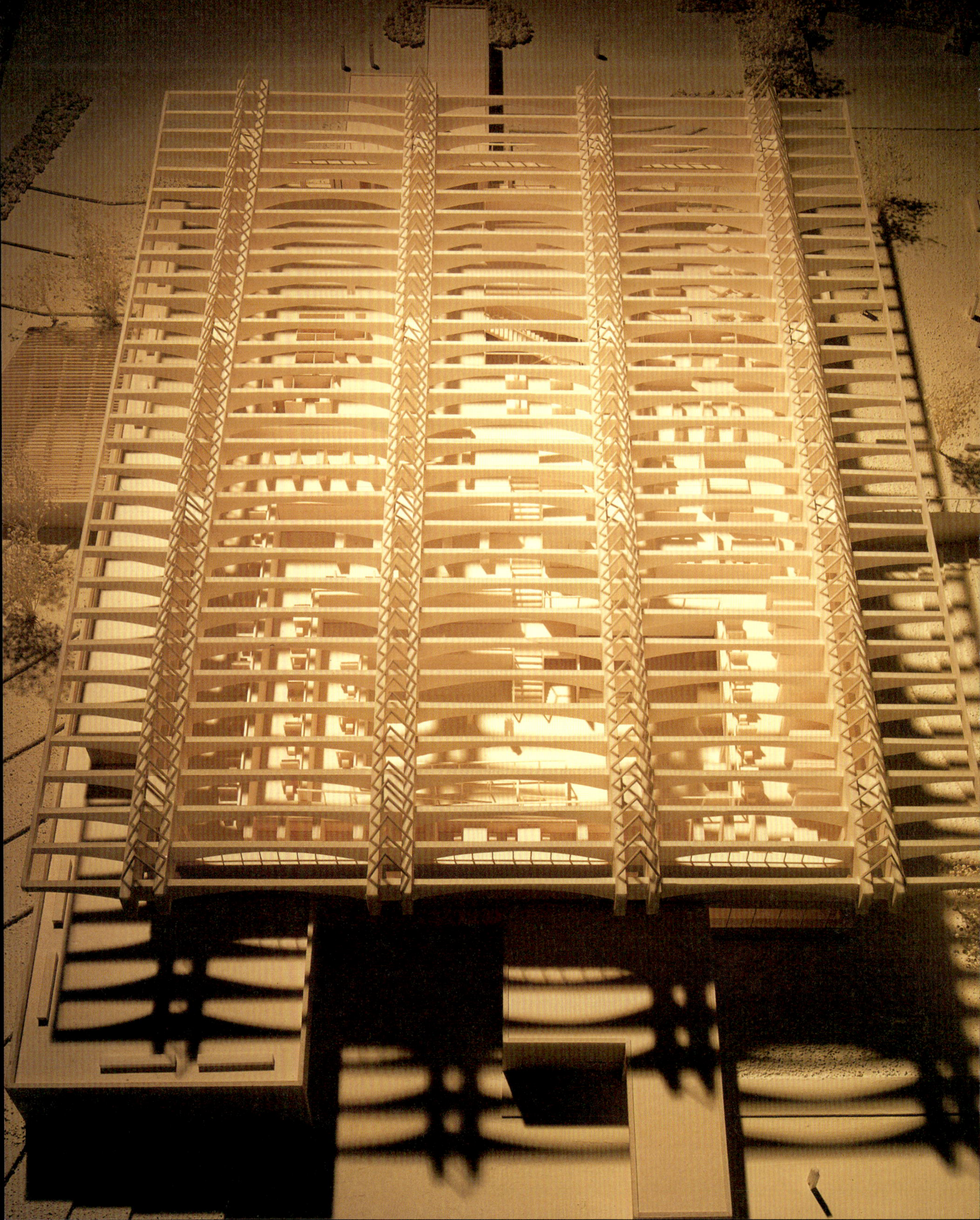

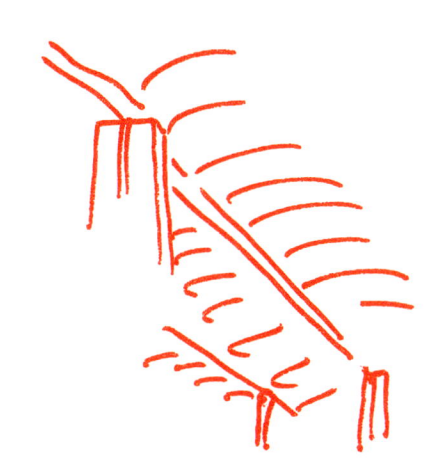

1	entrance hall	12	machine room
2	reception room	13	garage
3	office	14	open stack room
4	children's books area	15	reading area
5	children's room	16	tatami room
6	meeting room	17	cafe
7	study room	18	information corner
8	hall	19	exhibition area
9	reference desk	20	audiovisual library
10	stack room	21	outside reading area
11	auditorium		

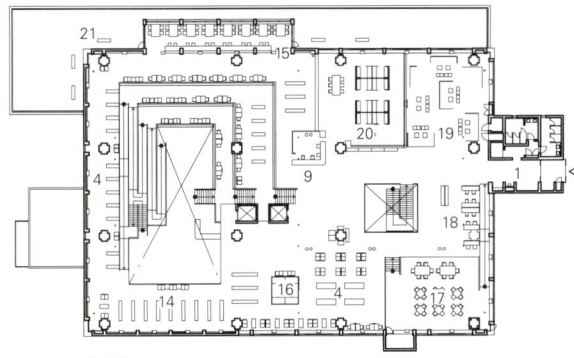

2F Plan

1F Plan 1/1000

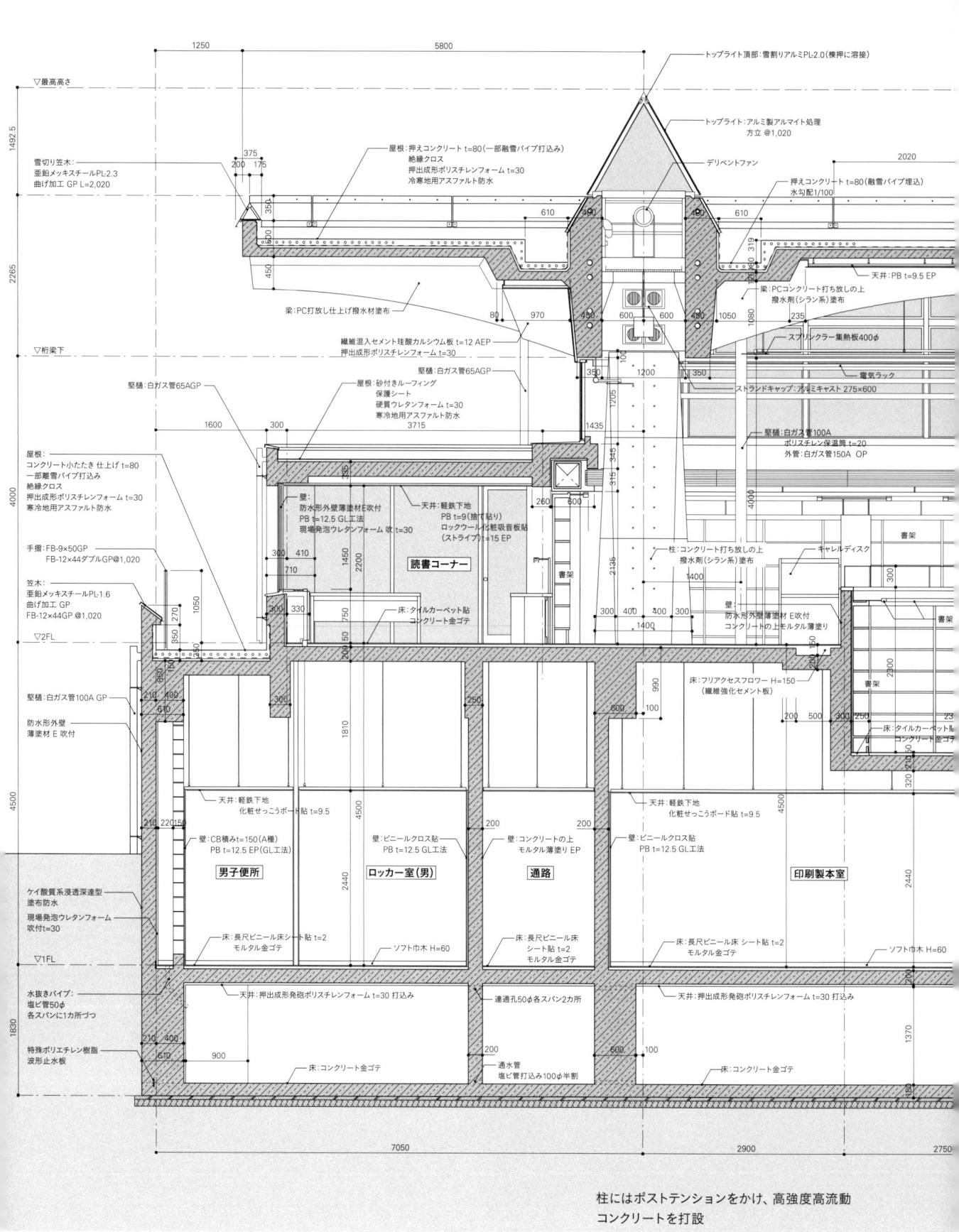

Detailed section 1/75

柱にはポストテンションをかけ、高強度高流動
コンクリートを打設

The columns were post-tensioned and cast with
high-strength high-fluidity concrete.

時間は場所に堆積する。
Time accumulates upon place.

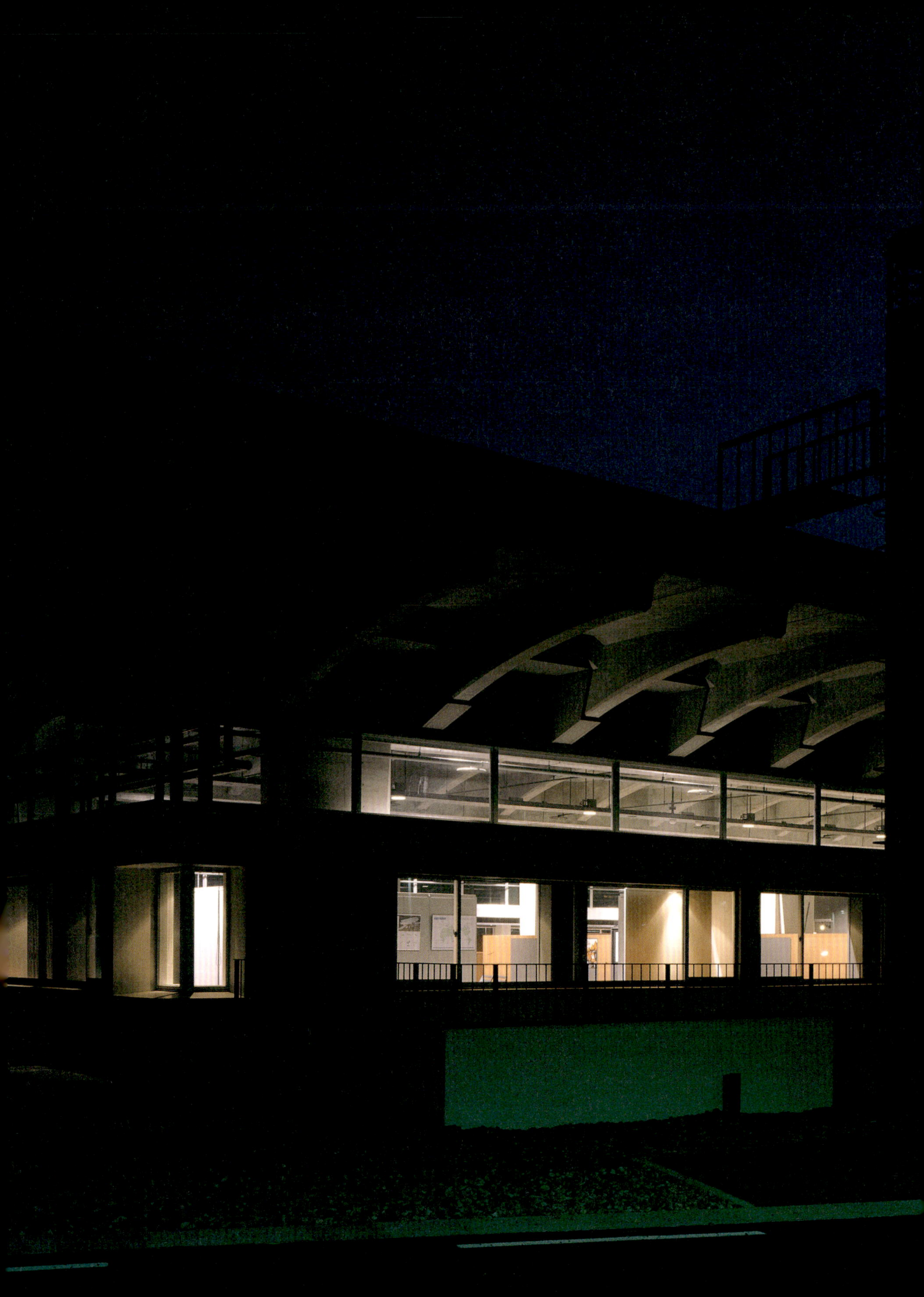

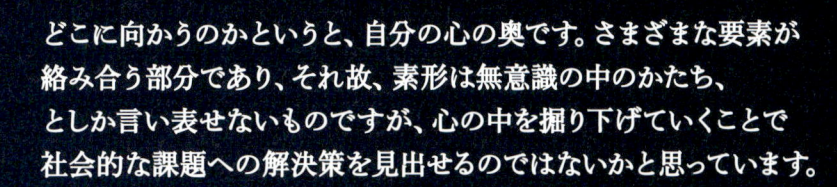

どこに向かうのかというと、自分の心の奥です。さまざまな要素が
絡み合う部分であり、それ故、素形は無意識の中のかたち、
としか言い表せないものですが、心の中を掘り下げていくことで
社会的な課題への解決策を見出せるのではないかと思っています。

Where I am heading towards is the depths of my own mind. It is where various
elements are entangled together. I can only express the protoform as a form within the
unconscious, but I believe that solutions to our social problems can be found through
delving into the mind.

牧野富太郎記念館
Makino Museum of Plants and People

1999
高知県高知市 Kochi

「消える建築」が自己否定の構図を取るのに対して、「隠れる建築」は、周囲との関係を受け入れ、それと強く切り結ぶことによって初めて成り立つ。そのことによって、敷地や環境がもっている生来の矛盾や不透明さを、建物の仕組みの根底に、色濃く引き受ける宿命をもつことになる。

"Disappearing architecture" positions itself in alignment with self-denial, whereas "hidden architecture" bases itself upon accepting its relationship to its surroundings and binding tightly together with it. Through the latter, a building is destined to adopt the innate contradictions and obscurities of its site and environs into the very basis of its existence.

森に包まれ、森に帰る

不思議な縁で生まれた激烈な仕事であった。わたしの40代を象徴する仕事である。

自らを「花の精」と呼び、植物をこよなく愛した牧野富太郎（1862-1957）は、『牧野日本植物図鑑』で知られ、40万点もの植物標本を残し、1,500種以上の植物を命名したとされる。植物分類学の祖とも言われる巨人だ。破天荒でとても魅力的な人物だったらしく、いまだに熱狂的なファンも多い。その牧野博士を記念する博物館が、高知市郊外にある五台山の牧野植物園内にひっそりと建っていた。同じ植物園内に、牧野博士を顕彰する展示館と植物研究のための建物を建てる、というのが計画であった。

この仕事には幾つもの縁で引き寄せられた。まず初めに、「海の博物館」の展示をやった展示デザイナーの里見和彦君が相談にやってきた。聞けば、遠縁の親戚である牧野植物園の園長が、県立の博物館を考えているので会ってほしい、という。里見剛園長は、動物行動学の日高敏隆先生から、「博物館を作るなら海の博物館を参考にするように」と言われてすでに見学していた。そして、県立美術館の鍵岡正謹館長は、セゾン美術館にいた頃からの知り合いだ。橋本大二郎知事は、「海の博物館」に見学に来られたことがあるので、すでに面識があった。

知事の計らいで県議会で議決してもらい、特命で設計委託を受けた。それだけ責任も重い。何としても牧野博士に相応しい建物を作りたかった。取り掛かった時、県の担当者が作成していたのは、4階建ての四角いビルのような建物の案だった。それはあんまりだ。博物館の機能からも、五台山の風景を乱さないためにも、可能な限り低層が好ましい。管理・研究・収蔵を担う棟と展示を担う棟を分け、分棟で案を作った。

もとは県の役人だった里見園長は60過ぎ、いかにも高知県人らしく、明るく、激しやすく、この上なく頑固な人であった。牧野博士をこよなく敬愛し、収蔵物もままならない植物園の現状に憤っていた。この里見園長が、県の担当部局である文化環境部の清田康之部長とソリが合わなかった。後に県の役人のトップである総務部長になる清田さんは30代後半、自治省からの出向で、若いがバリバリの本省キャリアである。

里見園長は10,000㎡は最低必要だと主張する。一方、財政を気にする清田さんは3,000㎡を譲らない。ふたりが目の前でつかみ掛からんばかりの激論を交わし、間に入ってなだめたことも一度ならずあった。実は、大きく庇を張り出し、屋根の下に建物の3分の1近く半外部空間を抱え込んだ建物の特異な形式は、いつまでも面子にこだわって譲らぬこのふたりを妥協させるために編み出した苦肉の策だった。内部空間は6,000㎡、半外部空間も入れれば8,000㎡以上になる。架構を木造にしたのは、木材振興を掲げていた知事からのたっての希望である。

幾つものスタディを重ねた末、それまでの架構の整合性を中心に据えた硬い作り方では、目標とする空間には届かないと考えるに至った。牧野博士の自然に対する態度にどうしても空間が響かないのだ。造成を極力抑えた平面配置にし、山肌を這うような有機的な形態を木造で作る。そして、いずれは木々に隠れて森に帰っていくような建物にしようと決めた。

有機的な屋根には苦労した。台風がよく来ることでも知られる高知、おまけに山の上である。高知の雨は滝のように、しかも下から降る、と現地の建築家から幾度も脅かされた。原寸のスタディを重ね、現場に入ってからは現物サンプルを作って確認を重ねた。複雑きわまりない納まりにもかかわらず、いまだに雨は一滴も漏っていない。

建物が出来て10年以上の歳月が流れた。展示の設計をした里見和彦君は、竣工後、県職員の試験を受け、植物園の展示担当の学芸員になった。今はフィールドを担当するようになって植物と格闘している。年々歳々、建物の周囲に植えられた牧野博士ゆかりの木々や植物が豊かに育っていく。その様を見るととても幸せな気持ちになる。最近では、建物は森に守られ、その命に包まれてすっかり安らいでいるようにも見える。(Eng. p.278)

Site Plan 1/1500

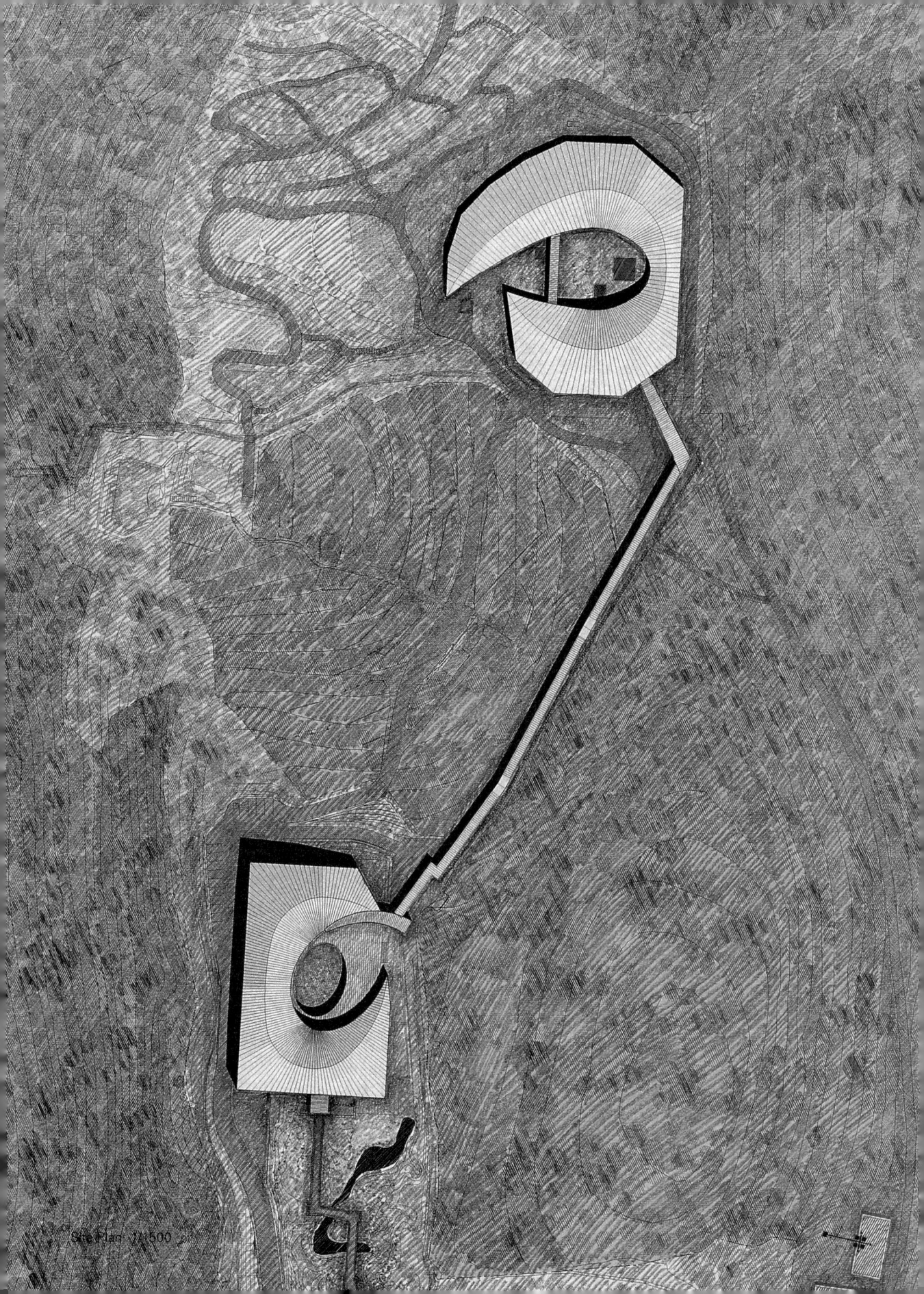

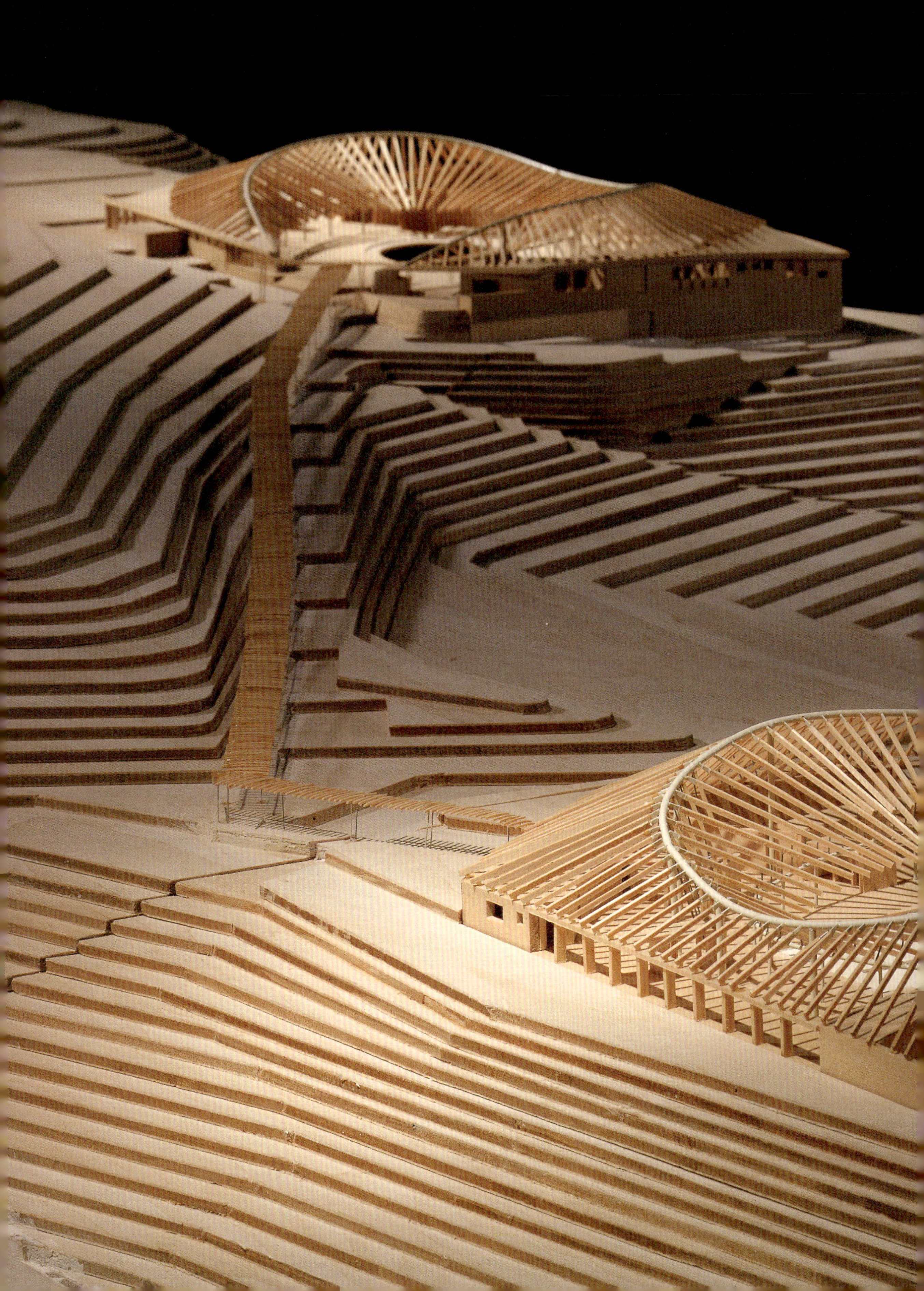

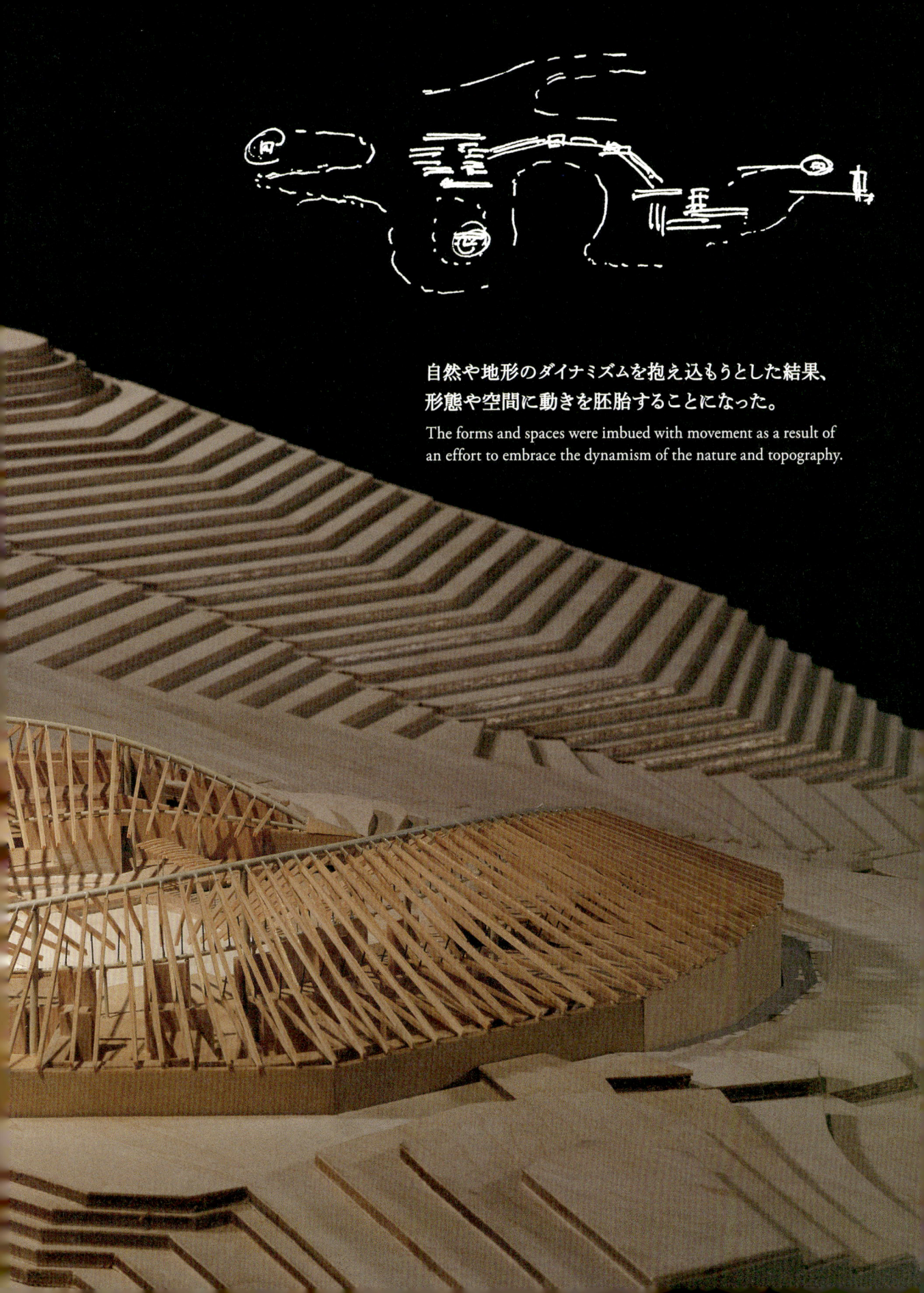

自然や地形のダイナミズムを抱え込もうとした結果、
形態や空間に動きを胚胎することになった。
The forms and spaces were imbued with movement as a result of
an effort to embrace the dynamism of the nature and topography.

外周にテンションを加える案(左)と
外周を固める案(右)

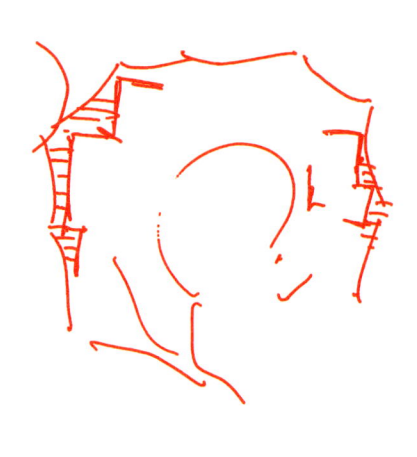

Sketches of schemes to apply tensioning along the perimeter (left) and to harden the perimeter (right).

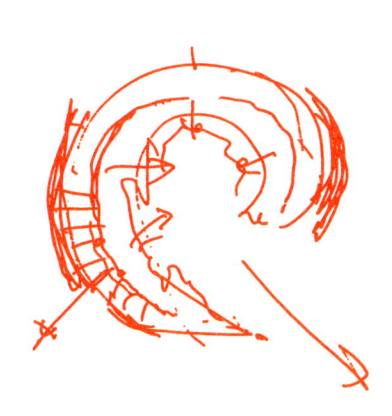

物としての建物をどんな形態にしたいのか、という願望はほとんどない。まだ建物が建ち上がってもいない段階で、いくら形になるスケッチを描いたところで、それは自分の欲しているものとは、ほとんど関係のないことのように思えてしまう。

I have almost no preferences regarding how to shape a building as an object. No matter how plausible a form may appear to be in a sketch made before the building has even emerged, I cannot but feel that it does not have much to do with what I truly want.

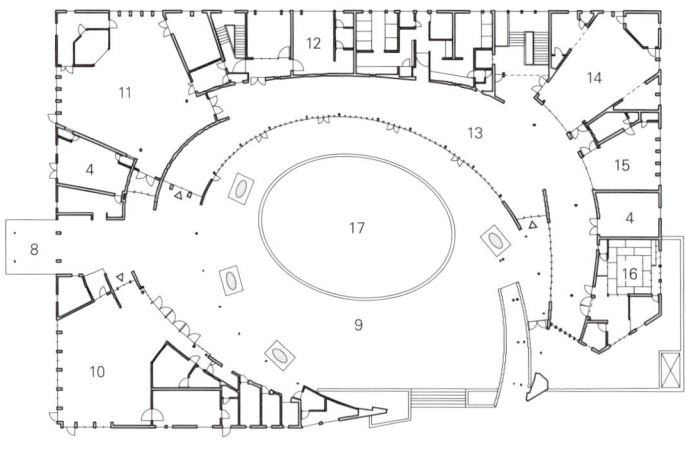

Museum Building 2F Plan

1	office
2	storage
3	laboratory
4	machine room
5	courtyard
6	library
7	stack room
8	main entrance
9	deck
10	shop/restaurant
11	auditorium
12	meeting room
13	Godaisan gallery
14	studio
15	study room
16	tatami room
17	void

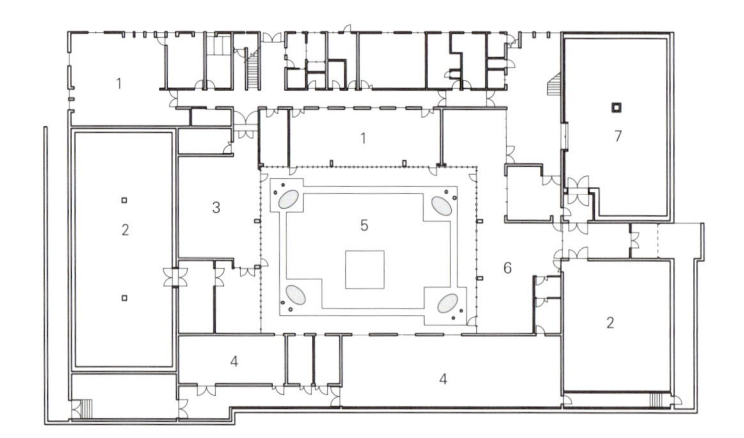

Museum Building 1F Plan   1/800

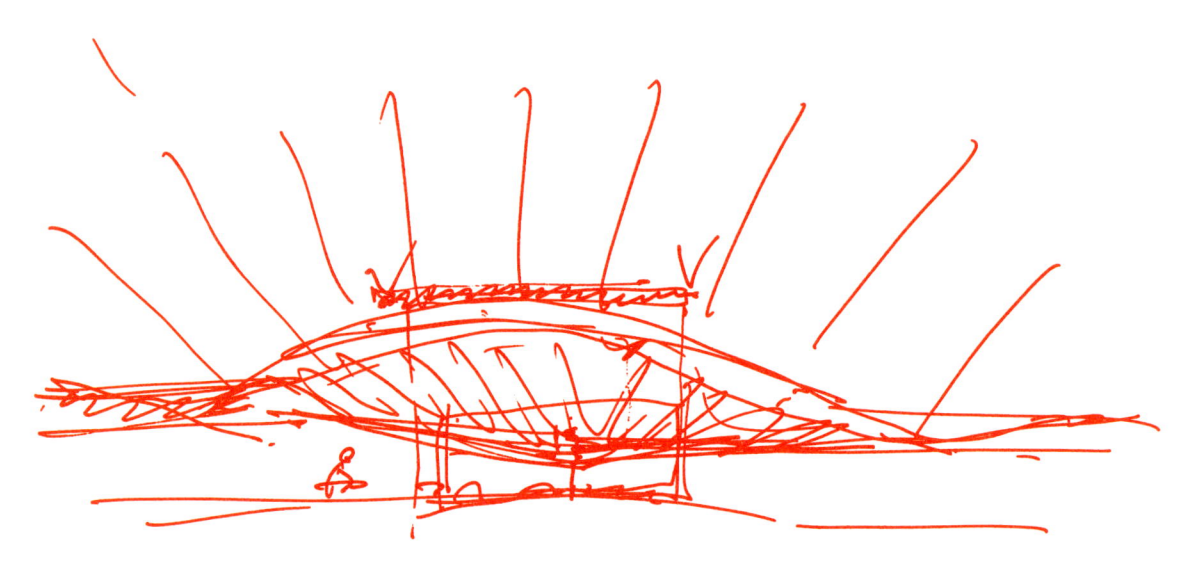

Hiroshi NAITO 1992-2004

わたしは、どこでも世界の中心になり得ると思っている。
I believe that any place has the potential to become the center of the world.

この設計を通して、設計上の理念が
現実のものとなるよりも、こうしたさまざまな人の連なりが
建物に集約していくことの方が、はるかに重要なことだし
創造的なことだ、とより一層感じるようになった。

Through this project, I came to further believe that there is much more significance and creativity in realizing a building as a coalescence of a range of minds and talents, rather than as a manifestation of any certain design principles.

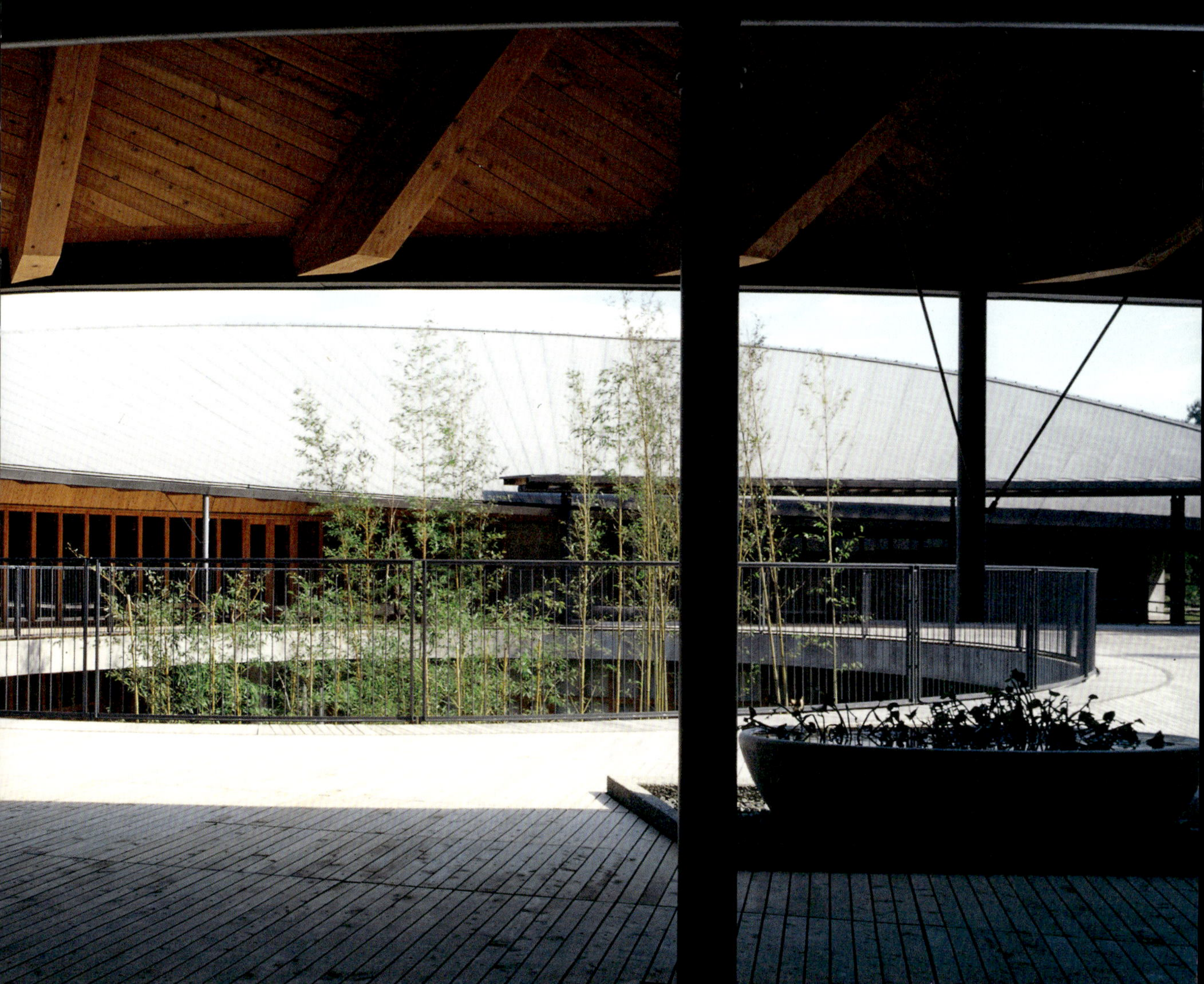

Museum Building Elevation 1/800

オープンから7年後の本館中庭
The courtyard of the main building in its seventh year after opening.

1 main entrance
2 Godaisan gallery
3 tatami room
4 storage
5 laboratory
6 courtyard
7 library

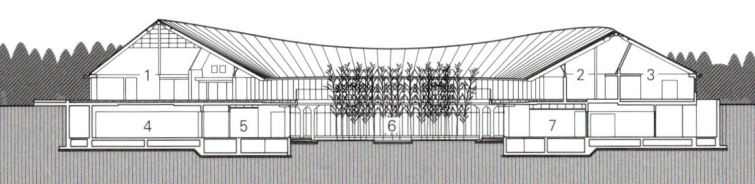

Museum Building Section 1/800

Detailed plan

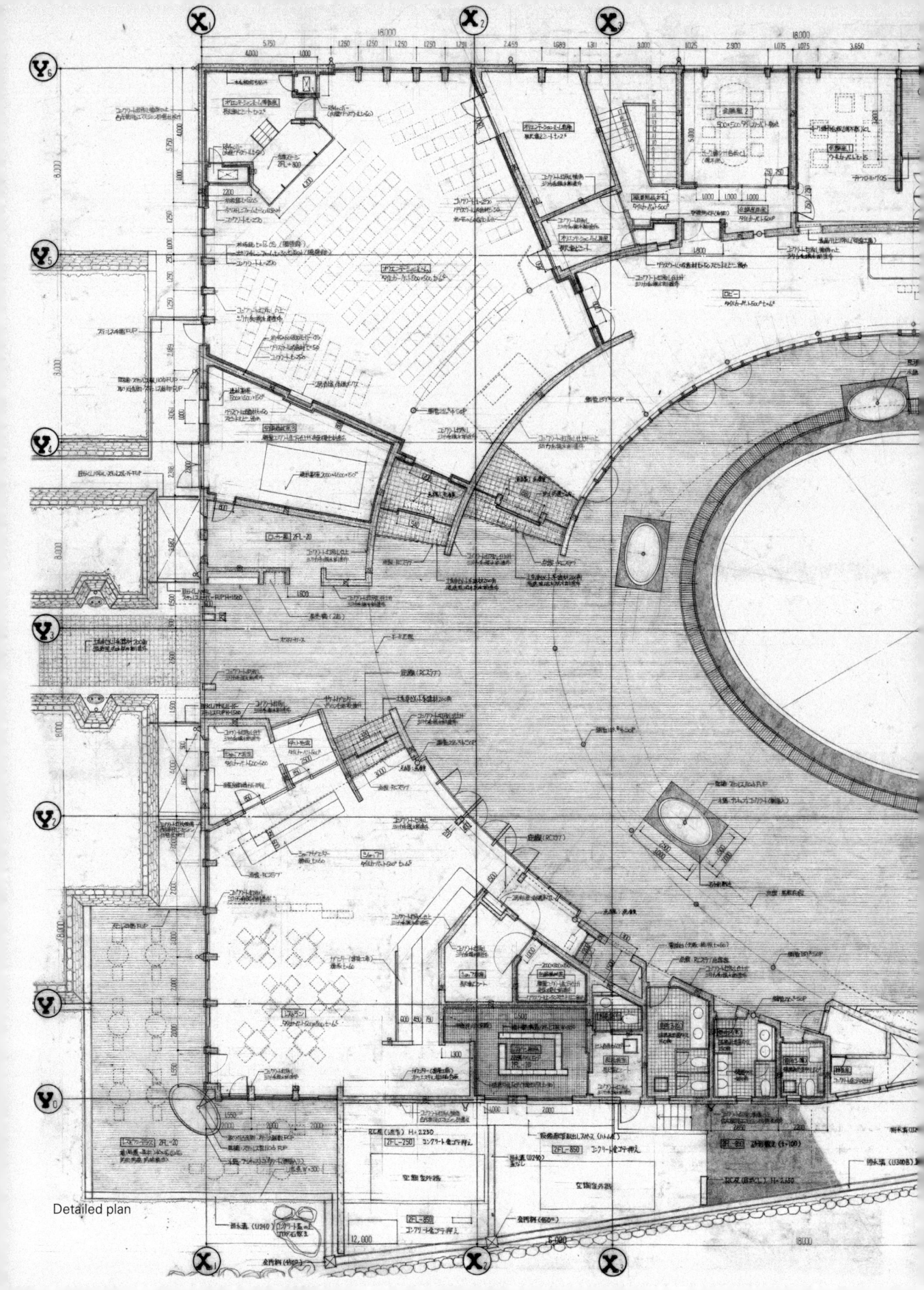

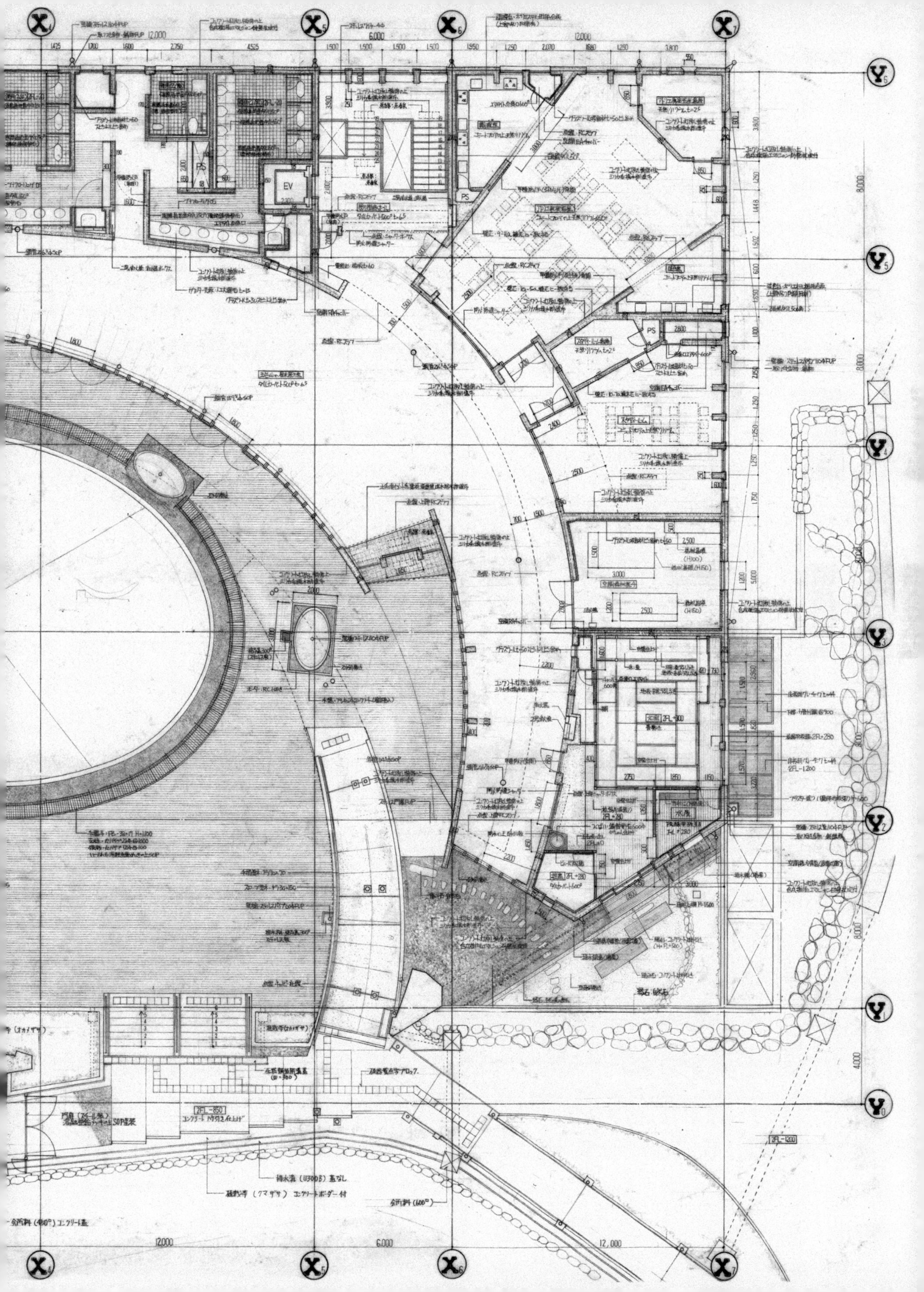

X4
X5
X6
X7
Y0
Y1
Y2
Y3
Y4
Y5
Y6
12,000
6,000
12,000
EV
PS
2FL-850
コンクリート ハケ引き仕上げ
2FL-1200
排水溝（U300B）蓋なし
植栽帯（クマザサ）コンクリートボーダー付
金網柵（600□）
金網柵（450□）コンクリート蓋
植栽帯（オカメザサ）

建物が建ち上がる前にはおよそ
見えにくかったさまざまな力や動きを顕在化させ、視覚や感覚に
訴えるものとして現実のものとする。その意味で設計は、
異なる言葉を行き来する翻訳という作業に似ている。

The various energies and movements that are generally difficult to see before a building emerges are actualized as real things that appeal to the sight and senses. To this end, design is similar to the act of translation, which involves going back and forth between different languages.

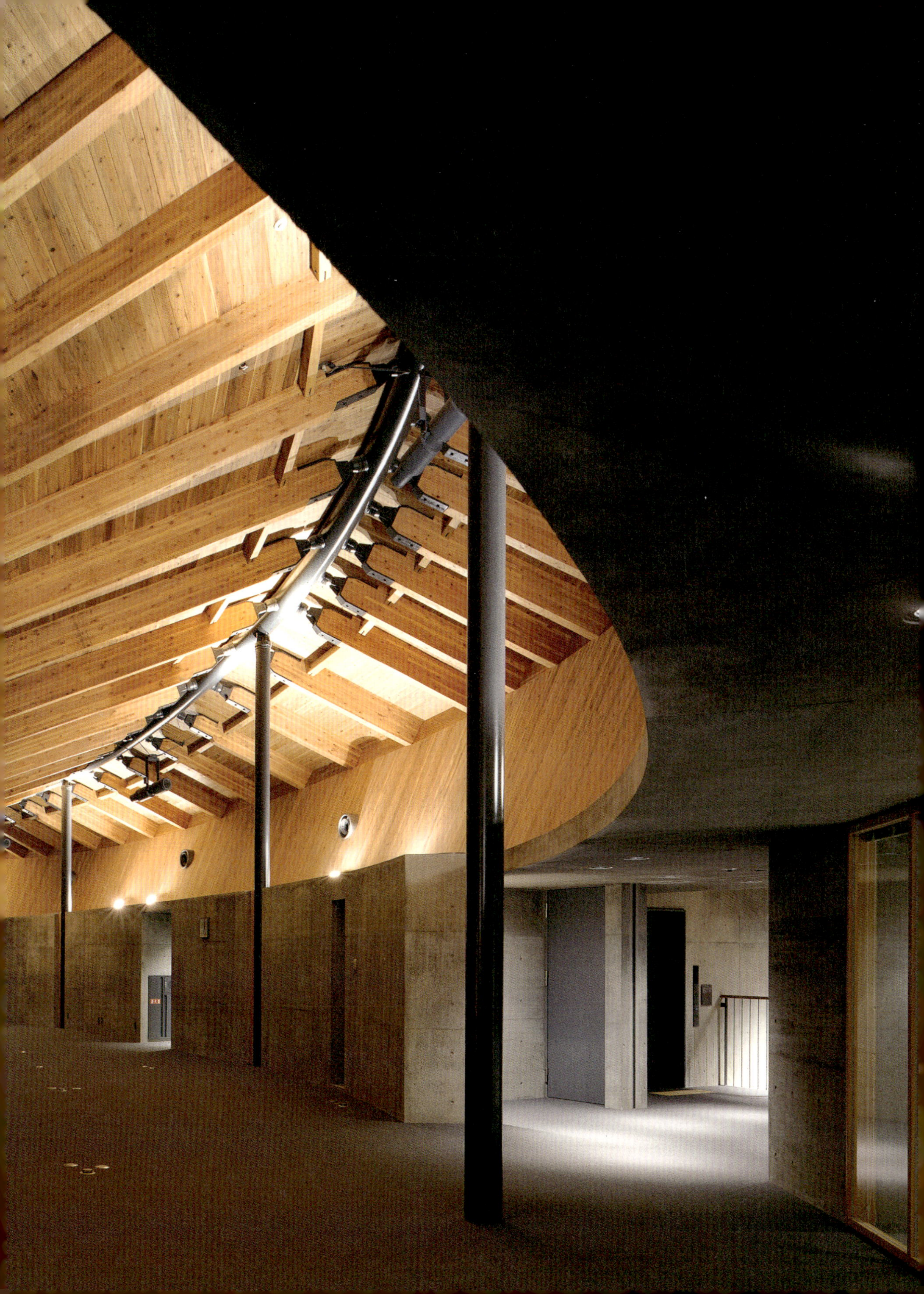

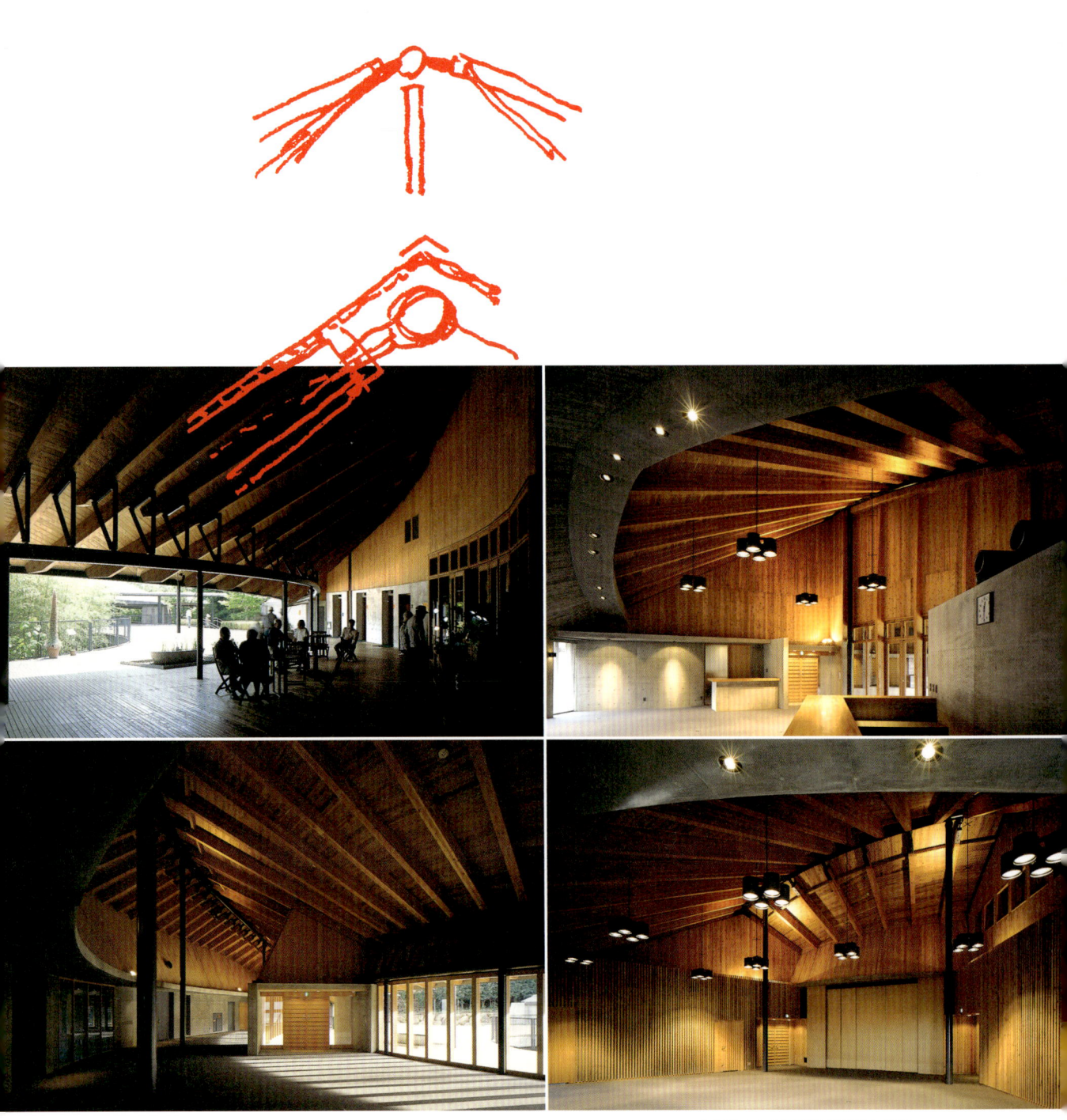

分節化された平面を連続的に覆う
フレキシブルな架構

The flexible structure provides a continuous cover over the segmented floor plan.

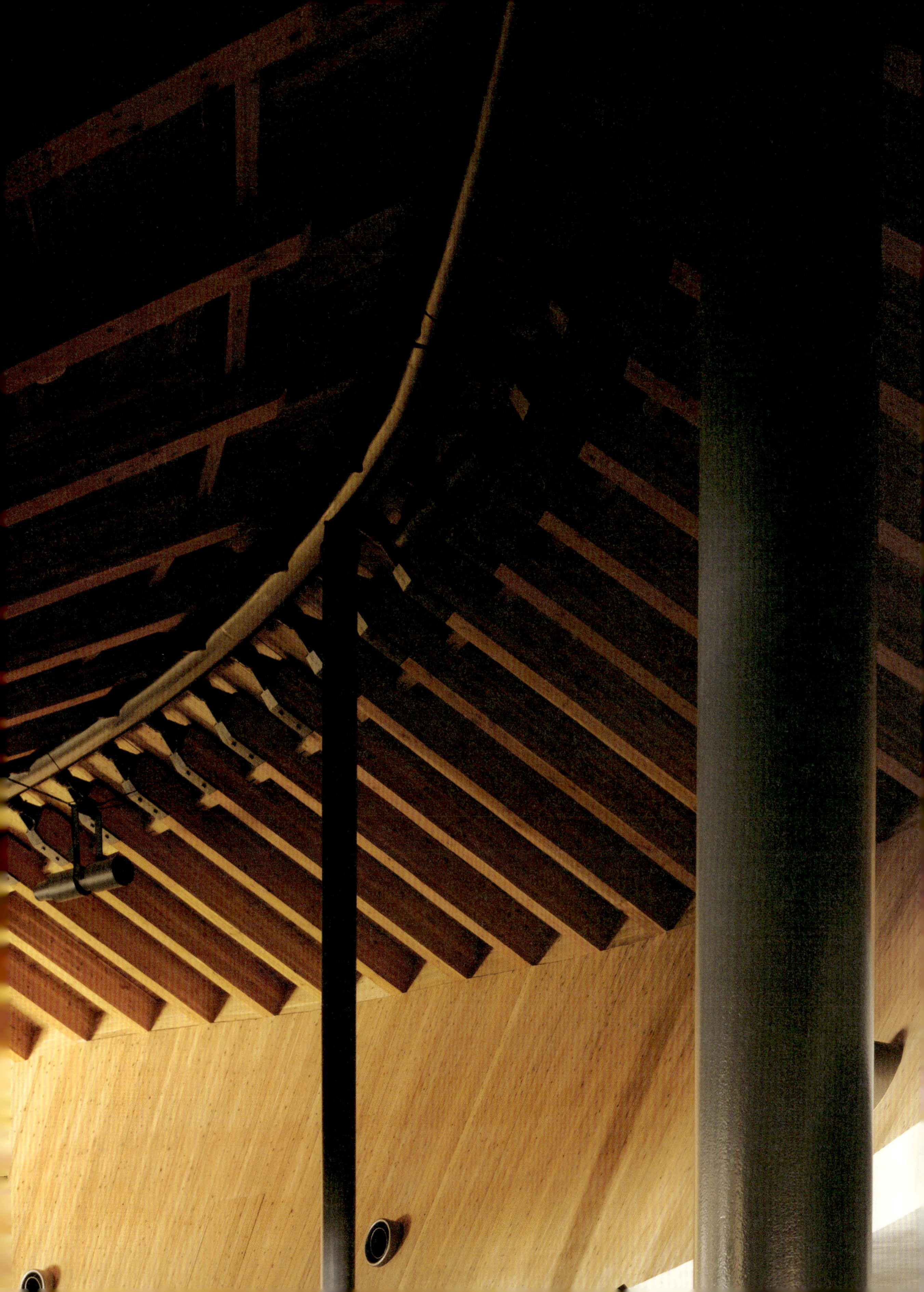

Exhibition Hall Elevation 1/800

傷跡が癒えるにつれ、建物を建ち上げるという宴は終わり、山は元のたたずまいに戻っていく。
The mountain gradually returns to its original appearance as its wounds heal after the party for constructing the building has now come to an end.

地面に伏せるようにして建つ展示棟
The exhibition wing was built to hug the ground.

1 exhibition room
2 courtyard
3 exhibition gallery

Exhibition Hall Section 1/800

人間が作った建築物と自然とを対立させて考える
ヨーロッパ的な建築の在り方とは違う、もう少し建築から
自然の方に寄り添う在り方がないだろうか。

Is there not a way for architecture to exist closer beside nature,
in a way that diverges from the European model of architecture in which
man-made structures are considered in opposition to it?

われわれは言葉によって思考し、理解する。
一方、自然や風土は饒舌だが言葉をもたない。設計という作業は、
この狭間にあって、直観によってその目に見えない価値を捉え、
誰にでも分かる形で提示することではないか。

We think and comprehend through words. Meanwhile, nature and the environment, although loquacious, have no words that they can speak. Is it not the role of design, which operates in-between these, to intuitively grasp value that is invisible to the eye and to present it in a form that can be comprehended by all?

自分の能力を使って、自然をどう身近にするか、本質に迫るか。
そういった牧野博士の精神は、われわれがとてつもない変化に
さらされる21世紀を生きる上で、大きな力になると思う。

How can one employ their faculties to bring nature closer to oneself and to approach its essence? I believe that this spirit that Dr. Makino held will provide great strength in our lives as we are exposed to the tremendous changes of the twenty-first century.

凡人は天才のやることをトレースしようなどと思ってはいけない。
An ordinary mind should not think about tracing the actions of geniuses.

Exhibition Hall Plan 1/800

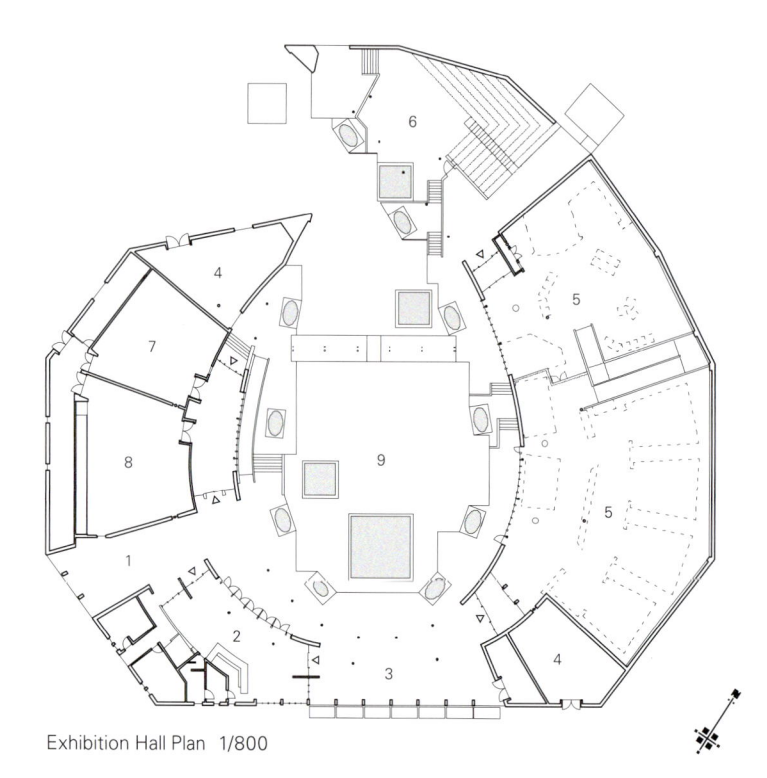

1 main entrance
2 cafe/information
3 observation deck
4 machine room
5 exhibition room
6 lecture hall
7 botanical illustration gallery
8 exhibition gallery
9 courtyard

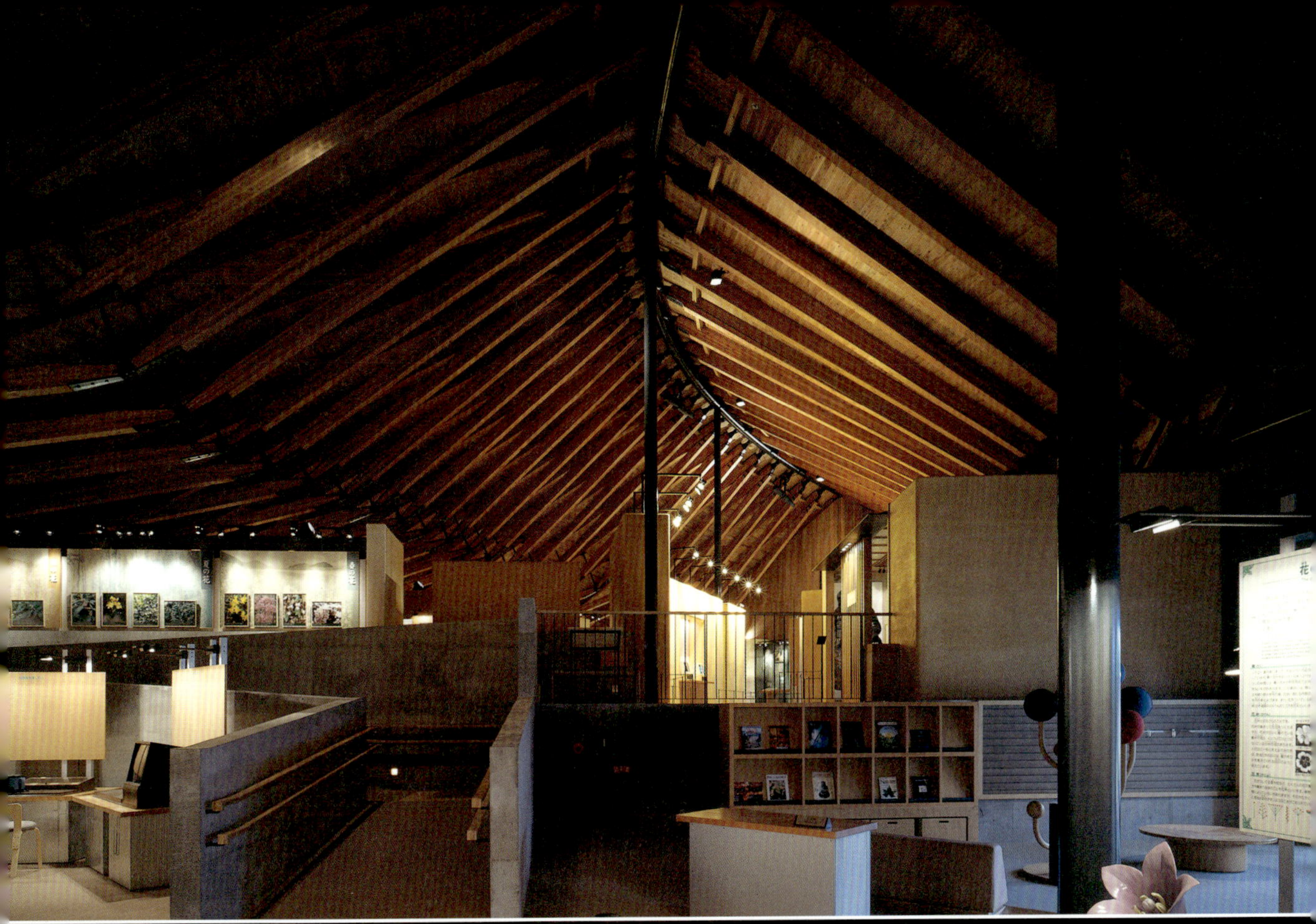

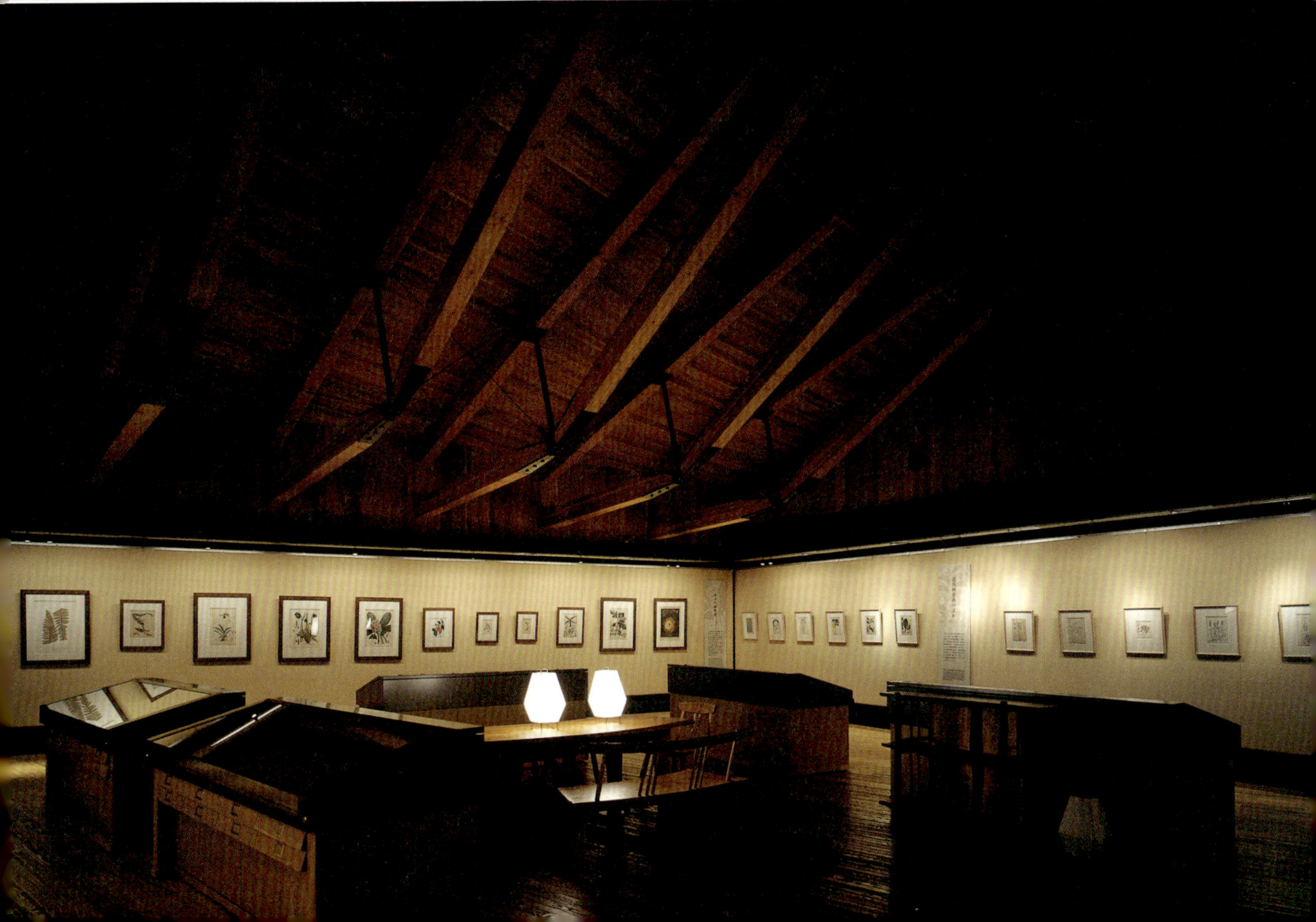

Detailed plan

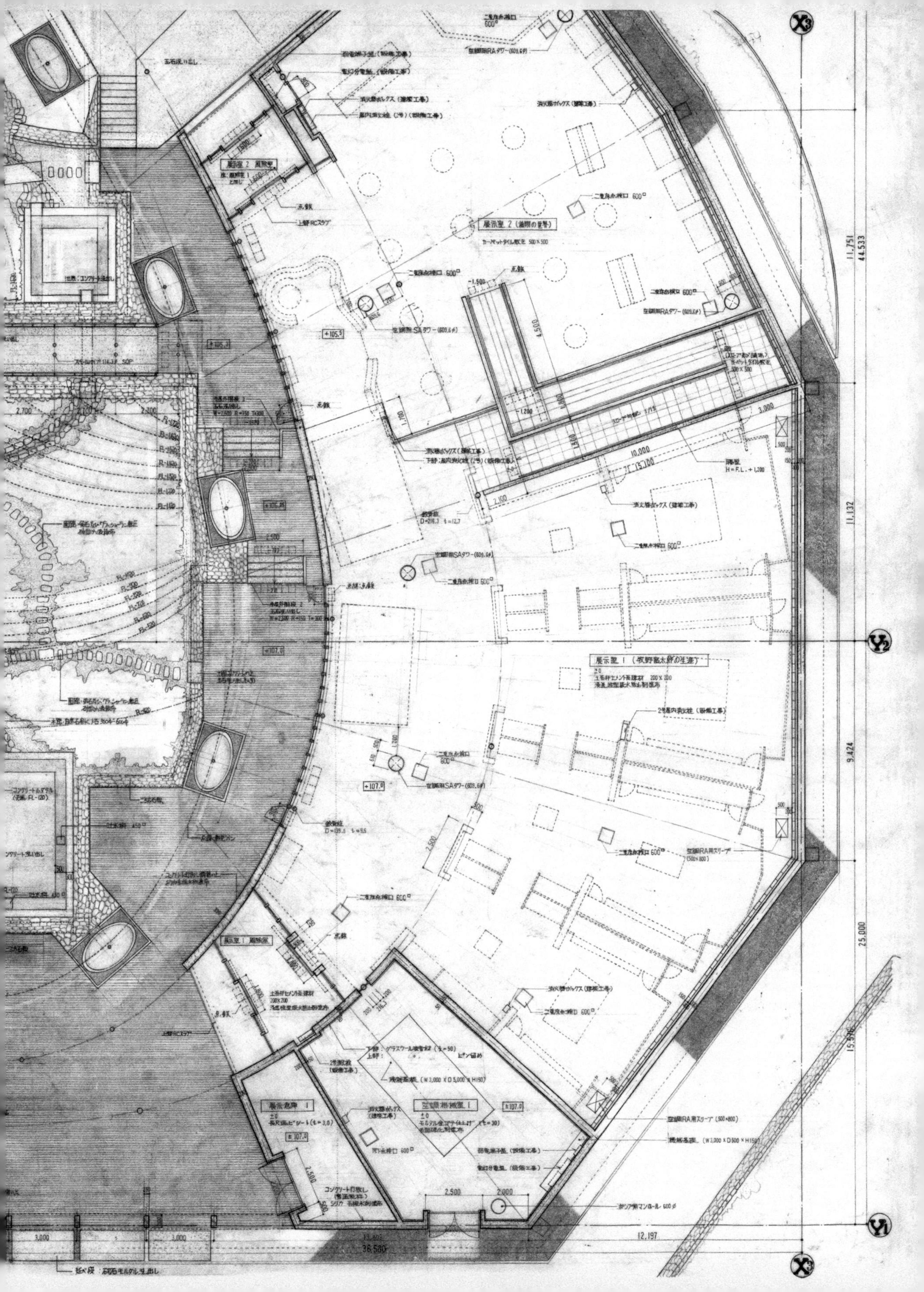

展示室 2（植物の世界）
カーペットタイル敷き 500×500
展示室 1（牧野富太郎の生涯）
展示倉庫 1
空調機械室 1
消火器ボックス（建築工事）
二重床点検口 600□
空調用SAタワー（609.6φ）
空調用RAタワー（609.6φ）
2号屋内消火栓（設備工事）
スロープ 勾配 1/15
3,000
10,000
2,100
2,500
2,000
12,197
36,580
11,751
44,533
11,132
9,424
25,000
15,576

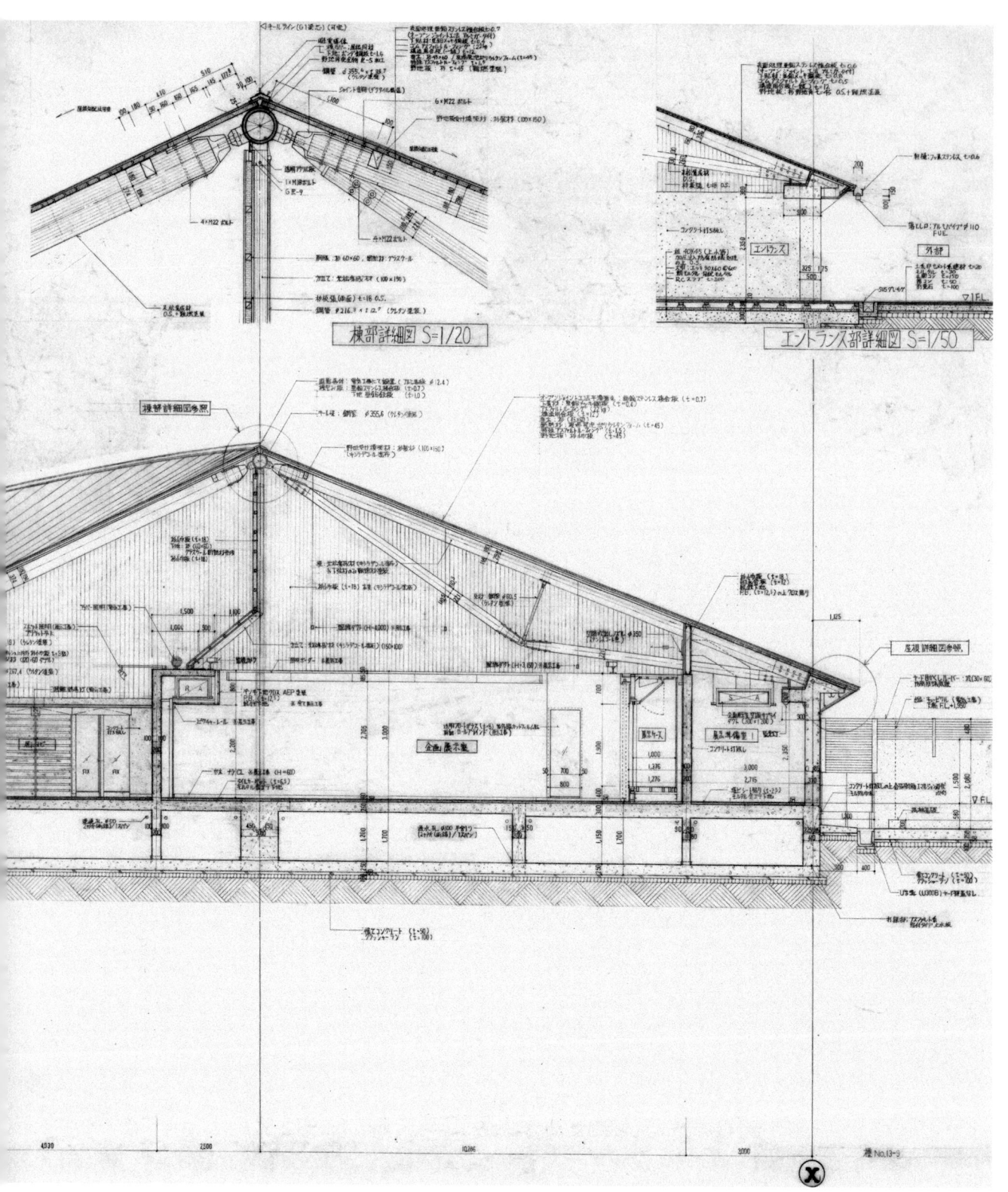

Detailed section

一本ごとに異なる集成材と
鋼管の合理的なジョイント

The efficiently-designed joints
connect each unique laminated wood
member to the steel tubes.

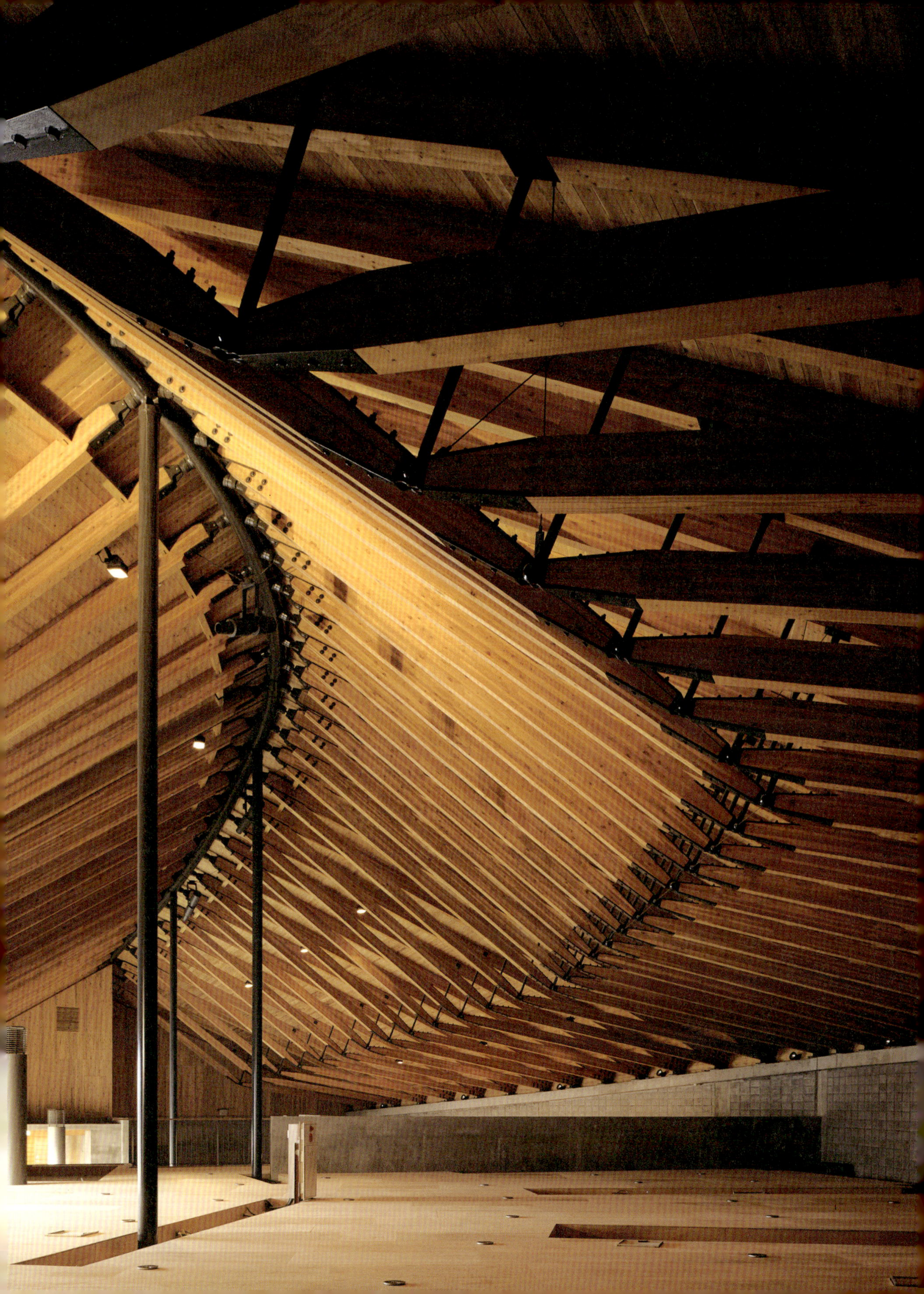

収蔵されている牧野博士の数多くの原画を見た時、
すごい感銘を背筋に受けた。これで十分、
後はこれを身体に取り込み、どう建築化するかということだった。
I was deeply moved when I saw the numerous original prints by Dr. Makino in the collection. This experience was enough—all that I then needed to do was to assimilate it into a basic concept and architecturalize it.

植物が育っていくにつれて建物も空間も成熟していく姿を
目の当たりにするとなぜか幸せな気持ちになる。
For some reason, I feel very happy when I see how the building and its
spaces are maturing alongside the growing vegetation.

住居No.22
House No.22

2000
東京都新宿区　Tokyo

時間をつないでいくことは、新しく作ることより
手間が掛かることだ。でも、それだけの価値はある。新しく建てる
のでは決して得られない特別な何かが空間に備わるからだ。

It takes more effort to connect time together than to newly create it. Still, it is worth this effort, because spaces gain a special something that cannot be achieved by building anew.

目立たず、渋く、いぶし銀

　クリエイティブ・ディレクターとして著名な小池一子さんから、自宅の改修を頼まれた。改築と増築である。小池さんは西武百貨店のさまざまなディレクションを手掛ける一方で、佐賀町エキジビット・スペースを主催するなど、デザインとアートを横断するようなスーパーな存在だが、気さくな人柄で知られる。80年代中頃、「海の博物館」を設計するきっかけとなった西武セゾングループの伊勢志摩芸術村構想に参画した時に知遇を得て以来のお付き合いである。人脈も広く、多くの著名な建築家と付き合いがあるはずなのだが、どういう訳かわたしにご下命が下った。こいつならあまり変なことはやらないだろう、と思ったのではないか。

　洋裁教育者として著名だったお母様が、大工さんと相談して建てたという木造平屋の住宅の奥に鉄骨2階建ての増築部分がある。木造部分はかなり傷んでいたが、戦後のモダンでハイカラな暮らしが空間に染み込んでいて貴重な文化遺産だ。半世紀の歴史を刻んできた空気が漂っている。これを残さない手はない。この部分を保存修復し、道路側手前のわずかに残された敷地に、鉄骨2階建てで増築することにした。難しかったのは、その下に2台分の駐車場を設けなくてはならないことだった。ある程度スパンを飛ばさねばならない。ご主人のケンさんはバイクと車が趣味なので、ここは必須アイテムだった。近年、倉庫が必要になり、やむなくこの駐車場の一部に増築をした。

　Lアングルを組み合わせて十字柱を作り、それにブレーシングを入れて鉄骨造とし、それを角波の薄板鋼板で覆った。オーソドックスで何の変哲もない構成だが、小池さんの自宅なのだから、やはり微妙に他とは違う一工夫が欲しい。道路に面する外壁は、目立たず、それでも存在感のある壁にするために、外壁の鋼板は塗装屋さんに色を調合してもらって微妙に光る鈍い黒の現場塗装とした。

　いずれにしても、主役は中央に残された木造部分であり、鉄骨部分はそれをサポートする脇役の位置付けだ。目立たず、渋く、それでもなくてはならないもの、いぶし銀とまでは言えなくても、建物はそんな役割が果たせればいい。竣工後、小池さんの友人の何人かのアーティストがオブジェを置き、インスタレーションを加え、空間に彩りを添えている。脇役はそれらの背景として何とか役割を果たせているようだ。(Eng. p.279)

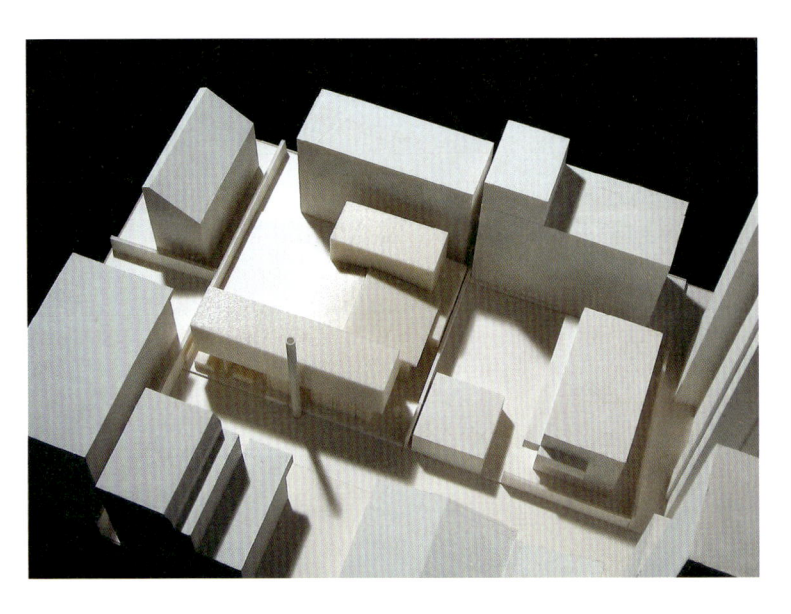

Site Plan 1/500

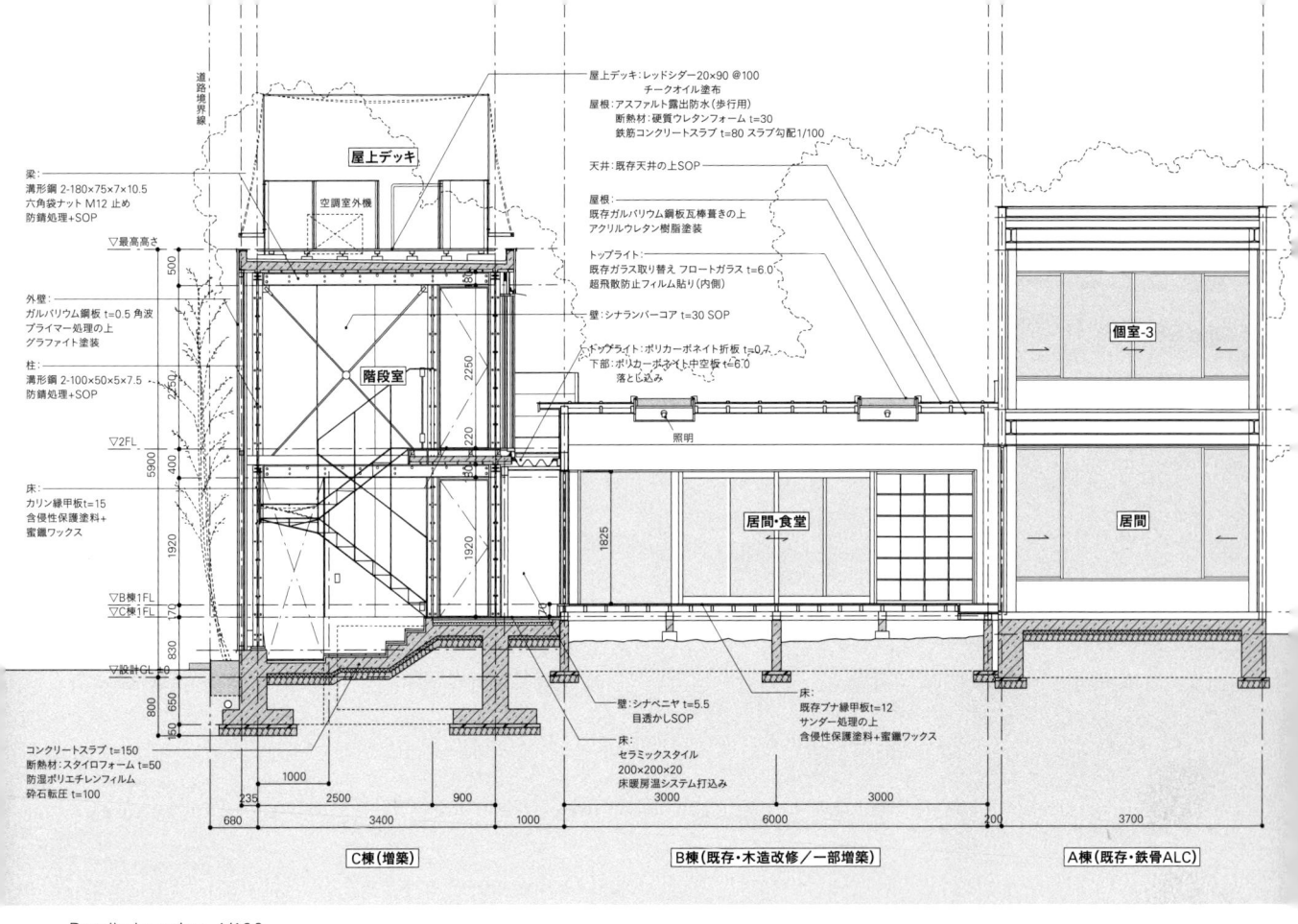

Detailed section 1/100

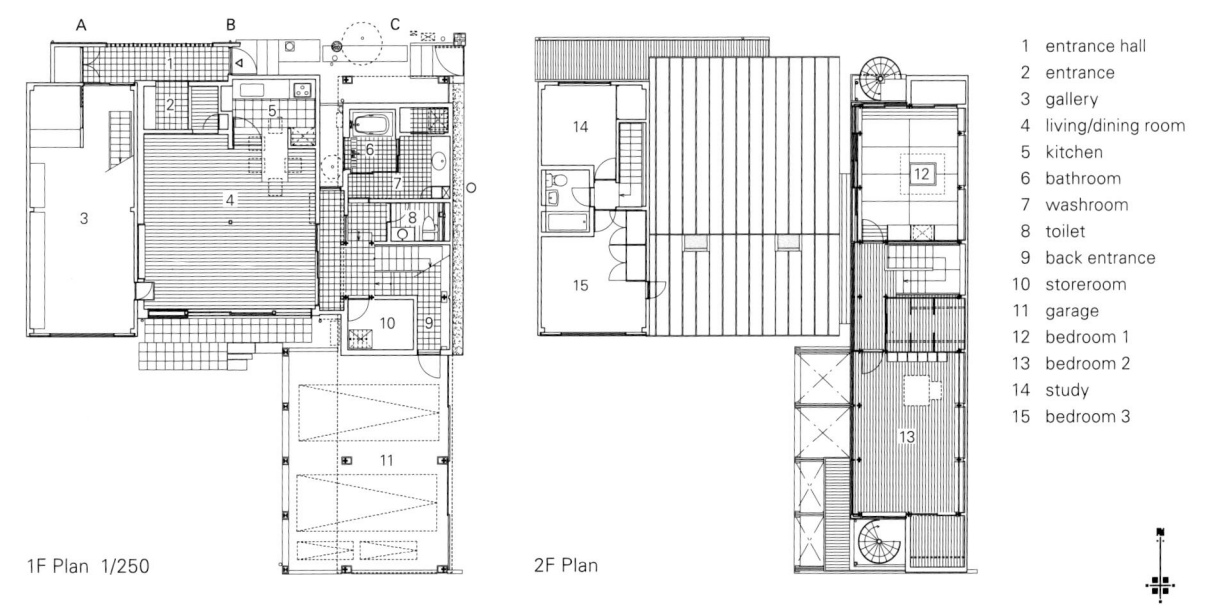

C棟(増築) — **B棟(既存・木造改修／一部増築)** — **A棟(既存・鉄骨ALC)**

Section labels/notes:
- 道路境界線
- 梁: 溝形鋼 2-180×75×7×10.5 六角袋ナット M12 止め 防錆処理+SOP
- 最高さ
- 外壁: ガルバリウム鋼板 t=0.5 角波 プライマー処理の上 グラファイト塗装
- 柱: 溝形鋼 2-100×50×5×7.5 防錆処理+SOP
- 2FL
- 床: カリン縁甲板 t=15 含浸性保護塗料+蜜蠟ワックス
- B棟1FL
- C棟1FL
- 設計GL±0
- コンクリートスラブ t=150
- 断熱材: スタイロフォーム t=50
- 防湿ポリエチレンフィルム
- 砕石転圧 t=100
- 屋上デッキ
- 空調室外機
- 階段室
- 屋上デッキ: レッドシダー20×90 @100 チークオイル塗布
- 屋根: アスファルト露出防水(歩行用) 断熱材: 硬質ウレタンフォーム t=30 鉄筋コンクリートスラブ t=80 スラブ勾配1/100
- 天井: 既存天井の上SOP
- 屋根: 既存ガルバリウム鋼板瓦棒葺きの上 アクリルウレタン樹脂塗装
- トップライト: 既存ガラス取り替え フロートガラス t=6.0 超飛散防止フィルム貼り(内側)
- 壁: シナランバーコア t=30 SOP
- ドウブライト: ポリカーボネイト折板 t=0.7 下部: ポリカーボネイト中空板 t=6.0 落とし込み
- 照明
- 居間・食堂
- 個室-3
- 居間
- 壁: シナベニヤ t=5.5 目透かしSOP
- 床: セラミックタイル 200×200×20 床暖房温システム打込み
- 床: 既存ブナ縁甲板 t=12 サンダー処理の上 含浸性保護塗料+蜜蠟ワックス

Dimensions: 680 / 3400 / 1000 / 235 / 2500 / 900 / 1000 / 3000 / 6000 / 3000 / 200 / 3700

1F Plan 1/250 2F Plan

1. entrance hall
2. entrance
3. gallery
4. living/dining room
5. kitchen
6. bathroom
7. washroom
8. toilet
9. back entrance
10. storeroom
11. garage
12. bedroom 1
13. bedroom 2
14. study
15. bedroom 3

Hiroshi NAITO 1992-2004

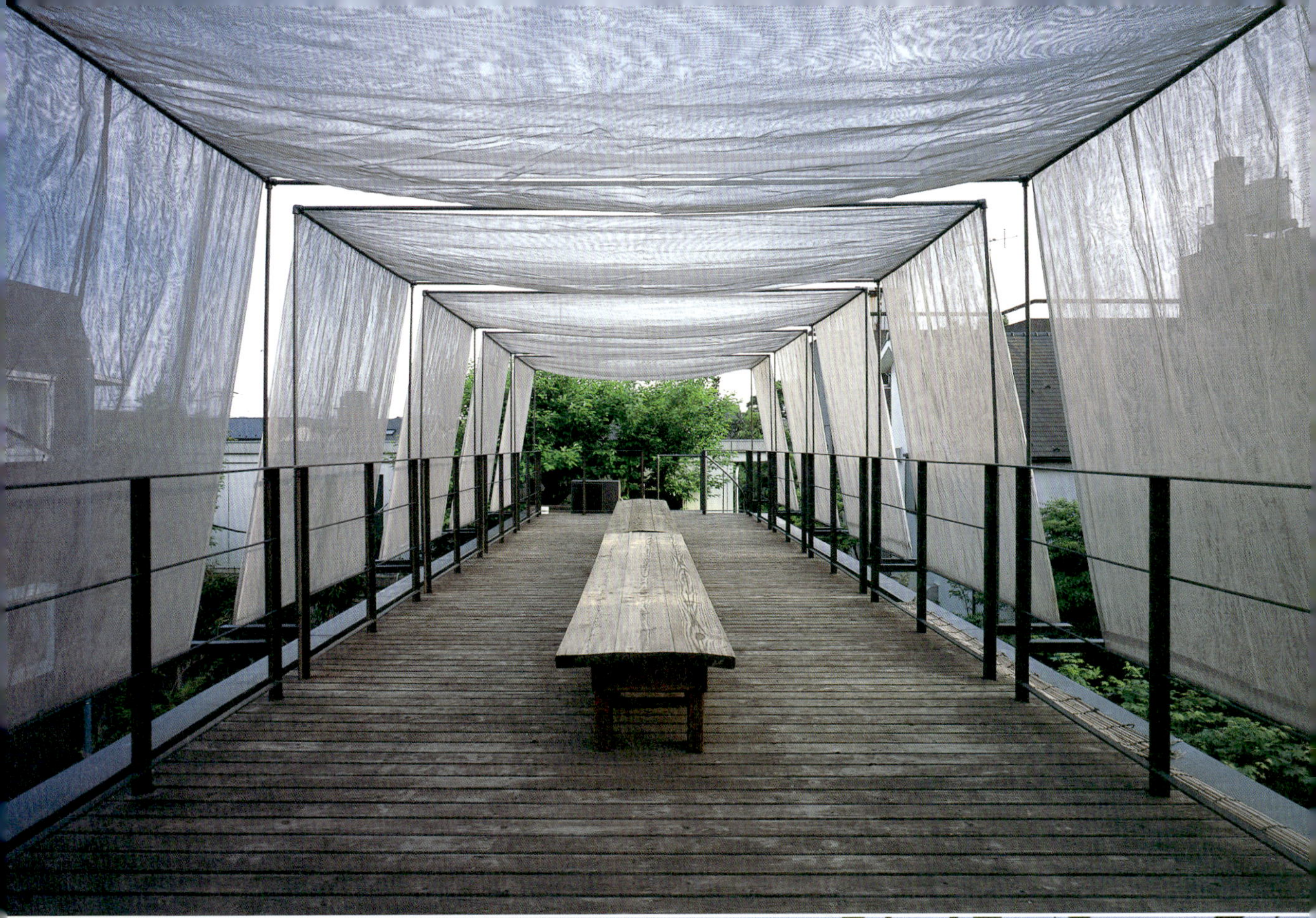
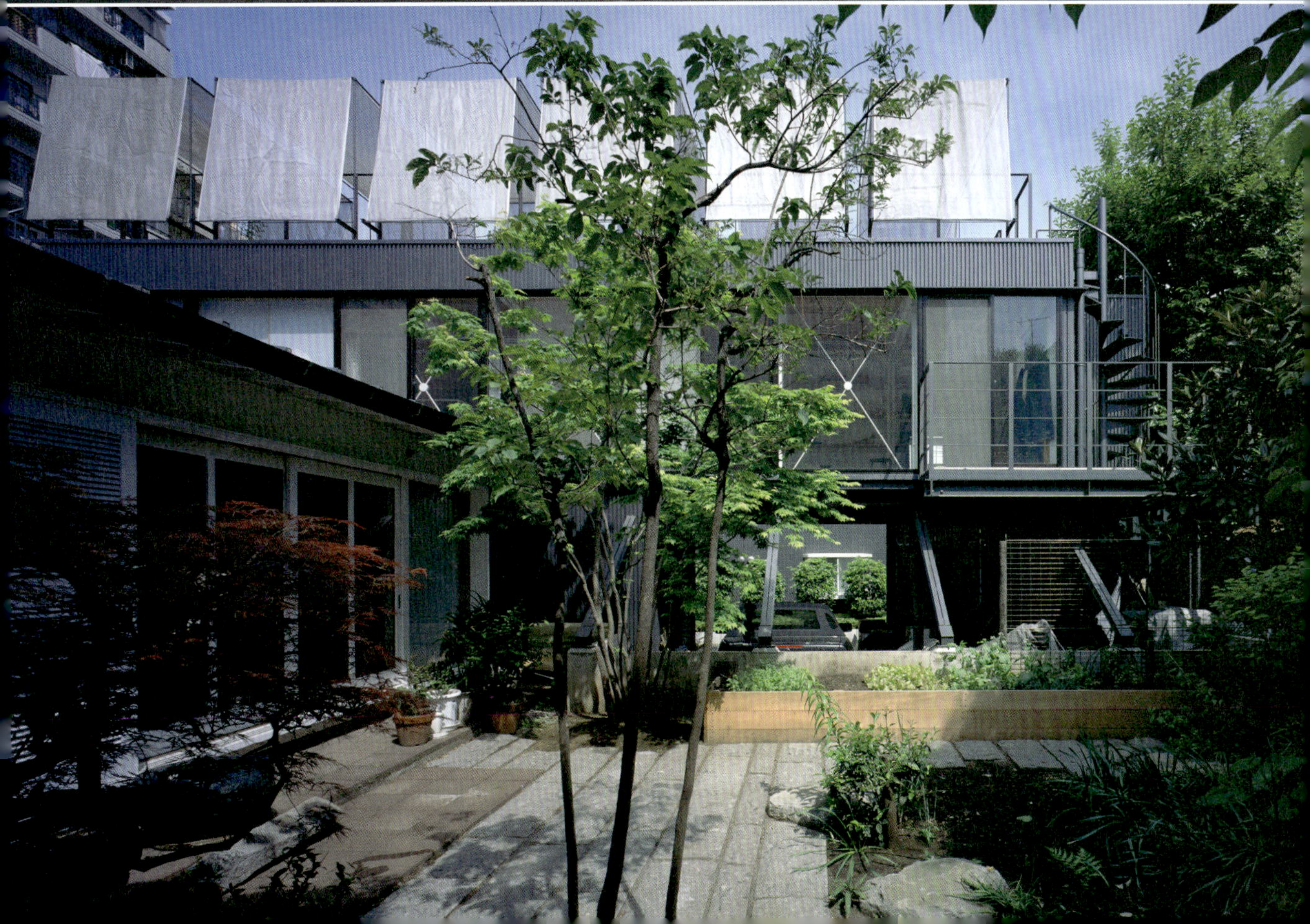

C棟個室2
A bedroom in the C Wing.

B棟リビング・ダイニング
The living/dining room in the B Wing.

「意図的に無為であること」、その度合いが高ければ高いほど、
空想は広がりをもつだろう。住宅の作り方は、
本来、そのようなものであるべきだったかもしれない。
Imagination gains greater breadth the more that one can be intentionally uncontriving. Perhaps this was originally how houses were supposed to be made.

倫理研究所富士高原研修所
Fuji RINRI Seminar House

2001
静岡県御殿場市 Shizuoka

9.11のすさまじい光景を見てからは、要領のいい
都市の解釈や面白半分の形態遊びはもうたくさんだ、
という気がするようになった。世界の現実を直視した上で、危うい
身近な日常を支える覚悟が必要だ。埋めようのない
その落差と乖離を耐える意志が必要だ。その意志こそが
建築的なるものの根幹かもしれない、と思い始めている。

After witnessing the terrible sights of September 11th, I became fed up with all of the form-playing and the clever readings of cities. We must look squarely at the realities of the world and have the determination to uphold our ever-fragile everyday lives. We must have a will to withstand the feeling of estrangement and the unfillable gap that lies between them. I am starting to think that this will may very well be what constitutes the basis of architecture.

折り目正しく新しく

根っからのチャキチャキの下町っ子の秘書の浅野恭子は、わたしが乞うて事務所に来てもらう前はセゾングループに勤めていた。その時の同僚であった山本透さんから浅野経由で、倫理研究所という団体が研修所の建て替えを考えているので相談に乗ってほしい、と頼まれた。もともと音楽の企画畑で辣腕プロデューサーであった山本さんは、この団体の理事長のアドバイザーをしていた。

そこで、理事長の丸山敏秋さんにお目に掛かった。ほぼ同世代で、わたしとも初対面から友人のように遇してくれる気さくな人柄の人だった。中年なのに青年のような容姿と精神をもっている。法人会員の増加や研修活動の拡大など、その時の実情を教えていただき、同時に建物に対する思いを語ってくれた。

倫理研究所は、古来よりもち合わせているこの国独特の気質や人間関係を見つめ直す中で生活を組み立てていこう、という運動を推進する社団法人である。荒っぽく説明したが、もちろん詳しく理解しているわけではない。ただ、建設業界に引き付けて考えてみると、思い当たる節が幾つかある。特にバブル経済以降、建設現場が荒れてきていることと重なって見えた。

経済性と効率化ばかりが表に立ち、建設会社も職人も、かつてもっていた誇りに自信がもてなくなりつつあるような気がした。モノにこだわり、少しでも良い仕事をしよう。そういうこの国の建設現場を陰で支えてきたモラルが崩れかけている。かつてイワン・イリイチがシャドー・ワークという言葉で語ったように、それこそが経済に絡めとられない文化なのだが、世の中がそのことに敬意を表さなくなっていた。同じ時代に起きていることは、どのようなことであれ相似形なのだ。

そこでこの建物では、折り目正しく精度を求め、その結果、端正な建物になることを目指した。現場にもそのことを求めた。また、この建物では、技術的に革新的なことも追求した。伝統を尊重するだけでなく、未来の空気もこの建物や場所に引き込みたい、というところで丸山理事長と意見が合ったからだ。

一番力を入れたのは、「海の博物館」以来、検討を重ねていた大断面集成材の究極的なジョイント、すなわちスチールプレートを介さないで木と木が直に力を伝え合うジョイントを作ることだった。それまで誰もやったことがない世界でも初めての試みだ。これをやるには、伝統工法のジョイントを勉強した上で、その中にある木材に対する考え方を、コンピューターを使った近代的な構造計算と構法に置き換えていかねばならない。このジョイントの特性を生かして有機的な架構を作り上げた。これはとてもうまくいった。

冬はマイナス20度にもなる厳しい寒冷地だが、中庭に向けて開放的で大きな開口部を作りたかったので、当時まだ開発中だった発熱ガラスを使った。微弱な電流を流すと発熱しペリメーターになる。ここではおおよそ18度に保たれるようにしている。これも初物だ。

出来上がって10年以上になるが、建物はいつも磨き上げられていて竣工時とあまり変わらない。これほどメンテナンスが行き届いた建物を他に知らない。大切に使ってもらっている。建築家冥利に尽きる。(Eng. p.280)

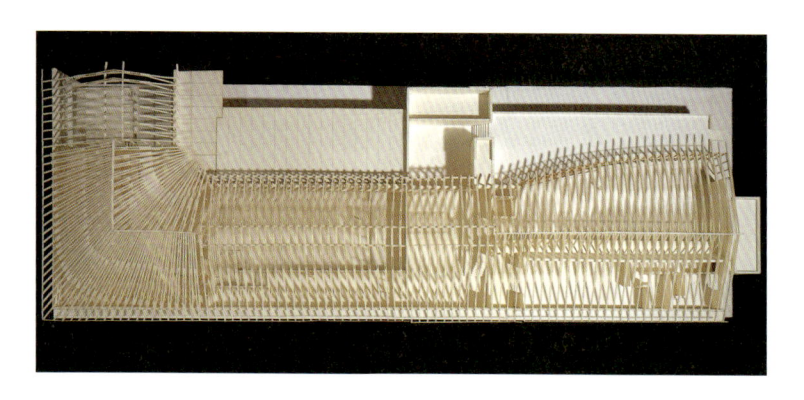

Site Plan 1/1500

エントランスホールから中庭を見る
A view of the courtyard from the entrance hall.

精神が抜け落ちてしまっては、論理的な整合性など
悪しき形式にしかすぎない。
If removed of its spirit, logical integrity would become merely an empty formality.

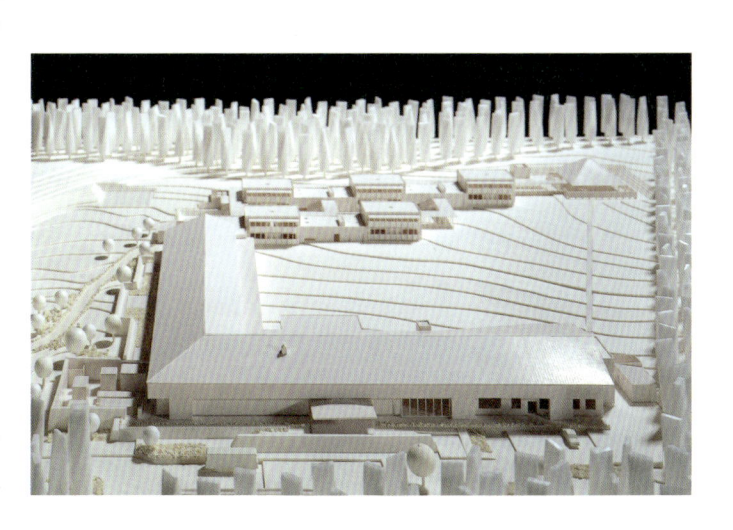

223　Fuji RINRI Seminar House

建築の折り目正しさのようなものが形になることが
重要だと考えました。建築の形態よりも、どのように作られているか
といった「仕組み」の在り方が、建物を構成する基本的な
骨組みになる方が良いような気がしたんです。

I believed that it was important for a precise and proper architecture to take shape.
I felt that it would be better if the building's basic framework was grounded in the
mechanism for how the architecture was created, rather than in its form.

サッシュマリオンを兼ねた
十字型熱押形鋼

The cruciform extruded
steel columns also serve
as mullions.

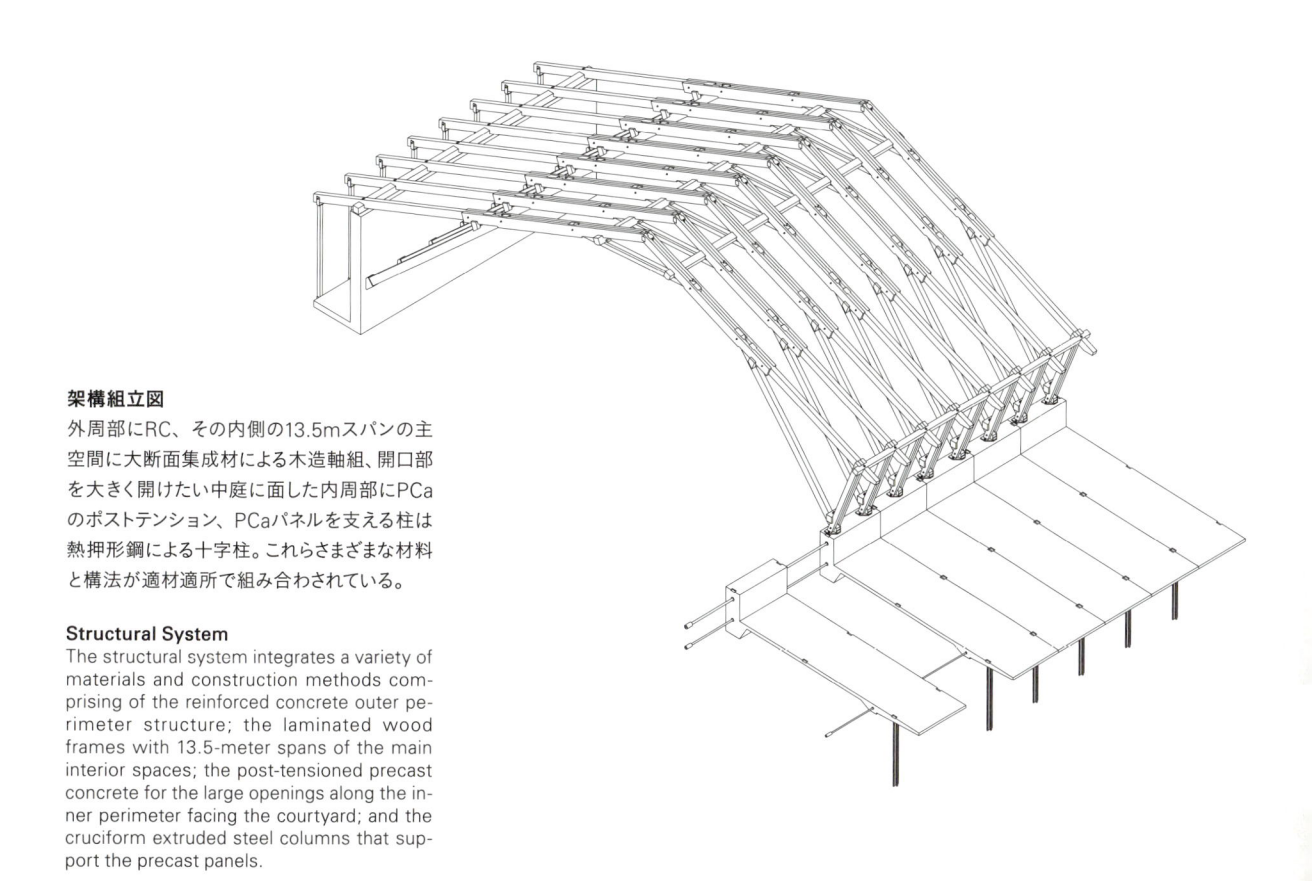

架構組立図
外周部にRC、その内側の13.5mスパンの主空間に大断面集成材による木造軸組、開口部を大きく開けたい中庭に面した内周部にPCaのポストテンション、PCaパネルを支える柱は熱押形鋼による十字柱。これらさまざまな材料と構法が適材適所で組み合わされている。

Structural System
The structural system integrates a variety of materials and construction methods comprising of the reinforced concrete outer perimeter structure; the laminated wood frames with 13.5-meter spans of the main interior spaces; the post-tensioned precast concrete for the large openings along the inner perimeter facing the courtyard; and the cruciform extruded steel columns that support the precast panels.

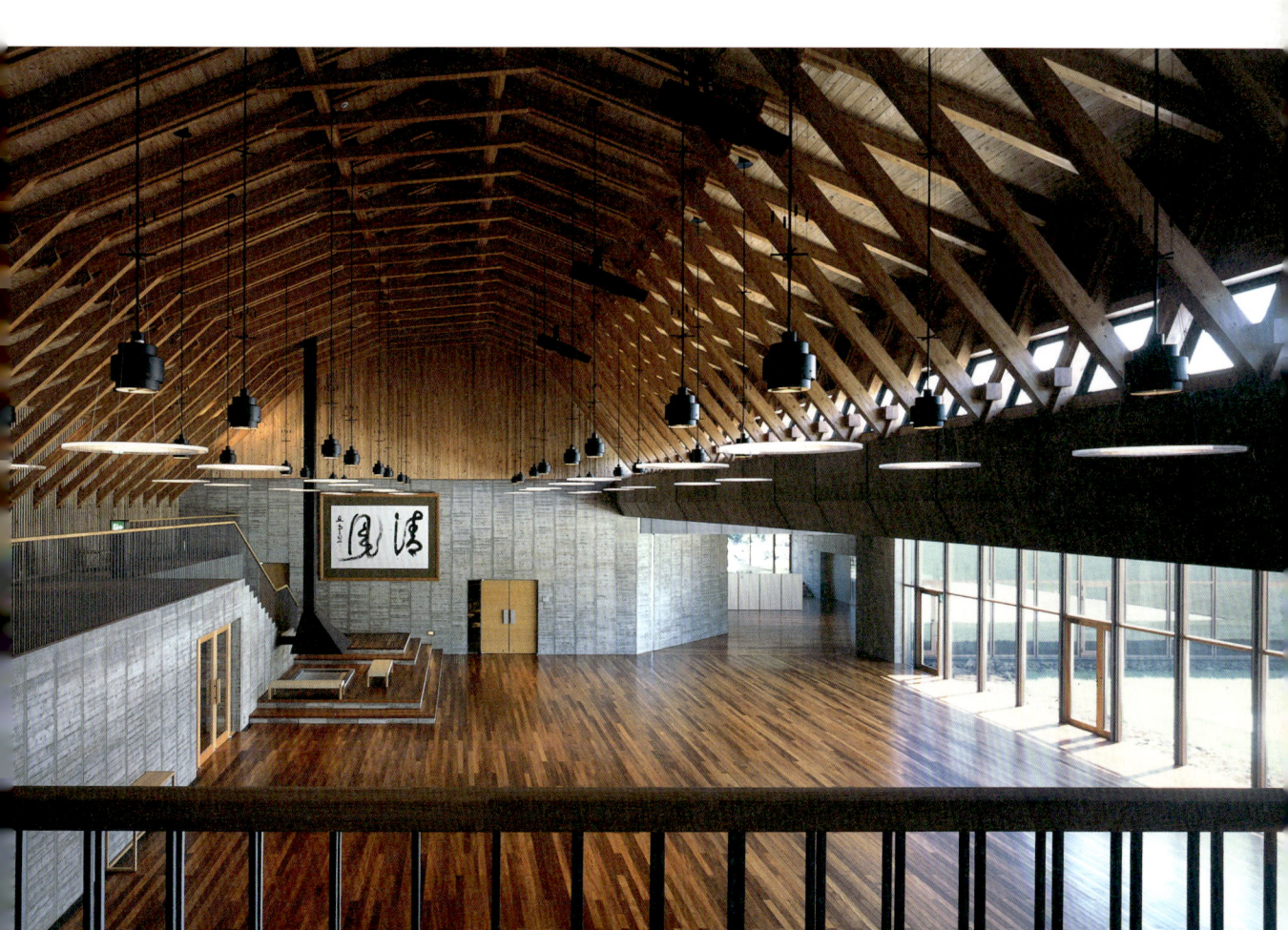

Section 1/800

躯体と外壁の間に設けたライフライン
The building's utilities occupy the space between the structure and the envelope.

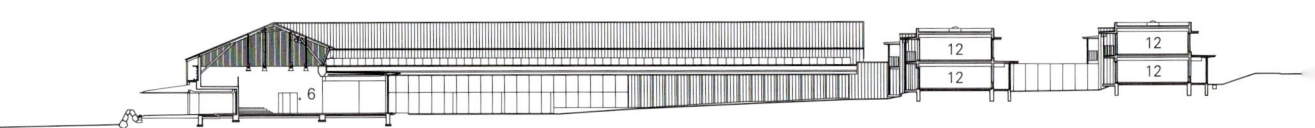

Section 1/800

226 Hiroshi NAITO 1992-2004

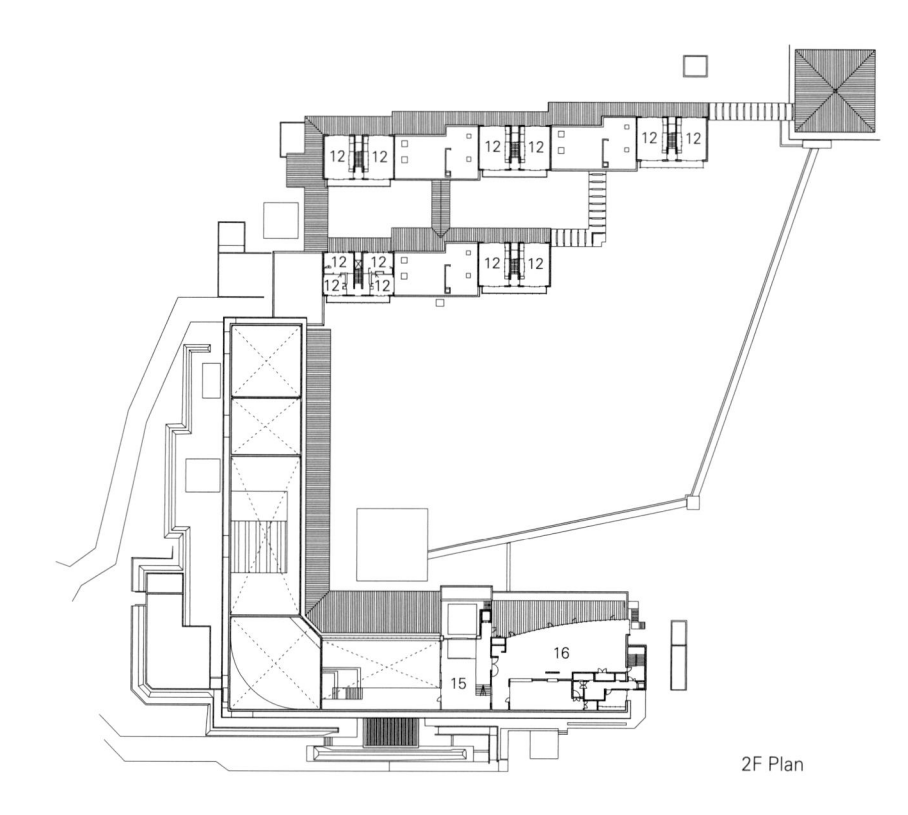

#	
1	stack room
2	reception room
3	meeting room
4	office
5	main entrance
6	entrance hall
7	auditorium
8	east lecture room
9	west lecture room
10	gallery
11	library
12	guest room
13	restroom
14	SEIDO hall
15	parlor
16	dining hall
17	courtyard

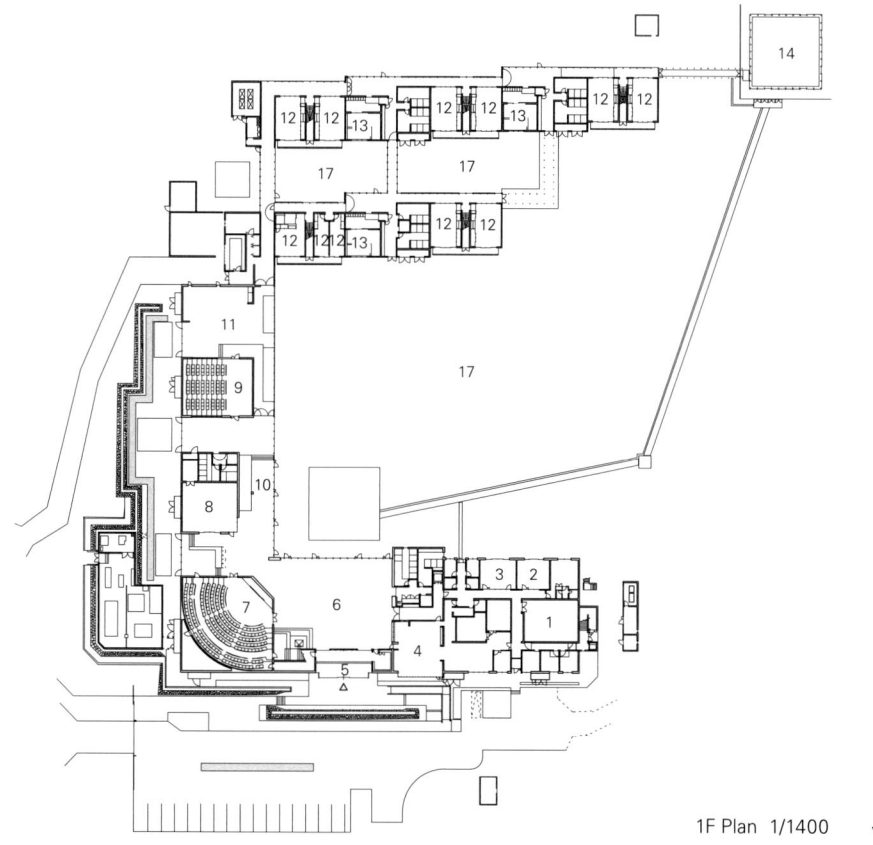

2F Plan

1F Plan 1/1400

Fuji RINRI Seminar House

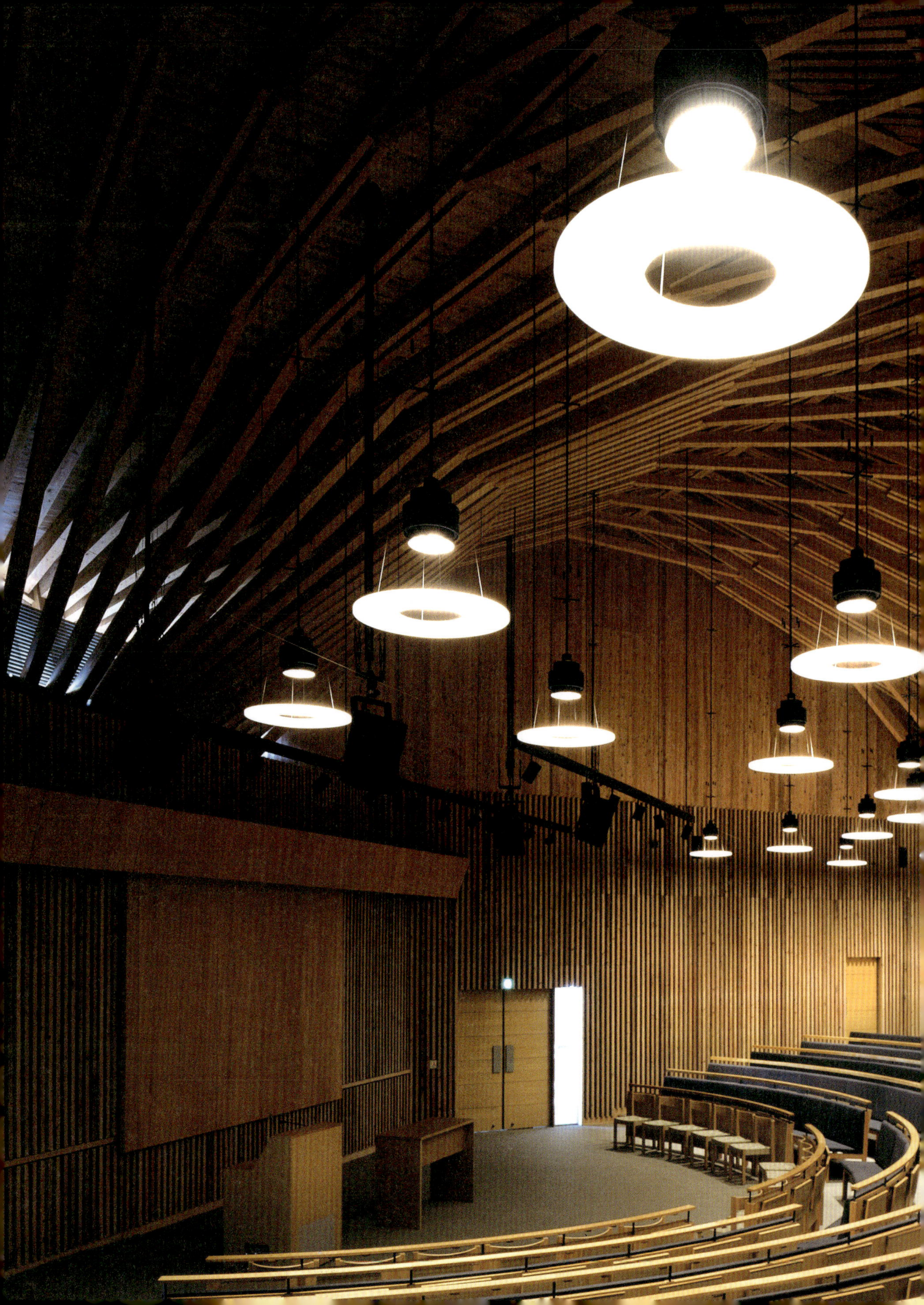

デザインは流転するが、技術の進化は決して後戻りしない。
たとえ小さな一歩でも、技術を積み上げるべきだ。
While design meanders, the evolution of technology never regresses.
Technology must be continually advanced, even if by small steps.

東教室とギャラリー
The east lecture room and gallery.

西教室
The west lecture room.

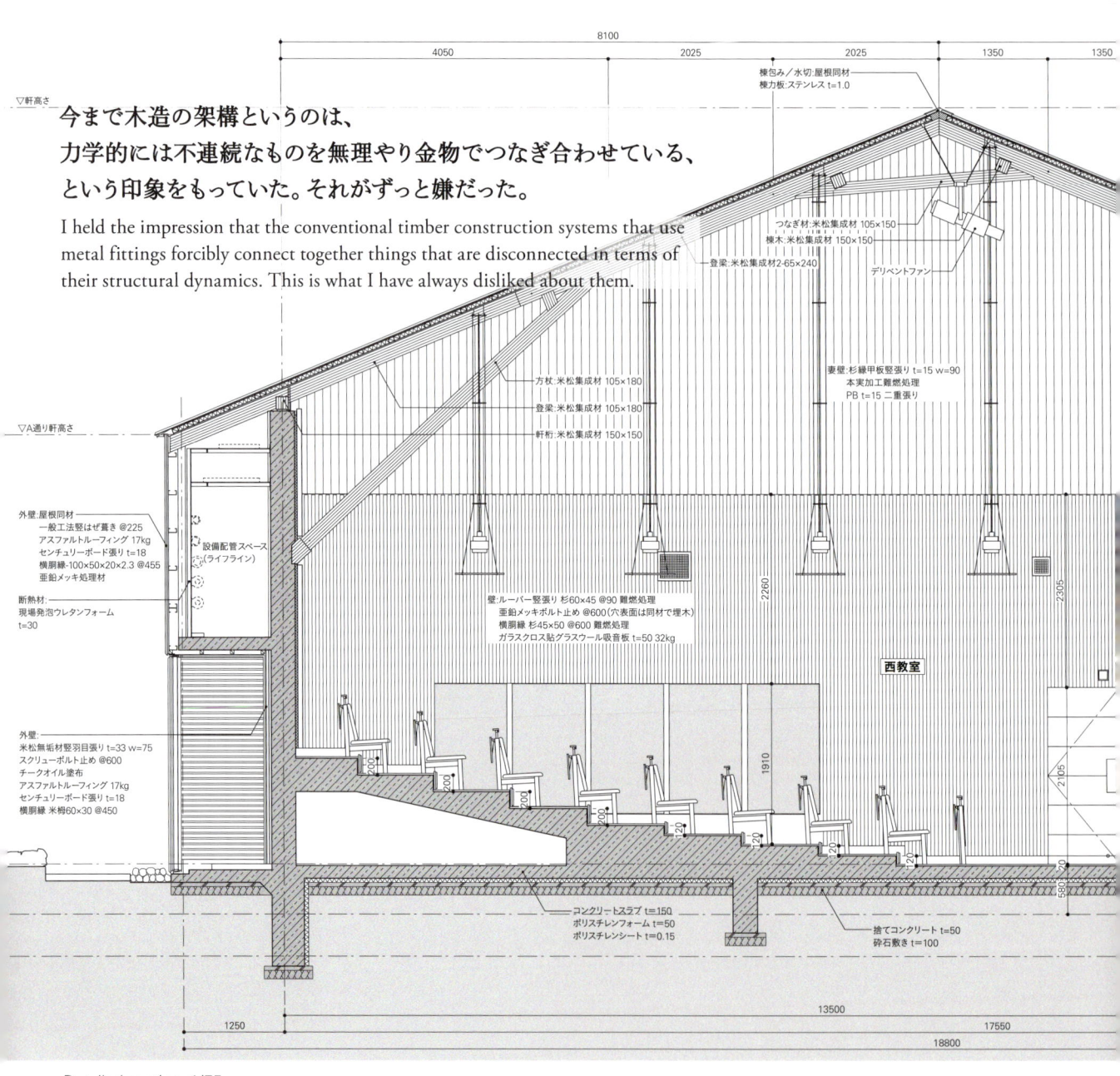

今まで木造の架構というのは、
力学的には不連続なものを無理やり金物でつなぎ合わせている、
という印象をもっていた。それがずっと嫌だった。

I held the impression that the conventional timber construction systems that use metal fittings forcibly connect together things that are disconnected in terms of their structural dynamics. This is what I have always disliked about them.

Detailed section 1/75

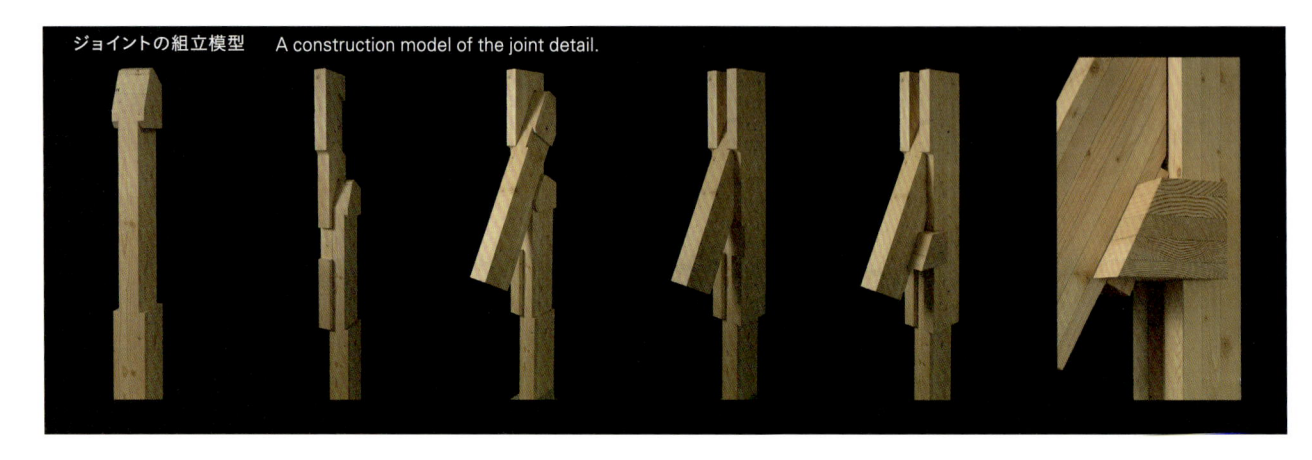

ジョイントの組立模型　A construction model of the joint detail.

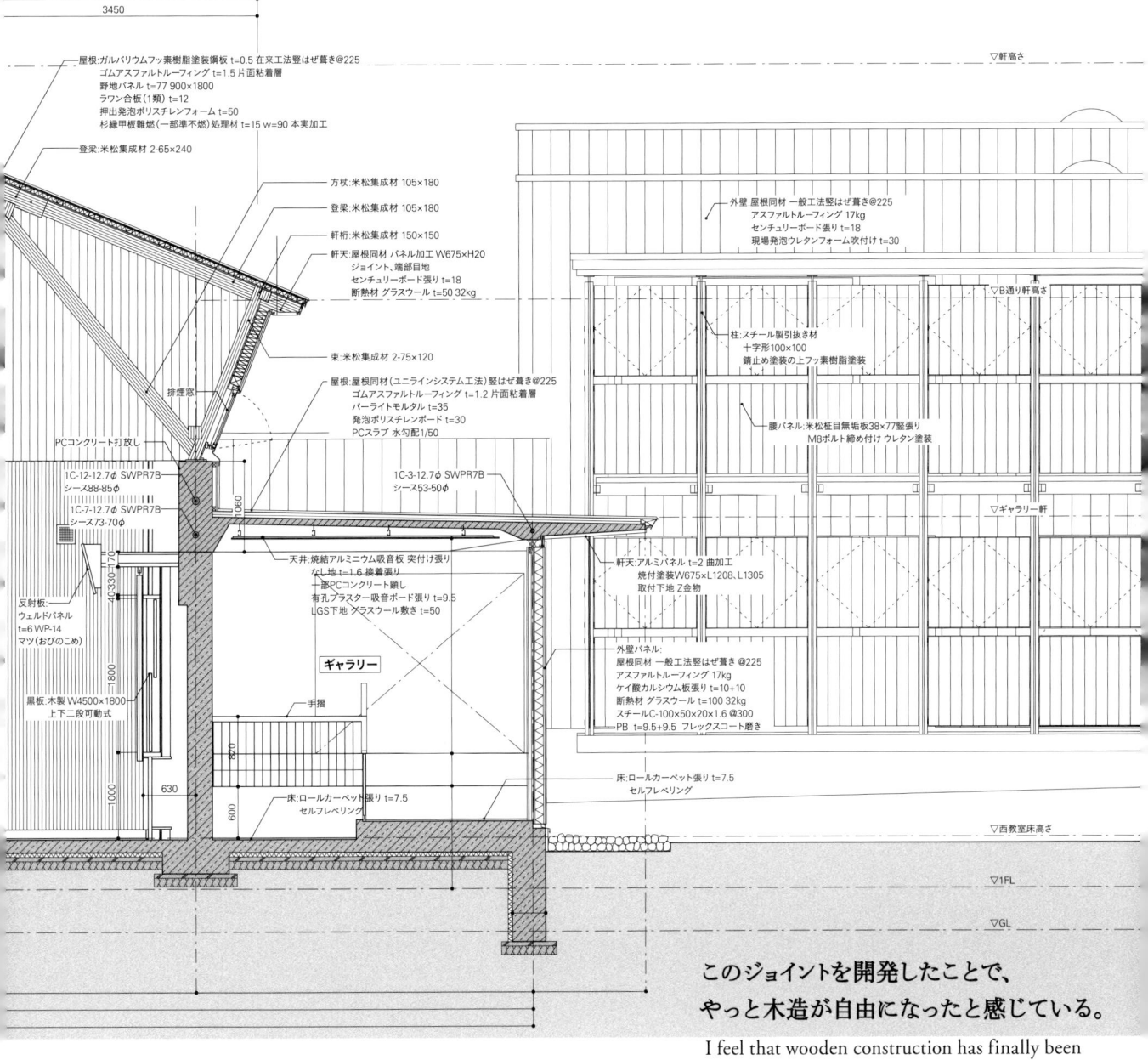

このジョイントを開発したことで、やっと木造が自由になったと感じている。

I feel that wooden construction has finally been freed with the invention of this joint detail.

ジョイント組立図

ひとつの木架構のモジュールに対して4つの木同士のジョイントが出てくる。これを金物を使わずに組み上げる。伝統的な在来構法の仕口の力の伝え方を参考に、CADによる設計とCAD・CAMによる製作で、木と木が直接力を伝え合う新たなジョイントを作った。

Joint System

Each module of the wooden frame has four wood-to-wood joints that were assembled without the use of metal fittings. A new joint system for transmitting loads directly between the wood was developed by referencing the behavior of loads in traditional wood joinery techniques and through using CAD and CAD/CAM tools for design and production.

Fuji RINRI Seminar House

不整形な敷地を囲むような配置計画

The building volumes were positioned to encircle the irregularly-shaped site.

清堂
The SEIDO Hall.

やはり木は優れた材料だ。
まだまだ可能性がたくさん秘められていると思う。
Wood is a decidedly superb material. I think it still holds many possibilities.

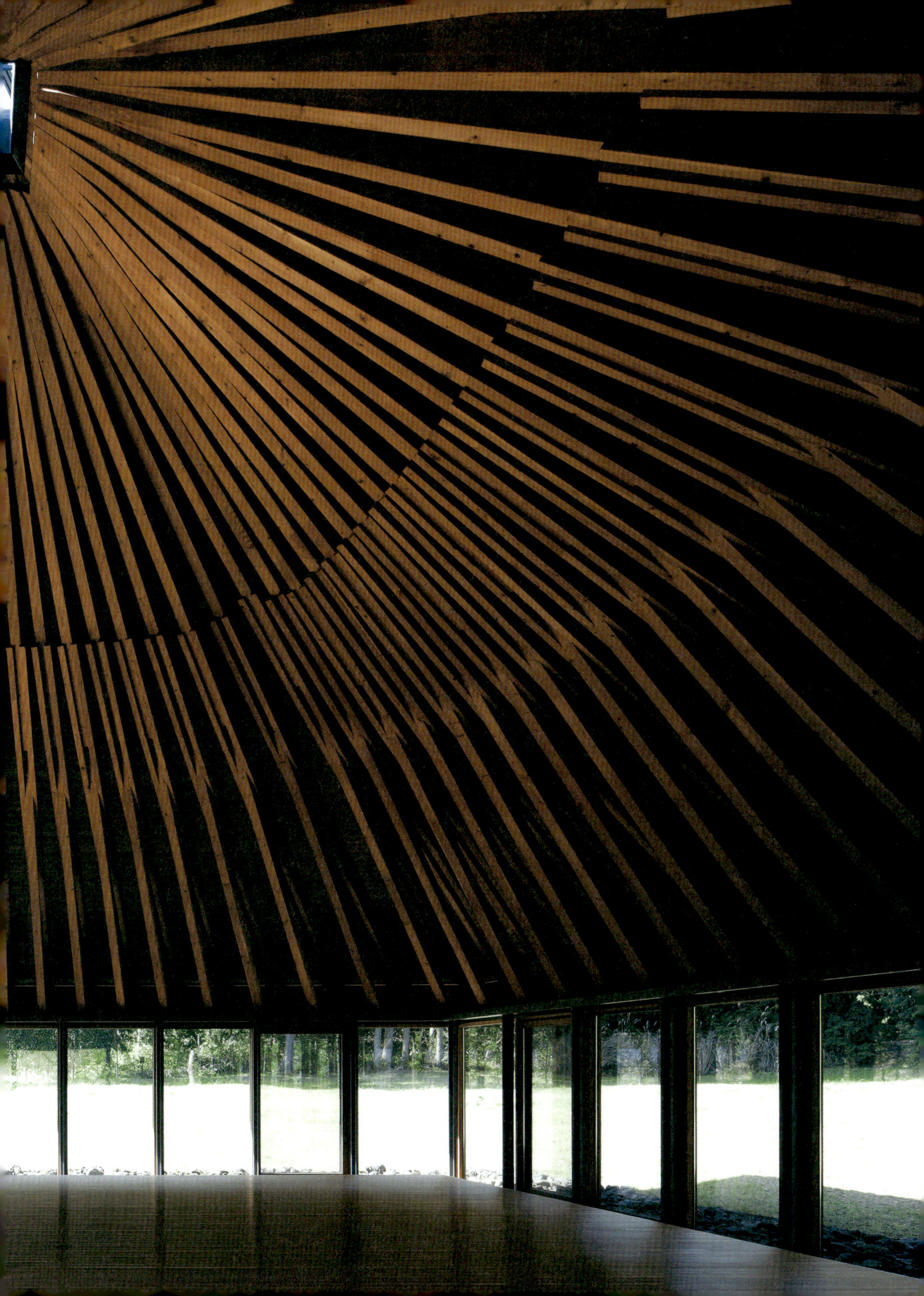

最上川ふるさと総合公園センターハウス
Mogamigawa Park Center House

2001
山形県寒河江市 Yamagata

ある秋の日の夕暮れに築山に登った。遠くに月山と朝日岳が
冠雪しているのが見え、最上川が光りながら流れていく。
その風景の中で、天空を映した建物の屋根は、緩やかな
起伏のあるランドスケープの中に舞い降りた三日月のようだった。

I climbed up onto the hill on one autumn evening. The sparkling Mogami River flowed by and the snow-capped Mount Gassan and Mount Asahidake were visible in the distance. Amidst such a scene, it appeared as if the building's roof that reflected the heavens was a crescent moon that had descended upon the gently undulating landscape.

ガラスの三日月

篠原修さんの縁で知り合った東大教授の堀繁さんは、農学系の景観の専門家だ。気さくな人柄からだろう、研究活動の傍ら、銀山温泉の修景など山形県の街づくりの相談に乗ることが多かった。県内をくまなく歩くなど、たいそうな熱の入れようである。その堀さんから、「委員長を務める委員会に建物の提案が欲しいのだが協力してもらいたい」との要請があった。

内容は不思議なものだった。最上川沿いの公園用地に全国緑化フェアの催しを誘致したい。緑化フェアでは催事の中心となるパビリオンが必要なのだが、催事のときはさまざまな展示をしたい。緑化フェアが終わってからは、地域のコミュニティ施設として使用するが、温室としても使いたいとのこと。まったく矛盾する機能を盛り込んだ与件だった。緑化フェアが催されるのは6〜8月。山形の内陸部はフェーン現象でわが国の最高気温を記録したところである。夏は存外暑い。そしてこのあたりは、冬は積雪がかなりある。冬は温室でありながら、それ以外の季節は通常の利用にも供さなければならない。これは前代未聞の無理難題である。いかにもラジカルな堀さんらしい。温室のための大スパン、通常利用のための遮熱と冷房、換気による熱抜き、冬期利用のための領域暖房、落雪屋根、そして景観とランドスケープ。解決しなければならない問題は盛りだくさんである。

温室の機能をもたせるには、ガラス張りにせねばならない。透明度の高い架構にする必要があったが、同時に雪の荷重も考慮に入れなければならない。また、矛盾するようだが、巨大なガラス面から落雪させるためのディテールを練り上げなければならなかった。同時に、広大な公園のシンボルなのだから、それなりにハッキリしたフォルムももたせたかった。最上川沿いの公園のランドスケープに合わせるように、流れるような形。遠くに月山が見える。だから三日月のような流れる形はどうか。それが初めに抱いたイメージだった。

有機的な形は、すでに「牧野富太郎記念館」で経験済みだったが、雪を落雪させるとなると屋根の水勾配は正確に上から下へと作らねばならない。思い付いたのは円錐形である。すり鉢状の屋根であれば、雪は正確に底へと流れ落ちる。円錐形の屋根面を保ったまま三日月型を切り出せば、牧野に近い有機的なフォルムが幾何学的に作り出せる。落雪に関しては、かなりうまくいったと思う。温室として使わないときは、暖気を可能な限り早く頂部から外に逃がす。手前には大きな池を作り、そこでクーリングした冷気を内部に誘引する。さらに居室には背後の土盛りを使ってクールチューブで空調負荷を減らす。冬は居住域暖房とし、大空間は暖めない。まだ稚拙だったコンピューターによる空気シミュレーションをし、空気の流れに関して検討を重ねた。ともかく、当時在ったあらゆる手段を駆使した。

一面が雪景色になり、朝日岳や月山が幻のように輝き、最上川が滔々と流れ、そこにとても温室とは思えないようなガラスの三日月が舞い降りた風景。それはなかなかのものではないかと思っている。しかし、この辺りの冬は豪雪で寒い。この風景を目にする人はあまりいないのが残念だ。(Eng. p.280)

Site Plan 1/1500

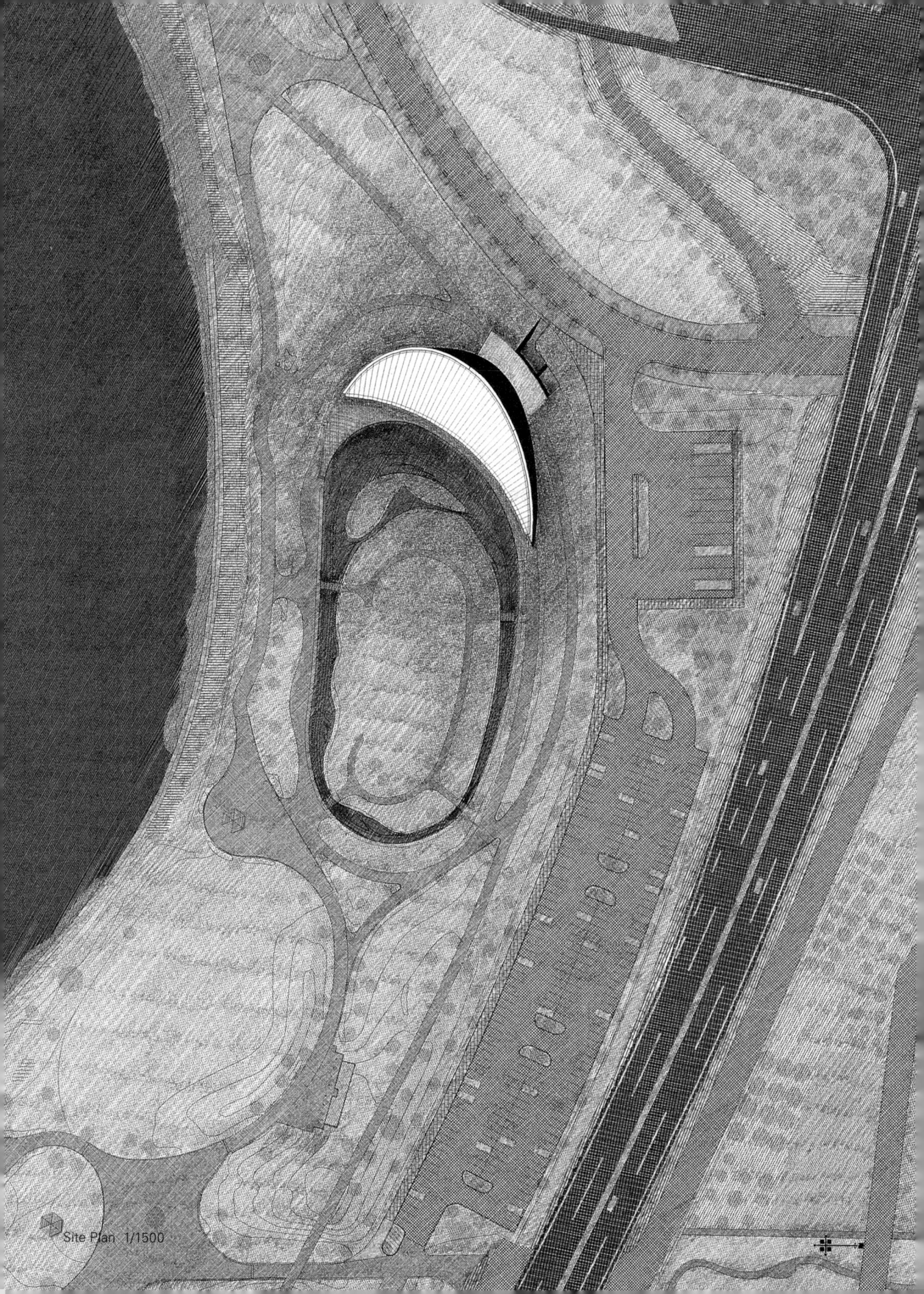

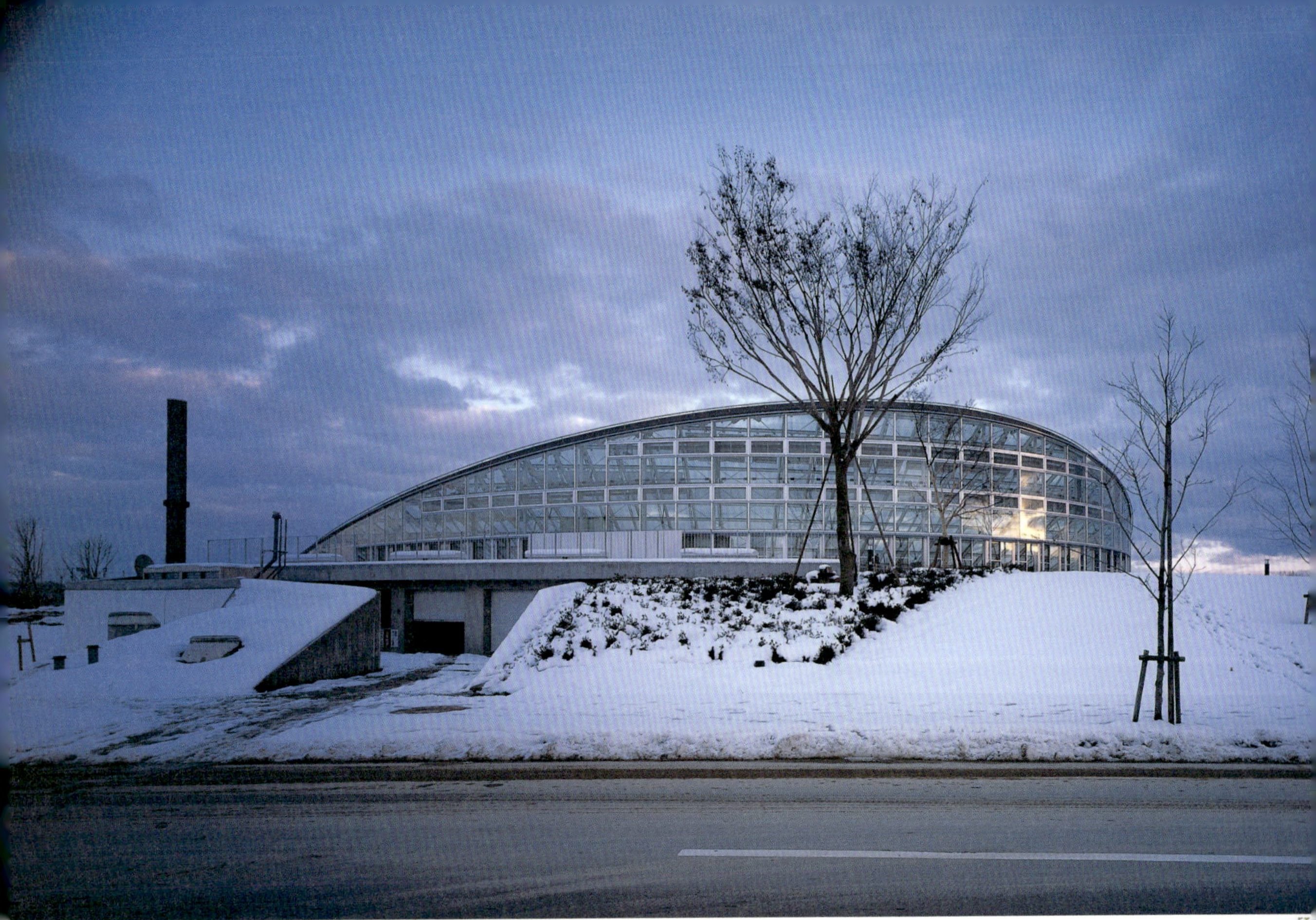
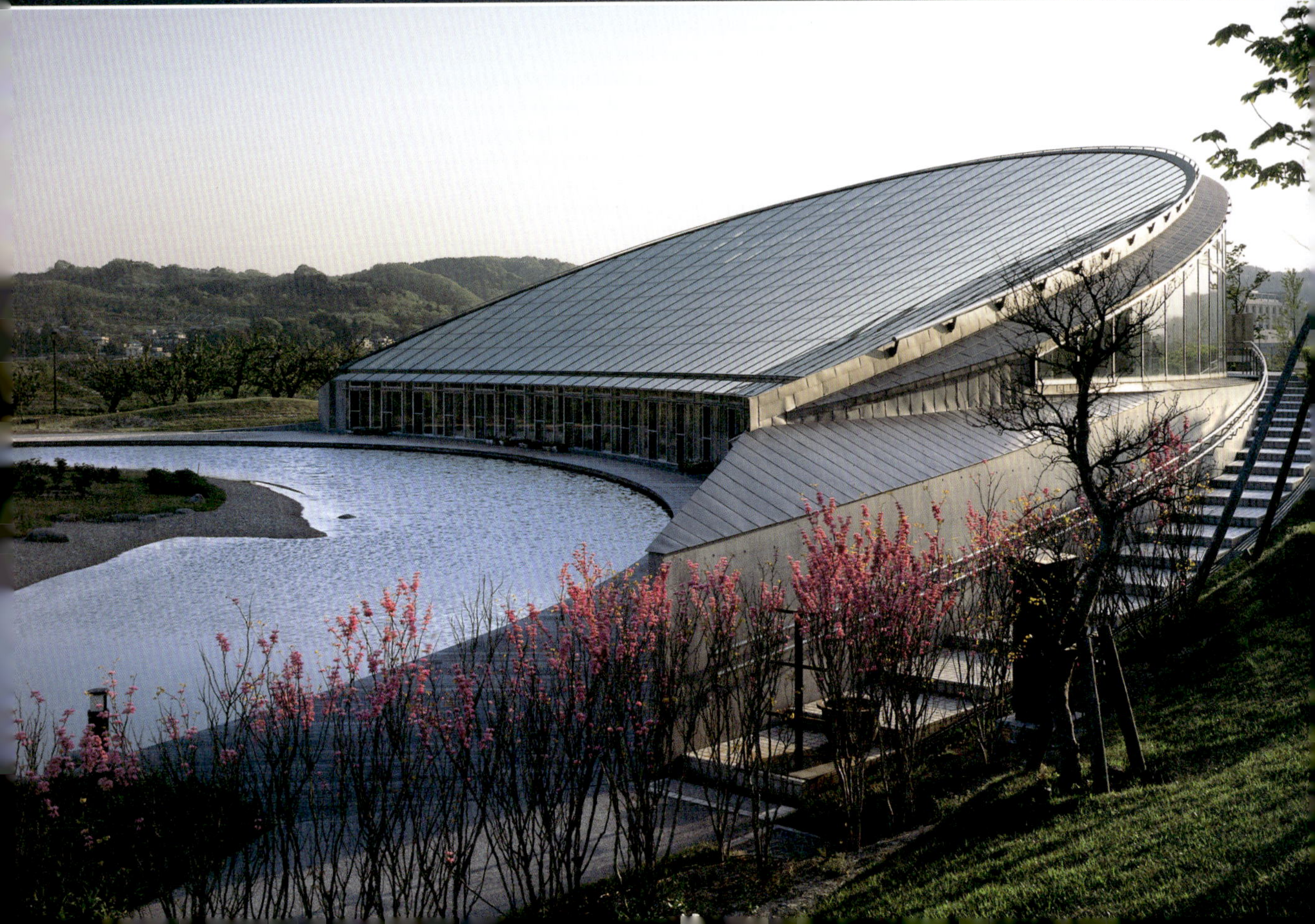

素形、シェルター、倉庫のようなもの、という脈絡は、
イデー、手段、現象というように置き換えられる。
The terms "protoform", "shelter", and "shed-like object" can be
interpreted respectively as the "idea", "means", and "phenomenon".

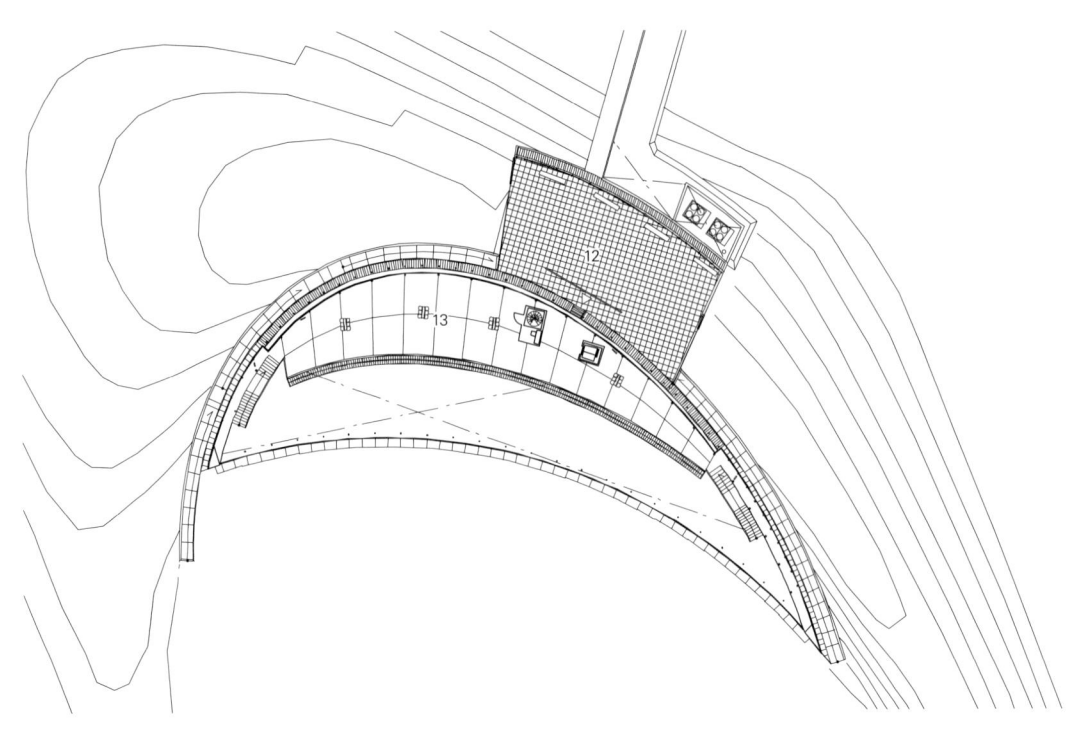

2F Plan

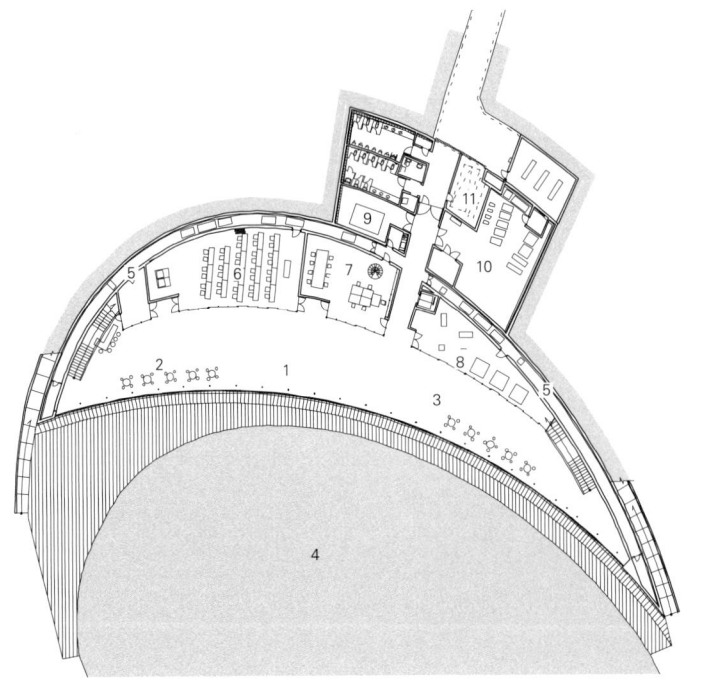

1. special exhibition gallery
2. cafe
3. rest area
4. pool
5. sustainable duct
6. seminar room
7. office
8. exhibition gallery
9. electorical room
10. HVAC mechanical room
11. garage
12. entrance terrace
13. entrance hall

1F Plan 1/800

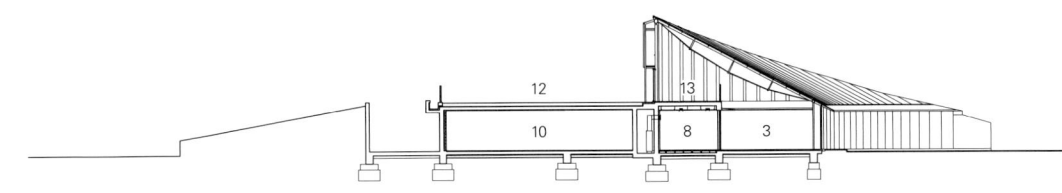

Section 1/500

244   Hiroshi NAITO 1992-2004

網目状の張弦梁と鋳物のジョイント
The cast-metal joints of the tension cross-cables.

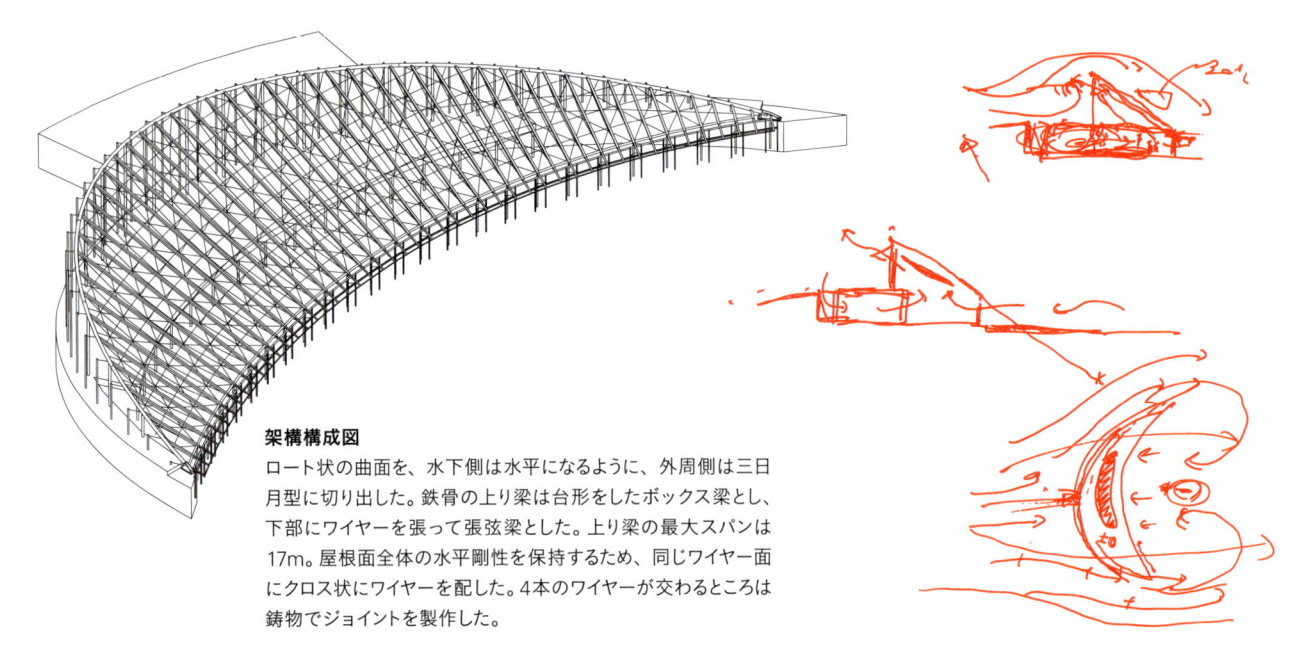

架構構成図
ロート状の曲面を、水下側は水平になるように、外周側は三日月型に切り出した。鉄骨の上り梁は台形をしたボックス梁とし、下部にワイヤーを張って張弦梁とした。上り梁の最大スパンは17m。屋根面全体の水平剛性を保持するため、同じワイヤー面にクロス状にワイヤーを配した。4本のワイヤーが交わるところは鋳物でジョイントを製作した。

Structural Composition
A crescent shape with a horizontal lower edge was cut out from a funneled surface. The diagonal steel members are formed from trapezoidal box beams and behave as arched beams tensioned by underside cables. The beams span a maximum length of 17 meters. Cross-cables were also fixed to the underside of the roof in order to sustain lateral loading to its entire surface. Cast-metal joints were made for where the four cables meet.

気流スケッチ
風の流れをイメージしたもの。気流模型を作り、コンピューターシミュレーションをした。

Wind Flows
Sketches visualizing the flow of wind. Building models were made to conduct computer wind flow simulations.

でも、建築はそうした時間とは違う次元の時間を
生きているのだ、と思いたい。違う次元、それは、遠くに見える山々、
悠々と流れる大河、そこから運ばれてくる風の中にある。

Yet I want to believe that architecture lives within a different dimension of time. A different dimension—one that exists within the wind carried from that great river flowing steadily from the mountains in the distance.

ちひろ美術館・東京
Chihiro Art Museum Tokyo

2002

東京都練馬区 Tokyo

時間をつないでいくことが、
これからの大きなテーマになってくるだろう。

I believe that the idea of connecting time together will
become the next major theme.

Chihiro Art Museum Tokyo

**追憶することと
創造すること**

「安曇野ちひろ美術館」を完成させて数年後、安曇野の見通しがついたので、本拠地である東京のいわさきちひろ絵本美術館を改装することになった。1977年に松本夫妻が美術館を立ち上げてから25年、増築と改築を重ねて来た迷路のような建物だから、あちこち老朽化が進んだことはもちろん、いわさきちひろ絵本美術館が大きな目標のひとつとして掲げているバリアフリーに対する対処が難しくなっていたことも改装の大きな理由だった。

　もっとも、わたしはこの建物の複雑怪奇な迷路のような空間がとても好きだった。歩いていると自分がどこにいるのか分からなくなるし、思いもかけないシーンが展開する。建物のデザインもルシアン・クロールのようなバナキュラーなテイストがあった。この良さはできるだけ残したかった。

　積み上げてきた歴史を大切に、迷路のような空間を整理することを目的に幾つもの改装案を理事会に提出した。概ね了解が得られ具体的な設計に入る前に、念のため構造のチェックをしておこう、ということになった。ところが確たる図面が残っていない。念のためコンクリートの抜き取り検査をやってみると、とても質が悪く、そのままで耐震補強をやったところで何とかなるレベルではなかった。構造体がひどい骨粗鬆症のようなものだった。また、仮に補強をやったとして、地盤が悪いので増えた建物総重量にはとても耐えられないことが判明した。結論は、建て替えざるを得ない、ということである。

　新しく設計し直すことになったが、美術館がこの地で刻んできた記憶は尊重したい。複雑な条件下で形を整える方向で仕事をすることが多かったのだが、ここではあえて形を崩すことを心掛けた。もとの建物のバナキュラーな感じを継承し、斜めの線を多用し、中庭を生かして人を迎え入れるような配置にした。

　「赤い外壁がいいわ」と理事の黒柳さんが言った。とても困った。いくら何でも外壁に赤は難しい。途方に暮れた。しばらくして、黒柳さんがいつも持っている肩掛けバックに目が止まった。おそらく南米のインディオが編んだものだろう。鮮やかな横縞の品の良い模様で、その中に渋い赤のストライプが何本か入っていた。黒柳さんに、「赤っていうのはこの赤ですか」と聞いたら、「そうだ」と言う。この赤なら建物の外壁にもってきてもおかしくない。そこで、その赤をベースに塗装サンプルを作り、現場で決めてもらった。ここが最大の綱渡りだった。

・今までのやさしいIntimateなカンジ。ほっとできるカンジ。
　ひそむカンジなど考慮してほしい。
・絵を見る人の関係は、なるたけ近く、親しく見られる雰囲気を残したい。
・ちひろさんが22年間生活をして、描いて、亡くなった所だ、という
　ここだけ（安曇野とは違った）のものでありたい。
・それでいて個性的であり、新しいというイメージを与えられる建物。
・カフェ、ホールなどについては副次的で、ちひろの絵が主役だけど商売という点から末長く収入を得られるものにしたいので、若い人にも好かれるものが望ましい。（以上、黒柳徹子館長）
・子供専門の石とか、ニコニコしたくなるような美術館がいい。（山田洋次監督）
・子供がうまく背伸びをしないで見られるような展示になるといいと願っている。
・子供が自由にふるまえ、堅苦しくない美術館がいい。（以上、松本善明氏）

　山田さん、黒柳さん、松本善明さんら理事が建物に対して出した要望である。こんな想像力豊かな設計に対する希望を聞いたのも初めてである。ホテルの喫茶店での雑談を黒柳さんがまとめ、テーブルの上に敷いてあった紙に書いて、それぞれが署名した。今でもその紙は大切に保管してある。建物がそのように出来上がっていればいいのだが。(Eng. p.281)

Site Plan 1/1500

容易に消費される面白さよりも、消費されにくいつまらなさの中に
わたしなりの価値を見出したい。それを目指す方が性分に合っている。

I want to find value within the trivial things that are not easily consumed, rather than within the curious things that are easily consumed. It better fits my disposition to strive for the former.

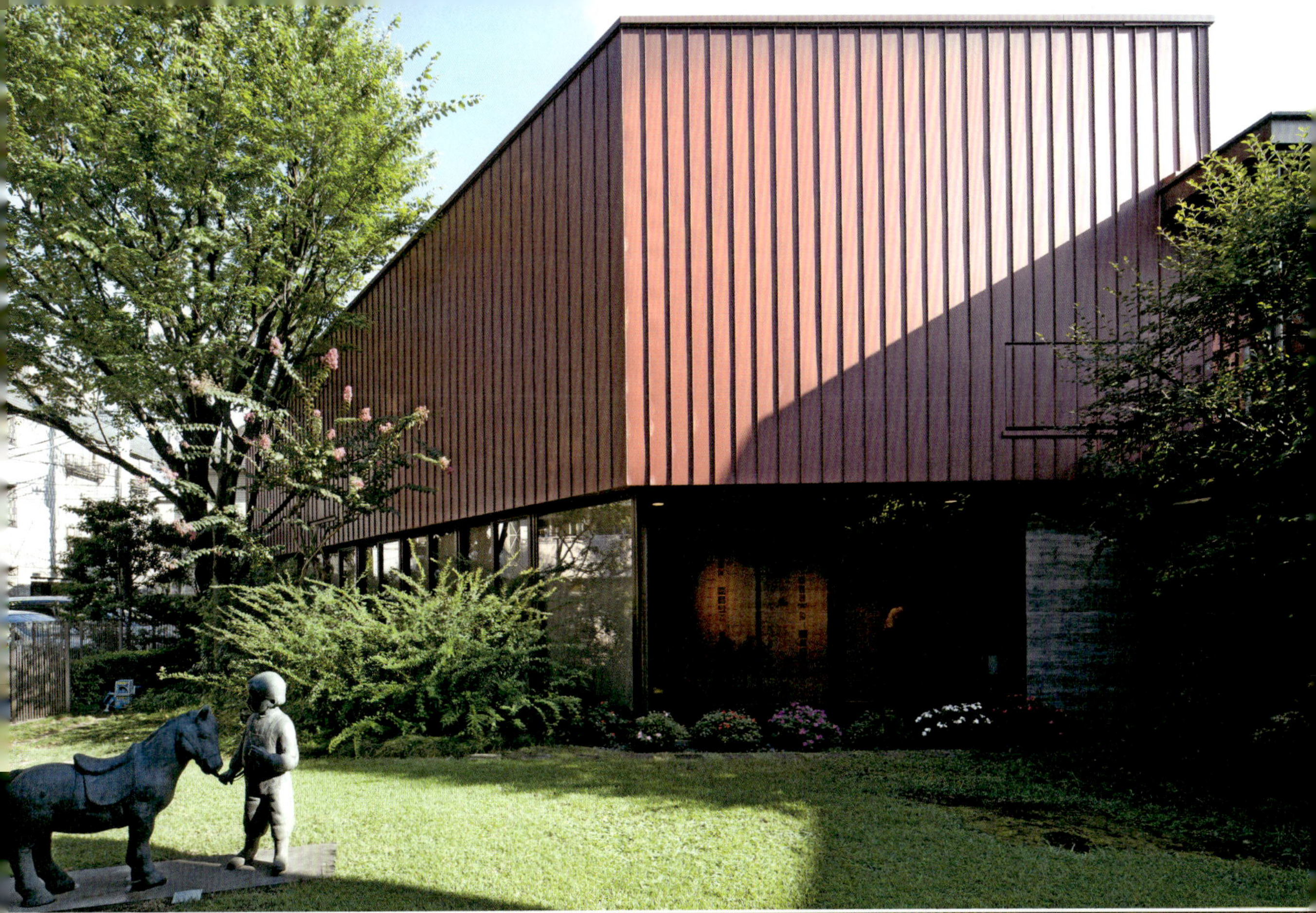

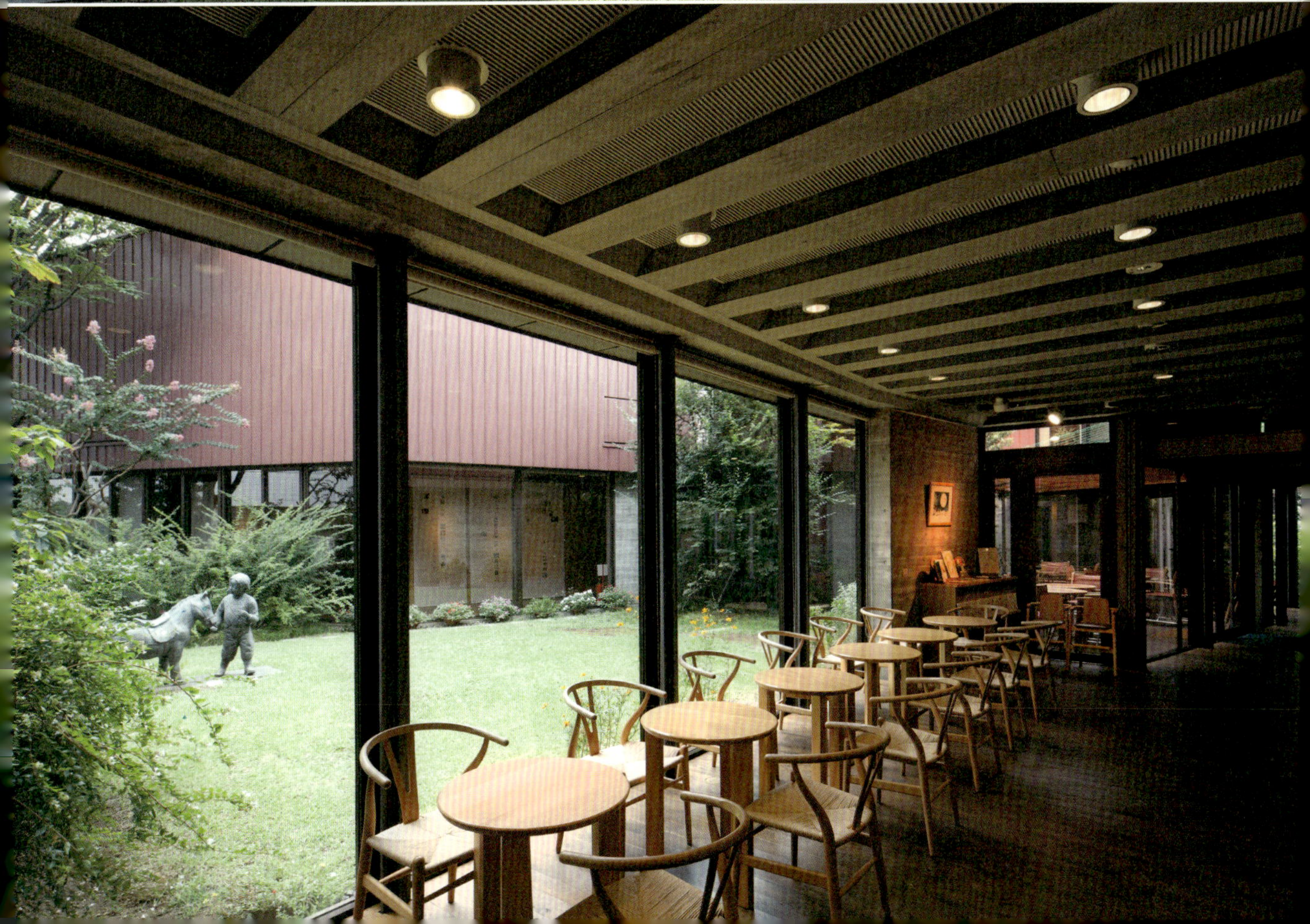

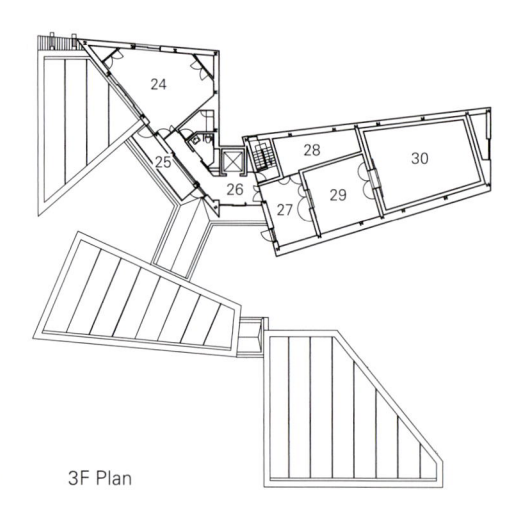

24 director's office
25 terrace
26 hall
27 unpacking room
28 machine room
29 stack room
30 collection storage

3F Plan

14 exhibition room
15 hall
16 reception room
17 restroom
18 office
19 vice-director's office
20 library
21 playroom

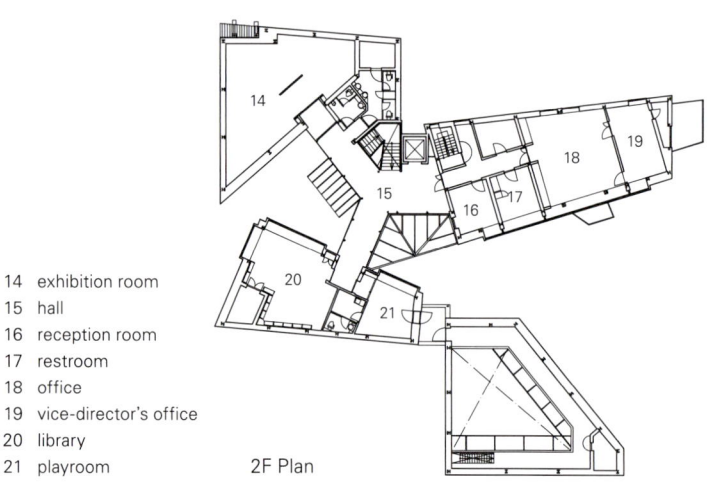

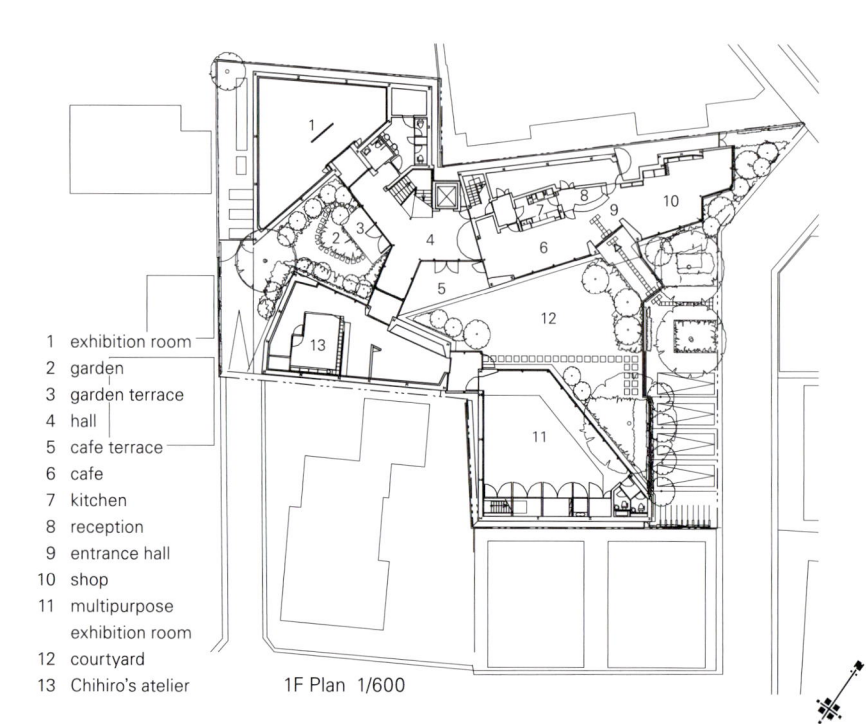

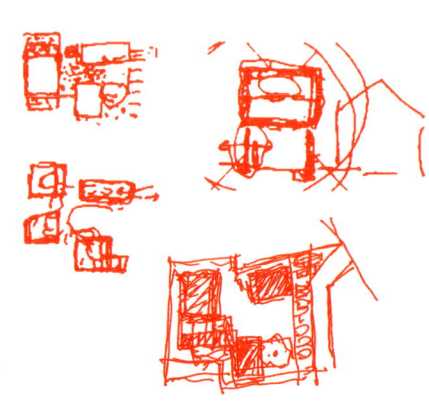

2F Plan

1   exhibition room
2   garden
3   garden terrace
4   hall
5   cafe terrace
6   cafe
7   kitchen
8   reception
9   entrance hall
10 shop
11 multipurpose exhibition room
12 courtyard
13 Chihiro's atelier

1F Plan 1/600

254   Hiroshi NAITO 1992-2004

旧美術館の記憶を残した配置計画
The site layout plan maintains the
memories of the original museum.

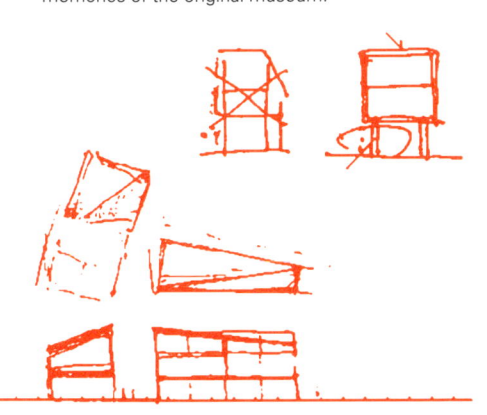

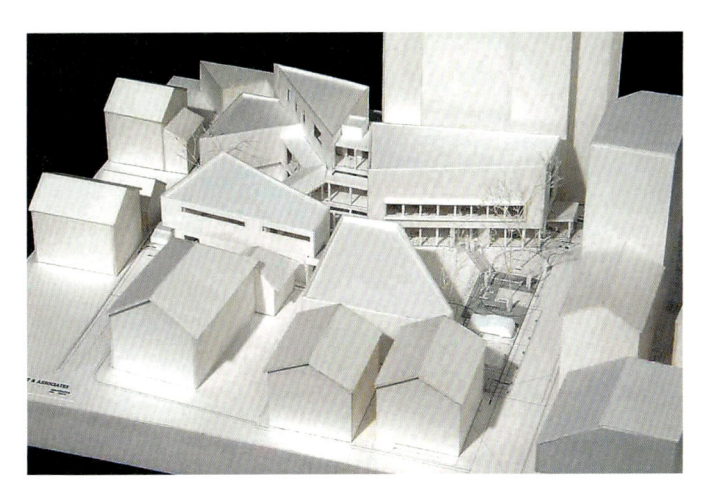

Chihiro Art Museum Tokyo

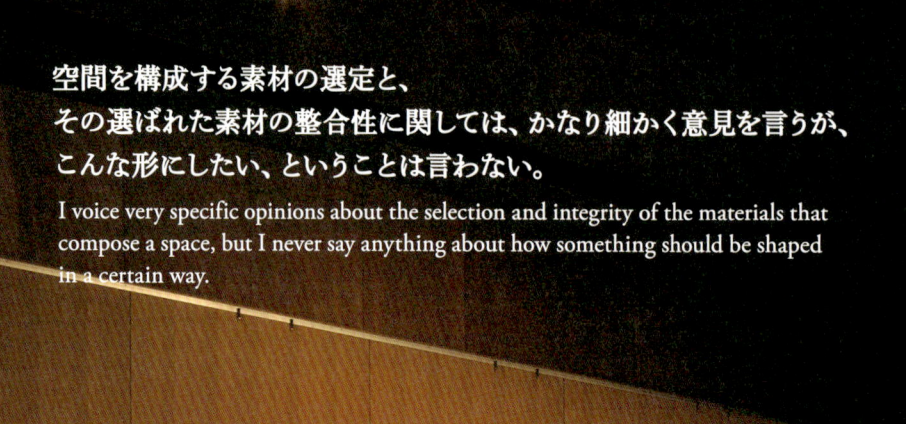

空間を構成する素材の選定と、
その選ばれた素材の整合性に関しては、かなり細かく意見を言うが、
こんな形にしたい、ということは言わない。
I voice very specific opinions about the selection and integrity of the materials that compose a space, but I never say anything about how something should be shaped in a certain way.

多目的展示室
The multipurpose exhibition room.

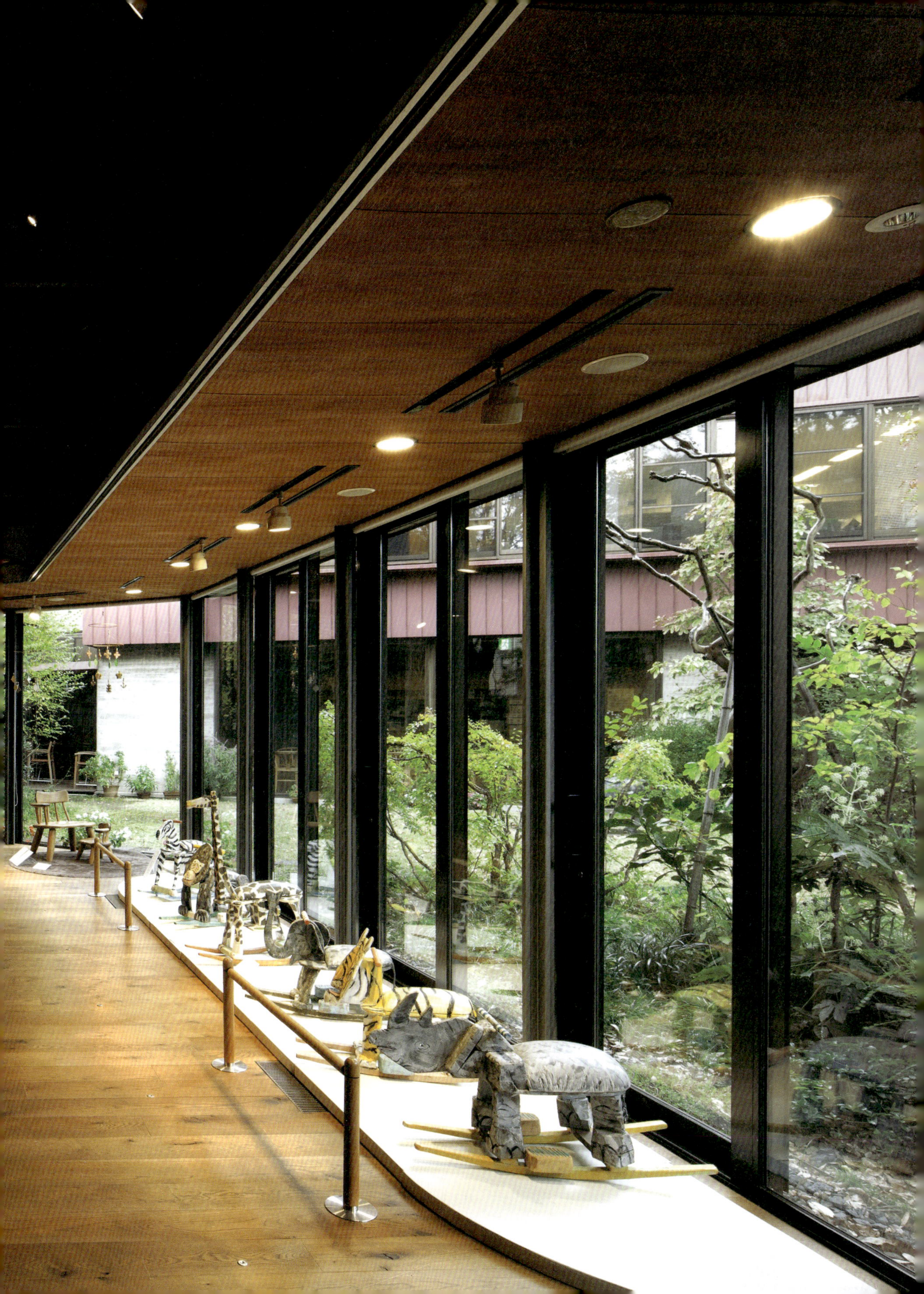

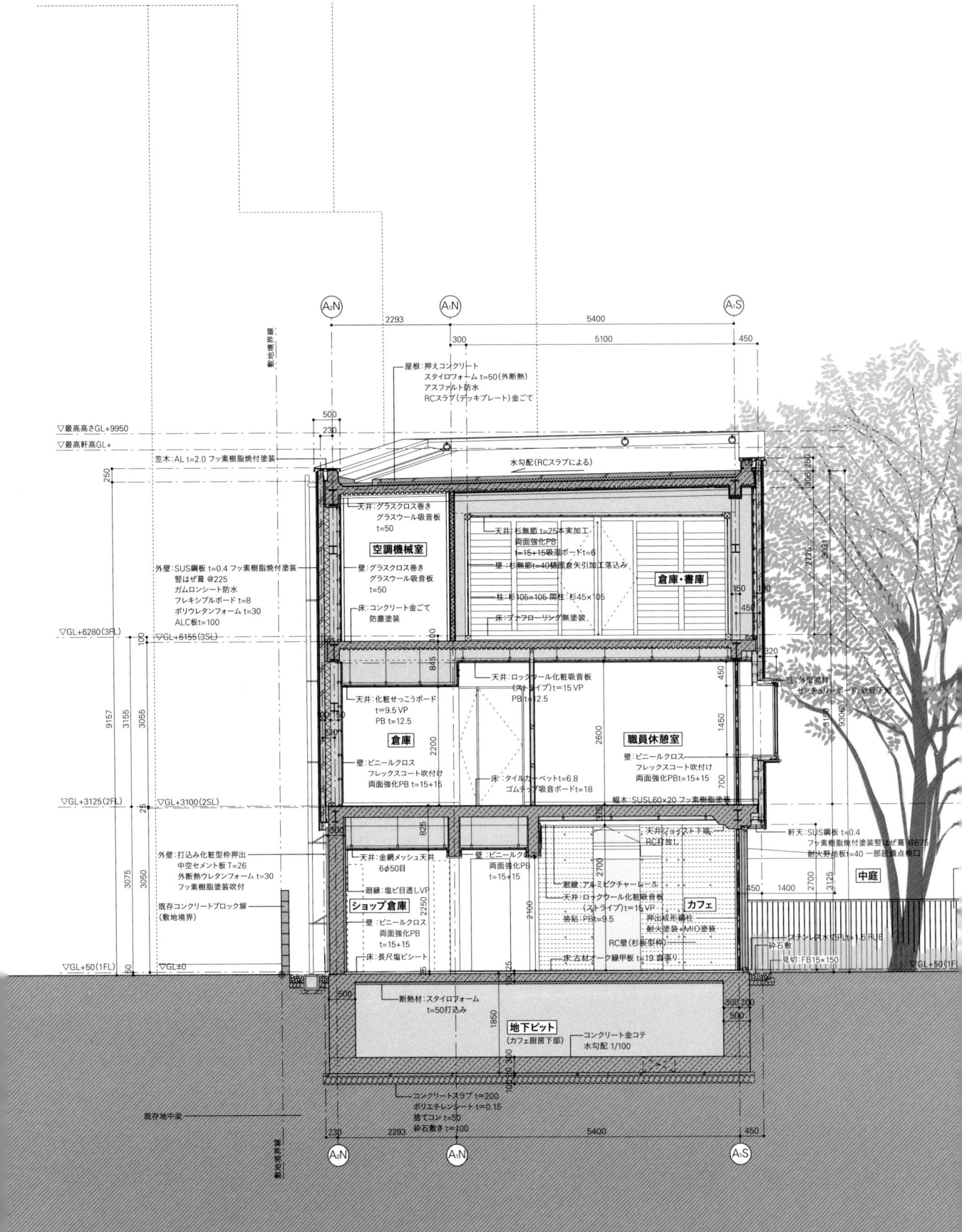

Detailed section 1/100

実際、ひとつの建物を作るに際して、
イメージスケッチのようなものは、まったくと言っていいほど描かない。
与えられた条件のもとで、何に重点を置くか、という言葉での
指示がほとんどだ。プロジェクトに作為や
嗜好を優先させると、何かが決定的に抜け落ちる。

When designing a building, I draw almost no sketches of how I imagine it to look like. I mostly only give instructions through words regarding where importance should be placed in light of the given conditions. Something critical is lost from a project when priority is given to contrivances or preferences of taste.

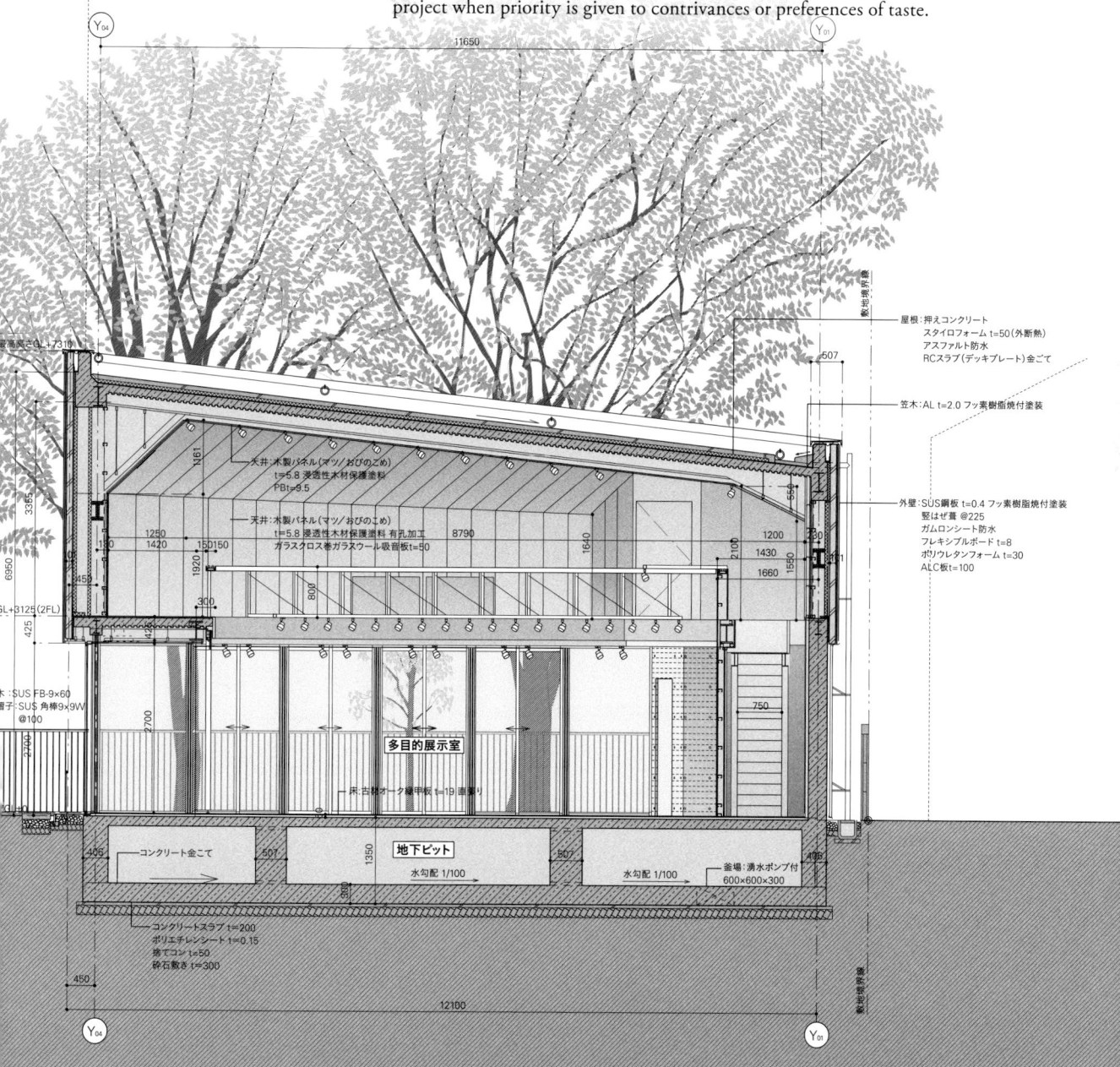

ジョイストスラブが露出する1階展示室
The first floor exhibition room with an exposed joist slab ceiling.

ちひろの復元アトリエ
Chihiro's recreated atelier.

建築を作る行為の抽象的側面を、
直接的に表現につなげることが不得手だ。

I am inept at linking the abstract facet of the act of
creating architecture directly to expression.

われわれにせいぜいできることは、現実に忠実であること、
時間の微かな囁きが、騒がしい意匠や設計者の浅はかな思い入れで
かき消されないようにすることだけだ。

The most that we can do is to remain faithful to reality and to try to keep the
noisy designs and the shallow ideas of designers from drowning out the faint
whispers of time.

住居No.27
House No.27

2004
東京都大田区 Tokyo

デザインを意図的に後退させること、こだわりすぎないこと、価値を捏造しないこと、やりすぎないこと、可能であれば未完成のまま投げ出すこと、建物として無理をしないこと、意識的に凡庸であること、などを心掛けるようにしている。

I take care to intentionally allow design to recede to the back; to not be too particular about things; to not fabricate value; to not overdo things; to let go of things while they are still incomplete, if possible; to not force out a building; and to be consciously mundane.

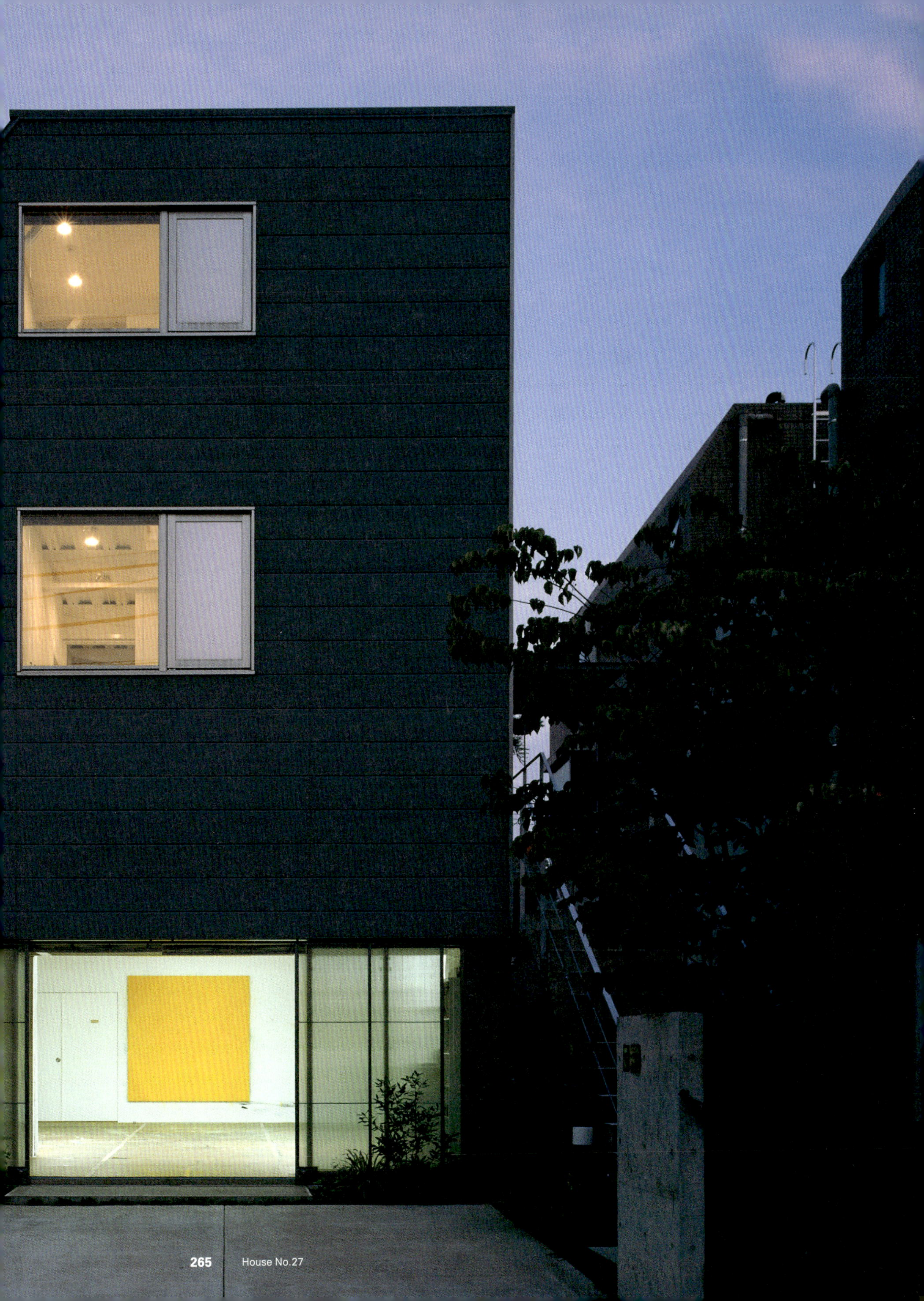

つくり、そだて、くらす

　堂本右美さんと初めて会ったのは、懇意にさせていただいていた父君である画家の堂本尚郎さんのお宅だった。外国生活から帰国したばかり、ご主人のディーンさんと生まれたばかりの赤ちゃんと一緒の対面だった。それから10年後、自宅の設計を依頼された。その時には、右美さんは独特の抽象的な画風をもつ女流画家として活躍し始めたところで、子供はふたりになっていた。

　依頼の主要なテーマは、生活と創作をどのようにしたら両立させることができるかだった。右美さんの仕事は忙しくなる一方だったし、子育てもしっかりとやりたい。そうなると、職住近接の商店主のような生活にならざるを得ない。また、ディーンさんの趣味の木工製作のスペースも求められた。右美さんの旺盛な創作欲と子育て、多忙なご主人の籠るスペースの確保。これらを盛り込むと、なかなか充分なスペースは確保できなそうだった。

　細かく空間を切り分けることは得策ではない。たぶん、生活はどんどん変わっていくだろう。こういう時は、大きなシェルターのような建物をザックリと作るのがいい。北側斜線をクリアしながら最大限スペースを求めた末、鉄骨造の3階建てとし、1階をアトリエと木工製作のスペースとした。

　クリエーターの創作する場所を作るのには独特の神経を使う。建築の形や空間が何らかの言葉を発してしまえば、それが生み出すものに影響を与えてしまう。一方、何もしなければ、それはそれである種の欺瞞を抱えてしまう。ニュートラルの在り方が難しい。こういう時は、構造と性能を中心に考えてまとめる。そこには、建築家の恣意性が入り込む余地が少ないからだ。

　この8年間、シェルターのような建物は、何とか創作と生活を支えてこれたのではないかと思う。創作は幅を広げ、ふたりのお子さんもずいぶん大きくなった。最近では、お母様を引き取り、1階部分を改装して同居が始まり、新たな変化の時期を迎えている。(Eng. p.281)

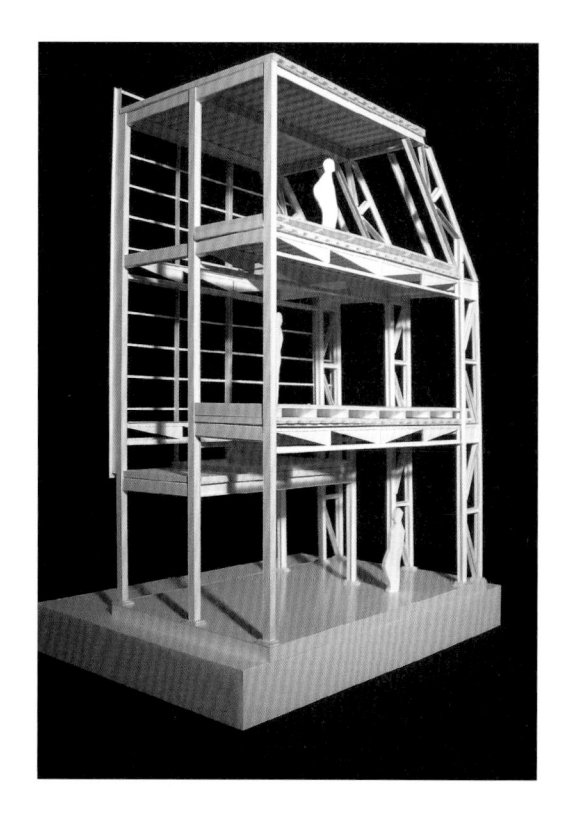

Site Plan 1:2500

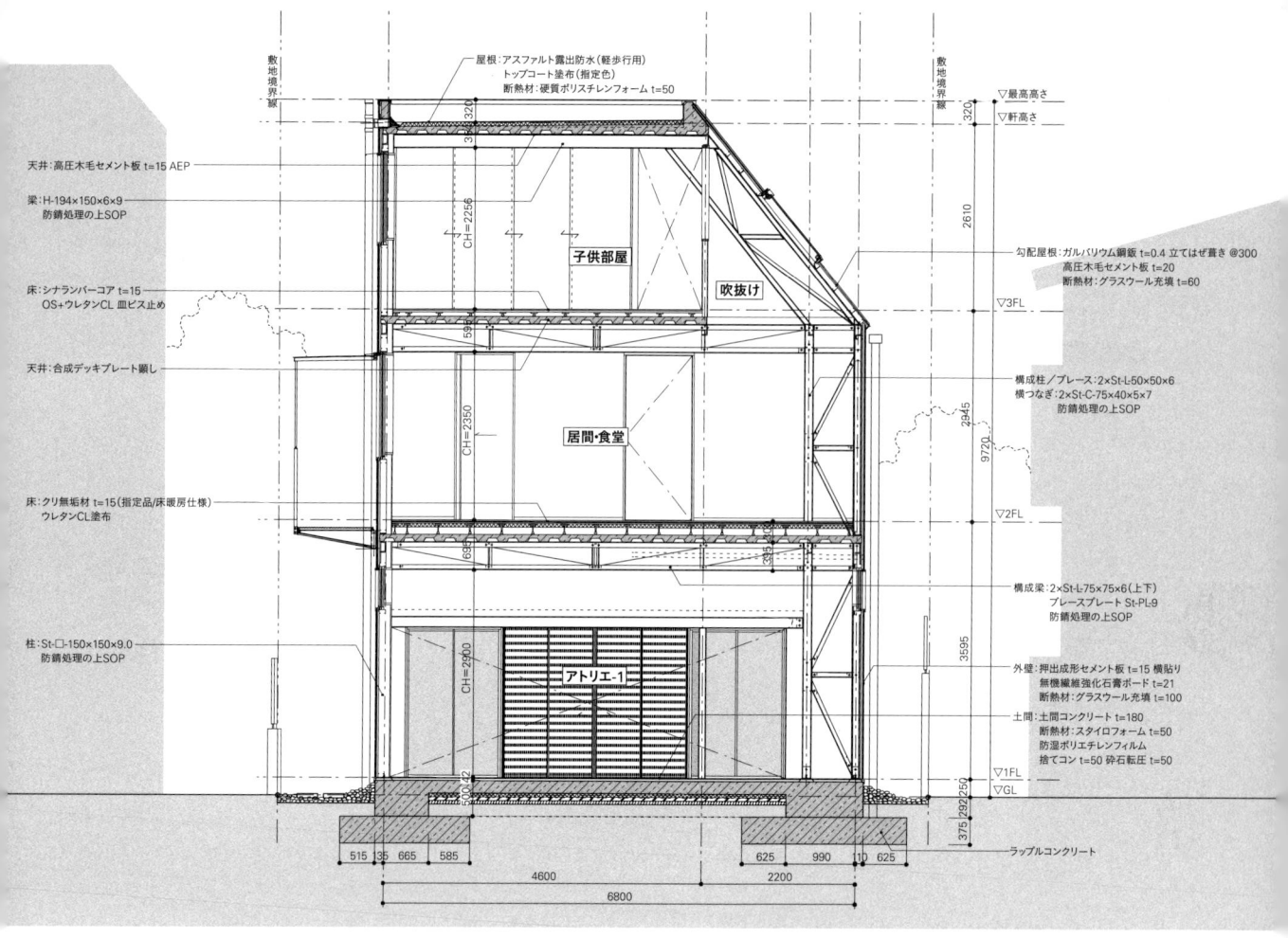

Detailed section 1/100

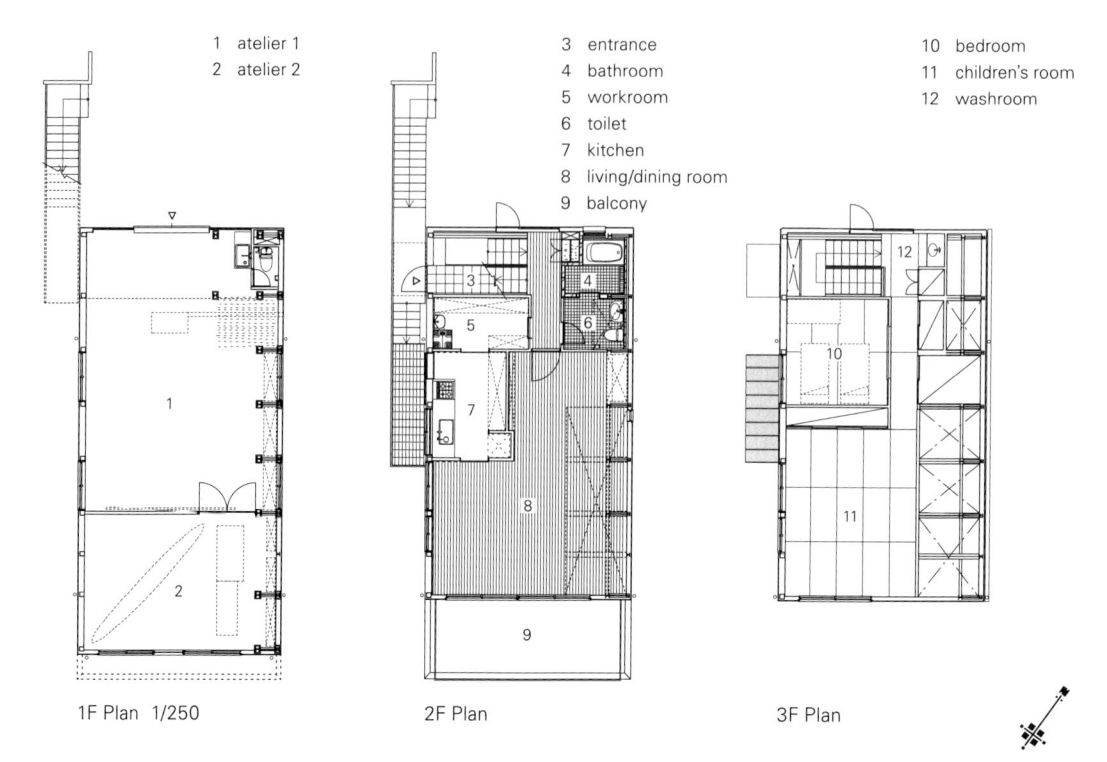

天井:高圧木毛セメント板 t=15 AEP
梁:H-194×150×6×9
　防錆処理の上SOP
床:シナランバーコア t=15
　OS+ウレタンCL 皿ビス止め

天井:合成デッキプレート顕し

床:クリ無垢材 t=15(指定品/床暖房仕様)
　ウレタンCL塗布

柱:St-□-150×150×9.0
　防錆処理の上SOP

屋根:アスファルト露出防水(軽歩行用)
　トップコート塗布(指定色)
　断熱材:硬質ポリスチレンフォーム t=50

子供部屋　吹抜け

居間・食堂

アトリエ-1

勾配屋根:ガルバリウム鋼板 t=0.4 立てはぜ葺き @300
　高圧木毛セメント板 t=20
　断熱材:グラスウール充填 t=60

構成柱/ブレース:2×St-L-50×50×6
横つなぎ:2×St-C-75×40×5×7
　防錆処理の上SOP

構成梁:2×St-L-75×75×6(上下)
ブレースプレート St-PL-9
　防錆処理の上SOP

外壁:押出成形セメント板 t=15 横貼り
　無機繊維強化石膏ボード t=21
　断熱材:グラスウール充填 t=100

土間:土間コンクリート t=180
　断熱材:スタイロフォーム t=50
　防湿ポリエチレンフィルム
　捨てコン t=50 砕石転圧 t=50

ラップルコンクリート

#	Room	#	Room
1	atelier 1	7	kitchen
2	atelier 2	8	living/dining room
3	entrance	9	balcony
4	bathroom	10	bedroom
5	workroom	11	children's room
6	toilet	12	washroom

1F Plan 1/250　　2F Plan　　3F Plan

Hiroshi NAITO 1992-2004

どのような時間を織り上げていくか、
空間を生み出す主体は住み手に委ねられている。
I left it up to the residents to weave their own time and to create their own spaces.

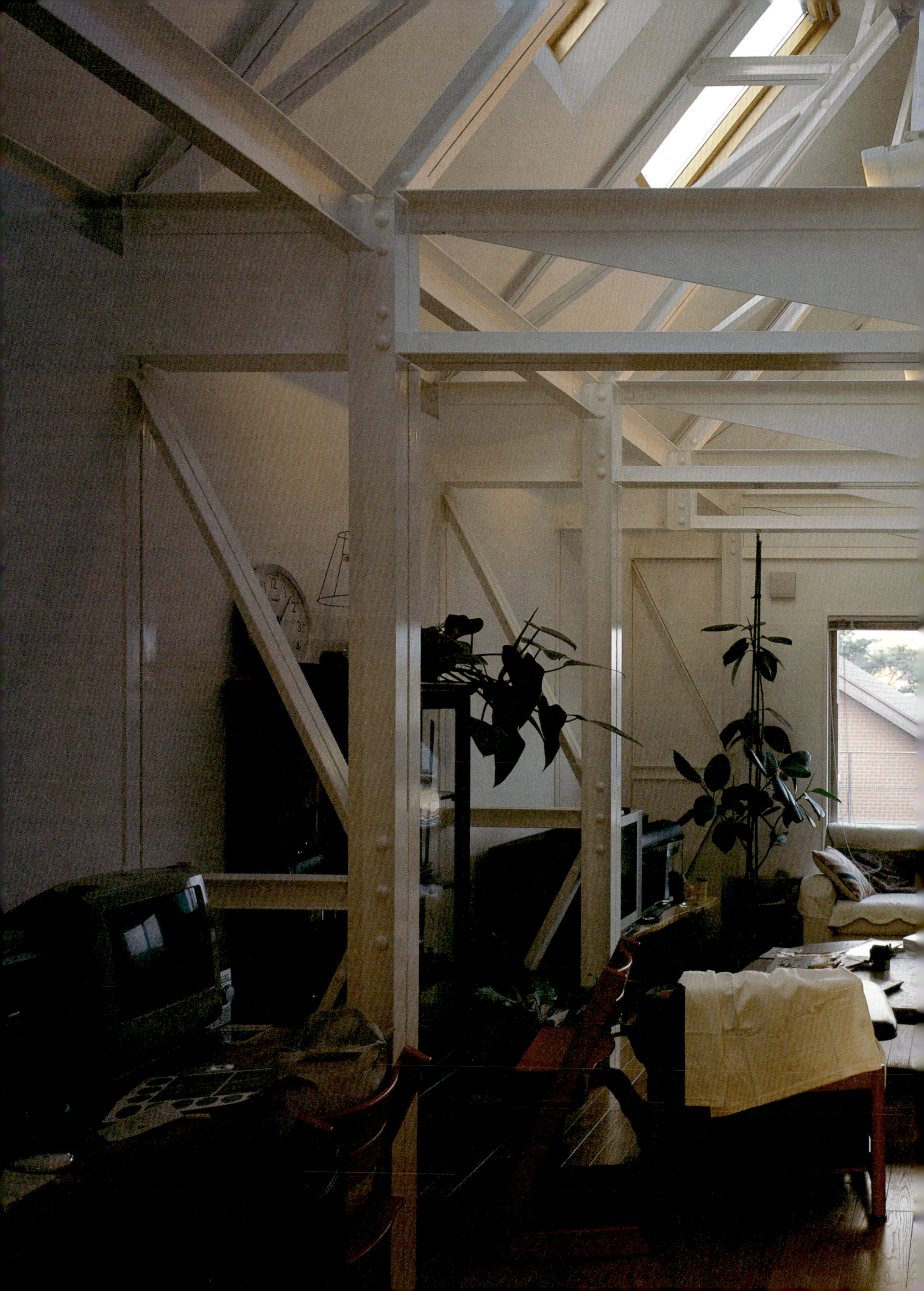

モノを作りつつ、意図的に無為であることは難しい。
It is difficult for one to intentionally not be contriving while making things.

[内藤廣 言葉のかけら 1992-2004]

建築が本当の意味での精神を宿すには、目新しさや面白さは邪魔なんですよ。[001]

われわれは図面上で空間を設計しているが、実は無意識のうちにその背後にある時間を設計している。時間を問題にすると、空間の成り立ち方は途端に変わる。にもかかわらず、建築はこのことをあまりにも無視し続けてきた。[002]

完結させずにおいた余白が、想像の中で埋められ、空間の像を結ぶかどうか。これは賭のようなものだが、それをこの場所で行われる一期一会の集いに託したい。[003]

構造体は、きわめて原始的な建築の由来を想起させるには有効な手段だ。その意味では、構造は建築にとって、最後の頼みの綱、と言えるかもしれない。[004]

依頼し使う側、設計者、作り上げる現場の人たち、それらをつなぎ止める共通の基盤は、同じ時代に生きているという実感でしかないと思う。[005]

建築がテニスのような個人戦だとすると、土木や都市はサッカーのような団体戦なのだ。[006]

自然と対立するかたちの重力系の思考に対して、自然と共生する風系の思考を、建築の中に積極的に取り入れていくことで、この硬直したパラダイムを解いていけるのではないか。風の側から建築を眺めれば、当たり前に思えていたことが異様に見える。[007]

建物に取り組むときに、あらかじめ戦略を立てたりしないので、むしろ終わってから冷静になって、その間の自分の無意識を探ることが多い。[008]

建築は孤独だ。[009]

形を作らないようにしたいという確かな衝動がある。特に、住宅を設計するときにはそういう思いが強い。[010]

住宅を離れればどんなにか楽になるだろうと、暗中模索のつらい作業の中でよく思う。しかし同時に、ここを離れてしまえば、すべてのことが見えなくなるような気もしている。臍の緒は切らない方がいいのだ。[011]

建築は、細部に宿る時間を複雑に組み上げた織物のようなものだ。[012]

建築はひとりでは作れない。[013]

内と外をつないでいく方法を見出さなければ、空間は永遠に「閉じられた箱」の中での遊戯に終始するしかない。[014]

大袈裟でもなく、さほど大きくもない建物の密度のある空間体験は、わたし自身の精神を幾度か解き放ってくれた。[015]

本やインターネットで得られる知識を超えないと、本当の情報は手に入らない。[016]

わたしの設計した建物に来て、みんなが違ったいろいろなことを考えてくれて構わない。[017]

突破しようと思えば、多少は痛い目に遭う。[018]

わたしが理想としている建築とは、何でもないように見えて、凄いものを作りたいということなんです。[019]

むしろ、これまでもったことのないような感覚をもちうるような場所をどうつくるか。それこそが新しいものだと信じているのです。[020]

住まう空間の隙間に建築的な空間を滑り込ませることができたからといって、何の意味があるというのだろう。[021]

死を語ることによって、都市は記憶を胚胎し、時を生きることを許される。[022]

わたしが正しいと思っていることはたぶん世の中では正しくない。[023]

建築家の作品の中にその時代の深層が象徴的に現れることは、確かなことだと言ってもいいのではないか。[024]

時の不在が、空間の多様化を導き寄せているのではないか。[025]

できることなら、無為の建築とでも呼べるようなものを作ってみたい。[026]

建物が建たない自然や裸の敷地に優るものはない。[027]

「素形」のディテールの無数の集積が、素形の建築となるのです。「素形」へと向かう作業は、物質と空間との信頼関係を回復する作業です。[028]

空気や環境はどこかでつながり連続しているのに、それらを建物の外皮で断ち切られた別個のものとして扱うのは異様なことだ。[029]

何かを思い付いても、常に物質の論理に帰って、細部から全体を修正し、問い直していくことが必要です。ノンフィクションである細部は、そして時間の織物でもある細部は、時の経過と共にその建築全体に対して正直に答えを出していくのだと思います。[030]

わたしは建築家が考えていることなんて、どうでもいいと思っているのです。つまり、その建物に誰かが来た時に、建築家の考えを押し付けて、コントロールするようなものにしたくない。[031]

建築では、外的な諸条件に囲い込まれて内的な必然性が浮上する、という側面もあるからです。[032]

住宅は時間を胚胎するシェルターでありさえすればいい。[033]

住宅を建てるというのは、ひとつの精神的な病なのではないかと思う。[034]

木は時間の経過と共に、それにかかわる人たちの記憶が染みつき、表情が豊かになっていく。[035]

ひとつの建物、それも手の内に入るほどのあまり大きくない建物に長い時間かかわっていると、自分の意識の底にあるものが次第に姿を現し始める。[036]

都市に埋め込まれる建築も、本来はその中に消費速度の体内時計のようなものをもつべきだと思う。[037]

空間を感じること、それは紛れもなく、われわれの明日の糧になるだろう。[038]

建築をつくることは、新しい現実をつくることだ。[039]

モダニズムの旗手たちの作品の素晴らしさはその群を抜いた個別性であって、普遍性においてではない。[040]

どんな時代でも、技術の飛躍的な進歩は、建築のパラダイムを変え、新しい価値と活力を建築の分野に与えてきた。[041]

設計という行為は、木や鉄やコンクリートといった物質を、建築の生成から消滅までの時間の中に置くためのプログラムだ、と考えるようにしている。[042]

住宅を設計することは、その時代の無意識を探ることだ。[043]

全体からディテールに至るまで、われわれは空間を設計しているようで、実は時間を設計しているのだ。形は見えやすく、時間は見えにくい。それゆえ、意識が空間に引きずられているにすぎない。[044]

構造を露出することの意味は、建築全体の中で与えられる位置づけと必然性によって支えられているべきだ。[045]

唯一の目的は、建てられた建物が何を語るかしかないのだから、それに向かわないあらゆる作業は意味がない。[046]

設計をまとめるとき、そこに迷いがないと不安になる。[047]

「素形」とは意識化された時間の姿、それが建築という形式の中に氷結したものなのではないかと思う。[048]

多くの建築は、かつてのような雄々しく自信に満ちた表情を失っている。[049]

空間を過剰に意識すれば、建築の形態は多様化していく。しかし時間を問題にすれば、形態の選択肢は狭まり、建築の輪郭ははっきりしてくる。[050]

設計という限られた時間の中でベストを尽くすが、一番適正な解が得られるとは限らない。[051]

わたしが考える住宅は住み替わりの一時的な滞留地ではなく、人がそこで生まれ、死んでゆく場所のことである。[052]

作りたいのは、事実だけを背負った倉庫のような存在、だ。[053]

建築は過去から流れる時間の流れを建てられる場所から引き継いでいる。それを受け止めなければ、いかなる建築の生み出す物語も捏造の誹りを免れない。[054]

今、世界は何かの支えを求めている。それは都市かもしれないし、建築かもしれない。われわれの果たせる役割は大きいと思うのです。[055]

「住むこと」と「建てること」は違う。「住むこと」は、どう取り繕おうと、結果としてこの制度を受け入れることであり、「建てること」は、制度の臨界点を確認する作業なのではないかと思う。[056]

建築は骨格の統一体としてではなく、流れ、つながる空間の統一体として成立しはすまいか。それがもし可能なら、このとき建築は物としてではなく、時の介在を許す空間を胚胎する。このときおそらく、差異化のゲームは忘れ去られたものとして終わる。[057]

建築という概念の中に潜む根本的な矛盾、錯誤、を自分の建物を通してあぶり出すことを試みたい。否定的な意味で言っているわけではない。それを意識化した上で、受け入れることが、設計の立っている現在の場所だと思うからだ。[058]

建築はさまざまな現実を許容する。その結果として多様化した建築空間の様相は、数億種類の生物が共存する混沌とした自然に似ている。[065]

English Project Descriptions

わたしは足の遅い建築家なんです。それがいい方に出る場合もあるし、悪い方に出る場合もある。まあここまでやってきたんだから、変わらないでしょうけど。[059]

デザインというのは心の病だと思う。[060]

もっと当たり前でいいはずだといつも思う。[061]

構造、構法、素材の選定を、自然条件の中で一番良いと思われる方向に向けていくと、建築はどんどん不自由なものになっていく。それは、ゆっくりと流れる自然の営み、自然のつくり出す時間の流れの中に建築を埋め込んでゆく作業だ。[062]

建築の力や役割を社会に対して開いておきたい。[063]

風景は、観光客や文学者や絵描きのためにあるのではない。そこに365日住まう人のためにある。[064]

Sea-Folk Museum

A Return to Protoform

It could be said that everything had begun with my encounter with the director of the museum, Yoshikata Ishihara. His father, Enkichi Ishihara, was a figure that had served as the head of the fishery union of Mie prefecture and had even become a member of the House of Representatives. He was known for having been held in high regard among the fishermen of the Ise-Shima region. It was in his father's wish that Director Ishihara established the museum centered on fishing culture in Toba in 1971. Plans for relocation were considered after the original museum had been heavily worn by the sea nearby and because its collection had become cramped with the rapid accumulation of items such as fishing tools.

Director Ishihara was of a lean build and had an exceptionally quick mind, but he was also innately competitive and did not have an ear for others. As an utter empiricist, he would actively travel anywhere and he held a wide breadth of knowledge. Moreover, because of this, the man had a firm backbone and soundly resisted all common social conventions and bureaucratic systems. He had even spearheaded the protests against the construction of nuclear power plants in Mie. He believed that they would not benefit the fishermen. Additionally, he was the owner of a particularly frugal spirit distinctive to the people of Ise. Yet he was also a person who kept coming up with new ideas and his thoughts changed with every meeting. He joked about it himself. It follows that it took a while for the basic requirements for the project to be set. He was fascinating, but was an extremely difficult person to work with.

In short, the Sea-Folk Museum was made by transcribing the character and ideas of Director Ishihara. He had a habit of saying, "make it as low-cost as possible" and "I have no money". At the same time, he requested a durability of over a century under the terrible environment that was close to the sea and exposed to the effects of salt damage. This was a project that presented me with these two mutually contradictory factors.

Design work was started in 1985 at around the time when the emerging bubble economy had given out its first cry. The project that had befallen upon me was completely anachronistic to the period. In those days, it was considered impossible to make a storage room that only cost 420,000 yen per *tsubo* (approximately 3.11 square meters). It did not help that the director had added further requests one after another. The building was not to have any columns so that its interior could be used freely like a gymnasium; the storage room, which needed to be protected at all costs, was to be positioned 12.5 meters above sea level following the historical records of tsunamis and had to be fireproofed with reinforced concrete; and its roof, speaking from experience, had to be gabled, and considerations for salt damage called for it to be thatched with a non-metallic material.

I could not figure out how to resolve the plan or how to even position the building. I reworked it again and again. What settled the design was the budget. The possibilities converged as the inessentials were cut away from around the most crucial project requirements. There were only so many solutions that were possible with a budget so low.

Hitoshi Watanabe was the member of my staff that was given charge of the project. Watanabe was an "*otaku*" in today's terms. He was clumsy at dealing with people and practically hopeless at reading situations. However, the level of determination and concentration that he exhibited when working out how to fulfill the required objectives of a plan was extraordinary. The fact that this odd character was treated like a son by Katsuhiro Onishi, the carpenter that had played a major role in the building's construction, made a great difference for the project. Indeed, one can even credit it as being their joint work.

The collection continued to grow after the building's completion. I have been told that what had first started as a collection of 20,000 items had grown to 60,000 over the course of two decades. The repository has reached its capacity and extra shelves have been inserted into the room for fishing tools in the form of mezzanine floors. Fishing tools that are no longer being used are flooding into the museum. This is telling of the great pace at which our times are changing. While all of the items are precious primary sources of folk culture, they would be discarded as bulk waste if they are not taken in by the museum. There is thus no choice but to accept them. The museum now has one of the nation's greatest collections of valuable items related to fishing that include boats, nets, and tools.

In inverse proportion to the growing collection, the museum's finances are becoming increasingly strained with each coming year. It is an obvious challenge for a private foundation to manage what really should be a publicly-funded operation. It is a very absurd situation. But what is to be done? The museum is now facing a critical moment.

House No.14, Tsukuba

A House Named by its Owner

This is also a house that represents an extreme of low-cost projects. The clients, Masayuki Inoue and Yuki Nakaigawa, were a pair of active contemporary ceramic artists and also friends. I held a liking for the pure and unworldly nature of the couple. Influenced by his teacher, Kimpei Nakamura, Inoue made fired objet pieces colored gaudily in gold and red which were sure to make anyone exclaim, "What in the world is this!" Nakaigawa's work was characterized by their textures and strange shapes that resembled fruits or viscera. They both created large-scale work. They have even made quite a few pieces that almost reach two meters.

I was asked to design their house on a lot that they had found in the mountains of Tsukuba after having been forced to relocate when their former home was caught in the path of a newly planned road. They were both starting to become known as artists at the time, yet avant-garde ceramics do not sell easily. While they could have made a decent income from making bowls and plates, they never made such things. They had their hearts firmly set on making ceramic objet pieces only. They were determined about being artists and not potters. But what could I say; it was this stubbornness that appealed to me. There was thus no money. I had just recovered my breath after completing the Sea-Folk Museum, and again I was faced with a sigh-inducing budget.

The first thing that came to mind was a rented house that I had lived in when I was young. It was an extremely crude and simple house that a farmer had carpenters build for him, but it was sufficient as a place to live in. A four-and-a-half *tatami* mat room, six-mat room, kitchen, and bathroom were squeezed brilliantly into the square one-story house that measured 3 ken on each side (1 ken is approximately 1.8 meters). It was arranged in a four-square plan that was proportioned to the 1.5-ken module that carpenters were most comfortable working with. As it should be, a plan that can be easily made by a carpenter is cheaper. Moreover, the cost of the framework of a wooden building up to its ridgepole is relatively inexpensive to begin with. Once the frame is completed, one just needs to add a roof and partitions and then you have a house. In considering this, I decided that instead of designing the house, it would be better to leave the majority of the plan to the carpenter's control, such that the house would be only "half-designed".

I composed the spaces using a grid of 1.5 ken, 1 ken, and 1.5 ken. The atelier space was positioned on the ground level in order to allow heavy objects such as the kiln to be placed on the floor. I put the living spaces on the upper level, which could be entered by a bridge from the road. As the second floor was to be a private zone, I extended a terrace beneath the eaves and enabled it to be closed off as needed with a shutter window. Inoue himself had inserted the acrylic panes in the slits of the shutter to save expenses.

The carpenter, Teiichi Sugita, read into our intentions well and put sturdy rounded columns in place of the four somewhat bulky square columns that were drawn in the plans where the beams came together at the center of the house. He put so much of his energy into the project that he actually collapsed after the building was completed.

Due to the fact that I dislike giving titles to the houses that I design, we have referred to them bluntly in my office according to the order in which they were designed. This house was supposed to become "House No.14". Inoue, however, must have felt that this did not do it justice for the effort that was put into building it. He named it the "Black House" and this has since become its alias.

A small single-story wooden house was built afterwards as a separate wing for accommodating the client's father who had been displaced by the Great Hanshin Earthquake. A garage shed was also added several years later. The artists' works have grown larger and larger since they acquired their new atelier and garden. To this day, there is still no sign of an end to the pair's creativity.

House No.15, Suginami

The Black Room that is Not Black

I was asked to renovate an apartment unit by Akiko Moriyama, who had made a dazzling career switch from being a vigorous professional bureaucrat to a keen editor. I could not put down the offer from this friend of ten years' standing. Moriyama owned a flat in an apartment building that was about twenty years old, but she had acquired a separate, smaller room in the same building and wanted it to be remodeled as a guest room. A look at the room revealed that it had the common "2LDK" layout [with two bedrooms and a living/dining/kitchen area] and was as generic a room as could be. It had an off-the-shelf metal door at its entrance, silver aluminum door and window frames, vinyl wallpaper, and a prefabricated bathroom unit. It is tough to make something substantial out of such things.

She told me that she had a budget of five million yen; she wanted a big Yayoi Kusama pumpkin painting on the wall; she wanted to put a glass piece by Yukio Nakagawa in the room; she needed me to make the space suitable for these things; she was going to let me take care of the rest; and she was purposely not going to look at the design. Moriyama's requests were frank, just like her personality. This is the most difficult kind of order for any architect to deal with. It was the first and last time that I was ever given requests like this. I followed her words anxiously and never showed her the design, while she, too, never once came to check on the project even during construction.

There was no way to make a Yayoi Kusama or Yukio Nakagawa piece look to be in place by working with half-heartedly made walls. An experiment to peel the vinyl cloth and plasterboard backing off the walls fortunately revealed solid concrete. There was no way not to make use of it. While being careful around the joints of the door and window frames, I shaped the space by peeling away at that vinyl wallpaper that was so full of ostentation and deceit. This was all that was done to the room, but the concrete walls, which must have been made without ever even dreaming of being exposed, gave off a nice sense of presence. They were raw, rough, deep, and warm. They gave me a feeling like that of meeting an elderly farmer in the fields of the countryside. After denuding the walls, I simply just built storage units and lay *tatami* mats on the floor.

When all was done, Kusama's pumpkin appeared to have settled in comfortably and Nakagawa's objet seemed to have found its spot. I casually named the project the "Black Room" simply because it immediately followed the "Black House", but for some reason its name seems to fit the space perfectly. Perhaps it is because of the atmosphere in the room. The only color that comes to mind inside the room is black. Indeed, I have never once been asked why it is called the Black Room, despite the fact that black was not even used anywhere in the space.

House No.18, Ito

Like A Woven Story

I met the client couple through an acquaintance. The husband, Masahiro Takahashi, worked at the public office of Yokohama and was an avid reader. One could tell that he was well-learned just from his appearance. His wife, Emiko Hirasawa, was known as a textile artist. She was of a small build but operated an enormous wooden weaver. She was full of vitality and I was always overwhelmed by her energy. The couple had once lived in Egypt and their impressions from then had made them want to live in a large, airy space. They had decided to locate to Usami on the Izu Peninsula after acquiring a hillside lot there.

Having been assured oddly gleefully by Hirasawa that the site should not be any problem at all because it was not too steep, I was stunned when I visited it. The slope was so steep that it was difficult to even remain standing without grabbing hold of a tree. The site was on a north-facing slope and shaped like a disfigured fan. It was foreseeable that construction would be extremely difficult as the site narrowed where it met the road. Further concerns arose when a string of earthquakes promptly shook Izu and made it apparent that the cost of the foundations would be eating away a considerable portion of the budget.

The design process was arduous. Takahashi was knowledgeable about buildings to begin with because he had studied at an architecture school, while Hirasawa was very particular about her lifestyle in a way characteristic of artists. An architect must interpret the ideas of the client while giving them reality, but the difficulty of the site far exceeded their understanding of it. And there was also the issue of cost. Their ideas were not in agreement with their budget.

Regardless of which project, I always feel that the act of designing a house is like a combat sport. There were several moments when the project was about to be called off completely. The building was realized only because Rika Ota, the staff member from my office in charge of the project, worked with great perseverance as she tried to calm me whenever I was about to snap, soothed the client, and negotiated with the contractor. I truly appreciated her efforts. After a temporary steel-frame platform was built to aid the construction work, pylons were driven into the ground, a floor slab and retaining walls were made in reinforced concrete, and a simple two-story wooden house was placed upon it.

Again, it seemed that the client wanted a title for the house. The "Weaver's House" was the name that Ota and Hirasawa chose together. I think it is a good name as it brings to mind the character of the building and the client's work. Now, after about fifteen years since its completion, trees cover the site that had been dug up during construction and flowers grow on the approach path. The thick larch-wood flooring that was laid in response to the client's request for a sturdy floor has turned amber and emits a great quality. Every time I visit a project that was realized through a struggle, I feel very happy to be able to experience how its spaces have matured within the life of its client.

House No.19, Kanazawa

A Craftman's Labyrinth

Kimpei Nakamura, the prominent avant-garde ceramic artist, approached me about rebuilding his family home in Kanazawa. Kimpei-san (as I will refer to him from here on, with no disrespect) was the teacher of the aforementioned Masayuki Inoue of the

Black House in Tsukuba, but I have been acquainted with Kimpei-san for longer. Kimpei-san's house in Tokyo was designed by Yutaka Saito and is a masterpiece that could also be considered to be his debut project. It is a brilliant house. I was hesitant to take on the project as I knew how difficult it would be to make something that could match this house, but I found myself accepting Kimpei-san's offer as if drawn by the magnetic pull of his artwork.

My conjectures are always too optimistic. This is my innate fault and a terrible habit. I discovered the true difficulty of the project after I had accepted it. Kimpei-san was actually just one of four clients. Among them was his elderly father, Baizan Nakamura, who was a well-known potter in Kanazawa. He was laid-back and always smiling in front of guests. He seemed to be a good-natured elderly man with a humble demeanor at first sight, yet one could easily imagine that he held a highly strict eye for quality. I had been told that the man was savvy of the very essences of the deeply sophisticated Kanazawa culture. I recall a time when he served me green tea. Upon picking up a seemingly ordinary tea bowl, I was surprised by its exquisite texture and balance and astonished again by its subtle qualities when I put it to my lips. He was that kind of a person.

Kimpei-san and his younger brothers, Takuo-san and Kohei-san, were all prominent potters, but they made work of completely different styles. I somehow had to make a place for this family to live and work together within the confined area of the site. To make things even more difficult, Baizan-san and his sons each had their own opinions about the architecture. The given conditions for the project were dizzying. I did not think that I could measure up to them. I had felt like I really should not have accepted the offer.

There was a large aged pine tree near the entrance to the site and another stood further within it. I decided to leave them as they were. The former residence had been centered on an eight-*tatami* mat *shoin* room with an external *engawa* corridor that Baizan-san had arranged the design of. There was nothing extravagant or special about it, but the space held a wonderful sense of depth and density. I still cannot clearly explain how such an effect could possibly have been achieved. I suspect that it had to do with the subtle dimensioning of heights and widths and the thicknesses of the building members. The space needed to be dismantled, but I decided to reconstruct it and to set it at the center of the new house. Essentially, I had decided that the two pine trees and Baizan-san's *shoin* were all that should remain unchanged, while everything else was considered unimportant.

As the area available for the buildings to be placed was limited, I put the living and atelier spaces for Takuo-san in three stories on the left side of the entrance; the spaces for Kohei-san and Baizan-san in three stories on the right side; the *shoin* at front center where it could be used by Kimpei-san when he returned home; and the spaces for Kohei-san at the very back of the site. The ground floor levels of the living spaces were made in reinforced concrete, while the other levels were made in steel. The flat roofs made in consideration of snowfall gave the residence the appearance of a cluster of boxes. The exterior walls from the second level and above were finished with layered galvanized steel sheets in order to provide the pine trees with a subdued backdrop.

The design process proved to be extremely challenging as was expected, for I had to explain to each of them why things were shaped as they were and why certain materials were used. They were all very curious. I was barraged with questions, particularly by Takuo-san. As one who chooses forms and materials more through intuition than by logic, I was baffled in my attempts to explain these things. If I am any better at giving explanations for forms and materials now, a large part of that can be attributed to this project.

The residents are experts of culture. And as one might expect of such people, they have a very refined sense for how to live in a house. The plain buildings have become like galleries for exhibiting their works of art. Any shortcomings with the building have been satisfied by the artwork. A building is also a vessel, after all. Just as is true of Baizan-san's tea bowls, I have realized anew that it is the quality of the empty parts and the voids which are of most importance.

Chihiro Art Museum Azumino
From the Golden Rice Paddies

Kaoru Mende, the lighting designer, introduced me to Takeshi Matsumoto and his wife Yuriko who were thinking about building a museum. The couple and I were of about the same age. I met them roughly a year after the Sea-Folk Museum had been completed. Takeshi was the eldest brother of the famous picture book artist Chihiro Iwasaki. His appearance spoke of a good upbringing, while I could tell that Yuriko had a quick mind. The two of them had developed their museum together hand-in-hand, with Takeshi directing the museum operations and Yuriko conducting the administration.

The couple was thinking about making an annex in Chihiro Iwasaki's birthplace of Azumino after fifteen years had passed since they established the picture book museum on the property of Chihiro's former home in Nerima. They had told me that they were holding a competition by invitation. Considering that there was a lot of work in my office at the time and noting that the couple was not familiar with architecture or design competitions, I proposed to support them by taking up a position as a member of the jury. They must have discussed the matter together for several days. I was contacted a while later and was told that they instead wanted me to participate in the competition as a contender. Knowing that I was just one of about fifteen architects that they had invited, I decided to submit a proposal without putting too much concern into it.

A picture book can be broken down into many elements: the pictures like those drawn by Chihiro, the literary story, and the editorial design that structures them. As I thought about this, I came to feel that a conventional museum made to just display the artwork would not be adequate. As the competition only called for concepts and a general overview, I presented an idea to make an inconspicuous building that would function as something between a museum and library.

The jury was formed of board members of the foundation and included impressive characters such as the theatrical director Tadasu Iizawa, who was the committee's head; the film director Yoji Yamada; actress Tetsuko Kuroyanagi; and Zemmei Matsumoto, who was a member of the Diet. They selected me as the designer, perhaps because they had liked the vagueness of my proposal that allowed it to be developed into anything. One never knows what opportunities can arise from a simple encounter.

I will never forget about the first time I visited the project site when I was preparing my proposal. The Hakuba mountain range was visible in the distance, capped with the first snow under a clear autumn sky, and all around me there were golden fields of rice. It was like a gold carpet. Clear water bubbled along the gently terraced site through the irrigation channels. It was an enchanting scene.

I thought that there was something very unnatural about the plan to make a village-operated park there and to build the museum within it. Would it not be better to leave it as it is? I had sincerely felt so. Perhaps I should have been failed as a contestant at that point. If the fields needed to be destroyed to make a park and the building, however, I knew that I had to create something that was greater than what would be lost. This was quite a difficult challenge. Days of agony continued as I struggled with the design. I studied ideas while thinking only about how to make the building inconspicuous and to merge it with the surrounding landscape.

I realized that the overall volume of the building could be made to appear the smallest if I shaped the roof as a series of small gables. Creating these as modules ensured that the impression of the whole would not change with later expansions. By using local larch wood and finishing the walls with a mix of local sand, a strange museum was completed that looked like a birdhouse or a barn. It was obvious that it was best for the building to be inconspicuous in a place like that, where the greatest pleasures were in the mountains, rivers, fields, and the clear air.

Since its opening, the museum has been visited by many more people than was expected. The stream of visitors has not subsided even today, sixteen years after its completion. The first expansion was made eleven years ago when a multipurpose room and exhibition rooms were added for the museum's international collection of picture books. Collection storage and research areas were also added three years ago. The museum has grown from its original area of 1,580 square meters to a respectful 3,200 square meters after the repeated expansions. And yet, the impression of the whole has not changed at all from the start. Visitors may not even notice the changes.

Children run around in the park while their fathers, tired from long hours of driving the family, sleep leisurely on lounge chairs on the museum's terrace. I often witness such sights when I visit the museum. The building occupies only a small part of its backdrop. It is how it should be. In the brilliant landscape of Azumino, with its clear air, and under the warm light of the sun, one can find a scene of happiness that is unique to its site. I think it would have made Chihiro happy, too.

Tenshin Memorial Museum of Art, Ibaraki

The Building that Shortened My Life

I was invited to a competition to design a memorial museum for Tenshin Okakura in Izura, Ibaraki, where Tenshin had lived in seclusion with Taikan Yokoyama and Shunso Hishida. I had the fortune to beat the tough opposition and was allowed to design the museum. Having read Tenshin's *Book of Tea* like a bible from when I was a college student, this was a project that I definitely wanted to work on. I fished out the tattered book and re-read it to refresh my mind before making my proposal.

Although the competition only called for general block plans, I focused my proposal on presenting ideas for how to make the spaces all the way down to the exhibition rooms. I also pointed out how the conventional methods of exhibiting Japanese art were not very good. I had believed that the practice of using bright lighting only took away from the original brilliance of the artwork, which really needed to be viewed under dim, indirect side-lighting, much in the way that a *tokonoma* alcove is lit by the light reflecting off of a *tatami* mat floor.

I was shocked by what I was told when I went to the prefectural office upon winning the competition. They wanted the design to be completed in half a year. Moreover, the timeframe from the start to finish of construction was to be one year. And yet I was dealing with a 6,000 square meter building that was required to provide an atmospheric environment suitable for exhibiting the delicate Japanese art under terrible seaside conditions. It seemed practically impossible. When I asked what would happen if I told them that I could not do it, they said that another design office would take over and work from my scheme. Given no choice, I told them that I would do it. I just had to make do somehow by pulling together all of my knowledge and experience from the past. A preparation room was established where I engaged in meetings with Takeshi Okubo, who later became the museum's director, and Sadayuki Nagayama, who became a sort of a leader figure among the curators.

There was simply no time in the construction schedule. The experience that I had gained through the Sea-Folk Museum project proved to be useful. By using precast concrete, the building members could be fabricated in separate parts at several factories and carried in from a port nearby to be assembled on site. The greater quality of the concrete also promised a higher level of protection from salt damage. We broke down the complicated drawings into modules that could be prefabricated and worked out how the building should be assembled with the structural engineer Kunio Watanabe. The building consisted of 1,200 prefabricated components. The fabricators had to make detail drawings for each of the components. It was an enormous task that required a great amount of work on our side as well, as each of the drawings had to be verified. I spent countless late nights checking through them.

Construction was also rushed. A goshawk nest was found nearby the site soon after construction had begun. It became apparent from the standpoint of environmental conservation that dynamite could not be used for excavating the hard bedrock. We were told that the goshawk would be scared away. We could thus only dig with rock drills, but the underground mechanical space was of a considerable size. Much time was lost there. After that part was cleared, an error was discovered in the structural design for the prefabricated components. These then had to be fixed somehow. More time was lost. The situation was critical. The museum's opening day had already been set and highly treasured paintings associated with Tenshin were being planned to be displayed specially to commemorate the event.

I cannot forget the time when I visited the site on my own out of worry on the second day of the new year, just three months before completion day. The construction site was empty. The structure was almost the only thing that had been completed. The roof still had to be made and the exterior and interior had to be finished in three months. I recall bracing myself for the demise of my office that I had struggled to establish through all the years. But, miraculously, the building was completed at the end of March thanks to the full effort of the contractor, the representatives from the prefectural office, and my staff. It was a tightrope walk from start to finish in which we had just barely made every step. This was a project that literally shortened my life.

Although it was built in much turmoil, once opened, the building came to be known as one of the most visited public museums, despite its terribly inconvenient location at the northernmost tip of the prefecture. I think this was an achievement not only of Tenshin's notoriety, but also the museum's splendid exhibition projects. Without a doubt, a large role was played by Okubo and Nagayama, who had both witnessed what it had taken for the museum to be realized.

The building luckily suffered few damages at the time of the earthquake disaster of March 11th, 2011. When I called in the following morning, I was genuinely overjoyed to hear the security guard tell me, "Everything is fine. It is such a wonderful building!" This is something that I am still proud of. Unfortunately, a septic tank beneath the nearby parking area was damaged and it took several months for the museum to be reopened. I was deeply moved by the efforts that the museum had made to quickly reopen the public facility for the community during that time of great difficulty.

House No.21, Setagaya

Living on a Street

Kenichi Okuno, the client of the house and a close friend of mine, was an editor of a pottery magazine before he later became the director of a crafts gallery operated by the Seibu Department Store. He was a hard drinker and also extremely shy, but he would say bold things to compensate for this. Okuno suddenly dropped by one day and joyously announced, as though if to make a great confession, that he had bought some land. I was happy to hear about my friend's decision, but I was stunned when he showed me the plan of the site. It was the narrow portion of a flag-shaped site that had been part of a small-scale residential development. He had bought the section of the site that had been the private approach path to the housing lot behind it, which had been connected to another street.

We shared a laugh when I jokingly pointed out to him that he was going to end up living in the streets after all. The lot was 4 meters wide and 18 meters deep. Furthermore, its north side was under a setback regulation. Even while I knew that it was for Okuno, I was anxious whether anyone could actually live on such a site. Despite his nonchalant appearance, he was the owner of quite a collection of books because of his job. He had also recently married a lacquer-ware artist and she needed to have a workspace. The house was to be just for the two of them because they had no plans for having children, but this situation changed midway through the design process and the number of residents grew.

I designed a wooden truss frame comprised of three tunnel-like tiers and covered its outer walls with metal sheeting. Although deep in length, the rooms were only 3 meters in width and were extremely narrow. I left the beams exposed and inserted boards between them to create bookshelves as a way of freeing as much space as possible. I asked the clients to use their books to finish the walls, which were made simply with structural plywood boards due to the limited budget. The ceiling heights were also set very low at 2 meters in order to fit the third story within the regulations on the building envelope. The staff member of my office in charge of the project was Paddy Tomesen from the Netherlands. He was over 190 centimeters tall and could almost hit his head on the rafters. I cannot forget the sight of this giant standing on the construction site of the miniscule house. It was particularly funny to watch the shorter carpenters scold the taller man who was still a novice at the time.

After construction was finished, the tiny house initially intended for two was occupied by four residents because the clients had decided to take in their mother who had been ill. The house was put on sale when my friend Okuno passed away ten years later due to illness and is now resided by a young couple that has taken a liking in the strange little building.

Tokamachi Public Library

A Large Roof in a City of Snow

I was given the opportunity to design this building after participating in an invited competition. The project was for making a library in Tokamachi, which is known as a snowy city where snowfalls of over 4.5 meters have been recorded. The area had once flourished from textile manufacturing, but no sign of this past can be discerned today. Both the city's population and its streets are in decline. One can already sense somewhat of a lonely feeling in the air when walking through it. The site was located outside of the city center on a gently sloping lot situated above the terraced embankment of the Shinano River.

There was a relatively large one-story supermarket called the Lion-do in front of the train station. I had wandered inside it while thinking about what kind of scheme I could propose. I noticed then that there were many tired middle-aged salary men, elderly people with bent backs, and some students and youths who did not seem to be shopping, but were there just to pass time. Perhaps they had been waiting for trains or buses, but I suspected that they were simply there to be among the bustle of other people. After all, it was cold outside and the streets were empty.

That was when I had thought, what if I made a space like a market where people could gather and be sheltered from the snow? It would be a waste for a library to only be a place for reading and borrowing books. Surely people would gather naturally if I could create a comfortable space open for anyone to lounge in. The building could be a place where people from various ages and professions would gather around the books.

Essentially, my idea was to create a snow shelter that could be used as a library. This plan called for a sturdy roof. I looked around the city and noted that buildings that had large roofs designed to shed snow, such as gymnasiums, were all heavily worn. It was because the snow had cut into their surfaces like files. The roofs designed to shed snow were also inconvenient as it took until spring for the large mounds of deposited snow to melt. Thinking about this, it seemed that the building needed to be designed to accumulate the snow on its roof. Of course, as the site was in a heavy snowfall area, I needed to consider for a snow load of about 1 ton per square meter. Additionally, unbalanced loads needed to be accounted for because there was no guarantee that the snow would melt uniformly on the roof. A robust structural system with plenty of built-in redundancy was needed. It seemed that precast concrete was the obvious choice for making a strong flat roof with a large span. It was the best option, and the only one.

With the heavy snowfall, it was also important for a countermeasure to be considered against snow cornices. Large snow cornices can weigh over 1 ton. The parapets, which are a vulnerable part of buildings to begin with, could be damaged. The building took on a rather top-heavy appearance because I designed the parapets to prevent the formation of snow cornices by giving them pointed tops and running electric heating wires through them. The elevation may lack a sense of sharpness, but it did not matter as it was the space inside that was important. The main demographic expected to use the building were the youths. I went to several high schools to hold public hearings while working on the design. I asked questions to groups of about ten students. When I asked them what they did after school, they all gave the same reply as if it was fixed and told me that they went home to study. I could not get them to speak their true voices while their teachers were present at the gatherings. Things got interesting after I asked the teachers to leave.

The atmosphere in the room would brighten immediately. It turned out that most of the children actually went to chat at their friends' houses, where they said they had the most fun. When I asked them why they had to be at their houses, they said they had nowhere else to go. When I asked them whether they would go to a place where anyone could casually gather, they all said, "Definitely". This gave me confidence about everything I had been proposing through my design.

I had also asked the students where they would go if a friend came to visit them from Tokyo. They said there was nowhere that they could show them to. In other words, there were no places that they could boast about. While a library was what I had been asked to design, I reconfirmed at that moment that what was really needed was a place where people could gather and that they could be proud about.

I made a terraced atrium full of shelves so that the great number of books could be seen from anywhere within the large space beneath the big roof. After being given such a space, surely the students do not feel embarrassed about inviting their friends from Tokyo anymore. I am told that the number of users of the building exceeds 300,000 people every year. This is quite an impressive usage rate for a public facility. I would like to think that this was achieved because my ideas for place-making had worked effectively there.

Makino Museum of Plants and People

A Return to the Forest

This was a project that arose from a funny turn of fate. It is the representative project of my forties.

Tomitaro Makino (1862-1957) held a great affection for plants and called himself the "spirit of the flowers". Known for the *Makino's Illustrated Flora of Japan*, he left behind over 400,000 plant specimens and names for over 1,500 different plants. He is identified as the father of botany and is a giant of his field. He was such a fascinating and unparalleled character that he still has many passionate fans. A museum commemorating Dr. Makino has stood quietly within the grounds of the Makino Botanical Garden on Mount Godai in the outskirts of the city of Kochi. This project was for the construction of a new exhibition hall honoring Dr. Makino and a plant research facility within the botanical garden.

The project came to me through a series of chance connections. I was first approached by Kazuhiko Satomi, who was the designer of the Sea-Folk Museum's exhibitions. He wanted me to meet the director of the Makino Botanical Garden who was thinking about making a new prefectural museum and happened to be a distant relative of his. Director Takeshi Satomi had been advised by Toshitaka Hidaka, the renowned scientist of ethology, to look at the Sea-Folk Museum as a precedent for his new museum and had already visited the building. I had already been acquainted with Masanori Kagioka, who held an important role in cultural affairs in Kochi, from the time when he was the director of the Saison Museum of Art. I also already had met Mayor Daijiro Hashimoto of Kochi when he had visited the Sea-Folk Museum.

I was given a special commission to design the project with the help of the mayor, who had proposed the project to the prefectural council. Knowing that I had been given a great responsibility, I was keen to make a building suitable for Dr. Makino no matter what. The scheme that was being drawn by the prefectural office when I entered the project was a square, four-story building. It was much too inappropriate. I figured that it would be better to lower the height of the building volume as much as possible in consideration of both the museum's functions and the scenery of Mount Godai. I made a scheme with detached buildings that set the management, research, and storage wing apart from the exhibition wing.

Director Satomi, who was formerly a civil servant, was in his early sixties and was a bright, volatile, and extremely stubborn character, just like a stereotypical Kochi citizen. As a dear admirer of Dr. Makino, he was unhappy with the state of the botanical garden that was inadequate for displaying its collection. The director did not get along with Yasuyuki Kiyota of the prefectural department of natural environmental preservation. Kiyota, who was on loan from the Ministry of Home Affairs and later became the prefectural chief of general affairs, was still in his late thirties but had an impressive career.

Director Satomi claimed that he needed a minimum area of 10,000 square meters. Contrarily, Kiyota, who held concerns for the budget, was set on a figure of 3,000 square meters. The two often argued before me and I had to calm them on more than one occasion to keep them from grappling with one another. The buildings' distinctively large eaves, which shelter exterior spaces accounting for almost one third of their area, was actually an idea that I had proposed in desperation to bring compromise to the two who would not bend their positions in fear of losing face. The eaves allowed for there to be an area of 6,000 square meters when only considering the interior space, but over 8,000 square meters with the semi-outdoor spaces included. I made the structure from wood in light of the mayor's wish to promote the use of timber in construction.

After conducting numerous studies, I arrived at the conclusion that the use of any conventional building system based on uniformity would be too rigid for realizing the spaces that I was striving to create. I could not get such spaces to resonate with the attitude that Dr. Makino had held towards nature. I thus decided to create organically-shaped wooden structures that would hug the mountain surface and to employ a site plan that could minimize the need for grading. I wanted the building to eventually be hidden by the trees and become one with the forest.

I struggled with designing the organically-formed roof. Kochi was known for the frequent passing of typhoons and the site was on top of a mountain. I was warned numerous times by a local architect that the rain in Kochi poured like a waterfall and that it would rise from below. I made studies at one-to-one scale and tested them by making actual samples on site. The roof was made with extremely complicated edge details, but it has yet to leak even a drop of rain.

Over ten years have passed since the completion of the building. Satomi, who had designed the botanical garden's exhibitions, took the prefectural civil servant examination and became a curator there after the project was finished. He has since planned many exhibition projects and has also been given charge of fieldwork assignments through which he works directly with the plants. The trees and plants related to Dr. Makino that have been planted around the buildings have grown fuller year by year. I have observed this with great joy. Today, the buildings appear to be at ease as they stand sheltered in the arms of the rich forest.

House No.22

Inconspicuous, Tasteful, and Refined

I was asked to refurbish the house of the renowned creative director Kazuko Koike. It was a renovation and expansion project. Known as a splendid character whose work crosses between the fields of design and art, Koike directs the various displays of the Seibu Department Store while even managing an exhibition space in Sagacho. She is also known for her friendly personality. We had been acquainted since the mid-80s, when I had participated in the Ise-Shima Art Village Project organized by the Seibu Saison Group. The occasion was also what had led to the Sea-Folk Museum project. She had an extensive network and was likely to be acquainted with many famous architects, yet for some reason she offered me with the commission. I suspect that she might have thought that I wouldn't do anything too eccentric.

Her single-story wooden house had a two-story steel-frame annex behind it that had been built to the requests of her mother, who had been known as a teacher of dressmaking. The wooden portion was in very poor condition, but it was like a precious cultural heritage site with spaces full of traces of the chic postwar lifestyle. The air inside it carried the history of half a century. There was no way not to preserve it. I decided to save and restore this portion while constructing a new two-story steel building on the sliver of land remaining alongside the road. This was complicated by the fact that two parking spaces needed to be fit underneath it. A considerable span of space had to be freed. The parking spaces were necessary because Koike's husband, Ken, had a hobby of riding bikes and cars. Unfortunately, part of this parking space recently had to be filled-in to meet their new need for a storage shed.

I created a steel-frame structure by bracing cruciform columns formed by joining L-angles and gave the building an envelope made of thin corrugated steel sheets. It was a plain and conventional composition up to there, but as it was Koike's house, I sought to give it a subtle twist that would set it apart from the others. I had the wall facing the street coated on site with a dull black paint containing a slight shine to make it emit a strong sense of presence while still keeping it subdued.

The steel frame structure was intended to only assume a secondary role, as the main feature of the house was the wooden structure preserved at its center. My hope was for it to be inconspicuous, tasteful, and refined. Some of Koike's artistic friends installed artwork in the building after it was completed and have given further color to its spaces. I am glad to know that the building is playing a part in providing their artwork with a backdrop.

Fuji RINRI Seminar House

Constructing the New and Proper

My secretary, Kyoko Asano, is a true *shitamachi* character that had worked at the Saison Group before I had requested her to come to my office. I was contacted through her by a former colleague of hers named Toru Yamamoto about a project to design a new training center for the RINRI Institute of Ethics. Yamamoto, who had originally been an able producer at a music production, was an advisor to the chairman of the organization's board of directors.

This was how I had met the chairman, Toshiaki Maruyama. He was of about my age and had a friendly personality, and he treated me like a friend from when we first met. He had both the appearance and heart of a youth despite being middle-aged. After informing me that the organization had been gaining members and were expanding their training activities, he shared his thoughts and visions that he held for the new building.

The RINRI Institute of Ethics was a corporation that promoted a movement to reshape our ways of living through reconsidering the distinct temperaments and human relationships that have been an attribute of the country from olden times. I give this rough description because I obviously do not really understand it in detail. I could, however, relate to their cause when thinking about it in relation to state of the construction industry. It seemed relevant to how ethics in the construction sites were deteriorating particularly after the era of the bubble economy.

I held a sense that the construction companies and craftsmen were increasingly losing their pride as economy and efficiency came to dominate the foreground. Cherish the craft and make things to the highest quality possible. This was the moral code that the construction practice of the country had been built upon, but it was falling apart. As illustrated by Ivan Illich's ideas of "shadow work", this was a culture that could not be mixed with economics and so the world no longer appreciated it. All things occurring in the same age are interrelated in some way.

And so I strived to make the project neatly and with precision, such that it could become, as a result, a noble building. I also demanded that this attitude be maintained on the construction site. Additionally, this was a building in which I sought for technological innovation, because I had agreed with Chairman Maruyama that the building and its spaces should not only respect tradition, but should also invite the future.

I put particular care into perfecting the joints of the large-section laminated wood members, which was something that I had been investigating since the Sea-Folk Museum. Specifically, I wanted to create joints that did not employ steel plates, so that the loads would be carried directly from wood to wood. This was a challenge that nobody had yet achieved. In order to realize it, I analyzed traditional joinery techniques and sought to translate the ideas behind them into modern structural formulas and methodologies by using computers. I succeeded to create an organic structural system by building off of the properties of the joints. This process went very well.

The site was in a cold area where temperatures dropped to 20 degrees centigrade below freezing in the winter. However, having wanted to create large openings along the courtyard, I used a type of thermal glass that was still under development at the time. Heat could be generated in the glass by passing a weak electric current through it. It was set to maintain a temperature of about 18 degrees inside. This experiment was also a first.

Over ten years have passed since the building's completion, but it has always been taken good care of and has not changed at all from when it was first built. I do not know of any other building that is so well maintained. It is really being used with tremendous care. I feel greatly fortunate for this as an architect.

Mogamigawa Park Center House

A Crescent Moon of Glass

Shigeru Hori was a specialist of agricultural landscapes and a professor at the University of Tokyo that I met through Osamu Shinohara. Probably owing to his sociable personality, Hori was often consulted alongside his research work about community-building projects initiatives in Yamagata prefecture such as the scenic restoration project of the Ginzan hot springs. He put enormous energy into his work and had traveled all over the region by foot. Hori asked me to design a building for a committee on which he served as the chairman.

It was an odd project. They wanted to invite a national tree-planting fair to a park area on the banks of the Mogami River. They needed a central pavilion as a venue for events held during the fair, but wanted to use it for various exhibits at the same time. The building was to be used as a local community facility after the fair was over, but they also wanted it to function as a greenhouse. Their requests were full of conflicting programs. The tree-planting fair was planned to be held from June to August. The inland area of Yamagata experienced the foehn phenomenon, however, and it was where the nation's hottest temperatures have been recorded. The summer there was hot beyond expectations. The area also experienced heavy snowfall in the winter. The building was to perform as a greenhouse in the winter, but it needed to permit regular usage in the other seasons as well. These things made it a task of unprecedented difficulty. It was a fittingly radical project for Hori to have proposed. The issues that needed to be addressed were aplenty—from the large spans for the greenhouse; heat insulation and cooling for regular use; heat exchange through ventilation; space heating for winter use; a snow-shedding roof; to the scenery and landscape.

The building had to be glass in order to function as a greenhouse. The structure had to be highly transparent, but also needed to be planned for the weight of the snow. At the same time, although seemingly contradictory, details had to be developed for the large glass surfaces so that they would shed snow. The building also needed to be given a distinctive form as it was to be a symbol for the expansive park. I imagined a fluid form that would echo with the park landscape along the Mogami River and the mountains in the distance. What if it took a fluid shape like a crescent moon? This was my initial vision.

I had already worked with organic forms in the Makino project, but the drainage slopes of this roof needed to be shaped accurately from top to bottom for it to shed snow. A conical form came to mind. A bowl-shaped roof could allow the snow to fall properly to the bottom. By cutting out a crescent shape from this bowl, I was able to geometrically extract an organic form similar to that of the Makino buildings. It was an effective solution in regard to shedding snow. The building was made to exhaust warm air as quickly as possible from the uppermost portion of its roof when not being used as a greenhouse. A large pond was created in front of the building to produce cool air that could be drawn inside. Cool tubes that utilize the earth mounds behind the building were made to reduce the burden of the mechanical thermal system inside the rooms. In the winter, only room heating was to be used while the large space was to be left unheated. Primitive computer software was employed to simulate and analyze air flows. We simply made use of whatever we could at the time.

Imagine the site covered in snow. Mount Asahi and Mount Gassan glisten like an illusion in the distance. The Mogami River flows by swiftly. And amidst it all sits what appears not to be a greenhouse, but a glass crescent moon that has descended from the sky. It is quite a scene. However, the area has deep snow and it is cold. It is unfortunate that few people will ever witness this sight.

Chihiro Art Museum Tokyo

To Reminisce and to Create

Once operations stabilized with the Chihiro Art Museum Azumino several years after it was built, a plan arose to renovate the main Chihiro Art Museum in Tokyo. The need for renovation arose because the labyrinthine building was aging in many areas after undergoing multiple expansions over the twenty five years since it was established by the Matsumoto couple in 1977. It had also become increasingly difficult for the building to meet the needs of visitors with disabilities, in spite of the fact that this had been an important goal of the museum.

I personally had really liked the labyrinthine spaces of the original building. I could lose track of where I was when I walked inside its spaces and encounter unexpected scenes. The design of the building also had a Lucien Kroll-esque vernacular taste to it. I wanted to maintain as much of its positive attributes as possible.

I presented the committee with several renovation proposals that aimed to respect the accumulated history of the building and to organize the maze-like spaces. When the actual designing was about to begin after we had reached a general consensus on the plan, a decision was made to inspect the structure of the existing building just to be sure. Yet there were no remaining drawings of the original building. Core samples of the concrete were thus taken for good measure. They revealed that the concrete was in poor shape, so much to the extent that the problem could not be remedied simply by adding anti-seismic reinforcement. It was essentially as if the building had suffered from a bad case of osteoporosis. It also became apparent that the soil quality was too poor to sustain the full weight of an enlarged building. In conclusion, there was no choice but to rebuild it anew.

Even though I had to design a new museum, I wanted to respect the memories inscribed into the site. It was usual for me to try to accommodate a complicated set of conditions by adjusting the shape of a building, but on this occasion, I purposely aimed to break the form. I maintained the vernacular taste of the original building, employed many diagonal lines, and positioned a courtyard so that it would welcome visitors inside.

But then, Kuroyanagi, a trustee, said she wanted the exterior to be red. I was baffled. Red on the exterior? I was lost. A little while later, my eyes caught the shoulder bag that Kuroyanagi always carried on her. It must have been made by the indigenous people of South America. It was finely woven in a pattern of vivid horizontal stripes in which there were several strands of an austere red. I had asked her if that was what she had meant by red, and she said yes. It was a shade of red that did not seem like it would be too strange to use on a building exterior. I had paint samples made based on it and had her make a selection on site. That was the most anxious moment of the project.

This was the list of requests for the building that the trustees Kuroyanagi, Yamada, and Zemmei Matsumoto gave me:
- Please consider that original sense of gentleness and intimacy; that sense of relief; and the sense of being hidden.
- The relationship between the artwork and observer should be made as close as possible to maintain the sense of an intimate viewing experience.
- It should be a one-of-a-kind place (different from Azumino) as it is the site where Chihiro lived for 22 years, drew her pictures, and passed away.
- The building should be unique and provide a sense of newness.
- Chihiro's drawings should be given the most importance, while the café and hall should be secondary; but they must sustain a profit from a business point of view and so should be designed to also appeal to young people.
(Kuroyanagi)
- The museum should make people smile. It could have things such as stone sculptures for children to play with.
(Yoji Yamada)
- The exhibits should be made properly so that children do not need to stretch their backs.
- It should preferably be a museum that is not uptight, where children can be free.
(Zemmei Matsumoto)

I have never heard of such imaginative requests for a design. Kuroyanagi had taken the notes during a casual meeting at a café in a hotel. She had written them on a paper table spread and each of the members had signed it. I have this saved preciously with me even now. It is my hope that the building lives up to their wishes.

House No.27

Creating, Nurturing, and Living

I met Yuumi Domoto for the first time at the home of her father, Hisao Domoto, who was a painter and a friend. She had just returned together with her husband Deane and her newborn child from living abroad. I was asked to design their house ten years later. Yuumi had become an active painter by that time and had a distinct abstract style of work. She also had another child.

The main theme of the project was centered on finding a balance between the everyday activities and the creative activities. Yuumi had been getting increasingly busy with her work, but she also needed to tend to the children. It was inevitable that she live like a shop owner who has their living quarters and work place close together. Deane wanted a space for his hobby of woodworking. The house thus essentially needed a room for Yuumi's creative work, a room for nurturing the children, and a room for the busy husband to seclude himself in. However, there did not seem to be enough space to provide for all of these things.

It would not have been wise to subdivide the house into small spaces. Their lifestyle was probably going to keep changing anyway. I think that it is better to make a large shed-like building in situations like these. After identifying the greatest building volume allowed by the zoning envelope regulations, I made a three-story steel-frame structure with an atelier and woodworking space on the first floor.

Special care must be taken when making spaces for the creative activities of an artist. Their work can be influenced by the form or space of the architecture if it is too strong or noisy. On the other hand, there would also be something deceitful about the architecture if nothing was done at all. It is difficult to assume a neutral existence. I think it is best to allow structure and function to shape these kinds of spaces. This approach leaves no room for the arbitrariness of the architect.

The shed-like building has managed to support the residents' creative and everyday activities for eight years. Their creative activities have expanded and their children have grown bigger. Recently, the house has entered a new phase of its life as the family has invited their grandmother to live together with them after remodeling the first floor.

作品データ
Data on Works

凡例 legend

1. 担当　staff
2. 所在地　location
3. 主要用途　principal use
4. 敷地面積　site area
5. 建築面積　building area
6. 延床面積　total floor area
7. 構造　structure
8. 規模　scale
9. 最高高さ　maximum height
10. 協力　assistance
11. 構造設計　structural engineers
12. 設備設計　facility engineers
13. 施工　constructor
14. 竣工　completion date

海の博物館
Sea-Folk Museum

1. 渡辺仁、川村宣元
   Hitoshi Watanabe, Nobuharu Kawamura
2. 三重県鳥羽市　Toba-shi, Mie
3. 博物館　museum
4. 18,058.83㎡
5. 収蔵庫　Repository：2,173.33㎡
   展示棟　Exhibition Hall：1,487.30㎡
6. 収蔵庫　Repository：2,026.30㎡
   展示棟　Exhibition Hall：1,898.83㎡
7. 収蔵庫：プレキャストコンクリート造、
   一部鉄筋コンクリート造
   Repository：precast concrete,
   partly reinforced concrete
   展示棟：木造、一部鉄筋コンクリート造
   Exhibition Hall：wood,
   partly reinforced concrete
8. 収蔵庫：地上1階　Repository：1 story
   展示棟：地上2階　Exhibition Hall：2 stories
9. 収蔵庫　Repository：9,400mm
   展示棟　Exhibition Hall：13,250mm
11. 構造設計集団
    Structural Design Group Co.,Ltd.
13. 収蔵庫：鹿島建設
    Repository：Kajima Corporation
    展示棟：大棚建設
    Exhibition Hall：Ohtane Corporation
14. 収蔵庫：1989年6月　Repository：June, 1989
    展示棟：1992年6月　Exhibition Hall：
    June, 1992

No.14 筑波・黒の家
House No.14, Tsukuba

1. 吉田多津雄　Tatsuo Yoshida
2. 茨城県新治郡　Niihari-gun, Ibaraki
3. 住宅＋アトリエ　house＋atelier
4. 1,322.51㎡
5. 82.50㎡
6. 201.30㎡
7. 木造　wood
8. 地上2階　2 stories
9. 9,110mm
13. 杉田建築　Sugita Kenchiku
14. 1993年5月　May, 1993

住居No.15 杉並・黒の部屋
House No.15, Suginami

1. 蛭田和則　Kazunori Hiruta
2. 東京都杉並区　Suginami-ku, Tokyo
3. ゲストハウス　guest house
6. 39.06㎡
7. 鉄筋コンクリート造　reinforced concrete
13. 稲泉建設　Inaizumi Kensetsu
14. 1993年6月　June, 1993

住居No.18 伊東・織りの家
House No.18, Ito

1. 太田理加　Rika Ota
2. 静岡県伊東市　Ito-shi, Shizuoka
3. 住宅　house
4. 852.24㎡
5. 151.74㎡
6. 239.22㎡
7. 木造、一部鉄筋コンクリート造
   wood, partly reinforced concrete
8. 地上2階　2 stories
9. 8,270mm
11. スタディ建築事務所
    Structure Technical Design Architect Office
13. 石井工務店　Ishii Komuten Co.,Ltd.
14. 1995年9月　September, 1995

住居No.19 金沢の家
House No.19, Kanazawa

1. 太田理加　Rika Ota
2. 石川県金沢市　Kanazawa-shi, Ishikawa
3. A：住宅＋アトリエ　house＋atelier
   B・C：住宅　house　D：アトリエ　atelier
4. A：315.23㎡　B：148.79㎡　C＋D：493.36㎡
5. A：158.76㎡　B：63.81㎡
   C：94.77㎡　D：134.90㎡
6. A：328.51㎡　B：51.03㎡
   C：226.49㎡　D：232.51㎡
7. A・C：鉄筋コンクリート造＋鉄骨造
   reinforced concrete＋steel frame
   B：鉄骨造＋木造　steel frame＋wood
   D：鉄骨造　steel frame
8. A・C：地上3階　3 stories　B：地上1階　1 story
   D：地上2階　2 stories
9. A：9,970mm　B：3,400mm
   C：9,880mm　D：8,700mm
11. スタディ建築事務所
    Structure Technical Design Architect Office
13. 竹中工務店　Takenaka Corporation
14. 1996年3月　March, 1996

安曇野ちひろ美術館
Chihiro Art Museum Azumino

1. 古野洋美、吉田多津雄、片山恵仁、山田まどか
   Hiromi Furuno, Tatsuo Yoshida,
   Yoshimasa Katayama, Madoka Yamada
2. 長野県北安曇郡松川村
   Matsukawa, Kitaazumi-gun, Nagano
3. 美術館　museum
4. 11,288㎡
5. 3,433.22㎡
   (1期 1st phase：1,768.42㎡＋2期 2nd phase：
   940.76㎡＋3期 3rd phase：724.04㎡)
6. 3,206.65㎡
   (1期 1st phase：1,581.01㎡＋2期 2nd phase：
   923.99㎡＋3期 3rd phase：701.65㎡)
7. 鉄筋コンクリート造＋木造（小屋組）
   reinforced concrete＋wood (roof frame)
8. 地上1階　1 story
9. 6,170mm
11. 構造設計集団
    Structural Design Group Co.,Ltd.
12. 明野設備研究所
    Akeno Engineering Consultants Inc.
    ライティングプランナーズアソシエーツ（照明）
    Lighting Planners Associates Inc.
    (lighting planning)
13. 前田建設工業　Maeda Corporation
14. 1期：1996年6月　1st phase：June, 1996
    2期：2001年2月　2nd phase：February, 2001
    3期：2009年1月　3rd phase：January, 2009

茨城県天心記念五浦美術館
Tenshin Memorial Museum of Art, Ibaraki

1. 川村宣元、有村和浩、田井幹夫、好川拓、
   堀岡勝、大西直子、蛭田和則
   Nobuharu Kawamura, Kazuhiro Arimura,
   Mikio Tai, Taku Yoshikawa, Masaru Horioka,
   Naoko Onishi, Kazunori Hiruta
2. 茨城県北茨城市　Kitaibaraki-shi, Ibaraki
3. 美術館　museum
4. 90,077.56㎡
5. 5,449.06㎡
6. 5,847.59㎡
7. 鉄筋コンクリート造＋プレキャストコンクリート造
   reinforced concrete＋precast concrete
8. 地下1階＋地上1階　1 basement＋1 story
9. 10,910mm
10. 茨城県土木部営繕課（設計・監理）
    Ibaraki Prefectural Government
    (planning and construction supervision)
11. 構造設計集団
    Structural Design Group Co.,Ltd.
12. 明野設備研究所
    Akeno Engineering Consultants Inc.
13. 松村・岡部 JV
    Matsumura＋Okabe Joint Venture
14. 1997年3月　March, 1997

住居No.21 千歳烏山の家
House No.21, Setagaya

1. 古野洋美、パディ・トメセン
   Hiromi Furuno, Paddy Tomesen
2. 東京都世田谷区　Setagaya-ku, Tokyo
3. 住宅　house
4. 71.83㎡

5. 28.60㎡
6. 51.89㎡
7. 木造 wood
8. 地上2階 2 stories
9. 7,950mm
11. スタディ建築事務所
   Structure Technical Design Architect Office
13. 稲泉建設 Inaizumi Kensetsu
14. 1997年8月 August, 1997

十日町情報館
Tokamachi Public Library

1. 有村和浩、横井拓、片山惠仁
   Kazuhiro Arimura, Taku Yokoi,
   Yoshimasa Katayama
2. 新潟県十日町市 Tokamachi-shi, Niigata
3. 図書館 library
4. 13,007.00㎡
5. 3,083.32㎡
6. 4,498.49㎡
7. 鉄筋コンクリート造＋プレキャストコンクリート造
   reinforced concrete＋precast concrete
8. 地上2階 2 stories
9. 12,357mm
11. 構造設計集団
    Structural Design Group Co.,Ltd.
12. 明野設備研究所
    Akeno Engineering Consultants Inc.
13. 鹿島・丸山 JV
    Kajima＋Maruyama Joint Venture
14. 1999年3月 March, 1999

牧野富太郎記念館
Makino Museum of Plants and People

1. 川村宣元、神林哲也、高草大次郎、加藤成明、
   好川拓、吉田多津雄、玉田源
   Nobuharu Kawamura, Tetsuya Kambayashi,
   Daijirou Takakusa, Nariaki Kato,
   Taku Yoshikawa, Tatsuo Yoshida, Gen Tamada
2. 高知県高知市 Kochi-shi, Kochi
3. 博物館 museum
4. 44,596.30㎡
5. 5,683.73㎡
6. 7,362.26㎡
7. 鉄筋コンクリート造＋鉄骨造＋木造（小屋組）
   reinforced concrete＋steel frame＋wood
   (roof frame)
8. 本館：地上2階 Museum Building：2 stories
   展示棟：地上1階 Exhibition Hall：1 story
9. 13,000mm
11. 構造設計集団
    Structural Design Group Co.,Ltd.
12. 明野設備研究所
    Akeno Engineering Consultants Inc.
13. 竹中・香長・中勝 JV
    Takenaka＋Kacho＋Nakakatsu Joint Venture
14. 1999年3月 March, 1999

住居No.22
House No.22

1. 蛭田和則 Kazunori Hiruta
2. 東京都新宿区 Shinjuku-ku, Tokyo
3. 住居 house
4. 282.87㎡
5. 167.38㎡
   （増築部分 extension part：79.68㎡）
6. 210.73㎡
   （増築部分 extension part：91.68㎡）
7. 木造＋鉄骨造（増築部分）
   wood＋steel frame (extension part)
8. 地上2階 2 stories
9. 5,900mm
11. スタディ建築事務所
    Structure Technical Design Architect Office
13. 大栄工務店 Daiei Construction
14. 2000年11月 November, 2000

倫理研究所富士高原研修所
Fuji RINRI Seminar House

1. 川村宣元、浅野恭子、古野洋美、好川拓、
   玉田源、太田理加、沼田恭子、田井幹夫、
   高草大次郎、宮崎俊行、大西直子
   Nobuharu Kawamura, Kyoko Asano,
   Hiromi Furuno, Taku Yoshikawa,
   Gen Tamada, Rika Ota, Kyoko Numata,
   Mikio Tai, Daijirou Takakusa,
   Toshiyuki Miyazaki, Naoko Onishi
2. 静岡県御殿場市 Gotenba-shi, Shizuoka
3. 研修所 seminar house
4. 19,510.37㎡
5. 5,192.78㎡
6. 5,777.19㎡
7. 鉄筋コンクリート造＋木造（小屋組）、
   一部プレキャストコンクリート造＋鉄骨造
   reinforced concrete and wood (roof frame),
   partly precast concrete and steel frame
   清堂：鉄骨＋木造（小屋組）
   SEIDO hall：steel frame＋wood (roof frame)
8. 地上2階 2 stories
   清堂：地上1階 SEIDO hall：1 story
9. 9,112mm
11. 空間工学研究所 Space and
    Structure Engineering Workshop Inc.
12. 明野設備研究所
    Akeno Engineering Consultants Inc.
13. 鹿島建設 Kajima Corporation
14. 2001年6月 June, 2001

最上川ふるさと総合公園センターハウス
Mogamigawa Park Center House

1. 川村宣元、玉田源
   Nobuharu Kawamura, Gen Tamada
2. 山形県寒河江市 Sagae-shi, Yamagata
3. 公園管理施設 visitor center
4. 87,900㎡
5. 1,312.82㎡
6. 1,546.60㎡
7. 鉄筋コンクリート造＋鉄骨造
   reinforced concrete＋steel frame
8. 地上2階 2 stories
9. 11,232mm
10. 堀繁（全体監修）
    Shigeru Hori (general supervision)
    山形県土木部営繕課（監理）
    Yamagata Prefecture Government
    (construction supervision)
11. 空間工学研究所
    Space and Structure Engineering Workshop Inc.
12. 郷設計研究所（設計）
    Goh Technical Design Studio (planning)
    明野設備研究所（監理）
    Akeno Engineering Consultants Inc.
    (construction supervision)
13. 升川建設 Masukawa Construction Co.,Ltd.
14. 2001年12月 December, 2001

ちひろ美術館・東京
Chihiro Art Museum Tokyo

1. 川村宣元、吉田多津雄、片山惠仁
   Nobuharu Kawamura, Tatsuo Yoshida,
   Yoshimasa Katayama
2. 東京都練馬区 Nerima-ku, Tokyo
3. 美術館 museum
4. 1,154.51㎡
5. 551.04㎡
6. 1,298.07㎡
7. 鉄骨造、一部鉄骨鉄筋コンクリート造
   steel frame,
   partly steel framed reinforced concrete
8. A・B：地上3階 3 stories
   C・D：地上2階 2 stories
9. 9,950mm
11. 空間工学研究所
    Space and Structure Engineering Workshop Inc.
12. 明野設備研究所
    Akeno Engineering Consultants Inc.
    ライティングプランナーズアソシエーツ（照明）
    Lighting Planners Associates Inc.
    (lighting planning)
13. 戸田建設 Toda Corporation
14. 2002年6月 June, 2002

住居No.27
House No.27

1. 蛭田和則 Kazunori Hiruta
2. 東京都大田区 Ota-ku, Tokyo
3. 住宅 house
4. 219.52㎡
5. 111.98㎡
6. 236.35㎡
7. 鉄骨造 steel frame
8. 地上3階 3 stories
9. 9,720mm
11. ロウファットストラクチュア
    LOW FAT structure Inc.
13. 大栄工務店 Daiei Construction
14. 2004年12月 December, 2004

作 品 年 表 Project Chronology

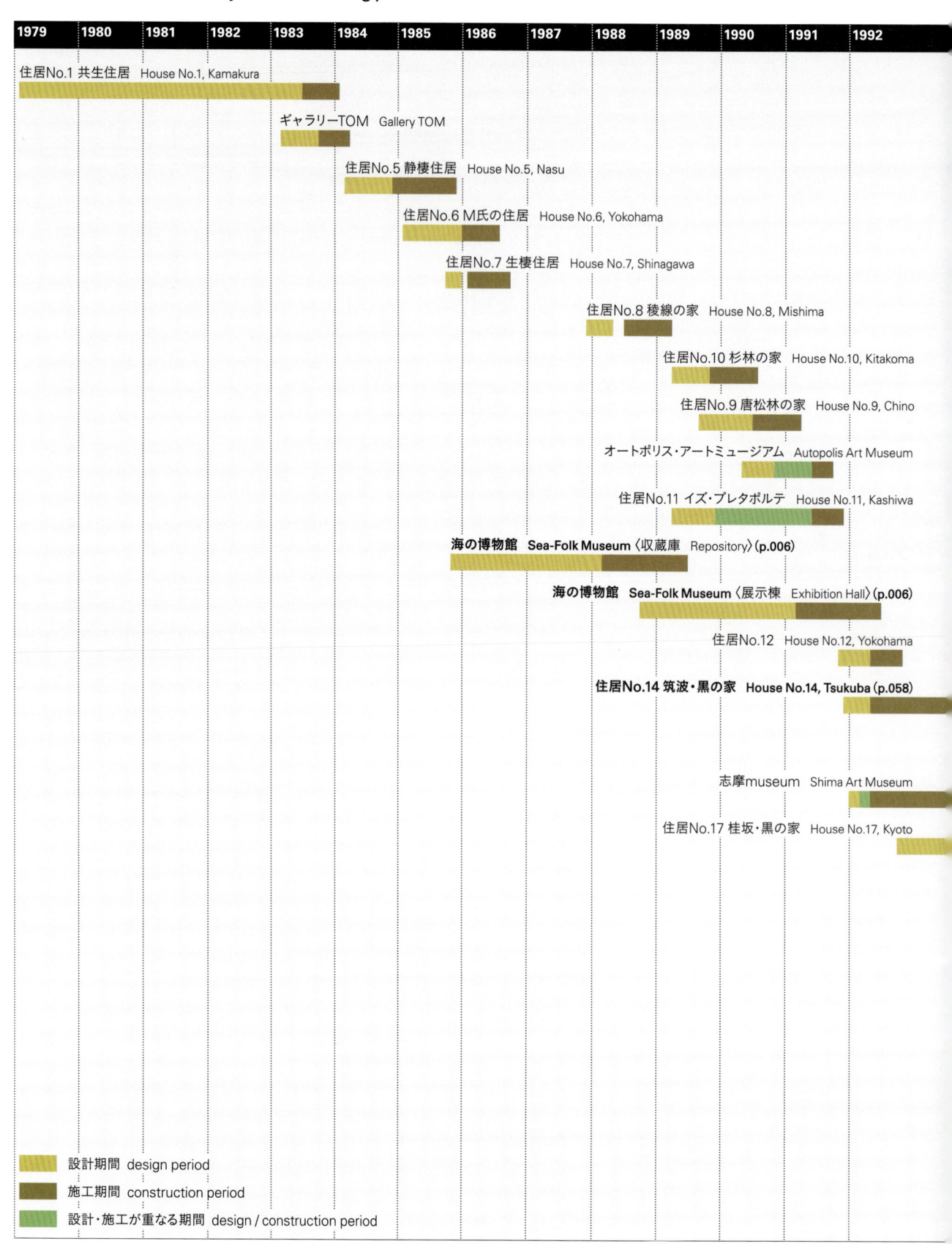

1979	1980	1981	1982	1983	1984	1985	1986	1987	1988	1989	1990	1991	1992

- 住居No.1 共生住居 House No.1, Kamakura
- ギャラリーTOM Gallery TOM
- 住居No.5 静棲住居 House No.5, Nasu
- 住居No.6 M氏の住居 House No.6, Yokohama
- 住居No.7 生棲住居 House No.7, Shinagawa
- 住居No.8 稜線の家 House No.8, Mishima
- 住居No.10 杉林の家 House No.10, Kitakoma
- 住居No.9 唐松林の家 House No.9, Chino
- オートポリス・アートミュージアム Autopolis Art Museum
- 住居No.11 イズ・プレタポルテ House No.11, Kashiwa
- **海の博物館 Sea-Folk Museum 〈収蔵庫 Repository〉(p.006)**
- **海の博物館 Sea-Folk Museum 〈展示棟 Exhibition Hall〉(p.006)**
- 住居No.12 House No.12, Yokohama
- **住居No.14 筑波・黒の家 House No.14, Tsukuba (p.058)**
- 志摩museum Shima Art Museum
- 住居No.17 桂坂・黒の家 House No.17, Kyoto

凡例:
- 設計期間 design period
- 施工期間 construction period
- 設計・施工が重なる期間 design / construction period

284 Hiroshi NAITO 1992-2004

Year	1993	1994	1995	1996	1997	1998	1999	2000	2001	2002	2003	2004	2005	2006

- 住居No.1 共生住居　House No.1, Kamakura 〈増改築　Expansion and Renovation〉
- ギャラリーNIKI　Gallery NIKI
- 住居No.21 千歳烏山の家　House No.21, Setagaya (p.150)
- 国立台湾史前文化博物館 卑南文化公園 遊客服務中心施設　National Museum of Prehistory, Peinan Culture Park Visitor Center
- 古河総合公園管理棟　Koga Municipal Park, Visitor Center
- 長野今井ニュータウン C工区　Imai New Town Area C
- 十日町情報館　Tokamachi Public Library (p.160)
- 安曇野ちひろ美術館　Chihiro Art Museum Azumino (p.108) 〈1期　1st Phase〉〈2期　2nd Phase〉
- 牧野富太郎記念館　Makino Museum of Plants and People (p.176)
- 茨城県天心記念五浦美術館　Tenshin Memorial Museum of Art, Ibaraki (p.132)
- 住居No.22　House No.22 (p.210)
- 雅樂倶・茶室　River Retreat GARAKU, Tea Ceremony Room
- 倫理研究所 富士高原研修所　Fuji RINRI Seminar House (p.218)
- 住居No.23　House No.23
- 最上川ふるさと総合公園センターハウス　Mogamigawa Park Center House (p.238)
- 住居No.15 杉並・黒の部屋　House No.15, Suginami (p.070)
- フォレスト益子　Forest Mashiko
- ちひろ美術館・東京　Chihiro Art Museum Tokyo (p.248)
- 住居No.18 伊東・織りの家　House No.18, Ito (p.078)
- 九谷焼窯跡展示館　Shelter for Remain of Kutani Kiln
- 住居No.19 金沢の家　House No.19, Kanazawa (p.092)
- 苫田ダム管理庁舎　Tomata Dam Control Center
- ギャラリー冊　Gallery SATSU
- うしぶか海彩館　Ushibuka Fisherman's Wharf
- 倫理研究所船橋社宅　Rinri Institute of Ethics Funabashi Housing
- みなとみらい線馬車道駅　Minatomirai Line, Bashamichi Station [基本　Schematic Design] [実施　Execution Design]
- [デザイン検討　Design Studies]
- 住居No.27　House No.27 (p.264)
- リストランテ・マッカリーナ　Restaurant Maccarina
- 住居No.20 極楽寺の家　House No.20, Kamakura

285　Project Chronology

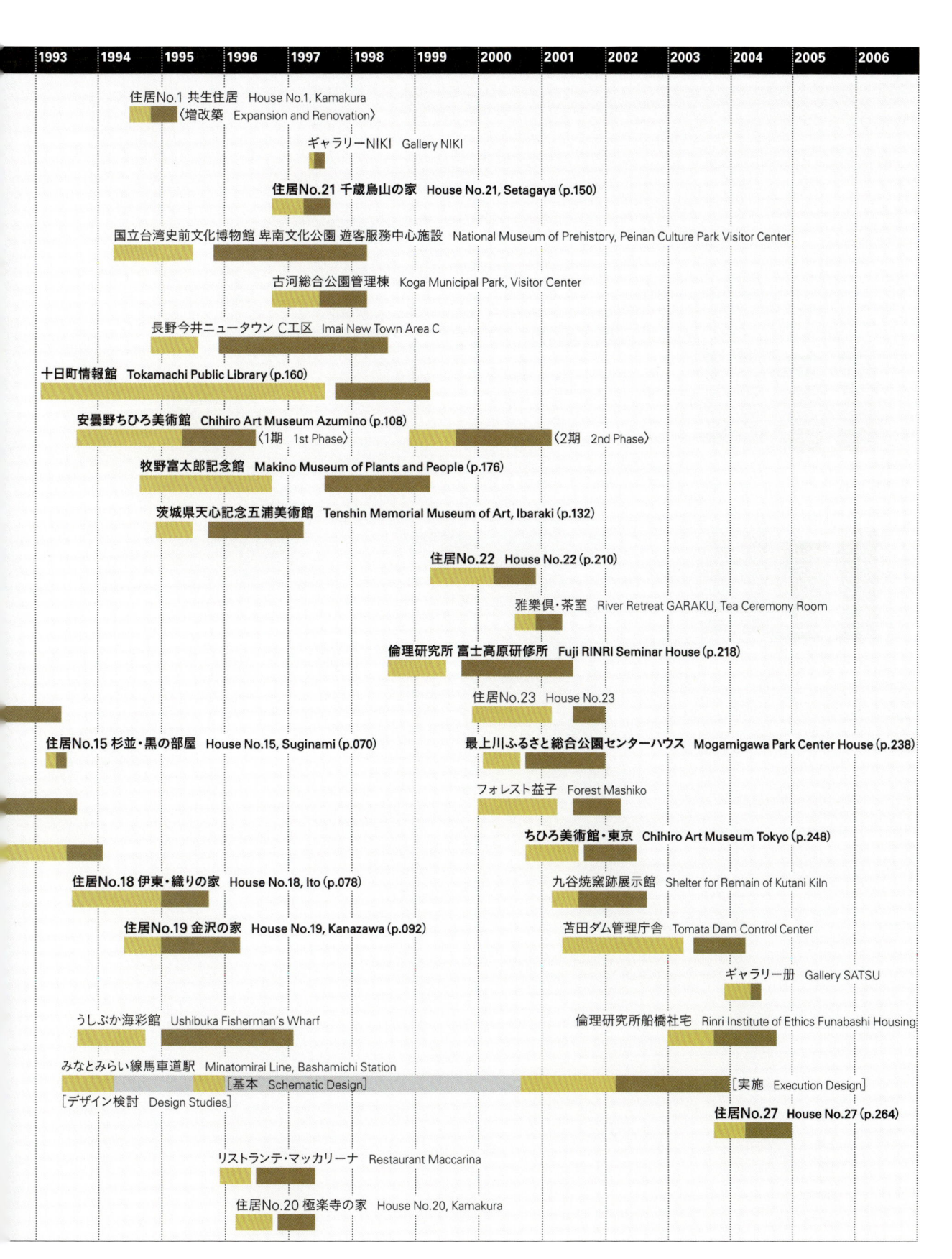

内藤 廣　Hiroshi NAITO

[経歴]
- 1950　神奈川県横浜市に生まれる
- 1974　早稲田大学理工学部建築学科卒業
- 1976　早稲田大学大学院にて吉阪隆正に師事、修士課程修了
- 1976-78　フェルナンド・イゲーラス建築設計事務所勤務(スペイン・マドリッド)
- 1979-81　菊竹清訓建築設計事務所勤務
- 1981　株式会社内藤廣建築設計事務所設立
- 2001　東京大学大学院工学系研究科社会基盤工学　助教授
- 2002-11　東京大学大学院工学系研究科社会基盤学　教授
- 2007-09　グッドデザイン賞　審査委員長
- 2009-　TOTOギャラリー・間　運営委員
- 2010-11　東京大学　副学長
- 2011-　東京大学　名誉教授・総長室顧問

[Biography]
- 1950　Born in Yokohama, Kanagawa, Japan
- 1974　Graduated from Waseda University (B. Arch.) in Tokyo
- 1976　Completed studies under Prof. Takamasa Yoshizaka at the Graduate School of Waseda University (M. Arch.)
- 1976-78　Chief Architect at the office of architect Fernando Higueras (Madrid, Spain)
- 1979-81　Worked at the office of architect Kiyonori Kikutake (Tokyo, Japan)
- 1981　Established Naito Architect & Associates
- 2001　Associate Professor, The University of Tokyo
- 2002-11　Professor, The University of Tokyo
- 2007-09　Chairman of the Good Design Award Judging Committee
- 2009-　TOTO GALLERY·MA Planning and Management Committee Member
- 2010-11　Executive Vice President, The University of Tokyo
- 2011 -　Emeritus Professor and Senior Advisor to the Office of the President, The University of Tokyo

[主な著書　Publications]
- 1993　『海の博物館(SEA-FOLK MUSEUM)』
　　　写真:石元泰博／Photographer:Yasuhiro Ishimoto
- 1995　『INAX ALBUM 30　素形の建築』LIXIL出版
- 1996　『建築文化1996年4月No.594
　　　内藤廣　シェルタリング・アース』彰国社
- 1997　『建築文化1997年11月No.613
　　　内藤廣　サイレント・アーキテクチュア』彰国社
　　　Silent Architecture Aedes
- 1999　『安曇野ちひろ美術館(CHIHIRO ART MUSEUM AZUMINO)』
　　　写真:石元泰博／Photographer:Yasuhiro Ishimoto
　　　『建築のはじまりに向かって』王国社
- 2000　『牧野富太郎記念館(Makino Museum of Plants and People)』
　　　写真:石元泰博／Photographer:Yasuhiro Ishimoto
　　　『住宅という場所で』共著、TOTO出版
- 2002　『JA46:内藤廣(JA46:Hiroshi Naito)』新建築社
　　　『倫理研究所 富士高原研修所(Fuji RINRI Seminar House)』
　　　写真:石元泰博／Photographer:Yasuhiro Ishimoto
- 2003　『建築の終わり』共著、TOTO出版
- 2004　『建築的思考のゆくえ』王国社
- 2006　『内藤廣／インナースケープのディテール』彰国社
　　　Hiroshi Naito : Innerscape Birkhauser
　　　『建土築木1 ―構築物の風景―』鹿島出版会
　　　『建土築木2 ―川のある風景―』鹿島出版会
- 2007　『内藤廣対談集 複眼思考の建築論』LIXIL出版
- 2008　『構造デザイン講義』王国社
- 2009　『建築のちから』王国社
- 2010　『著書解題――内藤廣対談集2』LIXIL出版
- 2011　『環境デザイン講義』王国社
　　　『NA建築家シリーズ03 内藤廣』日経BP社
　　　『内藤廣と若者たち 人生をめぐる一八の対話』
　　　東京大学景観研究室編、鹿島出版会
- 2012　『内藤廣の頭と手』彰国社

［主な受賞歴］

1993	芸術選奨文部大臣新人賞（海の博物館）
	日本建築学会賞（海の博物館）
	第18回吉田五十八賞（海の博物館）
1998	建設省選定公共建築100選（海の博物館）
2000	第13回村野藤吾賞（牧野富太郎記念館）
	IAA国際トリエンナーレ グランプリ（牧野富太郎記念館）
	第42回毎日芸術賞（牧野富太郎記念館）
2001	第42回BCS賞（牧野富太郎記念館）
2003	第4回織部賞
2004	第45回BCS賞（ちひろ美術館・東京）
	第3回日本鉄道賞 表彰選考委員会特別賞
	（みなとみらい線 ＊馬車道駅）
	第49回鉄道建築協会賞 国土交通省鉄道局長賞
	（みなとみらい線 ＊馬車道駅）
	グッドデザイン賞（みなとみらい線 ＊馬車道駅）
2006	International Architecture Awards（島根県芸術文化センター）
	土木学会デザイン賞2006 最優秀賞（牧野富太郎記念館）
	土木学会デザイン賞2006 優秀賞（みなとみらい線 ＊馬車道駅）
2007	優良木造施設表彰施設 林野庁長官賞（日向市駅）
	第48回BCS賞（島根県芸術文化センター）
	第52回鉄道建築協会賞 国土交通省鉄道局長賞（日向市駅）
	土木学会デザイン賞2007 最優秀賞（苫田ダム ＊管理庁舎）
2008	第14回薫賞 経済産業大臣賞（島根県芸術文化センター）
	第10回ブルネル賞（日向市駅）
	第7回日本鉄道賞 ランドマークデザイン賞（高知駅）
2009	第50回BCS賞（日向市駅）
	第54回鉄道建築協会賞 停車場建築賞（高知駅）
2010	第12回公共建築賞・特別賞（島根県芸術文化センター）
2012	グッドデザイン賞 地域づくりデザイン賞／グッドデザインベスト100
	（山代温泉・湯の曲輪 ＊総湯）
	グッドデザイン賞（渋谷駅街区東口二階デッキ）

［Awards］

1993	The Education Minister's Art Encouragement Prize for New Artists (Sea-Folk Museum)
	The Prize of Architectural Institute of Japan for Design (Sea-Folk Museum)
	The 18th Isoya Yoshida Memorial Prize (Sea-Folk Museum)
1998	The Ministry of Construction Best 100 Public Architecture Award (Sea-Folk Museum)
2000	The 13th Togo Murano Prize (Makino Museum of Plants and People)
	World Triennial of Architecture, Grand Prix of the International Academy of Architecture (Makino Museum of Plants and People)
	The 42nd Mainichi Art Award (Makino Museum of Plants and People)
2001	The 42nd BCS Prize (Makino Museum of Plants and People)
2003	The 4th Oribe Award
2004	The 45th BCS Prize (Chihiro Art Museum Tokyo)
	The 3rd Japan Railway Award Jury Committee Special Prize (Minatomirai Line ＊Bashamichi Station)
	The 49th Association of Railway Architects Award MLIT Director-General Prize (Minatomirai Line ＊Bashamichi Station)
	Good Design Award (Minatomirai Line ＊Bashamichi Station)
2006	International Architecture Awards (Shimane Arts Center)
	Civil Engineering Design Prize 2006 First Prize (Makino Museum of Plants and People)
	Civil Engineering Design Prize 2006 Second Prize (Minatomirai Line ＊Bashamichi Station)
2007	Japanese Council for Advancement of Timber Utilization (Hyugashi Station)
	The 48th BCS Prize (Shimane Arts Center)
	The 52nd Association of Railway Architects Award MLIT Director-General Prize (Hyugashi Station)
	Civil Engineering Design Prize 2007 First Prize (Tomada Dam ＊Control Center)
2008	The 14th Iraka Award Minister of Economy Trade and Industry Prize (Shimane Arts Center)
	The 10th Brunel Award (Hyugashi Station)
	The 7th Japan Railway Award Landmark Design Prize (Kochi Station)
2009	The 50th BCS Prize (Hyugashi Station)
	The 54th Association of Railway Architects Award Station Architecture Prize (Kochi Station)
2010	The 12th Public Building Award Special Prize (Shimane Arts Center)
2012	Good Design Award Good Design Prize of the Japan Chamber of Commerce and Industry / Good Design Best 100 (Yamashiro Hot Spring "Yunogawa" ＊Soyu)
	Good Design Award (The pedestrian deck of the east gate in SHIBUYA)

[展覧会]

1987	TOKYO TOWER PROJECT（アクシスギャラリー／東京）
1989	海の博物館展覧会「夜の海」（西武渋谷店／東京）
1993	迷宮都市展（セゾン美術館／東京）
	内藤廣展（建築家倶楽部／東京）
1994	ハートで描く心のメッセージ展（メトロポリタンプラザビル／東京）
1995	世界建築トリエンナーレ奈良1995現代建築家展 （奈良県立美術館／奈良）
	素形の構図 還元する場のかたち（ギャラリー・間／東京）
1996	ギャラリー・間10周年記念 出展作家の原点作品展 （ギャラリー・間／東京）
1997	Silent Architecture（Aedes West／ベルリン・ドイツ）
1998	Silent Architecture巡回展（Architektekammer der Freien Hansestadt／ブレーメン・ドイツ） Silent Architecture巡回展 （Zumtobel Staff LICHTFORUM／ウィーン・オーストリア） Silent Architecture巡回展（Kärntens Haus der Architektur／クラーゲンフルト・オーストリア） 世界建築トリエンナーレ奈良1998現代建築家展 （奈良そごう美術館／奈良）
2000	建築のはじまりに向かって（牧野富太郎記念館／高知） 日本／トータルスケープに向かって（The Netherlands Architecture Institute／ロッテルダム・オランダ）
2001	sur／FACE 14人の現代建築家展（BMW スクエア／東京） 『海の博物館』以降（海の博物館／三重） 英国―JAPAN2001「日本の建築家16人展」 （RIBA／ロンドン・イギリス）
2002	日本建築セミナー展（ボリビアカトリック大学／サンタ・クルス・ボリビア）
2005	内藤廣―the GENBA（島根県芸術文化センター／島根） Hiroshi Naito. Innerscape （Museum of Finnish Architecture／ヘルシンキ・フィンランド）
2006	TIMESCAPE（オカムラ・ガーデンコート・ショールーム／東京） 「山田脩二×内藤廣 写真×建築」展（南洋堂 N+／東京）
2010	建築はどこにあるの？ 7つのインスタレーション （東京国立近代美術館／東京）
2012	内藤廣：18800 pieces 2012.6.13（京都造形芸術大学／京都）

[Exhibitions]

1987	TOKYO TOWER PROJECT (AXIS Gallery / Tokyo)
1989	Sea-Folk Museum Exhibition: The Sea at Night (Seibu Shibuya / Tokyo)
1993	LABYRINTH (Sezon Museum of Art / Tokyo) Hiroshi Naito (Architecture club / Tokyo)
1994	Heartful Messages (METROPOLITAN PLAZA / Tokyo)
1995	Contemporary Architect Exhibition II (Nara Prefectural Museum of Art / Nara) Composition of the Protoform (GALLERY·MA / Tokyo)
1996	GALLERY·MA 10th Anniversary Exhibition The 53 Origins (GALLERY·MA / Tokyo)
1997	Silent Architecture (Aedes West / Berlin, Germany)
1998	Silent Architecture – Travelling Exhibition (Architektekammer der Freien Hansestadt / Bremen, Germany) Silent Architecture – Travelling Exhibition (Zumtobel Staff LICHTFORUM / Vienna, Austria) Silent Architecture – Travelling Exhibition (Kärntens Haus der Architektur / Klagenfurt, Austria) Contemporary Architect Exhibition III (Nara Sogo Museum of Art / Nara)
2000	Hiroshi Naito: Towards the Beginning of Architecture (Makino Museum of Plants and People / Kochi) Japan: Towards Totalscape (The Netherlands Architecture Institute / Rotterdam, the Netherlands)
2001	sur / FACE (BMW Square / Tokyo) Hiroshi Naito: Since the Sea-Folk Museum (Sea-Folk Museum / Mie) Japanese Avant-Garde: Reality / Projection 16 Young Japanese Architects (RIBA / London, UK)
2002	Japanese Architecture Seminar Exhibition (Catholic University of Bolivia / Santa Cruz, Bolivia)
2005	Hiroshi Naito – the GENBA (Shimane Arts Center / Shimane) Hiroshi Naito. Innerscape (Museum of Finnish Architecture / Helsinki, Finland)
2006	TIMESCAPE (Garden Court Okamura Showroom / Tokyo) Shuji Yamada × Hiroshi Naito / Photography × Architecture (Nanyodo N+ / Tokyo)
2010	Where is Architecture? Seven Installations by Japanese Architects (The National Museum of Modern Art, Tokyo / Tokyo)
2012	18800 pieces 2012.6.13 (Kyoto University of Art and Design / Kyoto)

初出一覧　Original Publication Data

キャプション以外の言説、ページ後の数字は掲載年、月、日
For writings except the captions.
Figures following page number indicate publication year, month, and date.

『建築文化』彰国社　*KENCHIKU BUNKA*　Shokokusha
p.7, 10, 12, 27, 33, 37, 45, 98, 136, 139, 140, 141, 143, 148, 149, 151, 159, 177, 262, 272[004][008], 273[045][058]：9808；p.192, 199, 223：0002

『新建築』新建築社　*SHINKENCHIKU*　Shinkenchiku-sha
p.13, 24, 29, 127, 131, 144, 173, 252, 263, 273[054]：0211；
p.43：0206；p.74, 90, 109, 115, 116, 122, 124, 183, 243, 256, 259, 273[053]：9706；p.161, 164, 167, 168：9911；p.181, 197：0001；
p.209：0605；p.218, 229, 272[015]：0111；p.247：0407；
p.272[003]：0201；p.272[002], 273[037][065]：9201；
p.272[006]：0306；p.272[007][009][014][029], 273[041]：9912；
p.272[023]：0004；p.273[035]：0012；p.273[036][050][064]：9211；
p.273[038]：9402；p.273[049]：0011臨時増刊
『node 20世紀の技術と21世紀の建築』；p.273[052]：8408

『COMPE & CONTEST』 TOTO出版　TOTO Publishing
p.25, 78, 93, 133：9711

『コンフォルト』建築資料研究社　*CONFORT*　Kenchiku Shiryo Kenkyusha
p.31, 155：9708

『新建築住宅特集』新建築社
SHINKENCHIKU JUTAKUTOKUSHU　Shinkenchiku-sha
p.32：9711；p.62：9401；p.71：9404；p.77, 211, 248：0207；p.100, 106：9711；p.217, 264, 269, 271：0612；p.272[005][011][013][021][033][034], 273[043][056]：9502；p.272[010], 273[040][057]：8702；
p.272[024][025][026], 273[044]：9112；p.273[060]：9309

『日刊建設工業新聞』日刊建設工業新聞社
The Nikkan Kensetsu Kogyo Shimbun
THE NIKKAN KENSETSU-KOGYO SHIMBUN, LTD.
p.35[top], 208：000609

『GA JAPAN』エーディーエー・エディタ・トーキョー
A.D.A. EDITA Tokyo Co., Ltd.
p.35[bottom], 224, 233, 236：0111-12；p.239：0407-08；
p.272[001][017][019][020][031], 273[055]：0309-10；
p.273[059]：0001-02；p.273[062]：9303-04

『芸術新潮』新潮社　*Geijutsu Shincho*　Shinchosha
p.58：0707

『いけ花 龍生』(社)龍生華道会　*Ikebana Ryusei*　Ryusei Kadokai Corp.
p.66：9407

『室内』工作社　*SHITSUNAI*　Kosakusha
p.69：9602

『BISES』編集、ビズ出版　BISES Publishing
p.86：9712

『まちなみ・建築フォーラム』市ヶ谷出版社　*Forum*　Ichigayashuppan
p.113, 118, 121：9712

『SD』鹿島出版会　Kajima Institute Publishing
p.129, 130：9312

『AXIS』アクシス　AXIS
p.175：0312

『高知新聞』高知新聞社　*The Kochi Shimbun*
p.185, 198, 201：991101；p.200：000402

『JIA news』(社)日本建築家協会　The Japan Institute of Architects
p.186, 272[032]：0107

『ディテール』彰国社　*DETAIL*　Shokokusha
p.272[012][028][030]：9704；p.272[016][018]：0407；
p.272[027]：9701

『迷宮都市 新しいイズムの建築家たち』セゾン美術館
LABYRINTH New Generation in Japanese Architecture
Sezon Museum of Art (1993)
p.272[022]

『JA』新建築社　Shinkenchiku-sha
p.273[039][042]：9402

『INAX ALBUM 30 素形の建築』LIXIL出版
Protoform LIXIL Publishing (1995)
p.273[046][047][048][051][061][063]

*文章は一部、内藤廣氏によって加筆・修正されたものです。
　A portion of the text has been revised / rewritten by Hiroshi Naito.

クレジット　Credits　　　　　　　　　　　　　　　内藤廣建築設計事務所

写真　Photographs
三島叡（日経アーキテクチュア1999年12月27日号掲載）
Satoru Mishima (*Nikkei Architecture*. 27 Dec. 1999.)
pp. 176-177
中川敦玲　Nobuaki Nakagawa
pp. 116-117
新建築社写真部　Shinkenchiku-sha
pp. 36, 50[right], 51[right], 100[top], 208-209, 215[bottom], 216[bottom right], 232
内藤廣　Hiroshi Naito
pp. 10-11, 14-17, 22-33, 37, 42-43
蛭田和則（内藤廣建築設計事務所）Kazunori Hiruta (NAA)
上記ページ以外すべて　All pages except above-mentioned.

図面・図版　Drawings
内藤廣建築設計事務所　Naito Architect & Associates

英訳　English Translations
アムスタッツ・ブライアン　Brian Amstutz
pp. 46-57
マチダ・ゲン　Gen Machida
上記ページ以外すべて　All pages except above-mentioned.

編集協力　Cooperation
内藤廣建築設計事務所：伊藤美智子、小田切美和、蛭田和則
Naito Architect & Associates : Michiko Ito, Miwa Otagiri, Kazunori Hiruta
南風舎　Nampoosha

所員
神林哲也　内藤鏡子
蛭田和則　小田切美和
細沼　俊　伊藤美智子
市村　駿　内藤晶子
福原信一
湯浅良介
五十嵐悠介
市川弥穂
増崎陽介
原田孝子
原　章史
有木陽一
小笹　泉
時田海士郎
橋本尚樹

古野洋美
沢里　正

旧所員
酒井信一郎　太田理加
瓦谷潤一　玉田　源
八島央子　河野貴臣
佐渡基宏　吉田多津雄
ウルリケ・リーブル　片山恵仁
榊　法明　河田麻美
石原弘明　原口　剛
渡辺　仁　垣内崇佳
下村有希子　北野博宣
相野律子　上原世恵子
カトリン・リンケルスドルフ　浅野恭子
加藤成明　宮崎俊行
大山美由紀　李　仁敦
塩田玲子　長田潤子
米本昌史　瓜生浩二
バディ・トメセン　加藤菜保
大西直子　山田まどか
堀岡　勝　國島明恵
竹中アシュ　大畠稜司
山中祐一郎　川村宣元
マルクス・ブリューゲル　好川　拓
横井　拓　間下奈津子
田井幹夫　野口健一
高草大次郎　池原靖史
有村和浩　山田　徹
沼田恭子　大島耕平
渡谷博美　熊切真知子
朝山宗啓　蘆田暢人
大坪和朗

内藤 廣の建築 1992-2004
素形から素景へ1

2013年3月19日 初版第1刷発行
2022年3月30日 初版第3刷発行

著者	内藤 廣
発行者	伊藤剛士
発行所	TOTO出版（TOTO株式会社）
	〒107-0062 東京都港区南青山1-24-3 TOTO乃木坂ビル2F
	［営業］TEL:03-3402-7138 FAX:03-3402-7187
	［編集］TEL:03-3497-1010
	URL:https://jp.toto.com/publishing
	編集：TOTO出版
	内藤廣建築設計事務所
アートディレクション&デザイン	工藤強勝＋渡部 周
プリンティングディレクション	高柳 昇
印刷・製本	株式会社東京印書館

落丁本・乱丁本はお取り替えいたします。
本書の全部又は一部に対するコピー・スキャン・デジタル化等の
無断複製行為は、著作権法上での例外を除き禁じます。
本書を代行業者等の第三者に依頼してスキャンやデジタル化することは、
たとえ個人や家庭内での利用であっても著作権法上認められておりません。
定価はカバーに表示してあります。

©2013 Hiroshi Naito

Printed in Japan
ISBN978-4-88706-332-7